Communications
in Computer and Information Science   1690

Kothe Doug · Geist Al · Swaroop Pophale ·
Hong Liu · Suzanne Parete-Koon (Eds.)

Accelerating Science and Engineering Discoveries Through Integrated Research Infrastructure for Experiment, Big Data, Modeling and Simulation

22nd Smoky Mountains Computational Sciences
and Engineering Conference, SMC 2022
Virtual Event, August 23–25, 2022
Revised Selected Papers

 Springer

Editors
Kothe Doug
Oak Ridge National Laboratory
Oak Ridge, TN, USA

Geist Al
Oak Ridge National Laboratory
Oak Ridge, TN, USA

Swaroop Pophale 🆔
Oak Ridge National Laboratory
Oak Ridge, TN, USA

Hong Liu
Oak Ridge National Laboratory
Oak Ridge, TN, USA

Suzanne Parete-Koon
Oak Ridge National Laboratory
Oak Ridge, TN, USA

ISSN 1865-0929   ISSN 1865-0937 (electronic)
Communications in Computer and Information Science
ISBN 978-3-031-23605-1   ISBN 978-3-031-23606-8 (eBook)
https://doi.org/10.1007/978-3-031-23606-8

This Springer imprint is published by the registered company Springer Nature Switzerland AG
The registered company address is: Gewerbestrasse 11, 6330 Cham, Switzerland

Preface

The Smoky Mountains Computational Sciences and Engineering Conference (SMC 2022) was organized by the Oak Ridge National Laboratory (ORNL). This year, due to a spike in COVID-19 cases in the community local to the conference venue, the organizers made the hard decision to turn SMC 2022 into an entirely virtual conference. The main conference was held during August 24–25, which was followed by the Scientific Data Challenge event held on September 21. The main theme of SMC 2022 was "Accelerating science and engineering discoveries through integrated research infrastructure for experiment, big data, modeling and simulation". Based around this theme the conference focused on four major areas—foundational methods, applications, systems and software, and advanced technologies for an integrated ecosystem. Reflecting the focus of the main theme of the conference, SMC 2022 created four distinct tracks for submission: Foundational Methods Enabling Science in an Integrated Ecosystem, Science and Engineering Applications Requiring and Motivating an Integrated Ecosystem, Systems and Software Advances Enabling an Integrated Science and Engineering Ecosystem, and Deploying Advanced Technologies for an Integrated Science and Engineering Ecosystem along with the Scientific Data Challenge (SDC).

We issued a call for papers (CFP) in February 2022 inviting scientists to share research breakthroughs in HPC centered around the different submission tracks and discuss ideas to contribute to our program via peer-reviewed papers. SMC 2022's Program Committee consisted of 62 leading experts from national laboratories, academia, and industry who helped advertise the CFP and reviewed papers for the main program and the SDC competition.

Using a single-blind review process, the Program Committee accepted 24 of the 74 submissions to be presented at the conference as well as included in these proceedings. All papers were peer-reviewed by at least three experts, and the majority had five reviewers. The overall acceptance rate of the conference was 32%. The accepted papers, which are compiled in these SMC 2022 conference proceedings, describe the most important directions for research, development, and production, as well as elucidating experiences and advocating for investment in areas related to the conference theme. These important areas were organized under the following sessions.

In Session 1: Foundational Methods Enabling Science in an Integrated Ecosystem participants discussed applications that embrace foundational and first-principle methods, focusing on converging AI with high-performance modeling and simulation applications. Topics included experiences, algorithms, and numerical methods development and integration with the edge. This session also focused on workflows, self-learning, simulations, linear solvers, AI guided explorations, and leveraging HPC data in integrated ecosystems.

In Session 2: Science and Engineering Applications Requiring and Motivating an Integrated Ecosystem participants discussed multi-domain applications developed in preparation of convergence of HPC, AI, and edge computing. Contributions on novel machine learning algorithms for domain specific scientific discoveries while employing large-scale compute capabilities, including sensors, actuators, instruments for HPC systems, data stores, and other network-connected devices were also solicited. This session centered on applications that focus on integration across domains and scientific datasets.

Session 3: Systems and Software Advances Enabling an Integrated Science and Engineering Ecosystem included topics related to systems and software technologies for novel computing processes, such as neutron scattering, instrumentation ecosystems, and other intra and inter-institutional frameworks are capable of developing and deploying federated architectures. In this session the latest ideas and findings in the programming and software ecosystems for these rapidly changing and emerging fields were presented.

Session 4: Deploying Advanced Technologies for an Integrated Science and Engineering Ecosystem addressed industry experience and plans for deploying both hardware and software infrastructure needed to support emerging AI and/or classical workloads. This session focused on how emerging technologies can be co-designed to support compute and data workflows at scale for next-generation HPC and AI systems.

The SMC 2022 Scientific Data Challenge featured tasks developed by scientific data sponsors based on eminent ORNL data sets from scientific simulations and instruments in physical and chemical sciences, electron microscopy, bioinformatics, neutron sources, urban development, and other areas for the competition. Students and data analytics experts submitted papers describing their strategies and solutions to a series of increasingly difficult challenge questions. Overall, 33 teams registered for the competition and a peer review process selected 14 finalists, all of whom presented lighting talks at SMC 2022. Finally, six papers were down selected to be included in the proceedings based on their merit and scores from the SDC judges.

SMC 2022 had an excellent lineup of speakers eager to engage with our attendees. Along with the paper presentations there was a keynote from Anthony Roscoe from HPE. He spoke about technical advances and touched upon the impact of the COVID-19 pandemic on the global supply chain and its impact on the HPC markets.

Lastly, SMC 2022 would not have been possible without our authors, Program Committee members, Session Chairs, and the scientific community, who once again came together in our shared mission to discuss solutions to the most complex problems in energy science and computing.

August 2022

Kothe Doug
Geist Al
Swaroop Pophale
Hong Liu
Suzanne Parete-Koon

Organization

General Chair

Doug Kothe   Oak Ridge National Laboratory, USA

Conference Chair

Al Geist   Oak Ridge National Laboratory, USA

Program Chair

Swaroop Pophale   Oak Ridge National Laboratory, USA

Data Challenge Chairs

Hong Liu   Oak Ridge National Laboratory, USA
Suzanne Parete-Koon   Oak Ridge National Laboratory, USA

Steering Committee

Doug Kothe   Oak Ridge National Laboratory, USA
Al Geist   Oak Ridge National Laboratory, USA
Kate Evans   Oak Ridge National Laboratory, USA
Theresa Ahearn   Oak Ridge National Laboratory, USA
Gina Tourassi   Oak Ridge National Laboratory, USA
Hong Liu   Oak Ridge National Laboratory, USA
Suzanne Parete-Koon   Oak Ridge National Laboratory, USA

Media and Communications

Scott Jones   Oak Ridge National Laboratory, USA
Elizabeth Rosenthal   Oak Ridge National Laboratory, USA

Session Chairs

James Nutaro   Oak Ridge National Laboratory, USA
Pablo Seleson   Oak Ridge National Laboratory, USA
Helia Zandi   Oak Ridge National Laboratory, USA
Dayle Smith   Oak Ridge National Laboratory, USA

Jack Lange	Oak Ridge National Laboratory, USA
Addi Thakur Malviya	Oak Ridge National Laboratory, USA
Sarp Oral	Oak Ridge National Laboratory, USA
Seth Hitefield	Oak Ridge National Laboratory, USA
Arjun Shankar	Oak Ridge National Laboratory, USA

Program Committee

Vassil Alexandrov	STFC Hartree Centre, UKRI, UK
Rick Archibald	Oak Ridge National Laboratory, USA
Ritu Arora	University of Texas at San Antonio, USA
Ron Brightwell	Sandia National Laboratories, USA
Michael Brim	Oak Ridge National Laboratory, USA
Ali Butt	Virginia Tech, USA
Sunita Chandrasekaran	University of Delaware, USA
Marshall Choy	SambaNova Systems, USA
Ryan Coffee	SLAC National Accelerator Laboratory, USA
Mathieu Doucet	Oak Ridge National Laboratory, USA
Katherine Evans	Oak Ridge National Laboratory, USA
Aric Hagberg	Los Alamos National Laboratory, USA
Steven Hamilton	Oak Ridge National Laboratory, USA
William Headley	Virginia Tech/National Security Institute, USA
Oscar Hernandez	NVIDIA, USA
Andreas Herten	Jülich Supercomputing Centre, Germany
Jeffrey Hittinger	Lawrence Livermore National Laboratory, USA
Ramakrishnan Kannan	Oak Ridge National Laboratory, USA
Gokcen Kestor	Pacific Northwest National Laboratory, USA
Olivera Kotevska	Oak Ridge National Laboratory, USA
Daniel Laney	Lawrence Livermore National Laboratory, USA
Kody Law	University of Manchester, UK
Piotr Luszczek	University of Tennessee, USA
Verónica Melesse Vergara	Oak Ridge National Laboratory, USA
Esteban Meneses	Costa Rica National High Technology Center, Costa Rica
Reed Milewicz	Sandia National Laboratories, USA
Bernd Mohr	Jülich Supercomputing Centre, Germany
Kathryn Mohror	Lawrence Livermore National Laboratory, USA
Misbah Mubarak	Amazon Web Services, USA
Hai Ah Nam	NERSC, USA
Sarah Neuwirth	Goethe University Frankfurt, Germany
C. J. Newburn	NVIDIA, USA
Sarp Oral	Oak Ridge National Laboratory, USA

Vincent Paquit	Oak Ridge National Laboratory, USA
Michael Parks	Sandia National Laboratories, USA
Kevin Pedretti	Sandia National Laboratories, USA
Laura Pullum	Oak Ridge National Laboratory, USA
Sreeranjani Ramprakash	Argonne National Laboratory, USA
Philip Roth	Oak Ridge National Laboratory, USA
Roxana Rusitoru	Arm Ltd., UK
Jibonananda Sanyal	Oak Ridge National Laboratory, USA
Vivek Sarkar	Georgia Institute of Technology, USA
Thomas Schulthess	ETH Zurich, Switzerland
Kathleen Shoga	Lawrence Livermore National Laboratory, USA
Susan Sinnott	Pennsylvania State University, USA
Suhas Somnath	Oak Ridge National Laboratory, USA
James Stewart	Sandia National Laboratories, USA
Tjerk Straatsma	Oak Ridge National Laboratory, USA
Devesh Tiwari	Northeastern University, USA
Feiyi Wang	Oak Ridge National Laboratory, USA
Jack Wells	NVIDIA, USA
Rich Wolski	University of California, Santa Barbara, USA
Qing Zheng	Los Alamos National Laboratory, USA

Data Challenge Program Committee

Oscar Hernandez	NVIDIA, USA
Andy Barres	Oak Ridge National Laboratory, USA
Piyush Sao	Georgia Institute of Technology, USA
Saheli Ghosh	University of California, Riverside, USA
Sajal Dash	Oak Ridge National Laboratory, USA
Ramakrishnan Kannan	Oak Ridge National Laboratory, USA
Arpan Biswas	Oak Ridge National Laboratory, USA
Tania Lorido	University of Deusto, Bilbao, Spain
Seung-Hwan Lim	Oak Ridge National Laboratory, USA

Contents

Foundational Methods Enabling Science in an Integrated Ecosystem

Computational Workflow for Accelerated Molecular Design Using Quantum Chemical Simulations and Deep Learning Models

Andrew E. Blanchard[1], Pei Zhang[1], Debsindhu Bhowmik[1], Kshitij Mehta[2], John Gounley[1], Samuel Temple Reeve[1], Stephan Irle[1(✉)], and Massimiliano Lupo Pasini[1]

[1] Oak Ridge National Laboratory, Computational Sciences and Engineering Division, Oak Ridge, TN 37831, USA
irles@ornl.gov
[2] Oak Ridge National Laboratory, Computer Science and Mathematics Division, Oak Ridge, TN 37831, USA

Abstract. Efficient methods for searching the chemical space of molecular compounds are needed to automate and accelerate the design of new functional molecules such as pharmaceuticals. Given the high cost in both resources and time for experimental efforts, computational approaches play a key role in guiding the selection of promising molecules for further investigation. Here, we construct a workflow to accelerate design by combining approximate quantum chemical methods [i.e. density-functional tight-binding (DFTB)], a graph convolutional neural network (GCNN) surrogate model for chemical property prediction, and a masked language model (MLM) for molecule generation. Property data from the DFTB calculations are used to train the surrogate model; the surrogate model is used to score candidates generated by the MLM. The surrogate reduces computation time by orders of magnitude compared to the DFTB calculations, enabling an increased search of chemical space. Furthermore, the MLM generates a diverse set of chemical modifications based on pre-training from a large compound library. We utilize the workflow to search for near-infrared photoactive molecules by minimizing the predicted HOMO-LUMO gap as the target property. Our results show that

Supplementary Information The online version contains supplementary material available at https://doi.org/10.1007/978-3-031-23606-8_1.

© The Author(s), under exclusive license to Springer Nature Switzerland AG 2022
K. Doug et al. (Eds.): SMC 2022, CCIS 1690, pp. 3–19, 2022.
https://doi.org/10.1007/978-3-031-23606-8_1

the workflow can generate optimized molecules outside of the original training set, which suggests that iterations of the workflow could be useful for searching vast chemical spaces in a wide range of design problems.

1   Introduction

The "design and perfection of atom- and energy-efficient synthesis of revolutionary new forms of matter with tailored properties" is one of five scientific grand challenges articulated in the Basic Energy Sciences Advisory Report on Directing Matter and Energy [1]. In chemical sciences, one of the most coveted and impactful targets is the ability to design molecular compounds with desirable properties such as biological activity for molecular therapeutics [2,3] or particular photo-optical properties geared towards photovoltaic applications [4], or the development of molecular dyes [5] or biomarkers [6]. While significant progress has already been achieved in the field of machine learning-assisted computational drug discovery [7,8], the use of artificial intelligence (AI) protocols for the design of photoactive molecules is still in its infancy [9]. This situation can be attributed in part to the fact that the prediction of photo-optical properties for a given molecular structure requires computationally expensive quantum chemical calculations, namely the computation of molecules in their ground and excited states [10]. The computational generation of sufficiently large databases containing molecular structure and their optical properties is therefore far more costly than the calculation of bioactivity, which is traditionally performed using computationally much cheaper empirical scoring or classical force field calculations of protein-ligand interactions [11].

A reasonable shortcut to predicting photo-optical molecular properties is to approximate electronic excitation energies with energy differences between molecular orbital (MO) energy levels [12]. Of particular interest here is the energy difference between the highest occupied MO (HOMO) and the lowest unoccupied MO (LUMO). This so-called "HOMO-LUMO" gap often correlates very well with the lowest-energy, and hence most accessible, excited state that a molecule typically adopts upon energy intake due to the absorption of photons. Thus, HOMO-LUMO gaps have recently become the target of AI-based approached to photoactive molecules [10,12,13]. However, as mentioned above, this approach is only a reasonable shortcut, since for the inverse design of molecular structures with desirable photo-optical properties the entire absorption and/or emission spectrum over the energy range of visible light is required [10]. *Ab initio* multireference wavefunction electronic structure methods such as CAS-PT2 [14] and NEVPT2 [15] are able to cover these energy ranges and provide a measure for absorption/emission intensity via the prediction of oscillator strengths, and therefore accurately predict molecular dye candidate photophysical properties. However, this capability comes with a substantial price: The calculation of an UV/Vis absorption spectrum for molecules containing only tens of atoms are impractical on standard laptop or even Linux-operated workstations, due to the enormous required computational effort and resources in CPU power and memory. Computationally less demanding methods are density functional theory (DFT)-based excited states time-dependent (TD)-DFT methods [16], with the approximate TD-density-functional tight-binding (TD-DFTB) method being one of the computationally most economical methods [17].

In this work we present a vision for a DFTB- and TD-DFTB-based computational workflow for the inverse design of molecules with desirable optical properties. As others before us, we start with an approximation of excitation energies by MO energy differences [12,13]. Besides the use of computationally efficient DFTB methods, our new inverse design algorithm has two major components: 1) Development of a multi-headed graph convolutional neural network (GCNN) approach that will allow the prediction of not only molecular orbital energy differences, but more complex properties such as multiple excitation energies and oscillator strengths for dye candidates [18,19]. The GCNNs surrogate models are sufficiently fast to supplant computationally expensive, explicit excited state calculations required for the inverse design step, which will be component 2): Development of a machine learning masked language model (MLM)-based generation of new dye candidates with subsequent evaluation against a target function (desirable optical properties). As proof-of-principle, we present here a study for the inverse design of molecules with the lowest-possible HOMO-LUMO gap, which is motivated by possible applications as biomarkers in biomedical applications [20]. We note that our choice to minimize the HOMO-LUMO gap in this proposed workflow is arbitrary and could be replaced by a particular energy range. Our choice of a multi-headed GCNN surrogate will allow in subsequent works to extend our molecular design algorithm to predict novel molecules with optical spectra containing user-defined target features, such as intense optical absorption or emission in particular regions of the visible light spectrum.

2 Computational Workflow for Molecular Design

2.1 Inverse Design of Molecules with Small HOMO-LUMO Gap

It is important to remember that we are using two AI components in our computational workflow, which can be trained jointly or independently from each other. In this proof-of-principle work, we started with an existing generative MLM model that originally targeted the generation of drug candidates for molecular therapeutics [21], while the GCNN surrogate for the prediction of HOMO-LUMO gaps was specifically trained as part of this work.

Figure 1 illustrates schematically a pipeline for the adaptive training of the GCNN surrogate model and the generation of new molecules with desirable HOMO-LUMO gap as predicted by the DFTB method. We begin by performing DFTB calculations on a subset of the 134,000 molecules contained in the QM9 database [22] to predict their HOMO-LUMO gaps, then train the GCNN surrogate which is subsequently utilized to score the newly generated molecules predicted by the MLM algorithm. In a final step, the newly predicted molecules are re-calculated using the DFTB method and their HOMO-LUMO gaps compared against the surrogate-predicted value (not shown in Fig. 1). In the following, we briefly discuss the center pieces of our workflow, namely the DFTB

calculations of HOMO-LUMO gaps from SMILES strings, the GCNN surrogate
and the MLM, and their interplay with each other, before elaborating the details
of each component in subsequent Sections.

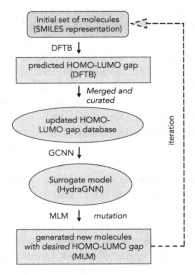

Fig. 1. Computational workflow for molecular design.

DFTB. To generate on-the-fly HOMO-LUMO gap predictions, we employ
the density-functional tight-binding (DFTB) method. DFTB is a fast and efficient quantum mechanical simulation technique that is implemented e.g. in the
DFTB+ program package [23], as well as in other popular quantum chemistry
packages. The required runs are performed in two stages. In the first stage we
generate the data for predicted HOMO-LUMO gaps from a Simplified Molecular Input Line Entry System (SMILES) string [24] representing the molecular
structure. If the structures are in PDB format they can be easily transformed
into SMILES representation using the RDKit software [25]. All of the results are
merged into a single file and curated for the GCNN surrogate operation.

GCNN Surrogate. To train a surrogate model for HOMO-LUMO gap prediction, we use the multi-headed HydraGNN package developed earlier by some
of our team [18,19]. This surrogate, allowing multi-headed output, is ideally
suited for the simultaneous prediction of multiple important molecular characteristics, such as electronic properties and synthesizability scoring. Training of
HydraGNN can be performed on multiple GPU nodes. The trained surrogate
model is then used to generate hydra score for subsequent molecule generation
operation. Details on the HydraGNN surrogate are given below.

Molecule Generation Using MLM. In our last step we use the masked language model (MLM) to generate novel molecules based on the surrogate model.

The MLM was trained following previously reported work [21] on the Enamine *REAL* database [26]. These new molecules are then used to validate the surrogate-predicted HOMO-LUMO gaps using the DFTB method.

3   The DFTB Method

The density-functional tight-binding (DFTB) method [27–29] is an approximation to traditional density functional theory (DFT) [30], roughly 2–3 orders of magnitude faster yet providing detailed electronic structure by solving Kohn-Sham equations using a parameterized Hamiltonian. DFTB methods can be employed in simulations of processes that involve chemical reactions, electron excitation, electron transfer, and mass and ion transport for systems containing several tens of thousands of atoms. Linear scaling algorithms exist [31,32] and have been developed and applied to systems as large as 100 million atoms [33].

One of the key features of DFTB is the use of a two-center approximation [27], which requires the pairwise generation of Hamiltonian element parameters and repulsive potentials. The Foulkes-Haydock approach to the expansion of electron density in a Taylor series around a reference density [28] gives rise to a hierarchical family of DFTB "flavors", starting with the simplest version DFTB1 [27] which is accurate to a first-order expansion, to the most involved DFTB3 flavor which contains the full third-order terms [29]. All DFTB flavors can be cast into a spin-dependent formalism using on-site spin coupling terms [34]. Moreover, a long-range corrected version of the second-order DFTB2 flavor has been developed [35] in order to overcome the infamous self-interaction error inherent to conventional DFT and DFTB methods. In addition, a variety of ad-hoc charge-charge interaction damping and dispersion interactions have been introduced that can be added to account for potential deficiencies in any of the DFTB flavors [36]. However, the performance of any of these resultant DFTB flavors are strongly dependent on the respective optimized electronic Hamiltonian parameters and repulsive potentials for the chemical element combination in question which need to be optimized for any of the DFTB flavors individually.

High-quality DFTB parameters allow a near-1:1 reproduction of molecular orbital (MO) electronic energy levels for molecules, as well as valence and conduction band structures for bulk solid materials relative to DFT [37]. Repulsive potentials can be optimized such that DFTB calculations are able to reproduce DFT geometrical parameters [29] as well as vibrational [38] and optical [39] spectra. In terms of computational accuracy and efficiency, DFTB is settled in between traditional DFT methods and classical force field approaches, although higher accuracy than DFT can be achieved at times when empirical data is employed in the parameterization, for instance for the prediction of band gaps [40].

In our automated workflow, the DFTB calculations are run as follows. A SMILES string corresponding to an arbitrary molecule is internally converted into a set of Cartesian coordinates that are handed to the DFTB+ code as input, along with the selected level of theory. A python script is started to perform the DFTB calculation via the "atomic simulation environment" (ASE) [41], which allows for software-agnostic electronic structure calculations. The DFTB calculation itself in our case is a geometry optimization with user-controllable convergence criteria. The geometry optimization is necessary since the HOMO-LUMO gap is sensitive to the selected geometry. Ideally, the global minimum energy structure should be identified since it is the molecular conformation likely adopted by the molecule in question. At the end of the calculation, the value of the HOMO-LUMO gap is collected from the output corresponding to the converged molecular structure. There are two shortfalls that may occur in the DFTB calculation step: i) failure to achieve self-consistent-charge convergence of the atomic charges in DFTB density calculations, and ii) failure to achieve a converged minimum energy optimized structure. Our algorithm automatically detects those cases and removes them from the database of molecules.

In the presented proof-of-principles applications, we selected the DFTB3 method [29] with the associated, so-called 3ob parameters [42] for the calculation of MO energies and molecular geometries.

4 Surrogate Models: Graph Convolutional Neural Networks

GCNNs are a class of deep learning models that can operate directly on graphs. Graphs, $G = (V, \mathcal{E})$, are data structures that consist of a finite set of nodes V and edges $\mathcal{E}$ connecting the nodes with their neighbour nodes. For example, an edge, $e = (u, v) \in \mathcal{E}$, connects node $u \in V$ with its neighbour $v \in V$.

Representing molecules in the form of graph is natural. The atoms can be viewed as nodes and chemical bonds as edges of the graph as in Fig. 2. Each node in graph is represented by a nodal feature vector such as atomic features in molecules and potentially label properties in the node-level tasks. For edges, in addition to representing the connectivity of nodes in graph, they can also have edge features such as the chemical bound types. Each graph can have global graph-level properties such as the HOMO-LUMO gap for a specific molecular graph.

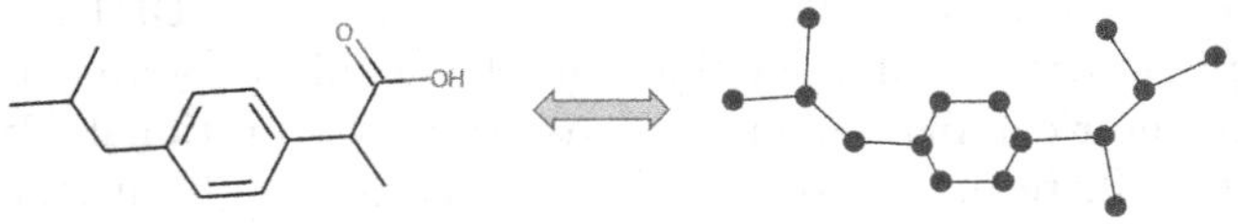

Fig. 2. Graph representation of a molecule.

GCNNs employ a message-passing framework to represent the interactions of nodes, the centerpiece of which is graph convolutional (GC) layers. In each GC layer, messaging passing is performed sequentially with three steps, i.e., message preparation, aggregation, and nodal state update. In message preparation, each node wraps a message, e.g., a vector, based on their current state with a message function and then sends out the message through edges to their neighbours. In message aggregation, the nodes collect the messages received from their neighbours and aggregate the messages with an aggregation function. The aggregated message is then used to update the node together with its current state via an update function. After the message passing in one GC layer, all nodal states are updated with information gathered from their immediate neighbour nodes. With multiple GC layers stacked together, messages are passed to nodes that are further away. In molecules, a single GC layer can be used to approximate pair-wise atomic interactions, while the many-body effects are implicitly represented by stacking many GC layers together. A variety of GCNNs have been developed to better represent the atomic systems, such as crystal GCNN (CGCNN) [43] for crystalline materials, MEGNet for both molecules and crystals [44], as well as ALIGNN [45] that adds the bond angles in the model. More details about GCNNs can be found in [18].

In this work, the GCNN model implemented in HydraGNN [18,19] is used as a surrogate model for HOMO-LUMO gap property. The GC layer used is principal neighborhood aggregation (PNA) [46]. HydraGNN is an open source software built on PyTorch [47,48] and PyTorch Geometric [49,50] library. It is capable of multitask prediction of hybrid node-level and graph-level properties in large batch of graphs with variable number of nodes. HydraGNN utilizes ADIOS [51], a data framework suitable for high performance computing, for data loading in order to handle large graph data set. It has been tested on multiple systems including ORNL's Summit and NERSC's Perlmutter with data sets larger than 100 GB.

Model Architecture and Training on Summit. The GCNN model used in the work consists of three parts, i.e., PNA convolutional layers, batch normalization layers, and fully connected layers. The model starts with a stack of six PNA layers of size 55, each of which is followed by a batch normalization layer, then goes through a global mean pooling layer, and ends with three fully connected layers with 100, 50, 25 neurons, respectively. ReLU activation functions are used.

The DFTB data set consists of 95k molecules with HOMO-LUMO gap generated using the method in Sect. 3. Ninety percent of the data set is used for model training and the other 10% is split equally for model validation and testing. The AdamW optimizer is used with the learning rate of 10^{-3} and the batch size of 64. The model is trained for 200 epochs and the final test MAE for HOMO-LUMO gap is 0.12 eV.

5 Molecule Generation: Masked Language Model

Research in natural language processing (NLP) has provided strategies to leverage large amounts of unlabeled data to train generalizable language models for text generation and prediction [52]. Masked language models are typically developed using two distinct stages, known as pre-training and fine-tuning. Pre-training is completely unsupervised (i.e., doesn't require any manual labeling) and, therefore, can be performed on very large data sets. In fine-tuning, the pre-trained model is further trained for a specific task (e.g., document classification) using a labeled data set that is typically much smaller. Using this two-stage approach, language models have achieved state-of-the-art results for a range of NLP tasks for multiple application areas [52, 53].

Pre-training language models on text sequences can be accomplished using a combination of tokenization and mask prediction. In tokenization, commonly occurring sequences are used to generate a vocabulary for the model [54, 55]. This vocabulary is used to map text to a sequence of integer token IDs which are used as input to the model. For mask prediction, tokens are randomly masked and the model is trained to reproduce the original sequence based on context. Therefore, for a given masked token, the model predicts a probability that each token in the vocabulary will occur at that location.

Advances in language models can be directly applied to molecular structures by using the Simplified Molecular Input Line Entry System (SMILES) text representation [24]. Using a SMILES string, atoms and bonds for a given molecule are converted to a sequence of characters. For example, benzene is given by c1ccccc1, where c represents an individual aromatic carbon atom and 1 represents the start and end of a ring. Similar to traditional text applications, tokenization can be used to split up a given molecule into commonly occurring subsequences [54, 55]. Mask prediction during pre-training then proceeds with the model learning to predict chemical structure based on context.

In our previous work [21, 56], we proposed a strategy to use pre-trained models to generate new molecular structures. Similar to pre-training, a given molecule, represented as a SMILES string, is tokenized and randomly masked. The model predictions are then sampled to generate a set of mutations to the original molecule as shown in Fig. 5. Therefore, in combination with the scoring provided by the surrogate model, the language model can be used to iteratively generate new molecules to search chemical space for a given optimization task. Most notably, the MLM can generate molecules that are much larger in the number of atoms relative to the original set of molecules. This is particularly important when considering the rapidly increasing chemical space with molecular size.

Pre-training on Summit. Following our previous work [21], we leveraged the Enamine *REAL* database [26] as a starting point for language model training. We then augmented the data set using a previously trained language model [21] to include approximately $3.6 \cdot 10^{10}$ molecules. A WordPiece tokenizer [54, 55] was then trained using the full data set. As described in [21], we used data parallelism with DeepSpeed's fused LAMB optimizer for mask prediction training on $3 \cdot 10^9$ molecules on the Summit supercomputer at the Oak Ridge Leadership Computing Facility using 1000 nodes (6 Nvidia 16 GB V100 GPUs per node). The data set was evenly partitioned with $5 \cdot 10^5$ molecules for each GPU. Pre-training was performed for 7 epochs using a batch size of 80 molecules with 3 gradient accumulation steps per GPU. The model is available for download at https://huggingface.co/mossaic-candle/adaptive-lm-molecules and can be used with the Hugging Face transformers library [57].

6   Application: Minimizing the HOMO-LUMO Gap

In this Section we describe our successful implementation of the end-to-end work-flow for accelerating the molecular design process by coupling the approximate quantum chemical methods (i.e. DFTB), surrogate GCNN model, and the generative MLM used as mutation operator for the molecule generation, for minimizing the HOMO-LUMO gap as the target property.

For future reference, we label the 95 k molecular compounds that were contained in QM9 and successfully processed by the DFTB calculations to generate their optimized molecular geometries and associated HOMO-LUMO gaps as the "original data set". As described in Sect. 4, this data set was split into training and test data sets.

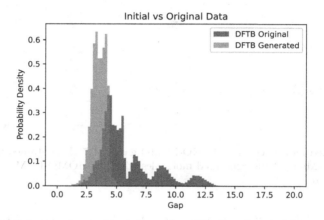

Fig. 3. Comparison of the DFTB-predicted HOMO-LUMO gap is shown for molecules contained in the original data set and for newly generated molecules. The population of molecules clearly shifted towards the target low values of the molecular HOMO-LUMO gap.

Figure 3 shows the comparison of the HOMO-LUMO gap as predicted by DFTB for the molecules contained in the original data set (blue) as well as for the newly generated ones (orange). At first glance it becomes apparent that the generated molecules possess much lower HOMO-LUMO gap values, following the user-defined constraint. It further appears that, while the molecules in the original data set show a multi-modal distribution of their HOMO-LUMO gaps corresponding to the different molecular classes (aliphatic molecules > olefinic molecules > conjugated molecules > molecules with double bonds and strained rings), the new predicted molecules have a more concentrated distribution centered near the 3–3.5 eV (see Figs. 4 and 5).

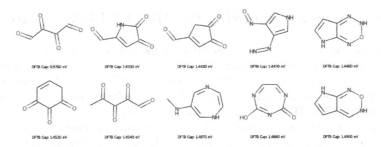

Fig. 4. Selected molecules with HOMO-LUMO gaps <1.7 eV that are already contained in the original QM9 data set. None of these molecules contains more than 9 "heavy" (C, N, O) chemical elements.

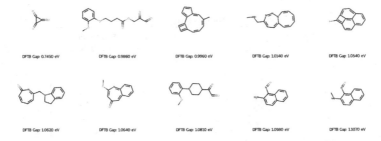

Fig. 5. Selected molecules with HOMO-LUMO gaps <1.7 eV contained in the generated data set. Many of the generated molecules with low HOMO-LUMO gaps contain more than 9 atoms.

The latter figure likewise indicates that most of the newly generated molecules contain more than 9 atoms, and that such structures were not at all included in the original training set of the GCNN surrogate. We do note that the generated molecules show a tendency towards including small, strained rings with double bonds included, such as three- and four-membered rings that are often fused to larger rings. Such molecules derive their small HOMO-LUMO gaps from their ring strains which typically pushes the HOMO levels up and the LUMO levels down, reducing the HOMO-LUMO gap [39], but at the same time increasing their chemical reactivity and the difficulty of synthesis.

Synthesizability is a quantity that can be calculated following the method as mentioned by Etrl et al. [58]. In this empirical technique the synthetic accessibility is estimated by coupling molecular complexity and molecular fragment effects as analyzed by processing a large collection of chemical structures that have already been synthesized before. This technique therefore contains at some level historical data on the synthesizability of a large collection of molecules. The method is then tested and validated by comparing with 'ease of synthesis' ranks. These values were gathered by domain expert chemists. The agreement between score and the ranks are generally reasonable, where a score close to 0 indicates low synthesizability and one close to 1 high synthesizability. This technique provides a good way to estimate the synthesizability for large molecules that have never been synthesized before.

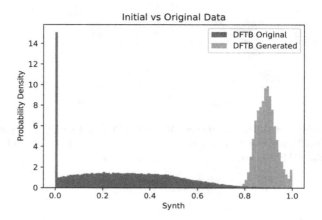

Fig. 6. Comparison of the synthesizability score for molecules contained in the original data set and for newly generated molecules. Molecules were selected according to both low HOMO-LUMO gap and high synthesizability scores. For discussion, see text.

Figure 6 indicates that, in contrast to the molecules in the original data set, the newly generated ones have much higher synthesizability scores, as both low HOMO-LUMO gap and high synthesizability was the criterion to select new molecules creating the new molecule population. This illustrates that a multi-objective search can be performed that will result in a Pareto-optimal set of molecules, combining a number of design targets such as low HOMO-LUMO gaps paired with high values of synthesizability.

Figure 7 gives an impression of the Mean Absolute Error (MAE) of the GCNN surrogate predictions against DFTB-calculated HOMO-LUMO gaps for the molecules contained in the original data set, separately for molecules of the training set and the test set. The MAE is nearly identical in both close to 0.11 eV, indicating an excellent performance of the HydraGNN surrogate for this task, and the homogeneity of the data set.

Such good agreement between surrogate- and DFTB-predicted HOMO-LUMO gaps is lost when considering the situation of the newly generated molecules, shown in Fig. 8. The MAE is increased to 0.45 eV as the now larger molecules, not contained in the original data set, lead to poorer performance of the HydraGNN surrogate which was only trained on the QM9 database containing molecules with up to 9 heavy chemical elements. This fact indicates the usefulness to perform adaptive surrogate training in iterative molecular design approaches, as indicated in Fig. 1 by the dashed arrow labeled "iteration". Nevertheless, it should be noted that the GCNN surrogate model, even without

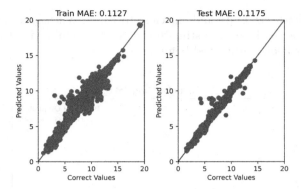

Fig. 7. Comparison of GCNN-predicted HOMO-LUMO gaps vs DFTB-computed ones ("Correct Values") for the training (left) and the test (right) data set of molecules contained in the QM9 database.

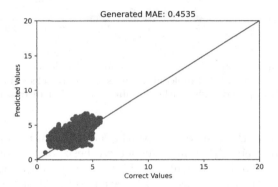

Fig. 8. Comparison of GCNN-predicted HOMO-LUMO gaps vs DFTB-computed ones ("Correct Values") for the MLM-generated molecules with smaller HOMO-LUMO gaps.

iterative improvements, was able to provide sufficiently reliable guidance to the MLM for generating new molecular structures with reduced HOMO-LUMO gap.

For completeness, and to give an impression of the chemical variability contained in the designed novel organic molecules with low HOMO-LUMO gap, we show their molecular structures in the associated supplementary information (SI). Figure S1 shows all molecules with HOMO-LUMO gaps <1.7 eV contained in the original data set (43) and Fig. S2 shows those in the data set of generated, novel molecules with the same HOMO-LUMO gap threshold (384).

7 Conclusions and Future Work

The current proof-of-principle shows that the combination of semiempirical quantum chemical electronic structure theory, GCNN surrogate, and MLM generative model succeeds to predict a plethora of novel molecular compounds with desirable optical properties, in this case HOMO-LUMO gaps that are as small as possible. First we wish to mention how well our multi-headed GCNN surrogate reproduced HOMO-LUMO gaps, the MAE was 0.11 eV for molecules both in the training as well as test set (both part of the QM9 database). This accuracy is similar to the one recently reported by Lilienfeld et al. [13] and is comparable, or even exceeds, the error bars that can be expected from traditional DFT methods in their prediction of excitation energies, and thus lays the foundation for an inverse design workflow focusing on HOMO-LUMO gaps. The surrogate lost accuracy when trying to predict HOMO-LUMO gaps of larger molecules that were not part of the training set, which indicates the necessity of adaptive surrogate training schemes in iterative molecular design. Our computational workflow for accelerated molecular design using quantum chemical simulations and deep learning models already possesses these capabilities, and we will exploit them in future applications.

Nevertheless, even in a single iteration, our workflow succeeded in predicting a significantly large number of molecules with very small HOMO-LUMO gaps <1.7 eV (384) which is much larger than the fraction of such molecules contained in the entire QM9-based original data set containing 95 k molecules (43). This constitutes proof-of-principle of our combined surrogate/generative model approach, even factoring in that the MLM was not even trained on molecules with particular optical properties.

The newly generated molecules have the caveat that the majority of them is likely not easy to synthesize or that they are unstable for other reasons, which underlines the necessity of multi-objective optimizations with suitable synthesizability scores. In future works, we will test the capability to perform adaptive training built into our workflow, and incorporate advanced property predictions such as the prediction of electronic excitation energies and oscillator strengths for real-world design applications targeting photoactive molecules and molecular dyes. Our workflow will be generally applicable to any type of molecular properties that can be predicted by quantum chemical electronic structure programs, such as molecular energies, electronic and magnetic properties, vibrational properties, and optical properties in general.

Acknowledgements. We thank Pilsun Yoo for fruitful discussions on the synthesizability score. This work was supported in part by the Office of Science of the Department of Energy and by the Laboratory Directed Research and Development (LDRD) Program of Oak Ridge National Laboratory. This research is sponsored by the Artificial Intelligence Initiative as part of the Laboratory Directed Research and Development Program of Oak Ridge National Laboratory, managed by UT-Battelle, LLC, for the US Department of Energy under contract DE-AC05-00OR22725. The research was supported by the Exascale Computing Project (17-SC-20-SC), a collaborative effort of the U.S. Department of Energy Office of Science and the National Nuclear Security Administration. This work used resources of the Oak Ridge Leadership Computing Facility, which is supported by the Office of Science of the U.S. Department of Energy under Contract No. DE-AC05-00OR22725.

References

1. Basic Energy Sciences Advisory Committee et al.: Directing Matter and Energy: Five Challenges for Science and the Imagination. US Department of Energy: Washington, DC (2007)
2. Sanchez-Lengeling, B., Aspuru-Guzik, A.: Inverse molecular design using machine learning: generative models for matter engineering. Science **361**(6400), 360–365 (2018)
3. Blanchard, A.E., Stanley, C., Bhowmik, D.: Using GANs with adaptive training data to search for new molecules. J. Cheminform. **13**(1), 1–8 (2021). https://doi.org/10.1186/s13321-021-00494-3
4. Sun, W., et al.: Machine learning-assisted molecular design and efficiency prediction for high-performance organic photovoltaic materials. Sci. Adv. **5**(11), eaay4275 (2019)
5. Pral, P.O., Barbatti, M.: Molecular excited states through a machine learning lens. Nat. Rev. Chem. **5**(6), 388–405 (2021)
6. Zhavoronkov, A.: Artificial intelligence for drug discovery, biomarker development, and generation of novel chemistry. Mol. Pharm. **15**(10), 4311–4313 (2018)
7. Jiménez-Luna, J., Grisoni, F., Schneider, G.: Drug discovery with explainable artificial intelligence. Nat. Mach. Intell. **2**(10), 573–584 (2020)
8. Bhowmik, D., et al.: Deep clustering of protein folding simulations. JBMC Bioinformatics **19**(484), 47–58 (2018). https://doi.org/10.1186/s12859-018-2507-5
9. Zhuo, Y., Brgoch, J.: Opportunities for next-generation luminescent materials through artificial intelligence. J. Phys. Chem. Lett. **12**(2), 764–772 (2021)
10. Cheng-Wei, J., et al.: Machine learning enables highly accurate predictions of photophysical properties of organic uorescent materials: emission wavelengths and quantum yields. J. Chem. Inf. Model **61**(3), 1053–1065 (2021)
11. Acharya, A., et al.: Supercomputer-based ensemble docking drug discovery pipeline with application to COVID-19. J. Chem. Inf. Model **60**(12), 5832–5852 (2020)
12. Meftahi, N., et al.: Machine learning property prediction for organic photovoltaic devices. NPJ Comput. Mater **6**(1), 1–8 (2020)
13. Mazouin, B., Schöpfer, A.A., von Lilienfeld, O.A.: Selected Machine Learning of HOMO-LUMO gaps with Improved Data-Efficiency. arXiv preprint arXiv:2110.02596 (2021)
14. Andersson, K., Malmqvist, P.Å., Roos, B.O.:Second-order perturbation theory with a complete active space self-consistent field reference function. J. Chem. Phys. **96**(2), 1218–1226 (1992)
15. Angeli, C., et al.: Introduction of n-electron valence states for multireference perturbation theory. J. Chem. Phys. **114**(23), 10252–10264 (2001)
16. Botti, S., et al.: Time-dependent density-functional theory for extended systems. Rep. Prog. Phys. **70**(3), 357 (2007)
17. Sokolov, M., et al.: Analytical time-dependent long-range corrected density functional tight binding (TD-LC-DFTB) gradients in DFTB+: implementation and benchmark for excited-state geometries and transition energies. J. Chem. Theory Comput. **17**(4), 2266–2282 (2021)
18. Lupo Pasini, M., et al.: Multi-task graph neural networks for simultaneous prediction of global and atomic properties in ferromagnetic systems. Mach. Learn. Sci. Technol. **3**(2), 025007 (2022). https://doi.org/10.1088/2632-2153/ac6a51
19. Pasini, M.L., et al.: HydraGNN. [Computer Software] (2021). https://doi.org/10.11578/dc.20211019.2, https://github.com/ORNL/HydraGNN

20. Li, B., Zhao, M., Zhang, F.: Rational design of nearinfrared- II organic molecular dyes for bioimaging and biosensing. ACS Mater. Lett. **2**(8), 905–917 (2020)
21. Blanchard, A.E., et al.: Language models for the prediction of SARSCoV- 2 inhibitors. bioRxiv (2021). https://www.biorxiv.org/content/10.1101/2021.12.10.471928v1, https://doi.org/10.1101/2021.12.10.471928
22. Ramakrishnan, R., et al.: Quantum chemistry structures and properties of 134 kilo molecules. Sci. Data **1**(1), 1–7 (2014)
23. Hourahine, B., et al.: DFTB+, a software package for efficient approximate density functional theory based atomistic simulations. J. Chem. Phys. **152**(12), 124101 (2020)
24. Weininger, D.: SMILES, a chemical language and information system. 1. Introduction to methodology and encoding rules. J. Chem. Inf. Comput. Sci. **28**, 31–36 (1998). https://doi.org/10.1021/ci00057a005
25. RDKit: Open-source cheminformatics (2022). https://www.rdkit.org
26. Enamine REAL Database. https://virtual-ow.org/, https://enamine.net/compound-collections/real-compounds/real-database. Accessed 01 Apr 2020
27. Porezag, D., et al.: Construction of tight-binding-like potentials on the basis of density-functional theory: application to carbon. Phys. Rev. B **51**(19), 12947–12957 (1995). https://link.aps.org/doi/10.1103/PhysRevB.51.12947, https://doi.org/10.1103/PhysRevB.51.12947
28. Elstner, M., et al.: Self-consistent-charge density-functional tight-binding method for simulations of complex materials properties. Phys. Rev. B **58**(11), 7260–7268 (1998). https://link.aps.org/doi/10.1103/PhysRevB.58.7260. https://doi.org/10.1103/PhysRevB.58.7260
29. Gaus, M., Cui, Q., Elstner, M.: DFTB3: extension of the self-consistent-charge density-functional tight-binding method (SCCDFTB). J. Chem. Theory Comput. **7**(4), 931–948 (2011). ISSN: 1549-9618, 1549-9626. https://pubs.acs.org/doi/10.1021/ct100684s. https://doi.org/10.1021/ct100684s
30. Jones. R.O.: Density functional theory: its origins, rise to prominence, and future. Rev. Mod. Phys. **87**(3), 897 (2015)
31. Nishimoto, Y., Fedorov, D.G., Irle, S.: Density-functional tight-binding combined with the fragment molecular orbital method. J. Chem. Theory Comput. **10**(11), 4801–4812 (2014). ISSN: 1549–9618. https://pubs.acs.org/doi/10.1021/ct500489d, https://doi.org/10.1021/ct500489d
32. Nishimura, Y., Nakai, H.: DCDFTBMD: divide-and-conquer density functional tight-binding program for huge-system quantum mechanical molecular dynamics simulations. J. Comput. Chem. **40**(15), 1538–1549 (2019). ISSN: 1096–987X. https://onlinelibrary.wiley.com/doi/abs/10.1002/jcc.25804, https://doi.org/10.1002/jcc.25804
33. Nishimura, Y., Nakai, H.: Quantum chemical calculations for up to one hundred million atoms using DCDFTBMD code on supercomputer Fugaku. Chem. Lett. **50**(8), 1546–1550 (2021)
34. Frauenheim, T., et al.: Atomistic simulations of complex materials: ground-state and excited-state properties. J. Phys. Condens. Matter **14**(11), 3015 (2002)
35. Lutsker, V., Aradi, B., Niehaus, T.A.: Implementation and benchmark of a long-range corrected functional in the density functional based tight-binding method. J. Chem. Phys. **143**(18), 184107 (2015)
36. Rezac, J.: Empirical self-consistent correction for the description of hydrogen bonds in DFTB3. J. Chem. Theory Comput. **13**(10), 4804–4817 (2017)
37. Cui, Q., Elstner, M.: Density functional tight binding: values of semi-empirical methods in an ab initio era. Phys. Chem. Chem. Phys. **16**(28), 14368–14377 (2014)

38. Nishimoto, Y., Irle, S.: Quantum chemical prediction of vibrational spectra of large molecular systems with radical or metallic electronic structure. Chem. Phys. Lett. **667**, 317–321 (2017)
39. Camacho, C., et al.: Origin of the size-dependent fluorescence blueshift in [n] cycloparaphenylenes. Chem. Sci. **4**(1), 187–195 (2013)
40. Chou, C.-P., et al.: Automatized parameterization of DFTB using particle swarm optimization. J. Chem. Theory Comput. **12**(1), 53–64 (2016)
41. Larsen, A.H., et al.: The atomic simulation environment—a Python library for working with atoms. J. Phys. Condens. Matter **29**(27), 273002 (2017)
42. Kubillus, M., et al.: Parameterization of the DFTB3 method for Br, Ca, Cl, F, I, K, and Na in organic and biological systems. J. Chem. Theory Comput. **11**(1), 332–342 (2015). ISSN: 1549–9618. https://doi.org/10.1021/ct5009137. Accessed 06 Mar 2021
43. Xie, T., Grossman, J.C.: Crystal graph convolutional neural networks for an accurate and interpretable prediction of material properties. Phys. Rev. Lett. **120**(14), 145301 (2018). https://link.aps.org/doi/10.1103/PhysRevLett.120. 145301, https://doi.org/10.1103/PhysRevLett.120.145301
44. Chen, C., et al.: Graph networks as a universal machine learning framework for molecules and crystals. Chem. Mater. **31**(9), 3564–3572 (2019). https://doi.org/ 10.1021/acs.chemmater.9b01294
45. Choudhary, K., DeCost, B.: Atomistic line graph neural network for improved materials property predictions. NPJ Comput. Mater. **7**(1), 1–8 (2021)
46. Corso, G., et al.: Principal Neighbourhood Aggregation for Graph Nets. en. arXiv:2004.05718 [cs, stat] (2020). arXiv: 2004.05718. http://arxiv.org/abs/2004. 05718. Accessed 21 Feb 2021
47. Paszke, A., et al.: PyTorch: an imperative style, high-performance deep learning library. Adv. Neural Inf. Process Syst. **32** (2019).http://papers.neurips.cc/paper/ 9015-pytorch-an-imperative-style-high-performancedeep-learning-library.pdf. Ed. by H. Wallach et al. Curran Associates Inc., pp. 8024–8035
48. PyTorch. https://pytorch.org/docs/stable/index.html
49. Fey, M., Lenssen, J.E.: Fast graph representation learning with Py-Torch geometric. In: ICLR Workshop on Representation Learning on Graphs and Manifolds (2019)
50. PyTorch Geometric. https://pytorch-geometric.readthedocs.io/en/latest/
51. Godoy, W.F., et al.: ADIOS 2: the adaptable input output system. A framework for high-performance data management. SoftwareX **12**, 100561 (2020). ISSN: 2352–7110. https://doi.org/10.1016/j.softx.2020.100561, https:// www.sciencedirect.com/science/article/pii/S2352711019302560
52. Devlin, J., et al.: BERT: pre-training of deep bidirectional transformers for language understanding. In: NAACL HLT 2019–2019 Conference of the North American Chapter of the Association for Computational Linguistics: Human Language Technologies–Proceedings of the Conference, no. 1, pp. 4171–4186. Mlm (2019). arXiv: 1810.04805
53. Gu, Y., et al.: Domain-specific language model pretraining for biomedical natural language processing. arXiv (2020). ISSN: 23318422. https://arxiv.org/abs/2007. 15779
54. Schuster, M., Nakajima, K.: Japanese and Korean voice search. In: 2012 IEEE International Conference on Acoustics, Speech and Signal Processing (ICASSP), pp. 5149–5152 (2012). https://doi.org/10.1109/ICASSP.2012.6289079
55. Wu, Y., et al.: Google's Neural Machine Translation System: Bridging the Gap between Human and Machine Translation (2016). arXiv: 1609.08144. http://arxiv. org/abs/1609.08144

56. Blanchard, A.E., et al.: Automating genetic algorithm mutations for molecules using a masked language model. IEEE Trans. Evol. Comput. (2022). https://doi.org/10.1109/TEVC.2022.3144045
57. Wolf, T., et al.: Transformers: state-of-the-art natural language processing. In: Proceedings of the 2020 Conference on Empirical Methods in Natural Language Processing: System Demonstrations. Online: Association for Computational Linguistics, pp. 38–45, October 2020. https://www.aclweb.org/anthology/2020.emnlp-demos.6
58. Ertl, P., Schuffenhauer, A.: Estimation of synthetic accessibility score of drug-like molecules based on molecular complexity and fragment contributions. J. Cheminform. 1(8) (2009). https://doi.org/10.1186/1758-2946-1-8

Self-learning Data Foundation for Scientific AI

Annmary Justine, Sergey Serebryakov⬚, Cong Xu, Aalap Tripathy⬚,
Suparna Bhattacharya⬚, Paolo Faraboschi⬚, and Martin Foltin^(✉)⬚

Hewlett Packard Labs, Hewlett Packard Enterprise, Spring, TX 77389, USA
{annmary.roy,sergey.serebryakov,cong.xu,aalap.tripathy,
suparna.bhattacharya,paolo.faraboschi,martin.foltin}@hpe.com

Abstract. The "Self-Learning Data Foundation for AI" is an open-source platform to manage Machine Learning (ML) metadata in complex end-to-end pipelines, and includes the intelligence to optimize data gradation, pipeline configuration, and compute performance. The work addresses several challenges: prioritizing data to reduce movement, tracking lineage to optimize complex ML pipelines, and enabling reproducibility and portability of data selection and ML model development. Off-the-shelf AI metadata management frameworks (such as MLflow or Weights & Biases) focus on fine-grain stage-level metadata, and only track parts of the pipeline, and lineage. Our proposed software layer sits between ML workflows and pipelines and storage/data access. The first implementation of the Data Foundation is the Common Metadata Framework (CMF), which captures metadata and tracks them automatically alongside references to data artifacts and application code. Its git-like nature allows parallel model development by different teams and is well suited for federated environments. It includes intelligence to optimize pipelines and storage, can learn the access patterns from pipeline execution to inform optimizations such as prestaging and caching. It also learns from model inference metrics to build iteratively more robust models. Through a data shaping use case for I/O optimization and an active learning use case to reduce labelling (on DeepCam AI model training on climate data running on NERSC Cori), we show the versatility of the data foundation layer, the potential benefits (4x reduction in training time and 2x reduction in labelling effort), and its central role in complex ML pipelines.

Keywords: AI metadata · Trustworthy AI · MLOps

1 Introduction

Over the last five years, Machine Learning (ML) methods have become an important tool in experimental and computational scientist toolbox thanks to their ability to learn complex relationships and infer results at a fraction of compute time of exact numerical solutions. Artificial Intelligence (AI) is helping in many areas of scientific discovery, including extracting structures from complex and noisy tomography images [1], accelerating simulations to make them viable for large systems with multi-scale physics [2], addressing inverse problem of predicting optimum experiment parameters [3], enabling complex modeling in high impact areas such as climate and drug discovery [4, 5], etc.

K. Doug et al. (Eds.): SMC 2022, CCIS 1690, pp. 20–37, 2022.
https://doi.org/10.1007/978-3-031-23606-8_2

Several challenges need to be addressed to further accelerate scientific discovery with the help of ML methods. First, *the process of learning new insights from scientific data needs to be more efficient and automated.* Today, scientists manually build complex pipelines for data and AI model engineering optimized for specific use cases. Each pipeline may contain multiple interdependent AI models interleaved with conventional data analytics [6], HPC simulation [4], or scientific experiment stages. The pipeline may include data augmentation stages to help avoid AI model overfitting and improve model trustworthiness. Some AI models may be built incrementally by active or continuous learning algorithms [1], where each pipeline iteration includes learning strategy, data selection, and labeling stages. These stages may be distributed between the edge (where the data is collected) and the HPC cluster. In complex pipelines, the parameter search space to optimize all pipeline stages can be very large and include learning strategy, data selection, data transformation and augmentation stage parameters and methods, AI model architectures, loss functions, model training parameters, etc. Tools are available to optimize individual pipeline stages, for example, Neural Network Architecture Search (NAS) and AutoML training hyper-parameter optimization tools [7–9]. However, these tools do not span across multiple pipeline stages and AI model engineering often requires considerable manual effort even when these tools are used. More critically, there is little cross-leverage and learning between different pipelines of similar type. Furthermore, large volume of parameters, branching and complex dependences of AI pipelines on input data (especially when AI models and built iteratively) makes it hard to achieve flow reproducibility. Second, *the process of building pipelines for AI models can be very computationally intensive* and suffer from computational and data access bottlenecks. AI model optimization for performance and trust metrics often requires many experiments that operate on large volumes of data. With continuing performance scaling of modern GPU and ASIC accelerators for AI model training, we anticipate growing need for intelligent data gradation to address I/O and data movement bottlenecks.

We argue that there is a *need for a new intelligence layer helping scientists to converge to trustworthy AI models faster while also reducing computational and data access bottlenecks.* This intelligence – a form of meta-learning - should help guide scientists and the AutoML tools towards the best strategies for building and optimization of pipelines and parameters for given problems. It should also help to identify and address compute and storage bottlenecks and help reduce data movement across storage tiers and between the edge and the HPC clusters. To enable this new intelligence, a common metadata infrastructure is needed that provides visibility to workflow lineages and metadata across all pipeline stages - from past executions of the AI pipeline, and for different pipelines of a similar type. This is to understand what worked well and what did not, and project the dependences of output metrics (precision, recall, inference time, etc.) on input data distributions and parameters from all pipeline stages, to provide informed initial guesses (seeds) and strategies for optimizations. This metadata infrastructure needs to be federated to enable access to metadata alongside with pipeline code for different team members working on different pipeline stages, and even for different teams to cross-leverage from each other's experience and historical knowledge.

In this paper we present the initial architecture of a Self-Learning Data Foundation framework that is our first step towards providing such meta-learning intelligence in the future. Another benefit of this infrastructure is that it enables reproducibility, audit trail, and ability to unwind incrementally developed models when bad data has been discovered, supporting rebuild of a model from last known good state. The paper is organized as follows: In Sect. 2 we describe Data Foundation for AI high level architecture. In Sect. 3 we discuss design and initial implementation of Common Metadata Framework – a "Git for AI" federated metadata infrastructure underpinning the Data Foundation for AI. In Sects. 4 and 5 we discuss first two intelligence tools built on top of this infrastructure – an AI model training aware storage tiering developed to reduce training I/O bottlenecks and an AI model uncertainty calibration to help with data selection and learning strategy in Active Learning pipeline. We conclude this position and architecture paper with a brief Summary in Sect. 6.

2   Self-learning Data Foundation for AI

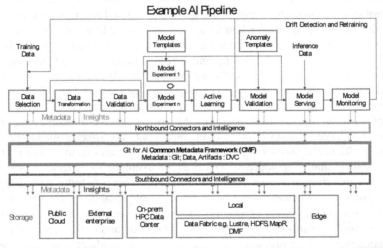

Fig. 1. Data Foundation for AI is composed of Common Metadata Framework (CMF), Northbound Connectors & Intelligence, and Southbound Connector & Intelligence software layers that are independent on AI platforms, frameworks, and storage. Shown in context of an example AI pipeline.

The self-learning data foundation is a new software layer situated between platforms that run AI pipelines or scientific workflows on the North and data storage and management back-ends on the South. It tracks AI workflow metadata (e.g. lineage graph, parameters, metrics) throughout the data and processing lifecycle and uses the metadata to achieve two key functions. The first function optimizes scientific data pipelines and models for trust and efficiency. The second function optimizes the underlying system by prioritizing data that would lead to high quality, trustworthy (e.g. robust and explainable) outcomes, throughout data transfer, retention, provisioning, and processing for AI. Figure 1 depicts the high-level architecture. The AI pipelines at the top could include multistage data driven scientific discovery workflows that may combine traditional HPC and AI processing including training, inference, and active learning. These pipelines could be distributed across locations and the stages could execute asynchronously. Typically, multiple AI pipelines are in operation within a given environment, potentially related to multiple ongoing scientific campaigns.

The data foundation software itself consists of two parts. The first, is the Git for AI Common Metadata Framework (CMF) that helps to track dependencies of AI outcomes on data lineage. The second comprises intelligence functions that learn from this metadata to optimize data, models and system resources for future AI training and inference workflows. For instance, these functions help select, prioritize, and optimize data, pipeline and model for trustworthy outcomes and runtime efficiency. Northbound optimizations improve AI application/pipeline performance metrics and southbound optimizations improve system/ infrastructure operational performance metrics.

3   The Common Metadata Framework (CMF)

A data-centric approach to AI (improve your data), in many cases, may result in better and more trusted AI models than a model-centric approach (tune model's parameters). Adopting a data-centric approach implies a transition from individual ML experiments to complex ML pipelines where heterogeneous artifacts (datasets, dataset slices, hyper-parameters, and ML models) interact with each other and tracking these interactions via metadata becomes critically important. Metadata provides insights into ML models and related artifacts at every stage of ML pipelines. It includes model selection among candidates (via hyper-parameter optimization analysis), model provenance (e.g., what is the base model this model was derived from, what is the learning rate?), model performance (is there a concept drift?), optimizations (reuse unmodified artifacts, such as pre-processed dataset), fairness (is there a bias in my dataset?), and trustworthiness (explainability and end-to-end observability). Metadata can be categorized into two buckets. The first bucket contains ML metadata associated with a standalone ML experiment. It includes information about ML artifacts, such as inputs (hyper parameters and datasets), and outputs (trained models and performance metrics). A broad range of solutions are available, among which the most notable ones are MLflow [10] and W&B [11]. The second bucket contains pipeline metadata that is used to provide data and ML model lineage by maintaining directed graphs of how artifacts are transformed into one another. Pipeline metadata tracking libraries are in early stages of adoption, and we are aware about two of them - standalone ML Metadata (MLMD) [12] library from TensorFlow ecosystem, and pipeline metadata tracking feature of W&B. Table 1 summarizes these two categories.

ML metadata tracking libraries can also be used to track metadata of pipelines consisting of one stage. Several factors contribute to the pipeline metadata tracking functionality becoming critically important in research and production environments. Complexity of ML pipelines has been constantly increasing, reproducibility issues have been the subject of active debates, end-to-end ML pipelines become distributed ("core" ↔ "edge") with complex interactions, and there are many opportunities to learn from positive and negative feedback loops ("train" ← "drift during inference"). Researchers have a rich

Table 1. Categories of machine learning metadata.

	Experiment metadata	Pipeline metadata
Target metadata	ML experiments	ML pipelines
Existing solutions	MLflow, W&B, Determined.AI	MLMD
Primary users	Research: data scientists, researchers	Production: researchers, ML engineers
Focus	Ease of use	Reproducibility
Want to know	How accurate is my model	What pipeline have I used to train this model?
Ease of use	Easy	Hard (unless users use TFX or similar frameworks)

set of libraries to track their ML metadata, but they lack such functionality for pipelines. Standalone libraries, such as MLMD, are hard to use, and require a wrapper to provide developer-friendly application programming interface (API). However, users get their pipeline metadata automatically tracked when these libraries are integrated with frameworks, such as TensorFlow and Kubeflow pipelines, which implies that users must use these frameworks in all stages of their ML pipelines.

To the best of our knowledge, no open-source end-to-end solution exists for data management and pipeline metadata tracking outside of ecosystem of the above-mentioned frameworks. Several challenges have not been addressed such as distributed pipelines (collect metadata, manage associated versioned artifacts, derive intelligence) self-learning across complex pipelines (learn from data drift, retrain ML models), and metadata-driven optimizations (recommend models, datasets, and hyper-parameters, reuse previously produced artifacts).

To address the challenges and meet the requirements outlined in this section, we have prototyped a Common Metadata Framework (CMF). Section 3.1 introduces the main principles behind CMF. Section 3.2 briefly describes the main components of the CMF. Section 3.3 outlines how users interact with the CMF, and Sect. 3.4 provides several ideas how CMF integrates with existing machine and deep learning frameworks, as well as with existing MLOps platforms such as MLflow. The CMF is an open source infrastructure available at https://github.com/HewlettPackard/cmf.

3.1 CMF Foundational Pillars

The CMF framework manages versioned artifacts, collects, and interlinks associated metadata either implicitly thought the input and output parameters of ML pipeline stages, or explicitly through metadata logging API. The CMF framework is built upon the following five foundational pillars:

Data Centricity. Data-centric AI views data as the first-class citizen and focuses on quality of datasets used to train and test ML models. We address challenges associated with tracking versioned data and maintaining artifacts lineage by supporting content-addressed artifacts and data slices. Content-addressed artifacts are uniquely identified by md5 hashes of their contents. Hashes eliminate chances of collisions between artifacts, support versioning of artifacts, and provide natural way to merge metadata from distributed, periodically disconnected, sites. We use data slices to track ML model performance for data sub-groups identified by, e.g., ethnicity, gender, or religion. We also ensure that ML pipelines can identify models that are biased for underrepresented examples by tracking data slices and performance of ML models on these data slices.

Support for Distributed Environments. ML pipeline stages can run in distributed environments spanning across many datacenters and edge sites. The metadata captured by the CMF framework can be stored directly in a central repository in a relational database or can be stored locally in local databases. Often, edge sites do not have reliable connections to the central datacenter. Also, for certain workflows, only metadata and artifacts associated with specific runs (e.g., best training experiments), need to be pushed to the central metadata repository and artifact store. To support these scenarios, the CMF framework can push local metadata to remote repositories and pull remote metadata into local repositories.

Implicit and Explicit Metadata Logging with Multiple Back Ends. The CMF framework automatically logs pipeline metadata for several ML use cases, including training and hyper-parameter optimization. Several back ends (metadata stores) are supported including MLflow and MLMD (proof-of-concept implementations). Developers can use CMF APIs if their use case is not supported, or they need to log extended information. We adapted a standard MLMD artifact schema. Since it is a standard, developers can use third-party tools (should they exist) to work with ML and pipeline metadata in CMF, for instance, visualizing or querying data.

Strongly Typed Artifacts. Following MLMD principles, every artifact has a type. The collection of artifacts forms a type system – a language that ML pipeline stages use to talk to each other. We provide a base set of artifacts, such as a dataset, a data slice, an ML model, and others. Developers can extend these base artifacts to meet their needs. For instance, we provide an abstract artifact for representing training reports, and provide two concrete implementations – for MLMD and MLflow. Users can provide their own train report artifacts, such as, for instance, pointing to Determined.AI or W&B tracking services. Visualization and analytic tools and querying engines that rely on standard interface of train reports will work with these new artifacts too.

Modular Architecture Built on Top of Open-Source Projects (to satisfy our requirements and facilitate adoption in AI community). We use several open-source frameworks: Data Version Control (DVC) [13], MLMD and, optionally, MLflow. DVC is an open-source framework for storing versioned artifacts. The framework computes the content hash of artifacts. It stores artifacts in the backend storage (Amazon S3, Google drive, HDFS, or a local filesystem) with an efficient content-addressed layout: an artifact is stored in the folder which is the first two characters of the content hash, and the artifact file is named as the remaining characters of this hash. This helps in easy retrieval and deduplication of content. In the future, other versioning back ends can be used in place of DVC if so desired, a DVC remote can be developed to serve as a Globus end point, and a DataFed integration can be considered. MLMD is an open-source library from TensorFlow ecosystem to store and manage pipeline metadata. The lineages built by the framework are stored in a database. The framework provides API to query the lineages. The type of queries that are supported includes but not limited to, queries to get the lineages for an artifact including the parent and child linkages, queries to get all artifacts involved (input/output) for an execution, queries to get all the stages in a pipeline and their latest executions etc. MLflow is a platform to manage the lifecycle of ML models – from training to deployment and serving. MLflow can be used as one of the back ends for storing pipeline metadata and could be a preferred choice during experimentation phase or in research environments due to its simplicity.

3.2 CMF Architecture

Main components of the CMF framework are shown in Fig. 2.

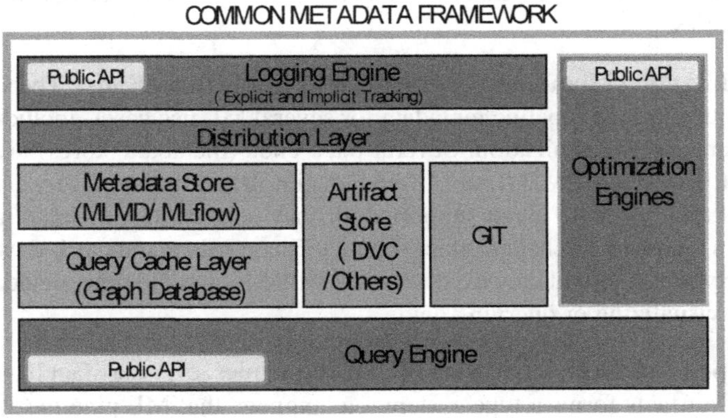

Fig. 2. CMF Architecture. Green highlighted are CMF components, gray highlighted are open source components leveraged in CMF. (Color figure online)

Developers interact with the CMF via public APIs exposed by logging, query, and optimization engines. The *logging engine* is responsible for logging various artifacts, such as datasets, machine learning models, performance metrics etc. The *query engine* is used to query artifacts' lineage. It can be used to answer such questions as what datasets were used to build this model. Or what models have been built using these datasets. The *optimization engine*, an experimental feature of CMF, can be used to optimize the execution of future pipelines. It can suggest, among other things, the initial set of hyper-parameters, or even a machine learning model for a new problem.

Internally, CMF is composed of three main components – metadata and artifact stores, and cache layer. The *metadata store* is responsible for storing artifact metadata. CMF uses MLMD (Machine Learning Metadata library from Google) as the metadata store layer. CMF can also use MLflow to store metadata, but this is an experimental feature. The *artifact store* is responsible for storing the actual artifacts – datasets, dataset slices and machine learning models. CMF uses data version control (DVC) for this. The *cache layer* is used to cache information about artifacts' metadata in such a way that it is easily accessible with minimal latencies. CMF uses Neo4J, a graph database, to implement this cache layer. This cache layer is optional.

3.3   Distributed CMF with Git-Like Experience

Tracking lineages of artifacts for complex ML multi-step pipelines is associated with several challenges. Pipeline steps can be executed in different datacenters or edge sites which are disconnected with each other and may have intermittent connection to the core datacenter. Pipeline steps can be managed by different teams. Artifacts which are not identical to each other can have the same names, or identical artifacts can have different names across different datacenters. The artifacts (inputs or outputs of pipeline steps) need to be uniquely identified across different sites and across multiple pipelines.

We solve these challenges by allowing artifacts to be identified by the hash of their content. This helps to uniquely identify an artifact anywhere in the distributed sites. Artifacts are associated with the execution of a step in the pipeline either as an input or an output. Other related metadata is collected about the artifacts and the pipeline steps. This metadata is journaled locally as and when steps in the pipeline are executed in their respective edge sites. These journals are transferred from the distributed edge sites to the central site.

Metadata collected from the various edge sites are merged into the central repository to create a single global view. An input artifact might have created multiple child artifacts and these child artifacts might have produced further artifacts on other sites. By identifying the artifacts with the content hash and associating metadata to the artifacts based on the content hash, we can merge metadata from multiple locations. Additionally, each artifact is associated with a step in the pipeline as an input or output artifact. This allows us to build the lineage chain across the distributed sites.

The artifact metadata also contains information that points to the physical location of the artifact and the git commit id of the code used to create the artifact. If the entire lineage chain needs to be cloned in a location, the nodes in the DAG are traversed and individual artifacts are pulled from the artifact repository to the local store along with the code.

The Fig. 3 demonstrates the use case for distributed CMF and shows how developers can take advantage of their knowledge of Git to start working with CMF.

Step 1.   The raw data, code and tracked metadata are collected in site 1. From site 1, it is pushed to the central repositories. The code used to acquire the data is pushed to the code repository. Content hash of the acquired data artifact is created, and additional metadata is collected. In this case, the data artifact is associated with execution of step 1 as an output event. The data artifact is pushed to the artifact repository (using data versioning software like Data Version Control (DVC)). The metadata for the data artifact is created. It contains the content hash and the pointer to the physical location in artifact repository. This metadata is pushed to the central repository, where a new metadata entry is created for this content hash as this is the first time this content hash is encountered in the central repository.

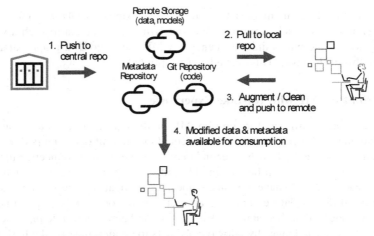

Fig. 3. Distributed CMF with git-like experience.

Steps 2 and 3. The raw data is processed to create a more distilled artifact. The raw data is pulled to the local site from the central repository. The metadata tracker calculates the content hash of the raw data and creates an artifact. This artifact is associated with the step as input artifact, and the new processed artifact is generated as output. The content hash of the newly generated artifact is associated with the execution of that step as an output artifact. The new artifact is pushed to the artifact repository. The generated metadata is pushed to the central repository. In the central repository, the metadata journaled at site 2 is merged with the existing metadata. Since the content hash for artifact 1 already exists in the central repository, the new event about artifact 1 (i.e., it is the input to stage 2 and parent of artifact 2) is merged to central repository. The artifact 2 content hash is an added content hash, hence a new metadata entry for artifact is added to the central repository and an output event is added to the artifact to associate it with stage 2.

Step 4. In this step, a user wants to inspect the artifacts generated by this pipeline for regulatory reasons or to debug the pipeline. The user clones the git code repository which stores the code related to the pipeline. The user issues a metadata pull command through the metadata client. The metadata client pulls the metadata associated with the data artifacts in the current repository from the metadata repository. The lineage graph associated with each artifact and its metadata is pulled from the central repository to local repository. Each node in the graph is traversed, and from the metadata information of the artifact, its physical location in the artifact repository is extracted and the artifact is pulled from the artifact repository. This brings the code, metadata, and data together in any site for inspection or debugging. Traversing the lineage graph and pulling all related artifacts ensures that not only the data associated with the pipeline is pulled, but its related lineage artifacts are also pulled into the local repository for inspection and analysis.

3.4   Integration with AI Frameworks and Experiment Tracking Tools

We have demonstrated how CMF can be integrated with other ML tracking platforms and ML/DL frameworks. In this section we briefly provide details of such integrations.

CMF Auto-logging for ML/DL Frameworks. Existing ML tracking platforms such as MLflow and W&B support auto-logging features. This feature enables researchers and developers, with just one line of code, to integrate theirs, e.g., PyTorch training scripts, with ML tracking platforms. We have implemented CMF auto-logging feature using ML tracking functionality available in open-source MLflow platform.

The key idea is that MLflow supports multiple so-called backend stores that store ML metadata. Supported backend stores are file-based store, REST store and SQL database-based store. MLflow selects one of these stores whenever developers set tracking endpoints for their experiments. The scheme prefix of their URLs specifies which store to use. When users enable auto-logging in MLflow, MLflow ingests callbacks into respective AI frameworks that call methods of these backend stores to do the logging.

We have implemented another backend store and registered its implementation and its scheme (*cmf://*) with the MLflow backend store registry. This enables CMF to intercept MLflow logging calls and redirect them to CMF to make this metadata part of the artifacts' lineage graphs.

CMF Integration with ML Tracking Platforms. Integrating CMF with third-party AI tracking platforms can be done in multiple ways. We have explored two options.

The first option is to replace metadata backend store, which is MLMD by default. We have implemented a proof-of-concept integration with MLflow. CMF tracks pipeline metadata with MLflow similarly to how MLflow tracks metadata of MLflow projects. MLflow uses the concept of a *run* to track metadata associated with the execution of a model training experiment. CMF creates one parent run to record the execution of a pipeline, and then it creates new child runs for each step on this pipeline. The parent run tracks metadata associated with the pipeline itself, while the child runs track metadata associated with individual steps (tasks), such as data downloading and preprocessing, model training, testing and deployment, etc. MLflow tracking API supports logging tags (general purpose key-value pairs), parameters (experiment parameters) and artifacts (datasets, models etc.) in each run. CMF uses tags to log information about input and output artifacts. In MLflow, tags' values are just strings, and CMF encodes input and output artifacts as JSON strings. This implies that we can reconstruct the lineage of artifacts by traversing runs within each pipeline execution. Since we use hashes and unique identifiers of artifacts, we can link the same artifacts in different pipeline executions. This is different to how metadata is stored in MLMD, and of course, this way of storing pipeline metadata is less efficient, however we see several advantages of using MLflow or similar backend in certain scenarios. For instance, a developer can already have access to a managed MLflow server in their enterprise environment and they can decide to use it to track pipeline metadata together with ML metadata of individual experiments.

The second option to integrate CMF with third-party AI tracking platforms that we have prototyped is to use CMF to track artifacts (metadata) that are managed and stored by these third-party AI tracking platforms. The idea is to let developers use whatever tools, frameworks, and platforms they are comfortable with, while CMF uses a strongly typed system of artifacts to reference experiments managed by external tools.

In a prototyped type system, a base *Artifact* class provides such fields as *uri* (unique artifact resource identifier), *labels* (collection of labels) and *properties* (collection of key-value items). Derived artifacts then are the following: *Reference* (general purpose reference to some external artifact), *Dataset* (is a collection of named references called splits), *MLModel* (machine learning model), *MLModelCard* (a reference to a ML model train/test/validation performance report), *HyperParameterSearch* (a reference to hyper-parameter search results). Third-party tracking tools are encoded in the *uri* field of each artifact, concretely, in its scheme part. Besides traditional schemes, such as *http*, *https* and *file*, CMF supports *mlflow://* (for MLflow-managed artifacts) and *aim://* (for AIM-managed artifacts). Other tracking tools can easily be added. We see several advantages and disadvantages of this approach. Since artifacts are managed by external third-party tracking tools, the CMF metadata store cannot guarantee that users can always access information about these artifacts – a reference will always be available in CMF, but actual artifacts may not be available. One advantage of this approach is that users are free to choose any tracking platform. Moreover, the metadata artifact classes provide backend-independent access to artifact parameters. For instance, the *MLModelCard* artifact can return performance metrics no matter what tracking tool is used (MLflow, AIM or W&B).

4   Southbound Intelligence

Training models for the real world could involve iterating through huge volumes of data (TBs to PBs), too expensive to fit in the performance tier of the underlying storage system. A recent study on data stalls shows that 10–70% of training time may be spent blocking on IO (fetch stalls) for several DNNs [15]. Model training with up to 90% sparsity further increases the I/O to compute ratio by an order of magnitude, making the problem even worse. The Data Foundation Southbound Intelligence methods leverage the metadata trails and historical experience to address some of these infrastructural challenges, e.g. improve data utilization, learn the relevance of data and help reduce the data movement between sites or between different storage tiers by prioritizing the right data.

As an example of an approach to tackle I/O bottlenecks during training, we describe a southbound intelligence technique, where we co-optimize the data tiering and model training in 3 dimensions.

Bandwidth Aware Iteration. We proposed a technique called mini-epoch training (MET) [15] to reduce the IO requirement of training without significant degradation of convergence. MET caches a subset of the training data, referred as a mini-epoch, in the performance tier of the storage system, and repeat the training over the mini-epoch for more than a few times. It adapts the repeating factor based on the feedback from the training convergence.

The size of mini-epochs depends on the space available in performance tier, while the repeating factor reflects desired IO reduction achieved. A higher repeating factor reduces the IO bandwidth demand, freeing bandwidth for other nodes and applications to share the same storage. However, repeating a mini-epoch trades some randomness (compared to shuffling a full epoch) which could affect model convergence in certain situations.

Model Convergence Feedback. As the repeating factor at which convergence is affected depends on the dataset and the model, we next introduce a feedback mechanism to adapt this:

Monitor the training loss/accuracy, validation accuracy and other metrics at the end of each mini-epoch. A score is calculated based on a combination of the monitored metrics.

If the score does not improve on repeating over mini-epoch i repeats for several times, early stop on this mini and wait until mini-epoch i + 1 is fully loaded then move forward.

Remember the optimal strategy for given dataset and model, so this gets automatically reflected in subsequent training runs.

Co-optimize Data Tiering Policies. Prefetching of mini-epochs is performed by the underlying storage tiering system at the bandwidth corresponding to the optimal strategy from the feedback module. Usually, the convergence is more sensitive to repeating factor at early phases during the training. As a result, the system will try to increase repeating factor as the training is making progress and the convergence is not impacted. Increasing data reuse further reduces the prefetching I/O traffic to the capacity tier of the storage. A high repeating factor tolerance also means that not all samples are needed/important and hence some importance sampling technique can be applied to further reduce I/O from capacity tier to performance tier. If the impact of repeating on convergence speed fluctuates across mini-epochs, more states will be tracked to enable adaptive repeating to different mini-epochs, and the prefetching rate also changes dynamically. If too much bias is added with large repeating of mini-epochs, there are two directions for co-optimization: (1) compose each mini-epoch randomly in each pass to reduce the bias; or (2) increase batch size to reduce the bias at every iteration.

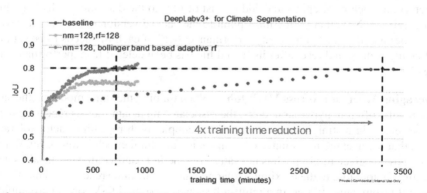

Fig. 4. IoU for training w/o MET, with MET and fixed repeating factor, with MET and adaptive repeating factor

Figure 4 shows that we can reduce training convergence time by 76.3% compared to its baseline implementation for Deep Learning Climate Segmentation Benchmark [16, 17] when trained on 4-nodes from NERSC Core-GPU system, each with 930 GB, 6.8 GB/s NVMe SSD and 500 MB/s HDD. Note that performance gains will be lower on a system with larger NVMe SSD capacity.

4.1   Integration with CMF

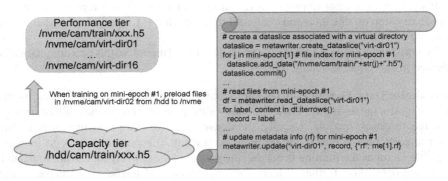

Fig. 5. MET with virtual directories and CMF

Design of a Metadata Layer. We add a metadata layer on top of MET to associate a virtual directory with each mini-epoch. The metadata of each virtual directory stores the general information about each mini epoch including its size, list of files, current location, status of the files, i.e., if it is present at the performance tier, and more importantly the MET characteristics such as repeating factor. CMF is integrated to implement the metadata layer for MET. First, the create_dataslice() API is used to create a virtual directory for each mini-epoch and add the list of files to the data slice at the beginning of the training. Note that all the links point to the cached version of files in the performance tier and the key "present_at_performance_tier" of each file needs to be set after preloading is done and reset after its linked file has been deleted from performance tier (Fig. 5).

Leveraging Metadata Across MET Jobs. When training the same model on the same dataset with different hyperparameters, the associated metadata such as repeating factor can be reused in a straightforward way. For example, high repeating factor tolerance means that the average importance of samples in each mini epoch is low. Even if a job training over a given mini-epoch is not saturating the I/O bandwidth, we can still set the repeating factor close to the maximum tolerant value (with value read from data slice) to reduce IO from capacity tier. In a multi-job scenario, parallel tasks on hyperparameter tuning can benefit from this technique if they share the I/O bandwidth from capacity tier.

The usage of metadata can be extended to train on a new model. We try to find a similar model that has been trained and has recorded metadata available. Here the model similarity is defined as the covariance between the prediction results on the validation dataset: if the covariance between two models is high, these two models are highly correlated and so are their behavior on the same data. Therefore, we can set repeating factor for each mini-epoch with the hint from the model that has been trained before, and then achieve desired I/O reduction.

5 Northbound Intelligence

The goal of Data Foundation Northbound Intelligence is to help develop trustworthy AI models that meet desired tradeoffs between accuracy, uncertainty, required training dataset size, development effort and inference runtime. We show here two example Northbound Intelligence applications that we are currently developing to inspire further work in this area by science teams and in the Open Source community.

Reduce the Human Effort to Train AI Models. Science flows impart specific challenges for AI trustworthiness. Research instruments and sensors may generate high velocity data streams that are preprocessed in real time by sophisticated AI algorithms (e.g., Variational Autoencoders, Generative Adversarial Networks, Convolutional Neural Networks, etc.) to reconstruct images and / or extract key insights from noisy data. The Exa.trkX high energy physics particle trajectory reconstruction flow from proton-proton collisions is one example [6], involving a sequence of Neural Network embedding, fully connected, and Graph Neural Network models combined with conventional analytics to identify detector cloud points belonging to the same particle trajectory. Training these inter-related models is challenging and requires considerable human effort due to highly dimensional parameter optimization space. We have integrated the Common Metadata Framework (CMF) with PyTorch Lightning workflow management tool used by the Exa.trkX team to enable logging lineage and metadata from the pipeline. This gives the team better visibility than before to complex dependences of output metrics – reconstruction efficiency, purity, and inference runtime – on pipeline parameters. The process of optimizing Neural Network model architectures and parameter involves multiple model training experiments – a laborious task taking months of engineering effort to iteratively arrive at the best configuration. With CMF supplying easy access to the metric vs. parameter dependences, we are working on development of an algorithm to suggest a set of parameters for the next model training experiment based on results from previous experiments (note that parameters include widths and depths of Neural Network models, filtering threshold for point pair and triplet intermediate results in different pipeline stages, model training hyper-parameters, etc.). This is complementary to conventional AutoML algorithms that only focus on optimization of one Neural Network model (in one pipeline training stage) at a time. We work on providing parameter suggestions for all stages in the pipeline and for different pipeline lineages (e.g., with different data preprocessing and analytic stages) that can be used as seeds to AutoML algorithms for more fine-grain, out-of-context refinement of individual models. This work will be extended in the future to learn not only from the current model training campaign but also to consider previous campaigns that may have used different cloud point distributions but similar concepts in assembling the cloud points to trajectories. Note that the science team still has complete control over the parameter sweep strategies. The Data Foundation will play just an advisory role in recommending the next set of parameters – an input that the science team can factor-in and combine with the domain specific empirical knowledge.

Improve AI Model Trustworthiness While Reducing the Volume of Labeled Data Required to Train AI Models. The pre-processed experimental or simulation data may flow to the next analysis stage designed to help model and understand the observed behaviors. For example, protein dynamics may be inferred from cryogenic electron microscopy density maps interpreted by AI models trained by molecular dynamics (MD) simulations [18]. Or, protein folding dynamics can be studied with the help of MD simulations accelerated by surrogate AI models [2]. Training of these AI models may involve smaller volume of labeled data than for deep learning models used in other commercial domains. The ground truth (the label) can be provided by a domain expert annotator, or it can be an output from an experiment or a simulation. Reducing the volume of labeled data therefore reduces the domain expert effort [1] or the number of simulations or experiment runs, e.g., the time on a light source beam. For example, Active Learning can be employed to build the Neural Network model incrementally, starting initially from a smaller labeled data set, then update the model based on inference results on unlabeled data. This adds the challenge of selecting the data of highest value for labeling in each iteration, for good generalization and robustness of the trained model, while also being representative of the entire modeled data distributions (i.e., do not introduce bias). Typically, either the most discriminative or the most representative samples are chosen, where information entropy is often used as a measure of discriminativeness to achieve good model generalization, and a distance from cluster centers representing different concepts in the input distribution is often used as a measure of representativeness (often also called diversity). The state of the art in Active Learning focuses on more sophisticated diversity assessment techniques, including training Adversarial Models to identify non-representative samples [1]. However, because of the relative simplicity, many Active Learning flows would simply use the inference prediction uncertainty as a measure of the information entropy, ignoring the sample diversity. For classification problems, the prediction uncertainty can be derived from model inference output class probabilities (for regression problems, the model can be built to infer the standard deviation of the distribution besides the mean [19]). For example, the marginal uncertainty (the probability difference between the classes with the highest and the second highest probabilities), the predictive entropy, or one minus the probability value of the highest probability class are often used as measures of predictive uncertainties [20]. This oversimplification ignores two factors: first, the importance of sample diversity, and second, the poor calibration of class uncertainties resulting from the greedy soft-max normalization of class probabilities typically used in classification models [21]. This is where the Data Foundation Northbound Intelligence helps. First, running behind the scenes as a call-back it can calculate the sample representativeness even when the user pipeline does not take this factor into account, and, more importantly, it can learn the weighting factor between the uncertainty and diversity metrics by monitoring the progress of Active Learning model accuracy over multiple training iterations. To the second order, it can also calibrate the model uncertainty, for example using the Platt scaling calibration [21] or using model ensemble techniques [22, 23]. Figure 6 shows the active learning pipeline. The Data Foundation Northbound Intelligence handles the Uncertainty Quantification calibration and Diversity Assessment tasks, and provides diversity weighting for the Learning Strategy. The CMF records the metadata and lineage from all tasks for reproducibility and possible unwind.

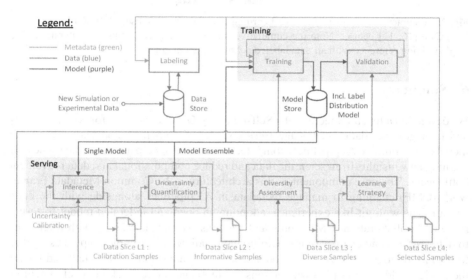

Fig. 6. Active learning pipeline

Figure 7 shows per-iteration accuracy improvements for a 10000 image sample subset of Deep Learning Climate Segmentation (DeepCam) benchmark [16, 17] using predictive entropy uncertainty metric only (no diversity weighting). The initial training run (iteration 1) is on 2500 images. The unlabeled dataset for Active Learning has 7500 images. The labeling effort is reduced by ~2x while the IOU accuracy metrics suffers by ~0.02. Note that training on the full DeepCam dataset with > 50K data samples achieves IOU accuracy of only ~0.73 [17], i.e., ~0.06 higher than our Active Learning with ~5K labeled samples. To further improve the accuracy of Active Learning, we are currently working on an effective method of identifying representative samples from a latent space projection generated by DeepLabv3+ image segmentation Neural Network model [17] during DeepCam inference.

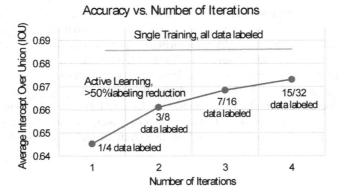

Fig. 7. Accuracy vs. number of Active Learning iterations for a subset of 10000 images from DeepCam [16, 17] dataset. Note the cumulative fraction of labeled samples per iteration. The single training reference with all data labeled is highlighted in green.

6 Summary

We developed a first architecture of a Self-Learning Data Foundation for AI that records and manages metadata and lineage from complex AI pipelines and learns from this metadata to optimize AI pipelines, compute, and storage to help automate the process of learning new insights from scientific data and reduce computational and data movement bottlenecks. The core component of this architecture is the Common Metadata Framework (CMF) enabling to manage metadata in AI pipelines alongside with the code and artifacts with git-like experience, adopting an open and federated model fostering reuse and collaboration. CMF stores and versions AI metadata along with references to data artifacts and enables reproducibility and audit trail in complex pipelines, ability to rewind to older versions of AI models when bad data has been detected, and restart the model build from last known versions. To motivate future work in development of intelligent tools using metadata and lineage for pipeline, storage, and compute optimizations, we also show examples of Southbound and Northbound intelligence running on top of CMF. In Southbound Intelligence example, we show 4x reduction of training time on a Cori-GPU for Deep Learning Image Segmentation Benchmark [16, 17] by intelligently overlapping AI computation with data movement between volume and performance storage tiers, while dynamically adjusting data reuse repeating factor to minimize accuracy impact. In Northbound Intelligence example, we discuss work in progress help scientists converge faster to best AI models and parameters in Exa.trkX high energy physics pipeline [6] by recording dependences of outcomes on pipeline lineage and parameters in CMF and guiding the user exploration in a complex optimization problem. We also discuss work in progress on improving robustness of Active Learning pipelines by calibrating inference uncertainty scores, providing diversity scoring, and learning best uncertainty and diversity scores for selecting the most valuable data for labeling and model retraining. It is our hope that this example will serve as a motivation for science teams to develop further intelligence on top of this infrastructure.

References

1. Du, X., et al.: Active learning to classify macromolecular structures *in situ* for less supervision in cryo-electron tomography. Bioinformatics **37**(16), 2340–2346 (2021)
2. Lee, H., et al.: DeepDriveMD: deep-learning driven adaptive molecular dynamic simulations for protein folding. In: 3rd DLS, pp. 12–19 (2019)
3. Jacobs, S.A., et al.: Parallelizing training of deep generative models on massive scientific datasets. In: CLUSTER 2019, pp. 1–10 (2019)
4. Partee, S., et al.: Using machine learning at scale in HPC simulations with SmartSim: an application to ocean climate modeling. J. Comput. Sci. **62**, 101707 (2022)
5. Jimenez-Luna, J., et al.: Drug discovery with explainable artificial intelligence. Nat. Mach. Intell. **2**, 573–584 (2020)
6. Ju, X., et al.: Performance of a geometric deep learning pipeline for HL-LHC particle tracking. Eur. Phys. J. C **81**, 876 (2021)
7. https://docs.ray.io/en/latest/tune/index.html
8. https://www.kubeflow.org/docs/components/katib/overview/
9. https://www.determined.ai/
10. https://mlflow.org
11. https://wandb.ai
12. https://www.tensorflow.org/tfx/guide/mlmd
13. https://dvc.org
14. Mohan, J., et al.: Analyzing and mitigating data stalls in DNN training. Proc. VLDB Endow. **14**(5), 771–784 (2021)
15. Xu, C., et al: Data-aware storage tiering for deep learning. In: PDSW 2021, pp. 23–28 (2021)
16. Kurth, T., et al.: Exascale deep learning for climate analytics. In: SC 2018, vol. 51, pp. 1–12 (2018)
17. Prabhat, et al.: ClimateNet: an expert-labeled open dataset and deep learning architecture for enabling high-precision analyses of extreme weather. Geosci. Model Dev. **14**, 107–124 (2021)
18. Matsumoto, S., et al.: Extraction of protein dynamics information from Cryo-EM maps using deep learning. Nat. Mach. Intell. **3**, 153–160 (2021)
19. Nix, D.A., et al.: Estimating the mean and variance of the target probability distribution. In: ICNN 1994, pp. 55–60 (1994)
20. Nguyen, V.-L., et al.: How to measure uncertainty in uncertainty sampling for active learning. Mach. Learn. **111**, 89–122 (2022)
21. Guo, Ch., et al.: On calibration of modern neural networks. In: 34th ICML, vol. 70, pp. 1321–1330. PMLR (2017)
22. Lakshminarayanan, B., et al.: Simple and scalable predictive uncertainty estimation using deep ensembles. In: NIPS 2017, pp. 6405–6416 (2017)
23. Chitta, K., et al.: Large-scale visual active learning with deep probabilistic ensembles. https://arxiv.org/pdf/1811.03575.pdf

Preconditioners for Batched Iterative Linear Solvers on GPUs

Isha Aggarwal[1], Pratik Nayak[1(✉)], Aditya Kashi[1], and Hartwig Anzt[1,2]

[1] Karlsruhe Institute of Technology, Karlsruhe, Germany
`pratik.nayak@kit.edu`
[2] Innovative Computing Laboratory, University of Tennessee, Knoxville, USA

Abstract. Batched iterative solvers can be an attractive alternative to batched direct solvers if the linear systems allow for fast convergence. In non-batched settings, iterative solvers are often enhanced with sophisticated preconditioners to improve convergence. In this paper, we develop preconditioners for batched iterative solvers that improve the iterative solver convergence without incurring detrimental resource overhead and preserving much of the iterative solver flexibility. We detail the design and implementation considerations, present a user-friendly interface to the batched preconditioners, and demonstrate the convergence and runtime benefits over non-preconditioned batched iterative solvers on state-of-the-art GPUs for a variety of benchmark problems from finite difference stencil matrices, the Suitesparse matrix collection and a computational chemistry application.

Keywords: Sparse linear systems · Batched solvers · Batched preconditioners · GPU · GINKGO

1 Introduction

Batched functionality for the data-parallel processing of many small- to medium size items on hardware that has more parallelism than what can efficiently be used for processing a single item has become an important building block for many applications. A common example for the use of batched functionality is the parallel solution of a set (batch) of independent linear systems of the form shown in Eq. (1)

$$A_i x_i = b_i \qquad i \in (1, \cdots, n) \tag{1}$$

where A_i is the system matrix of the i-th linear system and x_i and b_i are the solution vector and the right hand side, respectively. n denotes the number of independent linear systems that need to be solved. The solution of batched systems occurs, for example, in combustion simulations where the interaction

This research was supported by the Exascale Computing Project (17-SC-20-SC), a collaborative effort of the U.S. Department of Energy Office of Science and the National Nuclear Security Administration.

of multiple chemical species in each cell gives rise to multiple linear systems that are independent and housed in an outer non-linear loop which couples the ODE solution of the species concentrations with the fluid flow in the combustion simulations [5]. Another example is the set of linear systems to be solved in the collision kernel of a gyrokinetic particle-in-cell (PIC) code for nuclear fusion plasma simulation such as XGC [15].

On a high level, one distinguishes between two strategies for solving linear systems: direct methods, which involve factorization and direct triangular solves, and iterative methods which successively try to approximate the solution in an iterative scheme. Due to their deterministic nature, direct methods are the easier candidates when implementing batched linear solvers, and there exists a plethora of production-ready batched direct solver functionality Sect. 2. Iterative solvers come with the challenge of unknown convergence properties and flexibility requirements in terms of (sparse) matrix data format, stopping criterion, and preconditioners. At the same time, recent research has demonstrated that depending on the system characteristics and the accuracy requirements, batched iterative solvers can be significantly faster than batched direct solvers [2,16]. In non-batched settings, a popular strategy for improving the convergence of iterative solvers is to enhance the algorithms with sophisticated preconditioners. An open question is whether preconditioning can help also to reduce the time to solution of batched iterative solvers. At a first sight, this can be unclear as adding a preconditioner to a batched algorithm can increase complexity, memory traffic, and memory footprint. The increase in resource usage can potentially dramatically increase the iteration time and/or reduce the multiprocessor occupancy. To advance the field of batched iterative solvers, we develop preconditioners tailored toward batched iterative solvers and investigate whether the use of preconditioners can accelerate the time-to-solution process of batched iterative solvers for problems where un-preconditioned solvers exhibit slow convergence. In particular, we focus on the batched BiCGStab [20] solver available in the GINKGO math library, and accelerating the convergence using different preconditioners[1].

The novel contributions of this paper are:

1. We batched develop batched Jacobi preconditioners, batched incomplete LU factorizations, batched triangular solvers, and batched Incomplete Sparse Approximate Inverse (ISAI) preconditioners.
2. We evaluate the performance of the different preconditioners for a wide range of matrices from the finite difference discretization of the 1D Laplace problem, Suite Sparse Matrix Collection, and computational chemistry simulations.
3. We demonstrate the performance advantages over un-preconditioned iterative solvers and batched direct solvers on the NVIDIA A100 GPU.
4. We present a user-friendly interface to the batched preconditioner functionality available in the GINKGO math library.

---

[1] GINKGO features also batched versions of other Krylov solvers, BiCGStab is however the most lightweight Krylov solver for general problems available.

After a brief overview of relevant existing work on batched routines in Sect. 2, we review in Sect. 3 GINKGO's implementation of batched iterative solvers. Building upon this batched iterative solver functionality, in Sect. 4 we detail the design and implementation details for preconditioners that fit into GINKGO's batched iterative solver design. Experimental results are presented in Sect. 5.

We note that in the applications we target, all matrices in the batch share the same sparsity pattern, but but differ in the numerical values. This is typical for problems that use solve different problems using the same mesh, or the same chemical kinetics at different points in space.

2   Related Work on Batched Linear Solvers

For the data-parallel application of basic linear algebra subroutines (BLAS), batched BLAS functionality was developed by different hardware vendors and research groups. In an effort to synchronize the activities and enable interoperability, an interface for batched dense BLAS was proposed in a community effort [11]. Later, the set of batched routines has been expanded to LAPACK [1].

In the context of batched linear system solvers, significant efforts have been spent on developing functionality for the factorization, exact solution, and inversion of batched dense linear systems [4,10,12]. For sparse structured systems, methods tailored toward the solution of tri-diagonal and penta-diagonal problems have been proposed [6,13,19]. For general sparse matrices in compressed sparse row (CSR) format, a batched sparse QR factorization and solve is available in NVIDIA's cuSolver library [18]. For the iterative solution of batched sparse linear systems, batched Krylov solvers have been developed [2] and employed for the solution of chemical reaction systems [2] as well as plasma simulations [16]. Batched iterative solvers heavily rely on the efficient implementation of a batched sparse matrix vector product kernel [3]. Up to our knowledge, there exists no research on preconditioning for batched iterative solvers.

3   Design and Implementation of Batched Iterative Solvers

As the design of batched preconditioners needs to fit the characteristics and interface of the batched iterative solvers they are used in, we revisit the batched iterative solver design in GINKGO that was originally presented in [2,16]. In comparison to their direct solver counterparts, (batched) iterative solvers need to deal with a lot more parameters, and in this in section we elaborate on the design choices we made in GINKGO to make sure to maximize performance while maintaining flexibility and composability between the different components of batched iterative solvers: loggers, stopping criteria, preconditioners, solvers and sparse matrix formats.

While direct solvers always solve the system to the full precision of the underlying type, iterative solvers come with the option of tuning the tolerance to

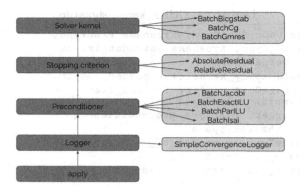

Fig. 1. The multi-level dispatch mechanism.

solve the systems to the required precision. This makes iterative solvers attractive when an 'exact' solve is unnecessary; this is the case in several engineering applications and especially when the linear solve is part of a nonlinear solver. Another advantage of the iterative solvers is that we can provide an initial guess. For an outer non-linear solver, using multiple calls to the linear solver, the solution of the previous linear step is usually a good initial guess for the subsequent linear solve.

In GINKGO, the solver is executed within a single kernel that is composed of the entire iterative algorithm. To avoid the overhead of launching a kernel at every iteration, we place the iteration stepping loop within the solver kernel. Each thread maintains a copy of the iteration count. As one thread-block solves one linear system and can synchronize at a relatively low cost, the value of the iteration count is the same for all threads in a thread-block. Further, in contrast with monolithic non-batched solvers, batched solvers can take advantage of the sparsity pattern, that is shared between the different batch entries.

To preserve flexibility in the choice of solver components in a single kernel design, we use C++ templating to generate kernels for the different combinations of preconditioners, solver, and stopping criteria. This incurs the cost of instantiation at compile time, while keeping the code maintainable and extensible. This also makes sure that the individual SpMV, solver, and preconditioner kernels are inlined, allowing the compiler to optimize the entire kernel as a whole. Figure 1 shows the multi-level dispatch mechanism used in GINKGO. This multi-level dispatch mechanism allows for flexibility of different options and allows us to launch a single templated device side kernel.

Listing 1.1: CUDA kernel signature

```
template <typename StopType, typename PrecType,
    typename LogType, typename BatchMatrixType,
    typename ValueType>
__global__ void apply_kernel(int padded_length,
    const StorageConf config, int max_iter,
    remove_complex<ValueType> tol,
    LogType logger, PrecType preconditioner,
    const BatchMatrixType a,
    const ValueType *__restrict__ b,
    ValueType *__restrict__ x,
    ValueType *__restrict__ workspace)
```

Listing 1.2: Kernel call site

```
apply_kernel<stop::SimpleRelResidual<ValueType>>
    <<<nbatch, block_size, shared_size>>>(
        shared_gap, config, max_its, residual_tol,
        logger, PrecType<>(), a,
        b.values, x.values, workspace);
```

Iterative solvers do not execute a pre-defined sequence of operations or iterations, but adapt the number of iterations to the problem at hand to provide a solution of the desired quality. Some systems of the batch may require more iterations than others for the same solution quality. In an implementation, either all the systems need to be iterated until each of them has achieved the desired solution quality, or each system is monitored individually, therewith allowing independent termination and logging for each linear system in the batch. Forcing all the systems to iterate until the "worst" system has converged in a SIMD fashion is inefficient because we are wasting resources on converged systems and additionally can also tend to diverge the already converged systems due to stability issues.

Monitoring the iteration process for all systems individually and scheduling the next system to the next available resource (where the iteration process has completed), on the other hand, makes more efficient use of the available resources. This breaks up the SIMD execution style of the batched routine as different items of the batch are potentially handled with a different iteration count. However, if each of these systems is handled by a distinct compute unit (streaming multiprocessor in NVIDIA GPUs), thereby removing the need to communicate between the compute units, it can provide optimal performance. Convergence monitoring requires a decision on which metric to monitor, and how to define the thresholds. We decided to integrate a simple but customizable stopping criterion for the residual norm. Currently available stopping criteria include a pre-defined relative residual norm reduction factor, as well as an absolute residual threshold.

4   Design and Implementation of Preconditioners for Batched Iterative Solvers

The design of the preconditioners for batched iterative solvers assumes that all matrices of the batch share the same sparsity pattern but differ in the numerical values, therewith potentially exhibiting different convergence properties. In the present work, all preconditioners expect the sparse matrices of the batch to be stored in the `BatchCsr` matrix format, which stores one copy of the sparsity pattern and a contiguous array of values for the distinct matrices in the batch.

Batched ILU(0) Preconditioner

The computation of an in-place exact ILU(0) factorization of a batched matrix A is shown in Algorithm 1. The algorithm follows the standard ILU(0) implementation [9]. In particular, the incomplete factorization is in-place, that is, after completion, the values in the lower and upper triangular parts of the matrix A are replaced with the values of the lower and upper incomplete factor L and U, respectively.

Algorithm 1. The batched Exact ILU(0) algorithm

```
 1: INPUT: A
 2: OUTPUT: Factorized (in-place) A ≈ LU
 3: N ← num_rows
 4: for b = 0 to num_batch_entries − 1 do
 5:     for i = 0 to N − 1 do
 6:         for k = i + 1 to N − 1 do
 7:             row ← 0
 8:             if (k, i) ∈ spy(A_b) then
 9:                 A_b(k, i) ← A_b(k, i)/A(i, i)
10:                 row ← A_b(k, i)
11:             end if
12:             for c = i + 1 to N − 1 and (k, c) ∈ spy(A_b) do
13:                 col ← 0
14:                 if (i, c) ∈ spy(A) then
15:                     col ← A_b(i, c)
16:                 end if
17:                 A_b(k, c) ← A_b(k, c) − (row ∗ col)
18:             end for
19:         end for
20:     end for
21: end for
```

The batched ILU(0) algorithm performs all computations in a single kernel, assigning one thread block to each matrix of the batch. If the nonzeros of a row in A are not sorted in increasing column index, a sorting step is invoked to enable efficient parallel processing in the factorization step. The batched matrix must not have any missing diagonal elements, and any missing diagonal elements are added using a separate batched diagonal addition kernel. An array containing pointers to the diagonal elements of A_0 is computed beforehand and passed in to the factorization kernel to avoid repeated computations.

The algorithm loops over all rows of the matrix A_i one by one and operates on all rows below the current row in parallel, using one warp per row, which enables coalesced accesses to the CSR values array. Moreover, the current

CSR row's elements are stored in a dense array in shared memory. This avoids repeated computations while searching for elements in the current row by their column indices; this operation is frequently required when updating the rows below.

Batched ParILU Preconditioner

Computations of a ParILU factorization of a batched matrix A with all the individual entries having a common sparsity pattern is shown in Algorithm 2. The algorithm implements the asynchronous ParILU algorithm [7], but adapts it for batched matrices.

The first step is to create and initialize the batched factors, L and U based on the given input matrix A. For efficient processing, A must be sorted with no diagonal elements missing. After computing the row pointers and subsequently allocating memory for L and U, the algorithm finds the column indices and values for the batched factors. As stated earlier, in order to take advantage of the shared sparsity pattern property while initializing the batched factors' values, we generate common patterns for $L_i s$ and $U_i s$ that contain pointers to the values array of matrix A_0. The common pattern generation kernel uses one warp per row of A_0 to enable coalesced accesses to the pattern arrays corresponding to both the factors and values array of A_0.

An effective strategy reducing the main memory access in the batched implementation of the ParILU algorithm is to analyze and store the dependency graph informing about the access to the matrix values.

The entire dependency graph is generated on the CPU as this process does not contain much parallelism and needs to be done only once for the shared sparsity pattern. To enable data locality in the factorization kernel while accessing the dependency graph, we store the dependencies for each non-zero element of A_0 in a contiguous fashion. The ParILU factorization kernel then employs one thread block per matrix to perform the ParILU sweeps. The sweeps are asynchronous as they use the most recent data available to update the elements without waiting for the dependencies. Each element of an individual matrix is handled by a separate thread. We copy the global values array of L_i and U_i to the shared memory to reduce the number of global memory writes while updating the elements.

Batched ISAI Preconditioner

The batched ISAI preconditioner is derived from the left general incomplete sparse approximate inverse [14]. An algorithm for the batched computation of an ISAI preconditioner with all matrices in the batch sharing the same sparsity pattern is shown in Algorithm 3. For convenience, we denote the left approximate inverse, A_{left}^{-1} by $\hat{A}$.

The algorithm initially generates a sparsity pattern for $\hat{A}$ as $\text{spy}(\hat{A}) = \text{spy}(|A_0|^k)$ as shown in Algorithm 3, where $|A_0|$ denotes a matrix with absolute values of A_0.

Algorithm 2. The batched ParILU algorithm. Note that '$idx \in A(i,j)$' denotes the position of the (i,j) entry of matrix A in its values (or column-index) array.

```
 1: INPUT: A
 2: OUTPUT:L, U
 3: spy(L) ← spy(lower_tri(A₀))
 4: spy(U) ← spy(upper_tri(A₀))
 5: PatternL ← lower_pattern(A₀)
 6: PatternU ← upper_pattern(A₀)
 7: for b = 0 to num_batch_entries − 1 do
 8:     Lb ← Ab(PatternL)
 9:     Ub ← Ab(PatternU)
10: end for
11: DepGraph ← []
12: for (i, j) ∈ spy(A₀)  do
13:     dep ← []
14:     if  i > j  then
15:         add(dep, idx ∈ L₀(i, j))
16:         for  k = 0 to j − 1  do
17:             if (i, k) ∈ spy(L₀) and (k, j) ∈ spy(U₀) then
18:                 add(dep, idx ∈ L₀(i, k))
19:                 add(dep, idx ∈ U₀(k, j))
20:             end if
21:         end for
22:         add(dep, idx ∈ U₀(j, j))
23:     else
24:         add(dep, idx ∈ U₀(i, j))
25:         for  k = 1 to i − 1  do
26:             if (i, k) ∈ spy(L₀) and (k, j) ∈ spy(U₀) then
27:                 add(dep, idx ∈ L₀(i, k))
28:                 add(dep, idx ∈ U₀(k, j))
29:             end if
30:         end for
31:     end if
32:     DepGraph[idx_in_A₀(A₀(i, j))] ← dep
33: end for
34: for b = 0 to num_batch_entries − 1 do
35:     for  sweeps = 0, 1, 2 · · ·  until convergence do
36:         for nnz = 0 to num_nnz  do
37:             dep ← DepGraph[nnz]
38:             len ← length(dep)
39:             sum ← 0
40:             for m = 1; m < len − 1; m = m + 2 do
41:                 sum ← sum + Lb[dep[m]] * Ub[dep[m + 1]]
42:             end for
43:             has_diag_dep ← (len mod 2) == 0
44:             if has_diag_dep == True then
45:                 diag ← Ub[dep[len − 1]]
46:                 Lb[dep[0]] ← (Ab[nnz] − sum)/diag
47:             else
48:                 Ub[dep[0]] ← Ab[nnz] − sum
49:             end if
50:         end for
51:     end for
52: end for
```

Next, a large number of small linear systems corresponding to each row of the matrices in the batch $\hat{A}$ is generated by extracting the target entries in batched matrix A given by the non zero locations in the inverses's row. Since all matrices $\hat{A}$ share the same sparsity pattern and all the matrices A share the same sparsity pattern, the computations to extract the small linear systems corresponding to a specific row of the matrix entries in batch $\hat{A}$ are very similar. Thus, to avoid

Algorithm 3. The batched ISAI algorithm.
___
1: INPUT: A, k
2: OUTPUT: $\hat{A}$
3: $S \leftarrow spy(|A_0|^k)$
4: $spy(\hat{A}) \leftarrow S$
5: **for** $i = 0$ **to** $num\_rows - 1$ **do**
6:      $T_i \leftarrow find\_non\_zero\_locations(\hat{A}_0(i, :))$
7:      $Size_i \leftarrow length(T_i)$
8:      $M_i \leftarrow generate\_pattern(A_0(T_i, T_i))$
9:      $R_i \leftarrow find\_location\_one(I(i, T_i)$
10:        **for** $v = 0$ **to** $num\_batch\_entries - 1$ **do**
11:           $\hat{A}_v(i, T_i) * A_v(M_i) = get\_rhs(Size_i, R_i)$
12:        **end for**
13: **end for**
___

repetition, it is useful to extract the pattern as denoted by M_i, which contains pointers to the values array of matrix A_0, and store the location of one in the respective right-hand side (R_i as shown above). The algorithm then generates the small linear systems for all rows for all matrices of the batch by reading the values from the corresponding matrix A. The small linear systems are then solved, and the solutions are inserted back into the values array of batch $\hat{A}$ at appropriate locations. The solution process is handled with a triangular or a general solve, depending on the type of the system. As we store these small matrices in dense format, we are restricted to a `row_size_limit` or 32, which is the subwarp size. For rows with more than 32 elements, one would need to assemble the excess system into a CSR matrix and perform an additional solve.

Batched Sparse Triangular Solvers

Sparse triangular solvers form an important component of the ILU, ParILU and ISAI preconditioners, being used in either the generation phase of the preconditioners (for ISAI based on ILU) or for the application phase, once the triangular factors have been generated. Triangular solvers consist of two main components: a symbolic phase that consists of generation of a dependency graph during the preconditioner generation and a numerical phase that uses the numerical values and the dependency graph to solve the triangular systems. Synchronization due to dependencies, can harm the efficient parallelization of sparse triangular solves. In the batched sparse triangular solve implementation, we use a busy-waiting loop inside a thread block, where threads are scheduled continuously, but do not perform any work until all the previous dependencies are completed. This approach has been proposed in [17] fits well for the requirements of batched preconditioner application.

5   Experimental Evaluation

For the experimental evaluation we run GINKGO's batched iterative solver functionality on an NVIDIA A100 GPU with a main memory bandwidth of 1555 GB/s, with 108 SMs, L1 cache of 192 KB per compute unit and a L2 cache of

40 MB per compute unit. The theoretical peak performance for double precision is 9.7 TFlops/s. We perform our experiments on the HoreKa cluster with gcc-8.3.0 and with CUDA-11.4[2].

To showcase the need, effectiveness and scalability of the batched preconditioners, we consider different problems. Initially, we will focus on a stencil matrix that is characteristic for many particle and stencil-based codes. We then turn to benchmark problems from Suitesparse. We round up the experimental evaluation by using preconditioned batched iterative solvers in the batched solution of chemical reaction problems.

In all the experiments, we start the iterative process with an all-zero initial guess $x^0 = 0$. We use a residual stopping criterion $\varepsilon = 10^{-12}$, which means we iterate until the residual $\|b - Ax^k\|$ in iteration k is 12 orders of magnitude smaller than the initial residual $\|b - Ax^0\|$. We note that this reflects high accuracy requirements and a fair but pessimistic comparison against batched direct solvers. Many applications e.g. using nonlinear solvers can tolerate less accurate solution approximations. In the experiments with stencil and Suitesparse matrices, we use an all-one right-hand side vector $b = 1$ for the linear systems.

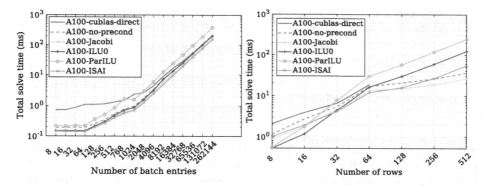

Fig. 2. (Preconditioned) BiCGStab runtime and for batches consisting of 3-pt stencil discretizations of the 1D Laplace problem. Left: Each problem is of size 64, the number of problems in the batch is increased. Right: The batch size is fixed to 20,000 problems, the size of the individual problems is increased from 64 to 512.

In the first experiment, we address the solution of a batch of linear system arising from the 3-point stencil discretization of a 1D Laplace problem and assess the runtime of the preconditioned batched iterative solvers for increasing batch size. The size of each individual linear system is 64. To reach the relative residual stopping criterion of 10^{-12}, an un-preconditioned BiCGStab solver needs 16

[2] This work was performed on the HoreKa supercomputer funded by the Ministry of Science, Research and the Arts Baden-Württemberg and by the Federal Ministry of Education and Research.

Table 1. Matrix and matrix set characteristics and iteration counts for the BiCGStab iterative solver using different preconditioners.

	size	nonzeros	No Precond	Jacobi	ILU(0)	ParILU	ISAI
1D Laplace							
3pt-stencil-64	64	190	16	11	1	1	6
Suitesparse							
LFAT5	14	46	80	33	7	8	16
bcsstm02	66	66	11	1	1	1	1
LF10	18	82	351	–	38	34	–
Trefethen_20	20	158	19	8	5	5	6
pivtol	102	306	16	13	2	2	7
bfwb62	62	342	30	15	6	6	9
olm100	100	396	–	–	36	98	26
bcsstk22	138	696	493	229	43	42	95
cage6	93	785	–	12	4	4	7
ck104	104	992	112	118	13	15	164
494_bus	494	1666	–	–	81	81	–
mesh3em5	289	1889	14	13	1	1	10
mhdb416	416	2312	–	37	2	2	41
bcsstk05	153	2423	325	124	32	32	149
steam1	240	3762	–	–	3	3	–
PeleLM							
isooctane	144	6135	–	38	3	4	–

iterations, while an ILU-preconditioned BiCGStab completes after the first iteration, see Table 1. In Fig. 2 (left) we increase the batch size from 8 systems in the batch to 262,144 systems in the batch. We note that the runtime in this graph reflects only the iteration time, that is, the BiCGStab iterative solver time and the preconditioner application time. The preconditioner generation is excluded.

The implementation assigns one thread block to each linear system in the batch. As a result, the iteration runtime is constant until the batch size exceeds the number of streaming multiprocessors (SMs) on the A100 and all SMs get busy executing a thread block. For larger batch sizes, the runtime increases with the number of linear systems in the batch.

For this problem, due to its cheap cost of application, we observe that the ISAI preconditioner wins over all other preconditioners. The Jacobi preconditioner is also very effective due to the fast application of the diagonal scaling. The ILU(0) and ParILU preconditioners suffer from the expensive triangular solves. They are usually more effective for problems with higher condition numbers. We also observe that the preconditioned BiCGStab variant completes faster than the CUBLAS batched direct solver.

In the next experiment, we fix the batch size to 20,000 and increment the size of the individual problems in the batch, see Fig. 2 (right). We note that the CUBLAS batched direct solver runs into memory issues for problems larger than 64 rows. For smaller problems, ILU0 and ParILU0 are very effective, while for larger problems, the cost of the exact triangular solves can not be compensated by the faster convergence. For large problems, the inexpensive Jacobi preconditioner is the best choice.

We now turn to benchmark matrices from the Suitesparse matrix collection [8]. The selected matrices are listed along with some key properties and the preconditioned BiCGStab convergence in Table 1.

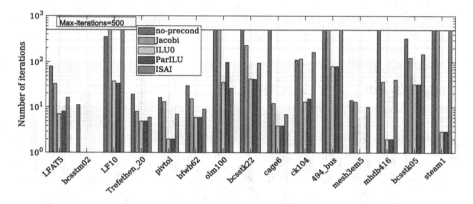

Fig. 3. Suitesparse matrix iteration count for the preconditioned BiCGSTAB solver.

Though repeating the information in Table 1, we visualize in Fig. 3 the BiS-GStab iteration counts for the relative residual stopping criterion 10^{-12} and an upper limit of 500 iterations. We consider configurations that do not converge within 500 iterations as failing. We note that for several problems, robust preconditioners are needed to ensure convergence, i.e. a non-preconditioned BiCGStab or a Jacobi-preconditioned BiCGStab fails.

In Fig. 4 (top), we visualize the time needed to generate the preconditioners for the distinct problems. The preconditioner generation generally increases with the size of the problems in the batch. As expected, the ILU(0) preconditioner generation is significantly more expensive than the Jacobi preconditioner generation. ParILU uses the fine-grained ParILU algorithm to approximate the incomplete factors of an ILU(0) preconditioner via fixed-point iterations. We use 20 fixed-point sweeps of the ParILU algorithm to generate good approximations of the ILU factors. In this setting, the ParILU algorithm is generally faster than the traditional ILU(0). Next, even though the ISAI preconditioner generation affords ample parallelism, it requires many operations and a lot of memory to store an explicit approximate inverse. Increased memory requirements leads to increased pressure on the L1 cache, reducing SM utilization. Thus we observe

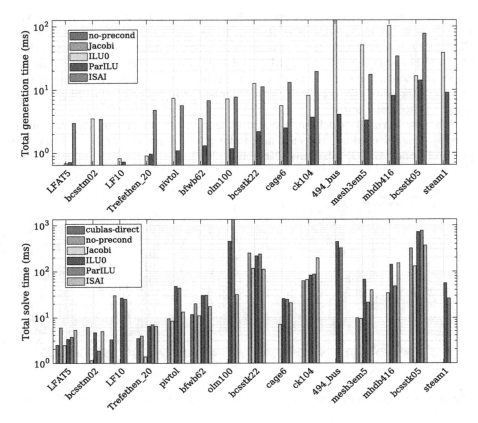

Fig. 4. Using batched preconditioners for Suitesparse benchmark matrices: Preconditioner generation time (top). Total solve time (including preconditioner generation) the preconditioned batched BiCGStab solver (bottom).

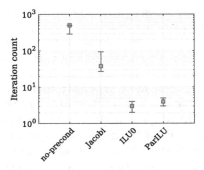

Fig. 5. Variation in the iteration count for the isooctane problem for different preconditioners, see Table 1 for median iteration counts.

6. Carroll, E., Gloster, A., Bustamante, M.D. and Náraigh, L.Ó.: A batched GPU methodology for numerical solutions of partial differential equations. arXiv, 2107.05395 (2021)
7. Chow, E., Patel, A.: Fine-grained parallel incomplete LU factorization. SIAM J. Sci. Comput. **37**(2), C169–C193 (2015). Publisher: Society for Industrial and Applied Mathematics
8. Davis, T.A., Hu, Y.: The university of Florida sparse matrix collection. ACM Trans. Math. Softw. **38**(1), 1:1–1:25 (2011)
9. Doi, S.: On parallelism and convergence of incomplete LU factorizations. Appl. Numer. Math. **7**(5), 417–436 (1991)
10. Dong, T., Haidar, A., Luszczek, P., Harris, J.A., Tomov, S., Dongarra, J.: LU factorization of small matrices: accelerating batched DGETRF on the GPU. In: 2014 IEEE International Conference on High Performance Computing and Communications, 2014 IEEE 6th International Symposium on Cyberspace Safety and Security, 2014 IEEE 11th International Conference on Embedded Software and System (HPCC, CSS, ICESS), pp. 157–160, Paris, France, August 2014. IEEE
11. Dongarra, J., et al.: A proposed API for batched basic linear algebra subprograms, April 2016. https://eprints.ma.man.ac.uk/2464/
12. Evstigneev, N.M., Ryabkov, O.I., Tsatsorin, E.A.: On the inversion of multiple matrices on GPU in batched mode. Supercomput. Front. Innov. Int. J. **5**(2), 23–42 (2018)
13. Gloster, A., Náraigh, L.Ó, Khang, E.P.: cupentbatch-a batched pentadiagonal solver for NVIDIA GPUs. Comput. Phys. Commun. **241**, 113–121 (2019)
14. Göbel, F., Grützmacher, T., Ribizel, T., Anzt, H.: Mixed precision incomplete and factorized sparse approximate inverse preconditioning on GPUs. In: Sousa, L., Roma, N., Tomás, P. (eds.) Euro-Par 2021. LNCS, vol. 12820, pp. 550–564. Springer, Cham (2021). https://doi.org/10.1007/978-3-030-85665-6_34
15. Hager, R., Yoon, E.S., Ku, S., D'Azevedo, E.F., Worley, P.H., Chang, C.S.: A fully non-linear multi-species Fokker-Planck-Landau collision operator for simulation of fusion plasma. J. Comput. Phys. **315**, 644–660 (2016)
16. Kashi, A., Nayak, P., Kulkarni, D., Scheinberg, A., Lin, P., Anzt, H.: Batched sparse iterative solvers on GPU for the collision operator for fusion plasma simulations. In: 2022 IEEE International Parallel and Distributed Processing Symposium (IPDPS) (2022)
17. Liu, W., Li, A., Hogg, J., Duff, I.S., Vinter, B.: A synchronization-free algorithm for parallel sparse triangular solves. In: Dutot, P.-F., Trystram, D. (eds.) Euro-Par 2016. LNCS, vol. 9833, pp. 617–630. Springer, Cham (2016). https://doi.org/10.1007/978-3-319-43659-3_45
18. NVIDIA: cuSOLVER–gpu accelerated library for decompositions and linear system solutions on NVIDIA GPUs. https://docs.nvidia.com/cuda/cusolver/index.html. Accessed 24 Aug 2021
19. Valero-Lara, P., Martínez-Pérez, I., Sirvent, R., Martorell, X., Peña, A.J.: cuThomasBatch and cuThomasVBatch, CUDA routines to compute batch of tridiagonal systems on NVIDIA GPUs. Concurrency Comput. Pract. Exp. **30**, e4909 (2018). https://doi.org/10.1002/cpe.4909
20. Van der Vorst, H.A.: Bi-CGSTAB: a fast and smoothly converging variant of Bi-CG for the solution of nonsymmetric linear systems. SIAM J. Sci. Stat. Comput. **13**(2), 631–644 (1992). Publisher: Society for Industrial and Applied Mathematics

Mobility Aware Computation Offloading Model for Edge Computing

Natnael Tefera[1]($\boxtimes$) and Ayalew Belay Habtie[2]($\boxtimes$)

[1] Department of Computer Science, Arba Minch University, Arba Minch, Ethiopia
natnael3872@gmail.com
[2] Department of Computer Science, Addis Ababa University, Addis Ababa, Ethiopia
Ayalew.Belay@aau.edu.et

Abstract. The technological advancement of mobile devices such as laptops, smartphones, wearable devices, and other handheld devices has resulted in the emergence of various user applications in the entertainment, learning, social networking, and community computing sectors. However, these devices have limited capacity and battery charge to process computation intensive tasks. As a result, offloading is one of the most important approaches for connecting mobile devices and powerful systems. It minimizes complexity and improves mobile computing capacity. Computation on cloud computing is a powerful solution for computation of tasks on devices with limited computing capacity. Still, due to the distance issue the energy usage for transmission and the network delay to send and receive computing requirement degrades the performance. As the result, edge computing is the promising enabler for latency sensitive and energy efficient computation in proximity. However, user mobility and the restricted coverage of Edge Computing (EC) server service pose new challenge for computation offloading. Delivering task offloading requests to servers and results to users is difficult in networks where user movement is frequent, resulting in increased latency, higher energy consumption, and inefficient resource utilization. The key problem in offloading computing to edge server is, determining how to efficiently decide to assign computation tasks to edge servers in such a way that the decision captures the mobility inherent in mobile devices and results in minimal latency, energy consumption and execution time during application running. In this paper, to tackle the constraints related to intermittent connectivity due to mobility, network changes, device heterogeneity, and resource load mobility aware computation offloading model is proposed. Dependency graph-based mobility prediction is adopted to trace next mobility locations and edge servers. Dependency graph with fuzzy logic algorithm is proposed which considers available computation and communication resources both on device and server. This fuzzy logic decision considers edge device battery level, data size, bandwidth, network coverage, delay sensitivity, edge server Virtual Machine (VM) utilization and load of the server. The proposed model is implemented using PureEdgeSim simulator with mobility traces. The simulation result was analyzed with respect to task failure rate, failure rate due to mobility, energy utilization and average task processing delay. The analysis of the simulation result is done using a comparative analysis with the state of the art works fuzzy decision-based cloud-MEC collaborative task offloading management system (FTOM) and a fuzzy decision tree-based task orchestration (FDT) considering task failure rate, energy utilization, task processing latency, and task completion delay. The proposed model performs better with minimum task failure rate, energy consumption and task processing delay compared to FTOM and FDT with an increase of mobile devices. For example, with an increase of mobile devices from 100 to 700, task failure rate increase from 2% to 70% in FTOM, 1% to 45% in FDT and from 0.9% to 40% in the proposed model. The simulation result also affirm that the proposed mobility aware computation offloading provided improved task failure rate with mobility when compared to FTOM, which is the worst one. The energy utilization with an increase of mobile devices and the task processing delay time (0.45 s for 700 mobile devices, 0.73 s for FTOM) for the proposed model is better than the other task offloading schemes.

Keywords: Edge computing · Mobility prediction · Computation offloading ·
Fuzzy logic-based computation offloading

1   Introduction

Dramatic increase and advancement in technology bring the emergence of Internet of Things (IoT), connected physical objects to collect and exchange information, which can greatly improve many aspects of our daily lives [1]. These mobile gadgets have become smarter with the introduction of new processing cores and memory architectures, but they are still limited to computing and residual battery capacity. Many computationally intensive applications, such as 3D modeling, augmented or virtual reality, online games, ultra-HD image and video processing, artificial intelligence, and the IoTs, are resource expensive and create massive amounts of data [2–4]. Such applications may generate a significant amount of computing workload, potentially draining the battery in smart/mobile devices [2]. High computational tasks can be offloaded to the nearby cloud and edge servers that have adequate computing resources [4].

The principle of computation offloading or cyber-foraging was originally introduced in Mobile Cloud Computing (MCC) [5, 6]. This principle is used to leverage powerful infrastructures (*e.g.,* remote servers) to augment the computing capability of less powerful devices (*e.g.,* mobile devices) [7] since, computation offloading allows low-resource devices (*e.g.,* smartphones) to run CPU-intensive applications like 3D gaming [8]. Computational offloading involves the delegation of computationally heavy tasks from mobile devices into central cloud data centers. While competing for computational offloading, mobile devices confront significant challenges. Offloading the computation task provides the possibility of supporting user equipment with ultra-low latency requirement, prolonging the device battery lives [9]. However, sometimes, time and resources saved by mobile devices are offset by the latency involved in locating an appropriate cloud server and migrating the workload. Several real-time applications, such as financial transactions, online gaming, video conferencing require high quality of service and low latency. Failing to provide desired result adversely affects the user experience [10].

Researchers introduced the concept of cloudlets to reduce network delays and increase user experience when compared to MCC. A cloudlet is a small-scale data center that is located near the users [11, 12]. To execute computing and offloading, a few fixed servers are connected via a wireless network in a micro cellular zone [13].

Various studies [20–22] have been conducted which cover the different computation offloading approaches, frameworks, schemes, methods, algorithms, strategies on Edge computing. Most of these studies considered the edge devices as static where user positions are considered to be time-invariant and user mobility-related information is not fully exploited. Some studies including [16–18] has considered mobility. In others study like [17] user mobility traces are considered as historical records of the mobile users at different geographic location. Still some literature considered user mobility using machine learning approach [18].

These mobility prediction approaches have limitation on the erroneous mobility record removal, leaning complexity and mobility feature learning as, mobility of the edge device is linear in machine learning and the mobility in reality is nonlinear due to random mobility of edge devices [26]. The studies lacks to address purely the mobility aware computation offloading in edge computing with noise tolerant and lightweight mobility prediction. This study considers fuzzy logic decisions on computation offloading in combination with graph dependency-based mobility prediction on edge computing for lightweight computation decision and noise tolerant mobility prediction.

The reminder of this paper is structured as follows. The related work on computational offloading is discussed in Sect. 2. The proposed mobility aware computation offloading is presented in Sect. 3. Section 4 discuses experimentation and result analysis. Section 5 depicts the conclusion and future perspectives.

2 Related Work

Computation offloading and resource allocation is an important issue in edge computing. Based on previous literatures, different computation offloading approaches were discussed including fuzzy logic based, machine learning, with mathematical modeling approaches and so on. For example, Hossain *et al.* [14] introduced a fuzzy decision-based cloud-MEC collaborative task offloading management system named as FTOM which is a collaborative task offloading management system based on fuzzy decision-based for using the remote cloud computing capabilities and utilizing neighboring edge servers. Selecting the best target node for offloading based on server capacity, latency sensitivity, and network state is the goal of the proposed approach. Based on the states of the server utilization, network condition, and delay sensitivity, FTOM makes dynamic decisions for offloading delay-sensitive computations to local or nearby edge servers, and delay-tolerant high resource-intensive computations to a remote cloud server. This approach was simulated and compared with other offloading schemes including local edge offloading (LEO), two-tier edge orchestration-based offloading (TTEO), fuzzy orchestration-based load balancing (FOLB), fuzzy workload orchestration-based task offloading (WOTO), and fuzzy edge-orchestration based collaborative task offloading (FCTO) for three different applications. The results of FTOM Simulation showed significant improvement on, rate of successful executed offloaded tasks and reduced task completion time when compared with LEO, TTEO, FOLB, WOTO and FCTO. Nguyen et al. [15], also introduced flexible computation offloading method in fuzzy based mobile edge orchestrator for IoT applications. The authors proposed three-tier architecture, mobile edge orchestrator, edge devices, edge orchestrator with edge server and cloud server. The edge orchestrator follows two stages in the proposed work. The first stage is application placement and the second stage is application deployment that places the incoming request either on the edge device, edge server, or neighbor edge server. The second stage deploys the application on either the edge server or the cloud server. The proposed work was simulated using four applications and showed an improved results from other techniques. However, the mobility of the edge device was considered as static and energy utilization was not given attention.

Shi et al. [16], proposed computation offloading based on reinforcement learning for mobility aware edge computing by considering mobility, deadline constraint, and available resource on edge servers. To learn servers' users power allocation policies, a deep deterministic policy gradient is proposed which is a reinforcement learning based approach. The researchers model the user mobility by contact time with user and server following the position distribution with mobility intensity parameters. Reinforcement learning is used to map the situation with actions to maximize the reward and in the meantime, the environment is formulated as a Markov decision process. When resource limitation occurs in MEC servers, the unprocessed tasks will be forwarded to the core network. The experiment was done taking the proposed deep reinforcement learning algorithm and random power allocation algorithm with different connect frequencies. The result of the experiment showed that the proposed deep reinforcement algorithm provides better allocation scheme. However, the proposed approach considers communication and computation cost only for edge servers and in the meantime, deep reinforcement learning introduces high time computation complexity as, space and complexity increase with the increase in number of heterogonous server and number of users present in the server. Moreover, Reinforcement learning models are essentially designed for linear mapping and systems with several input parameters and multiple features but user mobility traces are non-linear in nature.

Maleki et al. [17], proposed an offloading approach considering dynamic mobile applications features including mobility and changing specifications. Two forecasting methods, the drift method and the weighted moving average method was used to predict the mobility of device. The experiment was conducted for mobility traces of taxi cabs in San Francisco and the experimental results were compared with three baseline approaches. Results showed that the approach finds close to optimal latency and execution time. However, the researchers consider execution time and latency which is not sufficient as edge devices are constrained by the battery life as well.

Zhan et al. [18] Presented Heuristic Mobility Aware Offloading Algorithm (HMAOA) for mobility aware multiuser offloading optimization. HMAOA is used to optimize computation offloading in MEC contexts for fast moving users and maximizes the system utility under the constraints of user mobility, resource limitation, and task latency. The user's next expected base station is forecasted by taking into account not just the computing resources but also the channel fading, noise, interference, and distance from the end user to the base station. The researchers investigated multiuser single base station offloading decision and resource allocation considering mobility to achieve reduced task latency and energy consumption. The authors divide the original optimization problem into numerous local optimization problems and sub problems. The offloading choice is accomplished through the use of non-linear integer programming

(NLIP). To determine the approximate optimal offloading option, the NLIP sub problem is solved using a partial order based heuristic technique. The result of this approach is compared with six baseline algorithms and performs and demonstrated close to an optimal solution. The proposed method is found to improve latency and energy consumption, but its mobility prediction component only offers short-term results. Because of this limitation, tasks required to be offloaded cannot be assured to have optimal services.

Lu *et al.* [19], introduced a propagation based and cluster assisted computation offloading strategy considering mobility and social associations between edge device and edge server. To supply candidate edge servers, clustering is used. Channel conditions and available resources are considered to optimize offloading scheme. KALMAN filter with mobility model of mobile user is used to predict the location and trajectory of users. The clustering technique takes into account the historical connection as well as mobility prediction. The simulation was conducted and simulation results demonstrate that the proposed offloading strategy enhances the data processing capability of power-constrained networks and cut down the computation delay. Traditional mobility prediction techniques only consider a specific user's next expected location just based on its historical mobility patterns. However, the above-mentioned model does not consider new user who has not previous record.

3 Mobility Aware Computation Offloading Model

The design objectives of Mobile Aware Computation offloading model is concerned in the reduction of execution time, energy consumption, and latency. Computational task characteristics are concerning for both delay sensitive and computationally heavy activities. As a result, in the case of delay sensitive tasks, completion time reduction is an appropriate design target, whereas energy consumption minimization is a good design objective in the case of computationally intensive tasks. To develop the model, review of the architectures/models of the previous related literatures was made.

The developed model differs from state-of-the-art works in that, the offloading decision is comprised in edge device layer in the existing works which drains the battery of the edge device. As a result, to improve this limitation, the computation offloading decision is incorporated in the edge server layer in the proposed model. Moreover, the proposed model comprises combined fuzzy logic and dependency graph computation offloading decision, and mobility monitoring module on the edge server layer which is not included in the existing baseline studies. Additionally, local and regional edge server are identified based on the geographic distance from the edge device and included in the proposed model. A mobility aware algorithm for computation offloading is also developed.

3.1 The Proposed Model

The proposed mobility aware computation offloading model as shown in Fig. 1 comprises two major components. Edge device component which is the source of data to be processed either local by the edge device itself or by the corresponding edge server. This component includes the edge devices such as smart phones, laptops and other IoT devices like wearable devices and sensors. The second component contains the edge server which is responsible for running the tasks requested by the edge device. This component includes the local edge servers, regional edge servers and edge orchestrator.

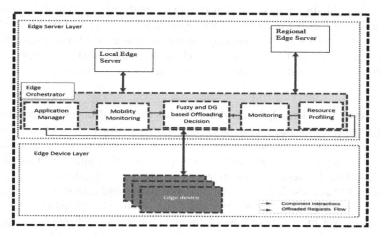

Fig. 1. The proposed mobility aware computation offloading model

Edge Device: The edge devices in the proposed model include IoT devices and edge user equipment, such as smart mobile phones, laptops, and watches. These devices are able to produce data, communicate with the upper layer through the WLAN network. Compared with the Servers in Data Canters, most of the IoT devices at the edge are somewhat limited in both computing capability and battery power. Edge devices can be connected directly to nearby edge servers via wireless links. Each node in the system can directly communicate its resources with the edge orchestrator. Besides, edge devices in our case are considered as heterogeneous in edge computing environment having different capabilities in power, memory size and CPU. Each device forwards offloading requests to the edge orchestrator which decides what to do with it. The resources such as CPU load, task size, remaining battery charge, and current mobility status are the decision-making parameters from the edge device's perspective. For offloading decisions, the volume of data to be transported is also taken into account. When the edge device requests task offloading, device characteristics and the request-related information are collected by the edge orchestrator.

Edge Server: The Edge Server has adequate computing and storage resources as compared to the edge computing and can be used to perform data analysis, and scheduling and computation activities/tasks. An Edge Server contains one or more physical machines hosting several virtual machines, covering the mobile users in proximity. These Edge Servers are interconnected with each other via MAN. The Edge Server is powered in computation and processing capacity in relative to edge devices and IoT gadgets. Edge servers contain the logic of the computation decision making strategy that is the edge orchestrator that is responsible for handling end user requests for computation offloading decision to reduce resource utilization and energy consumption as well as latency constraints. Based on the proximity of the edge servers to the edge devices, edge server can be local edge server, located near the source of the request initiated and regional edge server little bit distant from the edge device where the request is initiated. However, due to the mobility of the edge device the regional edge server will be the local when the user moves towards the regional edge server. The decision to offload is influenced by server-side aspects such as resources and characteristics. The size of users connected to the server and the number of virtual machines active are the server parameters taken into account.

Edge Orchestrator: The edge orchestrator (EO) is the main decision maker in handling incoming requests from end user devices. EO is a logic which is deployed in the edge servers that helps to reduce the latency as the edge server is powerful in resource in relative to edge devices. Basically, network resources, and the requirements of incoming application tasks, edge device information, mobility status of edge device is managed and controlled by EO and also it maintains a catalogue of the applications that are available. Furthermore, it is also responsible for deciding on whether to offload or not, selection of candidate server in the entire flow of computation based on fuzzy logic approach. Edge orchestrator determines the target computation server of the end user request by monitoring edge device features, edge server resources, the application characteristics, and the available network information factors such as the network bandwidth, edge server utilization, and task characteristics, predicted movement, network latency, and energy consumption to select edge servers.

For the mobility aware computation offloading, a fuzzy decision-based algorithm is proposed for a multiple of reasons. The edge computing environment is dynamic, with resource stages changing on a regular basis based on offload requests. As the quantity of incoming user requests is not known in advance, it's difficult to decide where a job should execute. Furthermore, task offloading management is primarily performed online and is regarded as an NP-hard problem [15, 20]. We require a low-complexity problem-solving technique to deal with these unpredictable environments. Furthermore, many input and output parameters are involved in the edge computing environment, and these parameters are part of the environmental behavior. This approach is inherently fuzzy. In this regard, fuzzy logic is one of the best alternatives for dealing with the aforementioned rapidly changing situation.

The main goal of the fuzzy decision-based computation offloading algorithm is to identify a target server for the offloaded task by monitoring various factors such as the size of the incoming task, the state of the network, and the resources already in use in the servers, energy of the user device and the mobility of the user. Figure 2, shows the fuzzy logic architecture together with dependency graph (DG) based Computation Offloading decision which is used in the proposed model.

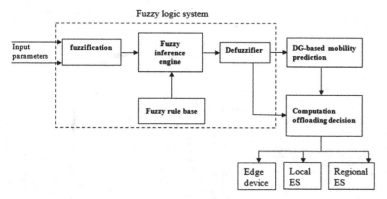

Fig. 2. Mobility aware fuzzy logic architecture with DG-based computation offloading decision

3.2 Mobility Prediction

To know the future station of the mobile edge device, Graph Dependency-based mobility route prediction is adapted from [21] which is noise tolerant while considering individual and collective behavior of mobile edge users. This approach represents paths as a graph, which is then used to accurately match road network arrangement with real-world Edge user movements. This mobility prediction approach is based on the assumption that edge user mobility is order dependent, as end users follow a specified order and Travers road segments in a specific direction to reach some destination of interest.

To forecast the next location of the edge device which is moving, for example as shown in Fig. 3, the current location of an edge device and its historical data are utilized, if available. In this mobility prediction, first, a prediction graph is constructed, in which nodes (vertices) represent road segments and arcs (directed edges) reflect the traversal order of road segments by edge users. The prediction graph is then used to anticipate the edge devices upcoming route by attempting to match its present trajectory with graph paths. However, due to the existence of noise in the graph, graph matching is problematic. In this case, the prediction graph creates graph edges with the following road segments lists appearing within a user-defined look ahead window. This is used to discard noise occurred in the data to increase prediction accuracy. To model collective and individual mobility behaviors, GMG (Global Mobility Graph) and the PMG (Personal Mobility Graph) prediction techniques, are presented to model both global and personal mobility patterns.

Data Preparation: The first edge device location data (GPS records) is collected periodically and sends it to EO. During collection, location data is split into trips by defining stay points. A stay point is a geographic area expressed as a set of consecutive GPS records where the distance from the first and last GPS records exceeds a distance threshold D_{thre} and the driver spent more time than a threshold T_{thr}. The resulting trips are then converted into mobility sequences by map matching GPS trajectories using a cloud map-matching based API.

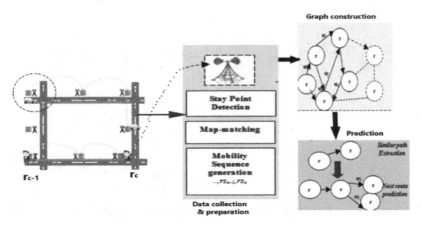

Fig. 3. Mobility aware computation offloading decision

Graph Construction: After obtaining mobility sequences, the EO incrementally updates its mobility graph. The mobility graph is initially built and then extended by inserting new road segments as graph nodes, whereas edge device movements between pair of road segment within the *lookahead* window size are represented by arcs. The weight of each new arc is set to 1. In the case where a road segment appears on newly collected mobility sequences, the weight of the corresponding arc is incremented accordingly.

Prediction: Once a mobility graph has been built, predictions can be performed using it. To predict the next route segment that will be visited by an edge device D, its current trajectory, denoted as CT (Current Trajectory), is required. It contains the current road segment where D is located in addition to its previous locations for the same trip, if available. Formally, let $RS = \{r_1, r_2, ..., r_n\}$ be the set of all road segments in a road network. $CT = \{p_j, pj + 1, ..., p_c\}$ is a sequence of road segments traversed by D where p_c is the current road segment of D. Having a trajectory CT, the prediction of the next route segment is performed in two steps.

Graph Matching: The first step consists of finding a path $SP = \{s_i, s_i + 1, ..., s_m\}$ in the mobility graph that matches with CT where $s_i \in RS$. We say that SP matches CT if and only if each road segment in SP appears in the same order in CT, that is $\forall_I, s_i = p$ and $m = c$. Note that graph matching is noise sensitive. Finding the path that exactly matches a trajectory CT can be challenging since erroneous positions may appear in location data. Using *MG,* built according to *lookahead* window, more flexibility to handle noisy data could be obtained.

For instance, if the first road segment *Ne* that comes after a given node *Nx* in a mobility sequence *s* is considered as noise, another arc will be created that skips *Ne* and go directly to next road segment, given that $w \geq 2$.

Next Road Extraction. The second step is to find the next road segment that edge device user will visit following *SP*, denoted as *Nr*. This road segment is predicted as the destination of the arc having the highest weight emanating from the last road segment in *SP*. More formally, let $E = \{a1, a2, ..., an\}$ be the set of outgoing arcs for the last node of *SP(sm)*. Then, *Nr* is defined as: $Nr = Dest(a_k)$ such that $W(a_k) \geq W(a)$ for $a \in E$ and $Uak \in E$ and $source(a_k) = sm$.

The mobility graph is adapted to consider both global (collective) and personal (individual) movement behaviors of drivers.

Global MG (GMG): GMG is used to represent global mobility behavior of a set of persons. The prediction graph is constructed from mobility data of all edge users. GMG is employed to perform predictions for an edge device user when no prior knowledge about his mobility pattern could be found such that edge users newly seen in prediction framework.

Personal Model (PMG): PMG consists of creating a mobility graph for each driver comprising his previous trajectories. Since each PMG only considers a single user, the prediction graph is only trained with his mobility sequences rather than the data of all users. A PMG is a sub-graph of the GMG. Therefore, a PMG can be considerably smaller than a GMG. By default, to forecast the next location of a given user device, the GMG model is used unless matching personal data is found in the PMG of the user. In such situation, the user's PMG is used for prediction.

After all this information is determined the computation offloading activity can be performed. Algorithm 1 represents the mobility aware computation offloading activity.

Algorithm 1: Mobility Aware Computation Offloading Algorithm

Input: Incoming task T with parameters $T_{Mobility}$, $T_{Baterry}$, $T_{Network}$, T_{Delay}, $T_{localVM\ utilization}$
output: Select target computational resource for offload O_{Edge}, $O_{Local\ ES}$, $O_{Regional\ ES}$
with minimum latency, minimum execution time, minimum energy;

1. *Read profile of incoming task*
2. *T; Read bandwidth;*
3. *Read network coverage;*
4. *Read VM utilization;*
5. *Read mobility speed;*
6. *Fg ← FuzzyLogic(τ, ι, d ,η, ω, e, m); // Output value that fuzzy logic returns*
7. *Calculate a crisp output value X← result of centroid defuzzifier;*
8. *If X<=8 then*
9. *If Required capacity < existing **then***
    O= edge device;
    else
10. *Check state of edge device **then***
11. *If device moving speed is low **then***
    O= Local edge server;
  else
12. *If mobility speed is medium and Local edge server network coverage is high*
    then
    O= Local edge server;
    else
13. *Predict_Next_Location by Graph dependency-based mobility route pre-*
    *diction **then***
    O=regional edge server
    else
14. *if X>8 **then***
15. *check mobility state **then***
16. *if not mobile **then***
    O=Local edge server;
    else
17. *if mobility speed is low **then***
    O= Local edge server;
    else
18. *if mobility speed is medium and Local edge server network coverage high*
    then
    O=Local edge server;
    else
19. *if mobility speed is medium and Local edge server network coverage meduim*
    then
    O= Regional edge server;
    else
20. *Predict_Next_Location by Graph dependency-based mobility route pre-*
    *diction; **then***
    O= Next_Regional edge server;
    end

Algorithm 1 describes the precise steps for determining the best target server for offloading computation based on fuzzy logic and mobility prediction. Initially, the tasks of edge devices and their characteristics, including task length, necessary number of cycles for task, and deadline requirement to finish task are collected from the edge device collected and from the available edge nearest edge servers (line 1–5). Based on the collected, parameter values are feed into the fuzzy logic system (line 6), then crisp values are calculated based on centroid defuzzification method (line 7). Offloading decision will be conducted based on the crisp output values and hence, if the result is less than 8 and if the device has required capability to compute the request, computation offloading will be handled there (*i.e.*, the edge device itself) line (8–9). However, the required capacity to handle request may not be in the device itself, in this case, the computation offloading will be granted based on the mobility status and network coverage of the available edge server (line 10–13). For crisp values greater than 8 computation offloading will be granted based on the mobility status, mobility prediction graph and network coverage of the available edge sever (line 14–20).

4 Experimentation and Result Analysis

In this section the evaluation of mobility aware computation offloading in edge computing through a simulator is presented in detail. The simulation tool, implementation of the proposed algorithm for the desired model and the parameters of the simulation and the simulation setup and the analysis result is presented.

4.1 Simulation Environment

To evaluate the performance of the proposed mobility aware computation offloading model, the most commonly known edge computing simulator – PureEdgeSim is used. PureEdgeSim is based on CloudSim Plus [22], which is event-driven simulation framework intended to simulate cloud, fog, and edge computing environments. It offers the necessary simulation components such as the network model, the mobility model, and the description of edge device characteristics (i.e. CPU capacity, battery, mobility, storage, and so on), making it usable for the proposed scenarios.

The simulation setup on this simulator comprises of an edge device including IoT devices, and a Local and regional server. The regional edge server is also emulated as a single data centre with one host and eight virtual machines, each with a processing rate of ten thousand MIPS. The number of mobile users is deployed equally among the edge servers. Each location is covered by a dedicated wireless network WLAN between edge servers and WLAN between edge device and edge server. Moreover, to investigate the performance when the system is overloaded, we vary the number of mobile devices from 100 to 1500. When they move to the related location, they will join WLAN, and they based on their offloading decision send tasks to the edge orchestrator for offloading to edge server or local processing or edge processing. The simulation parameters used is shown in Table 1.

Based on the application type, these parameters are random numbers with an exponential distribution. Following the creation of the list, the tasks are sorted by start time,

Table 1. Simulation parameters

Parameter	Measurement	Values
Edge devices range	Meter	15
Wan bandwidth	Mbps	400
WAN propagation delay	Second	0.1
WLAN bandwidth	Mbps	300
WLAN propagation delay	Seconds	0.2
Orchestrator deployment	–	Edge server
Orchestration algorithm	–	Mobility aware fuzzy logic, fuzzy logic, ECOOA
Architecture	–	Edge

and parameters such as the network model between the devices are initiated, and determined based on the average data task sizes, which differ for input and output. A network model is in charge of calculating the queuing delay of WLAN connections between edge devices and the edge orchestrator, as well as WAN connections between edge servers through edge orchestrator, in both uploading (task input) and downloading (task output) directions.

Finally, the virtual machines for the local and regional edge servers are launched, and the simulator's initialization step is completed and starts generating tasks automatically. For devices that are moving, based on the mobility speed the next location and edge server will be predicted based on the graph dependency method. When the simulation begins, the tasks are served depending on their start time and regardless of the application to which they belong. An end device manager is responsible in each IoT device for making the decision of where to process based on the decision algorithm.

4.2 Experiment Result and Analysis

The analysis of the simulation result is done using a comparative analysis with the state of the art works fuzzy decision-based cloud-MEC collaborative task offloading management system (FTOM) [14] and a fuzzy decision tree-based task orchestration (FDT) [23] considering task failure rate, energy utilization, task processing latency, and task completion delay. It is recalled that FTOM was proved to be a better computation offloading scheme compared to previous techniques including LEO, TTEO, FOLB, WOTO and FCTO in relation to success of task failure rate, task processing latency and task completion time.

To measure task completion time of the developed computation offloading model Fig. 4 shows the average task failure rate (the y-axis) versus the number of mobile devices (the x-axis, from 100 to 700). Task failure occur due to mobility, network delay or server capacity which are considered in the experiment. From analyzing Fig. 4. Task failure rate is approximately zero until mobile devices are 100. This is due to the fact that the mobility is low and the system is lightly loaded. However, when the mobility and edge device load increases the situation is changed as congestion is created. For example, the task failure rate increases from 2% at 100 mobile devices to 80% at 700 mobile devices in FTOM, from 1% at 100 mobile devices to 45% at 700 mobile devices in FDT and from 0.9% at 100 mobile devices to 40% at 700 mobile devices in our proposed model. Comparing all the models, the proposed model provided a lower task failure rather than the others because the proposed model uses mobility for computation offloading.

Further experiment on the task failure rate due to mobility indicated that the failure is increasing with an increase of mobile devices in FTOM and FDT as shown in Fig. 5. When 100 mobile devices are used in all the schemes, FTOM, FDT and the proposed mobility aware offloading computation model, the task failure rate due to mobility is almost similar approximately 10%. As the number of mobile devices increases the task failure rate due to mobility rapidly increases in all models but in FTOM is the worst. The proposed model offload task better that the others with very significant difference, it takes mobility as one of the parameters in task offloading.

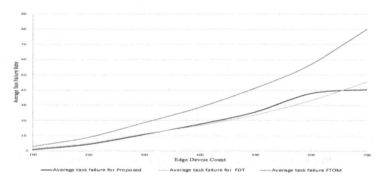

Fig. 4. Task failure rate for the proposed approach

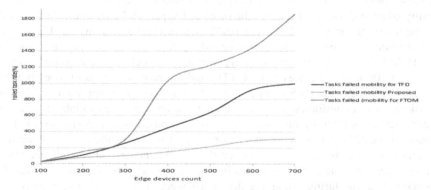

Fig. 5. Failure rate due to device mobility

Energy consumption utilization is one of the most critical parameters for edge devices specifically, for battery powered devices. As the result while delegating computation tasks battery consumption should be considered. In our experiment energy consumption was one of the parameters for task offloading decision which was not considered in the previous studies. Figure 6, show the battery consumption of the proposed study.

Analyzing Fig. 6, on energy utilization of mobile devices, the energy consumption rate (y-axis) increases with the increase of mobile device count (x-axis, from 100 to 700). For example, at 100 mobile devices all the models FTOM, FDT and the proposed model utilize 0.8% of energy. When the mobile device count is increase from 100 to 250, the energy consumption for FDT is higher that FTOM and the proposed model. From 250 to 420 mobile devices, the proposed model energy utilization is larger when compared to the other schemes. From 420 to 700 mobiles, energy consumption for FTOM is high. Comparing the overall energy consumption, the proposed model energy consumption at 700 mobile devices is 6.9% whereas FDT is 7.2% and FTOM consumption is 7.9%.

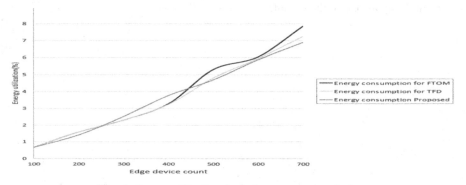

Fig. 6. Energy utilization for battery consuming devices

Another parameter considered in our experiment is task processing delay. It is true that the computation decision is handled considering the sensitivity of tasks and the mobility of edge devices. This gives the proposed approach better constraint from the baseline state of the art works, FTOM and FDT as shown in Fig. 7. Analyzing Fig. 7, when 100 mobile devices are used in the experiment the task processing delay (y-axis) for FDT and FTOM is 0.51 and 0,55 s respectively. But the time delay for the proposed model is 0.2 s. At 700 mobile devices FTOM, FDT and the proposed model processing time delay is 0.73 s, 0,7 s and 0.45 s respectively. Primarily, during computation offloading the task latency is considered as a fuzzy logic parameter and the available resource of the edge servers within the proximity is considered based on the device location and the state of the edge device either mobile or static. This makes the proposed approach to outperform from the other studies. Even though, the increase in edge device affects the task processing latency, as resources in edge servers are also limited, the available resource utilization during offloading decision lowers the task processing delay from other studies.

In relation to this, task completion time which is the summation of processing time and network delay was also considered in the experiment. With the increase in numbers of mobile devices, the overall, the average task completion time was increased. However, as the proposed model decision considers mobility and tasks size to balance the utilization of resources on the regional and local edge servers, the proposed approach showed better performance on average.

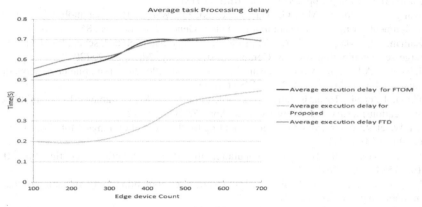

Fig. 7. Average task processing delay

5 Conclusion

In this study, we proposed mobility aware computation offloading model with fuzzy logic-based edge orchestration for edge computing applications, which controls computing resources to improve performance and the energy consumption. The EO selects where to compute the incoming client requests based on the available information on network connections and the status of the edge server and the application features. A fuzzy logic-based workload orchestrator is proposed in our system to give an efficient offload decision: a mobile device, a local edge server, or a regional edge server to assign edge resources to the incoming user requests.

Computation offloading to the nearest edge servers augments the capabilities of mobile devices and ensures lower-latency services and energy efficiency. However, a decision on computation offloading concerning uncertainties such as user highly scalable. Moreover, they reduce the number of migrations significantly compared to other non-optimal approaches.

The simulation results were analyzed with metrics, average task failure rate, and task failure rate due to mobility, average latency and average execution delay with state-of-the-art studies. Experimental evaluations showed that our proposed computation offloading model find energy efficient, latency reduction, and execution time minimization considering the mobility of the edge device in a reasonable time.

For future work, we plan to investigate the real data traces and propose efficient mobility-aware and energy efficient offloading methods while guaranteeing mobility of the edge device.

References

1. Chen, Y., Zhang, N., Zhang, Y., Chen, X.: Dynamic computation offloading in edge computing for internet of things, pp. 2327–4662. IEEE (2018)
2. Wang, Z., Zhao, Z., Min, G., Huang, X., Ni, Q., Wange, R.: User mobility aware task assignment for mobile edge computing. Future Gener. Comput. Syst. **85**, 1–8 (2018)
3. Zaman, S.K., Maqsood, T., Ali, M., Bilal, K.: A load balanced task scheduling heuristic for large-scale computing systems. Comput. Syst. Sci. Eng. **34**(2), 79–90 (2019)
4. Jehangiri, A.I., et al.: Mobility-aware computational offloading in mobile edge networks: a survey. Cluster Comput. **24**, 2735–2756 (2021)
5. Shuja, J., et al.: Towards native code offloading based MCC frameworks for multimedia applications: a survey. J. Netw. Comput. Appl. **75**, 335–354 (2016)
6. Yu, W., et al.: A survey on the edge computing for the internet of things. Mob. Edge Comput. **6**, 6900–6919 (2017)
7. Lin, L., Liao, X., Jin, H., Li, P.: Computation offloading toward edge computing. Proc. IEEE **107**, 1584–1607 (2019)
8. Messaoudi, F., Ksentini, A., Bertin, P.: On using edge computing for computation offloading in mobile network. IEEE (2017)
9. Guo, F., Zhang, H., Ji, H., Li, X., Leung, V.C.M.: An efficient computation offloading management scheme in the densely deployed small cell networks with mobile edge computing. IEEE/ACM Trans. Netw. **26**, 2651–2664 (2018)
10. Sheng, J., Hu, J., Teng, X., Wang, B., Pan, X.: Computation offloading strategy in mobile edge computing. Information **10**, 191 (2019)
11. Zhao, Z., Liu, F., Cai, Z., Xiao, N.: Edge computing: platforms, applications and challenges. J. Comput. Res. Dev. **55**, 327–337 (2018)
12. Sun, X., Ansari, N.: Latency aware workload offloading in the cloudlet network. IEEE Commun. Lett. **21**(7), 1481–1484 (2017)
13. Shi, W., Sun, H., Cao, J., Zhang, Q., Liu, W.: Edge computing-an emerging computing model for the internet of everything era. Comput. Res. Dev. **54**, 907–924 (2017)
14. Sonmez, C., Ozgovde, A., Ersoy, C.: Fuzzy workload orchestration for edge computing. IEEE Trans. Netw. Serv. Manag. **16**(2), 769–782 (2019)
15. Hossain, M., et al.: Fuzzy decision-based efficient task offloading management scheme in multi-tier MEC-enabled networks. Sensors **21**(4), 1484 (2021). https://doi.org/10.3390/s21041484
16. Spatharakis, D., et al.: A scalable edge computing architecture enabling smart offloading for location based services. Pervasive Mob. Comput. **67** (2020)
17. Lu, Y., Chen, Z., Gao, Q., Jing, T., Qian, J.: A mobility- aware and sociality-associate computation offloading strategy for IoT. Wirel. Commun. Mob. Comput. **12** (2021)
18. Maleki, E.F.: Mobility-aware computation offloading in edge computing using prediction. In: IEEE 4th International Conference on Fog and Edge Computing (ICFEC) (2020)
19. Nguyen, V.D., Khanh, T.T., Nguyen, T.D.T., Hong, C.S., Huh, E.-N.: Flexible computation offloading in a fuzzy-based mobile edge orchestrator for IoT applications. J. Cloud Comput. **9**(1), 1–18 (2020). https://doi.org/10.1186/s13677-020-00211-9
20. Shi, M., Wang, R., Liu, E., Xu, Z., Wang, L.: Deep reinforcement learning based computation offloading for mobility-aware edge computing. In: Gao, H., Feng, Z., Yu, J., Wu, J. (eds.) ChinaCom 2019. LNICSSITE, vol. 312, pp. 53–65. Springer, Cham (2019). https://doi.org/10.1007/978-3-030-41114-5_5
21. Zhan, W., Luo, C., Min, G., Wang, C., Zhu, Q., Duan, H.: Mobility-aware multi-user offloading optimization for mobile edge computing. IEEE Trans. Veh. Technol. **69**(3), 3341–3356 (2020)

22. Viger, P.F., Ouinten, Y., Lagraa, N., Amirat, H.: MyRoute: a graph-dependency based model for real-time route prediction. J. Commun. **12**(12), 668–676 (2017)
23. Silva Filho, M.C., Oliveira, R.L., Monteiro, C.C., Inácio, P.R., Freire, M.M.: CloudSim plus: a cloud computing simulation framework pursuing software engineering principles for improved modularity. Extensibility and correctness. In: IFIP/IEEE Symposium on Integrated Network and Service Management (IM) (2017)
24. Mechalikh, C., Taktak, H., Moussa, F.: A fuzzy decision tree based tasks orchestration algorithm for edge computing environments. In: Barolli, L., Amato, F., Moscato, F., Enokido, T., Takizawa, M. (eds.) AINA 2020. AISC, vol. 1151, pp. 193–203. Springer, Cham (2020). https://doi.org/10.1007/978-3-030-44041-1_18

Science and Engineering Applications Requiring and Motivating an Integrated Ecosystem

Machine Learning for First Principles Calculations of Material Properties for Ferromagnetic Materials

Markus Eisenbach[1]([✉])[iD], Mariia Karabin[1][iD], Massimiliano Lupo Pasini[2][iD], and Junqi Yin[1][iD]

[1] National Center for Computational Sciences, Oak Ridge National Laboratory, Oak Ridge, TN 37831, USA
{eisenbachm,karabinm,yinj}@ornl.gov
[2] Computational Sciences and Engineering Division, Oak Ridge National Laboratory, Oak Ridge, TN 37831, USA
lupopasinim@ornl.gov

Abstract. The investigation of finite temperature properties using Monte-Carlo (MC) methods requires a large number of evaluations of the system's Hamiltonian to sample the phase space needed to obtain physical observables as function of temperature. DFT calculations can provide accurate evaluations of the energies, but they are too computationally expensive for routine simulations. To circumvent this problem, machine-learning (ML) based surrogate models have been developed and implemented on high-performance computing (HPC) architectures. In this paper, we describe two ML methods (linear mixing model and HydraGNN) as surrogates for first principles density functional theory (DFT) calculations with classical MC simulations. These two surrogate models are used to learn the dependence of target physical properties from complex compositions and interactions of their constituents. We present the predictive performance of these two surrogate models with respect to their complexity while avoiding the danger of overfitting the model. An important aspect of our approach is the periodic retraining with newly generated first principles data based on the progressive exploration of the system's phase space by the MC simulation. The numerical results show that HydraGNN model attains superior predictive performance compared to the linear mixing model for magnetic alloy materials.

Keywords: Machine learning · Surrogate models · Material science · Solid solution alloys

This manuscript has been authored in part by UT-Battelle, LLC, under contract DE-AC05-00OR22725 with the US Department of Energy (DOE). The US government retains and the publisher, by accepting the article for publication, acknowledges that the US government retains a nonexclusive, paid-up, irrevocable, worldwide license to publish or reproduce the published form of this manuscript, or allow others to do so, for US government purposes. DOE will provide public access to these results of federally sponsored research in accordance with the DOE Public Access Plan (http://energy.gov/downloads/doe-public-access-plan).

K. Doug et al. (Eds.): SMC 2022, CCIS 1690, pp. 75–86, 2022.
https://doi.org/10.1007/978-3-031-23606-8_5

1   Introduction

The investigation of finite temperature properties using Monte-Carlo (MC) methods requires a large number of evaluations of the system's Hamiltonian to sample the phase space needed to obtain physical observables as function of temperature. Density functional calculations can provide accurate evaluations of the energies, but they are too computationally expensive for routine simulations. Surrogate models can alleviate the computational cost to complete classical MC simulations [16,24,25,30,33] since they can estimate finite temperature properties orders of magnitude faster than the original density functional theory (DFT) code. Although surrogate models generally do not attain the same accuracy as the physics-based model on which they are trained, a hybrid approach that combines initial inexpensive surrogate model evaluations with limited expensive DFT refinements can drastically reduce the computational time without significantly affecting the accuracy of the final inference with respect to running the DFT code throughout the entire classical MC workflow [27].

The identification of an appropriate surrogate model must take into consideration multiple factors such as (i) the dimensionality of the data space that needs to be explored, (ii) the amount of training data available, (iii) the complexity of the cause/effect relation that connects input features and target properties, (iv) the available computational resources. In situations similar to the ones addressed in this work where the training data is generated by running DFT calculations, (ii) and (iv) are strongly connected, as the computational resources available determine the amount of DFT data that can be generated for training.

Deep learning (DL) models have attracted a lot of attention in the material science community due to their ability to capture highly non-linear relations between input features and target properties [3,6,11,18,19,22,35]. However, their success relies on the a subtle connection between the complexity of the DL model and the amount of available training data.

In this paper we will investigate the capability of two different classes of surrogate models to describe the energy of a magnetic alloy system with sufficient accuracy needed to perform statistical mechanics investigations of alloy ordering.

We will first describe the two models we will be investigating, followed by a description of the physical alloy system, body-centered tetragonal FePt, that will provide the basis for our comparison. This will be followed by the results of our numerical experiments and finally we will discuss the results and conclude.

2   Surrogate Models

2.1   Linear Model

To model the energy of a refractory high entropy alloy system, the effective pair interactions (EPI) [17] was proposed. The energy is approximated by the summation of local energies as follows,

$$E \approx N \sum_{p'<p,m} V_m^{pp'} \Pi_m^{pp'} + V_i^p + V^0 + \epsilon, \qquad (1)$$

where N is the total number of atoms, V^0 is the bias term same for all sites, V_i^p is a single-site term depending only on the chemical component p of atom i, and $\Pi_m^{pp'}$ is the proportion of pp' interaction in the m-th neighboring shell. The EPI model has been shown [17] to work well for non-magnetic alloy systems.

2.2 Graph Convolutional Neural Network

GCNN models map atomic structure by naturally converting them into a graph, where atoms are interpreted as nodes and interatomic bonds are interpreted as edges, and outputs total (graph-level) and atomic (node-level) physical properties. The typical GCNN architecture is characterized by three different types of hidden layers: graph convolutional layers, graph pooling layers, and fully connected layers. The graph convolutional layers extract information from the graph samples about local features that model the short-range interactions of an atom with it neighbors. GCNNs embed the interactions between nodes (atoms) by representing the local interaction zone as a hyperparameter that cuts-off the interaction of a node with all the other nodes outside a prescribed local neighborhood. This is identical to the approximation made by many atomic simulation methods, including the LSMS-3 code used to generate the DFT training data, which ignore interactions outside a given cutoff range. Larger sizes of the local neighborhood lead to a higher computational cost to train the model, as the number of regression coefficients to train at each hidden convolutional layer increases proportional to the number of neighbors. The second set of layers extracts global features that describe long range weak interactions between atoms far from each other in the crustal structure. The architecture of a GCNN model is shown schematically in Fig. 1.

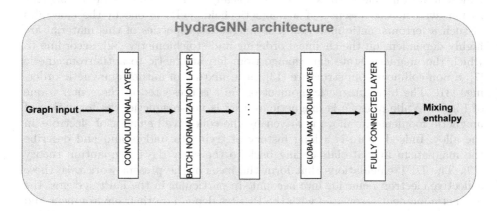

Fig. 1. HydraGNN architecture when used as a surrogate model for DFT calculations of mixing enthalpy.

Our implementation of GCNN, called HydraGNN, uses `Pytorch` [1, 26] as both a robust NN library, as well as a performance portability layer for running on multiple hardware architectures. This enables HydraGNN to run on CPUs and GPUs, from laptops to supercomputers, including ORNL's Summit and NERSC's Perlmutter. The `Pytorch Geometric` [2, 10] library built on `Pytorch` is particularly important for our work and enables many GCNN models to be used interchangeably. HydraGNN is openly available on GitHub [23].

A variety of graph convolutional layers, e.g., principal neighborhood aggregation (PNA) [4], crystal GCNN (CGCNN) [35] and GraphSAGE [12], have been developed. Previous studies using GCNN models for solid solution alloys [19, 22] showed that PNA better discriminates different atomic configurations which in turn improves the final accuracy of the model. Therefore, the Pytorch Geometric implementation of the PNA is used in this work as graph convolutional layer in HydraGNN. Batch normalizations are performed between consecutive graph convolutional layers along with a ReLU activation function. Graph pooling layers are connected to the end of the convolution-batch normalization stack to gather feature information from the entire graph to collapse the node feature into a single feature. This is achieved by summing the local interactions of each atom with its neighbors and use the result to estimate global properties such as the mixing enthalpy of an alloy. Fully connected (FC) layers are positioned at the end of the architecture to take the results of pooling, i.e. extracted features, and provide the output prediction.

Further details on the behavior of HydraGNN with different sizes of the local neighborhood have been previously reported [19].

3   Ferromagnetic Materials

Itinerant ferromagnetic materials are typically metals. They exhibit magnetization even in the absence of a magnetic field. FePt is one of the examples of such a ferromagnetic material. The magnetic properties of this material are highly dependent on the chemical ordering and stoichiometry [32], according to which the magnetic state can change from ferromagnetic to antiferromagnetic [7], a non-collinear spin structure [13], or a mixture of antiferromagnetic orderings [31]. The total magnetic moment of FePt is presented in the center frame of Fig. 2. While pure Fe is magnetic and Pt is non-magnetic, the formation of magnetic moments in alloys is driven by the collective behavior of electrons in the alloy. Indeed there is a long history of trying to understand and describe the magnetism in materials dating back to the early days of quantum theory [29]. The DFT calculations that form the basis of the present work take these collective electron behavior into account. In particular in the FePt systems, the magnetic moment associated with the Pt sites depend on their environment and the Fe concentration. This can be clearly seen in the center picture of Fig. 2 where the rate of change in the magnetic moment at Fe concentrations below $\approx 15\%$ depends on the amount of Fe in the system as the induced moments on the Pt site increases, whereas above this threshold the moments on the Pt sites have reached their saturated values and the total magnetization follows the Fe and Pt concentrations.

3.1   Solid Solution Binary Alloy Dataset

In this work we focus on a solid solution binary alloy, where two constituent elements are randomly placed on an underlying crystal lattice. We use a dataset for FePt alloys available through the OLCF Constellation [20] which includes the total enthalpy, atomic charge transfer, and atomic magnetic moment. Each atomic sample has a body centered tetragonal (BCT) structure with a $2 \times 2 \times 4$ supercell. The dataset was computed with LSMS-3 [8], a locally self-consistent multiple scattering (LSMS) DFT application [9,34]. The dataset was created with fixed volume in order to isolate the effects of graph interactions and graph positions for models such as GCNN. This produces non-equilibrium alloy samples, with non-zero pressure and positive mixing enthalpy, shown as a function of composition in the top picture of Fig. 2.

The input to HydraGNN for each sample includes the three components of the atom position and the proton number. The predicted values include the mixing enthalpy, a single scalar for each sample (graph), as well as the charge transfer and magnitude of the magnetic moment, both scalars per atom (node). Although the magnetic moment is a vector quantity, we treat it as a scalar because all the atomic magnetic moments in the dataset are co-linear (all magnetic moments point in the same direction).

The dataset consists of 28,033 configurations out of the 2^{32} available, sampled every 3 atomic percent. For this work, if the number of unique configurations for a specific composition is less than 1,000 all those configurations are included in the dataset; for all other compositions, configurations are randomly selected up to 1,000. In order to ensure each composition is adequately represented in all portions of the dataset, splitting between the training, validation, and test sets is done separately for each composition.

At the ground state, the total enthalpy H of an alloy is

$$H = \sum_{i=1}^{E} c_i H_i + \Delta H_{\mathrm{mix}}, \tag{2}$$

where E is the total number of elements in the system, c_i is the molar fraction of each element i, H_i is the molar enthalpy of each element i, and ΔH_{mix} is the mixing enthalpy. We predict the mixing enthalpy for each sample by subtracting the internal enthalpy from the DFT computed total enthalpy as a value more relevant to materials science (more directly related to the configuration). The chemical disorder makes the task of describing the material properties combinatorially complex; this represents the main difference from open source databases that have very broad elemental and structural coverage, but only include ordered compounds [5,14,28].

The range of values of the mixing enthalpy expressed in Rydberg is $(0.0, 65.92)$, the range of atomic charge transfer in electron charge is $(-5.31, -0.85)$, and the range of atomic magnetic moment in magnetons is $(-0.05, 3.81)$. Since different physical quantities have different units and different orders of magnitude, the inputs and outputs for each quantity are normalized between 0 and 1 across all data.

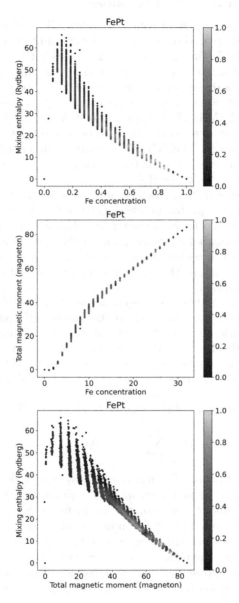

Fig. 2. Top: configurational mixing enthalpy of solid solution binary alloy FePt with BCT structure as a function of Fe concentration. Center: scatter plot of total magnetic moment against concentration of iron. Bottom: scatter plot of mixing enthalpy against total magnetic moment. The color map in each plot indicates the relative frequency of data.

The total magnetization of the binary alloy FePt is strongly correlated with the concentration of Fe in the alloy, as shown in center picture of Fig. 2, because only the Fe atoms have a non-negligible magnetic moment. This results in a strong (albeit nonlinear) correlation between the mixing enthalpy and the total magnetization of the alloy, as shown in the bottom picture of Fig. 2.

4   Numerical Section

This section first presents numerical results using a linear mixing model on portions of the training dataset associated with different compositions of the binary alloys FePt, and the performance of the linear model is interpreted in terms of the physical properties of the ferromagnetic system. Additionally, a more complex surrogate model represented by an HydraGNN model is used to simultaneously produce accurate estimates of total mixing enthalpy, atomic charge transfer and atomic magnetic moment over the entire compositional range of the binary alloy. The numerical results that use HydraGNN describe the accuracy of the model as a function of the volume of data used for training.

4.1   Numerical Experiments Using Linear Mixing Model

For binary alloy, there is only one term $V_m^{pp'}$ (see Eq. 1) for each shell, and we consider up to 6th shell. The dataset is randomly splitted with 80% for training and 20% for testing, and the model is cross validated among different splits. The reported model performance is evaluated on the test dataset. As shown in Fig. 3, the linear model fits perfectly to the total energy, but fails to capture the non-linear behavior of the mixing enthalpy. Since the linear model is designed for the fixed concentration, we first fit the model for each individual Fe concentration (i.e., 6.25%, 12.5%, 25%, 50%, 75%, 93.75%). The observation is that as the Fe concentration increases, the goodness-of-fit deteriorates, indicating the non-linear behavior coming from the magnetism. In Fig. 3, we fit the linear

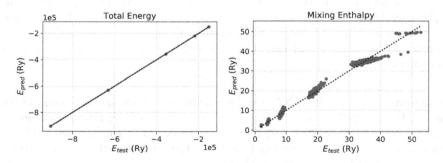

Fig. 3. The linear model predictions versus the test set of FePt data for total energy (left) and mixing enthalpy (right). Each cluster of data corresponds to a Fe concentration, ranging from 6.25% to 93.75%.

model to various Fe concentrations, and each cluster of data corresponds to a Fe concentration, ranging from 6.25% to 93.75%.

4.2 Numerical Experiments Using HydraGNN

Training Setup. The architecture of the HydraGNN models has 6 PNA [4] convolutional layers with 300 neurons per layer. A radius cutoff of 7 Å is used to build the local neighborhoods used by the graph convolutional mask. Every learning task is mapped into separate heads where each head is made up of two fully connected layers, with 50 neurons in the first layer and 25 neurons in the second. Periodic boundary conditions are implemented using the minimum image convention. The DL models were trained using the Adam method [15] with a learning rate equal to 0.001, batch sizes of 64, and a maximum number of epochs set to 200. Early stopping is performed to interrupt the training when the validation loss function does not decrease for several consecutive epochs, as this is a symptom that shows further epochs are very unlikely to reduce the value of the loss function. We reserve 10% of the total dataset for validation, which corresponds to 2,803 atomic configurations. The remaining 90% of the total dataset, which amounts to 25,230 atomic configurations, is used to generate different training subsets. Each training subset contains a percentage of the total training dataset, ranging from 10% through 100% with increments of 10% across successive data partitions. As discussed in Sect. 3.1, compositional stratified splitting was performed to ensure that all the compositions were equally represented across training, validation, and testing datasets. A larger partition contains the smaller ones as subsets. The training of the HydraGNN model was performed on one NVIDIA V100 GPU.

Performance of HydraGNN on the Entire Training Dataset. In Fig. 4 we show the parity plot of HydraGNN predictions against the LSMS-3 values for the mixing enthalpy. We notice that HydraGNN accurately predicts the mixing enthalpy for different compositions and atomic configurations associated with each composition, thus clearly outperforming the linear mixing model. This results corroborate that HydraGNN is an effective non-linear predictive model that accurately reads the dependence of the mixing enthalpy as a function of configurational entropy and chemical composition for a binary ferromagnetic solid solution alloy.

Performance of HydraGNN on Different Volumes of Training Data. The validation MSE is used to describe the accuracy of the HydraGNN model as a function of the volume of training data is shown in Fig. 5. The predictive performance shows that the validation MSE decreases linearly with the size of the training data for the mixing enthalpy.

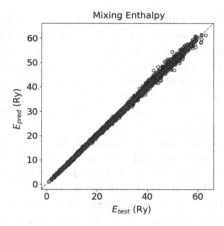

Fig. 4. The HydraGNN predictions versus the test set of FePt data for mixing enthalpy. The test set ranges over the entire compositional range by increasing the Fe concentration by 3%.

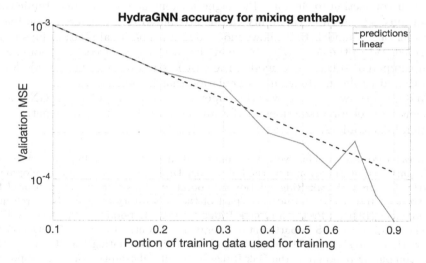

Fig. 5. Validation MSE of MTL training performed with HydraGNN for predictions of mixing enthalpy as a function of training data volume used for training.

5   Conclusions and Future Developments

In this work we have provided a comparison of two different surrogate models to fit first principles data for alloys. The goal is to provide effective models for the energy of the system that will allow the utilization in Monte-Carlo simulations of the finite temperature statistical mechanics of these systems to enable the quantitative exploration of phase transitions. The linear model has the significant advantage of faster evaluation and small number of model parameters, which reduces the training effort. While this linear model had been successfully applied to non-magnetic multi-component alloys [17] at fixed concentrations, the present work challenges the linear model. As can be seen in Fig. 3, the linear model shows deviation from the correct enthalpy prediction which is dependent on the concentration. Note that this deviation is not immediately apparent in the total energy, which in the all-electron LSMS calculations is dominated by the core-electron binding energy that does not contribute to the material behavior at the energy scale of condensed matter physics.

The use of GCNN allows the description of the interaction for a wide range of concentrations in a single network. As can be seen in Fig. 5 the model can be improved over a large range of set sizes in the training data without leading to over-fitting. As the HydraGNN architecture allows us to utilize additional physical information from the LSMS calculations, such as the site magnetization, for a multi-objective optimization of the model using multi-task training, which can lead to better physical prediction of the energy of the system. [21] Thus the HydraGNN model for the FePt system does not suffer the problems of the linear model. In particular, it can capture the changing atomic interactions and their connection to the local Pt magnetic moments at changing atomic concentrations. This greater capability can be attributed to the inherent non-linear character of NN models that allows more complex functional relationships to be described. While the advantages come at the cost of greater computational cost when compared to the linear model, the cost is still orders of magnitude lower than the fully selfconsistent DFT calculation that it models.

In summary, we have shown the superior performance of HydraGNN as a surrogate model for predictions of the mixing enthalpy in ferromagnetic solid solution binary alloys.

Acknowledgements. This work was supported in part by the Office of Science of the Department of Energy and by the Laboratory Directed Research and Development (LDRD) Program of Oak Ridge National Laboratory. This research is sponsored by the Artificial Intelligence Initiative as part of the Laboratory Directed Research and Development (LDRD) Program of Oak Ridge National Laboratory, managed by UT-Battelle, LLC, for the US Department of Energy under contract DE-AC05-00OR22725. This work used resources of the Oak Ridge Leadership Computing Facility and of the Edge Computing program at the Oak Ridge National Laboratory, which is supported by the Office of Science of the U.S. Department of Energy under Contract No. DE-AC05-00OR22725.

References

1. PyTorch. https://pytorch.org/docs/stable/index.html
2. PyTorch Geometric. https://pytorch-geometric.readthedocs.io/en/latest/
3. Conduit, B., et al.: Probabilistic neural network identification of an alloy for direct laser deposition. Mater. Des. **168**, 107644 (2019)
4. Corso, G., Cavalleri, L., Beaini, D., Liò, P., Veličković, P.: Principal neighbourhood aggregation for graph nets. arXiv:2004.05718 [cs, stat] (December 2020). http://arxiv.org/abs/2004.05718, arXiv: 2004.05718

5. Curtarolo, S., et al.: AFLOW: an automatic framework for high-throughput materials discovery. Comput. Mater. Sci. **58**, 218–226 (2012)

6. Dai, M., Demirel, M.F., Liang, Y., Hu, J.M.: Graph neural networks for an accurate and interpretable prediction of the properties of polycrystalline materials. NPJ Computational Mater.**7**(103) (2021). https://doi.org/10.1038/s41524-021-00574-w, https://www.nature.com/articles/s41524-021-00574-w#citeas

7. Bacon, G.E., Crangle, J.: Chemical and magnetic order in platinum-rich pt + fe alloys. Proc. R. Soc. Lond. A **272**, 387–405 (1963). https://doi.org/10.1098/rspa.1963.0060

8. Eisenbach, M., Li, Y.W., Odbadrakh, O.K., Pei, Z., Stocks, G.M., Yin, J.: LSMS. https://github.com/mstsuite/lsms, https://www.osti.gov/biblio/1420087

9. Eisenbach, M., Larkin, J., Lutjens, J., Rennich, S., Rogers, J.H.: GPU acceleration of the locally selfconsistent multiple scattering code for first principles calculation of the ground state and statistical physics of materials. Comput. Phys. Commun. **211**, 2–7 (2017). https://doi.org/10.1016/j.cpc.2016.07.013

10. Fey, M., Lenssen, J.E.: Fast graph representation learning with PyTorch geometric. In: ICLR Workshop on Representation Learning on Graphs and Manifolds (2019)

11. Fuhr, A.S., Sumpter, B.G.: Deep generative models for materials discovery and machine learning-accelerated innovation. Front. Mater. **9** (2022). https://doi.org/10.3389/fmats.2022.865270, https://www.frontiersin.org/articles/10.3389/fmats.2022.865270/full

12. Hamilton, W.L., Ying, R., Leskovec, J.: Inductive representation learning on large graphs. In: Proceedings of the 31st International Conference on Neural Information Processing Systems, pp. 1025–1035 (2017)

13. Higashiyama, Y., Tsunoda, Y.: Magnetism of pt0.67fe0.33 alloy. J. Phys. Soc. Jpn. **72**(12), 3305–3306 (2003). https://doi.org/10.1143/JPSJ.72.3305

14. Jain, A., et al.: Commentary: the materials project: a materials genome approach to accelerating materials innovation. APL Mater. **1**(1), 11 (2013). https://doi.org/10.1063/1.4812323

15. Kingma, D.P., Ba, J.: Adam: a method for stochastic optimization. arXiv:1412.6980 [cs] (January 2017). http://arxiv.org/abs/1412.6980, arXiv: 1412.6980

16. Lavrentiev, M.Y., Drautz, R., Nguyen-Manh, D., Klaver, T.P.C., Dudarev, S.: Monte Carlo study of thermodynamic properties and clustering in the BCC Fe-Cr system. Phys. Rev. B **75**(014208) (2007). https://doi.org/10.1103/PhysRevB.75.014208

17. Liu, X., Zhang, J., Yin, J., Bi, S., Eisenbach, M., Wang, Y.: Monte Carlo simulation of order-disorder transition in refractory high entropy alloys: a data-driven approach. Comput. Mater. Sci. **187**, 110135 (2021). https://doi.org/10.1016/j.commatsci.2020.110135

18. Louis, S.Y., et al.: Graph convolutional neural networks with global attention for improved materials property prediction. Phys. Chem. Chem. Phys. **22**, 18141–18148 (2020)

19. Lupo Pasini, M., Burĉul, M., Reeve, S.T., Eisenbach, M., Perotto, S.: Fast and accurate predictions of total energy for solid solution alloys with graph convolutional neural networks. In: Driving Scientific and Engineering Discoveries Through the Integration of Experiment, Big Data, and Modeling and Simulation. SMC 2021. Communications in Computer and Information Science, vol. 1512. Springer, Cham (2022). https://doi.org/10.1007/978-3-030-96498-6_5

20. Lupo Pasini, M., Eisenbach, M.: FePt binary alloy with 32 atoms - LSMS-3 data, February 2001. https://www.osti.gov/dataexplorer/biblio/dataset/1762742, https://doi.org/10.13139/OLCF/1762742

21. Lupo Pasini, M., Li, Y.W., Yin, J., Zhang, J., Barros, K., Eisenbach, M.: Fast and stable deep-learning predictions of material properties for solid solution alloys. J. Phys. Condens. Matter **33**(8), 084005. IOP Publishing (2020). https://doi.org/10.1088/1361-648X/abcb10

22. Lupo Pasini, M., Zhang, P., Reeve, S.T., Choi, J.Y.: Multi-task graph neural networks for simultaneous prediction of global and atomic properties in ferromagnetic systems. Mach. Learn. Sci. Technol. **3**(2), 025007 (2022). https://doi.org/10.1088/2632-2153/ac6a51

23. Lupo Pasini, M., Reeve, S.T., Zhang, P., Choi, J.Y.: HydraGNN. [Computer Software] (2021). https://doi.org/10.11578/dc.20211019.2, https://github.com/ORNL/HydraGNN

24. Lépinoux, J., Sigli, C.: Precipitate growth in concentrated binary alloys: a comparison between kinetic monte carlo simulations, cluster dynamics and the classical theory. Philos. Mag. **93**(23), 3194–3215 (2013)

25. Mohammadi, H., Eivani, A.R., Seyedein, S.H., Ghosh, M.: Modified monte carlo approach for simulation of grain growth and ostwald ripening in two-phase zn-22al alloy. J. Mater. Res. Technol. **9**(5), 9620–9631 (2020)

26. Paszke, A., et al.: Pytorch: an imperative style, high-performance deep learning library. In: Wallach, H., Larochelle, H., Beygelzimer, A., d'Alché-Buc, F., Fox, E., Garnett, R. (eds.) Advances in Neural Information Processing Systems, vol. 32, pp. 8024–8035. Curran Associates, Inc. (2019). https://proceedings.neurips.cc/paper/2019/file/bdbca288fee7f92f2bfa9f7012727740-Paper.pdf

27. Reitz, D.M., Blaisten-Barojas, E.: Simulating the nak eutectic alloy with monte carlo and machine learning. Sci. Rep. **9**(704) (2019). https://doi.org/10.1038/s41598-018-36574-y

28. Saal, J.E., Kirklin, S., Aykol, M., Meredig, B., Wolverton, C.: Materials design and discovery with high-throughput density functional theory: the Open Quantum Materials Database (OQMD). JOM **65**(11), 1501–1509 (2013)

29. Slater, J.C.: The ferromagnetism of nickel. Phys. Rev. **49**, 537–545 (1936). https://doi.org/10.1103/PhysRev.49.537

30. Tétot, R., Finel, A.: Relaxed Monte Carlo Simulations on Au-Ni Alloy, pp. 179–184. Springer, US, Boston, MA (1996). https://doi.org/10.1007/978-1-4613-0385-5_8

31. Tobita, N., et al.: Antiferromagnetic phase transition in ordered fept3 investigated by angle-resolved photoemission spectroscopy. J. Phys. Soc. Jpn. **79**(2), 024703 (2010). https://doi.org/10.1143/JPSJ.79.024703

32. Vlaic, P., Burzo, E.: Magnetic behaviour of iron-platinum alloys. J. Optoelectron. Adv. Mater. **12**, 1114–1124 (2010)

33. van de Walle, A., Asta, M.: Self-driven lattice-model monte carlo simulations of alloy thermodynamic properties and phase diagrams. Model. Simul. Mater. Sci. Eng. **10**, 521–538 (2002)

34. Wang, Y., Stocks, G.M., Shelton, W.A., Nicholson, D.M.C., Temmerman, W.M., Szotek, Z.: Order-N multiple scattering approach to electronic structure calculations. Phys. Rev. Lett. **75**, 2867 (1995). https://doi.org/10.1103/PhysRevLett.75.2867

35. Xie, T., Grossman, J.C.: Crystal graph convolutional neural networks for an accurate and interpretable prediction of material properties. Phys. Rev. Lett. **120**(14), 145301 (2018)

A Vision for Coupling Operation of US Fusion Facilities with HPC Systems and the Implications for Workflows and Data Management

Sterling Smith[1]([✉]), Emily Belli[1], Orso Meneghini[1], Reuben Budiardja[2],
David Schissel[1], Jeff Candy[1], Tom Neiser[1], and Adam Eubanks[3]

[1] General Atomics, 3550 General Atomics Ct., San Diego, CA 92121, USA
`smithsp@fusion.gat.com`
[2] National Center for Computational Sciences, Oak Ridge National Laboratory,
Oak Ridge, TN 37831, USA
[3] University of Virginia, 85 Engineer's Way, Charlottesville, VA 22903, USA

Abstract. The operation of large US Department of Energy (DOE) research facilities, like the DIII-D National Fusion Facility, results in the collection of complex multi-dimensional scientific datasets, both experimental and model-generated. In the future, it is envisioned that integrated data analysis coupled with large-scale high performance computing (HPC) simulations will be used to improve experimental planning and operation. Practically, massive data sets from these simulations provide the physics basis for generation of both reduced semi-analytic and machine-learning-based models. Storage of both HPC simulation datasets (generated from US DOE leadership computing facilities) and experimental datasets presents significant challenges. In this paper, we present a vision for a DOE-wide data management workflow that integrates US DOE fusion facilities with leadership computing facilities. Data persistence and long-term availability beyond the length of allocated projects is essential, particularly for verification and recalibration of artificial intelligence and machine learning (AI/ML) models. Because these data sets are often generated and shared among hundreds of users across multiple leadership computing facility centers, they would benefit from cross-platform accessibility, persistent identifiers (e.g. DOI, or digital object identifier), and provenance tracking. The ability to handle different data access patterns suggests that a combination of low cost, high latency (e.g. for storing ML training sets) and high cost, low latency systems (e.g. for real-time, integrated machine control feedback) may be needed.

Keywords: Fusion · Big data · High performance computing · Data management

K. Doug et al. (Eds.): SMC 2022, CCIS 1690, pp. 87–100, 2022.
https://doi.org/10.1007/978-3-031-23606-8_6

1   Introduction

When the DIII-D National Fusion Facility began operating, the PTDATA system [1] was used for acquisition, storage, archival, and retrieval of raw (write once) experimental data. Each plasma discharge, or shot, lasted from fractions of a second up to 10 s (although future machines' discharges will be much longer) and the experimental data was organized on a per shot basis. As operations expanded, the MDSplus data management system [2] was adopted at DIII-D to store analyzed data (data derived from raw data). Today, MDSplus has evolved into a complete data acquisition and management system that is used on numerous magnetic fusion experiments worldwide. These storage methods have served sufficiently well for data retrieval and usage of experimental data. However, on the high-performance computing (HPC) simulation side of fusion research, the requirements have been very different. Recent petascale simulations from the community have pushed the limits of machine storage, and presented challenges for data persistence and storage. These leadership *capability computing* jobs are typically done for a single experimental timeslice. In addition to expanding the number of timeslices and discharges for which capability jobs are performed, the modeling of discharges with an increasing number of *capacity computing* jobs will increase. It is thus anticipated that the production of HPC databases, from both capacity and larger capability simulations, will substantially balloon in the near future.

The intent of this paper is to describe the computing and storage requirements for both of these use-cases; namely, (a) large, complex magnetic confinement fusion (tokamak) experimental datasets and (b) GB and TB datasets generated by HPC numerical simulation results at various DOE facilities. This is followed by our vision for how to tie those requirements together across fusion user facilities (in particular, DIII-D at General Atomics in San Diego) and HPC facilities (typically OLCF and NERSC). These experimental and simulation datasets will form the basis for the development of both machine learning surrogate models and traditional semi-analytic reduced models. In addition, these datasets can be accessed to provide timely feedback to ongoing experiments during their inter-shot cycle.

The structure of the paper is as follows: in Sect. 2 we describe experimental data storage and analysis needs, in Sect. 3 we describe the challenges in maintaining a community database of HPC simulation results. Finally, in Sect. 4, we present our vision for managing these two seemingly different requirements using a single, centralized approach.

2   Data Needs for Experimental Databases

The **DIII-D National Fusion Facility** (DIII-D) operates in San Diego as a Department of Energy (DOE) Office of Science User Facility. Over its operating lifetime since 1987, about 300 TB of compressed raw data has been produced (see Fig. 1). An additional ~40 TB of standardized analyzed data has also been produced. The facility continues to run, and is accumulating additional data at the rate of about 20% year-over-year growth. Most data is associated with a unique sequential discharge number, where a DIII-D discharge lasts up to 10 s. The current discharge number is in the 190,000 range (although there have been some skips in numbers). Although the DOE FES has funded several fusion devices through the years that have accumulated smaller amounts of data, their overarching storage requirements are subsumed by DIII-D's.

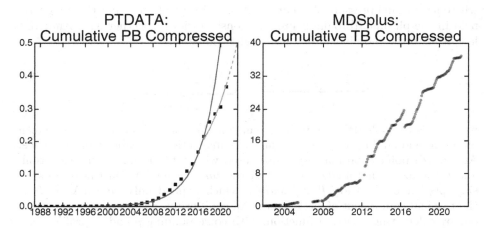

Fig. 1. Cumulative data at DIII-D by the given year for (left) PTDATA format and (right) MDSplus format. For MDSplus data, the drop in 2017 was due to an improved compression algorithm.

The traditional storage and analysis infrastructure for fusion data has been centered around looking at time traces of scalar quantities or contour maps of 1D array quantities versus time for a handful of related discharges. In particular, the analysis of the most recent discharge [3] can be helpful for planning which changes to make in the programming for the next discharge, where there is typically a 10–15 min interval between discharges. The traditional approaches are in stark contrast to the needs of the machine learning community, which digests the data from all available (tens to hundreds of thousands of) discharges simultaneously, and may also want to run various simulations for the relevant discharges.

Below are presented four recent experimental analysis machine learning workflows which have started to explore the boundaries of big data for magnetic confinement fusion experimental analysis:

1. Equilibrium reconstructions via machine learning
2. Event labeling via semi-supervised learning
3. Disruption predictions via random forest algorithm
4. Validation of the Trapped Gyro-Landau Fluid (TGLF) turbulent transport model [4].

After these we will touch on experimental uncertainty quantification.

2.1 Equilibrium Reconstructions via Machine Learning

At each time point during a tokamak plasma discharge, there is an equilibrium condition given to leading order as

$$\nabla p = \mathbf{J} \times \mathbf{B}, \tag{1}$$

where p is plasma pressure, $\mathbf{J}$ is current density in the plasma, and $\mathbf{B}$ is magnetic field in the plasma. Toroidal symmetry considerations, together with Amperè's law, lead to the (nonlinear) Grad-Shafranov equation

$$\underbrace{\frac{\partial^2 \psi}{\partial r^2} - \frac{1}{r}\frac{\partial \psi}{\partial r} + \frac{\partial^2 \psi}{\partial z^2}}_{\Delta^* \psi} = \underbrace{-\mu_0 r^2 \frac{dp}{d\psi} - F\frac{dF}{d\psi}}_{-\mu_0 r J_\theta}, \tag{2}$$

where F is the poloidal current function, ψ is the poloidal magnetic flux (which labels individual flux surfaces) and μ_0 is the magnetic permeability of free space. An (r, z, θ) polar coordinate system is used with r the radius, z the elevation, and θ the azimuthal angle (also called the *toroidal angle*). On the righthand-side, $p(\psi)$ and $F(\psi)$ are *flux functions* which depend only on ψ. Also, J_θ is the toroidal component of the current. An equilibrium reconstruction is carried out by calculating a $\psi(r, z)$ function, with corresponding p and F profiles, calculating the synthetic diagnostics that result from that trial function [such as magnetic coil sensor signals, powered poloidal field coil signals, total toroidal current signals, magnetic field pitch (ratio of poloidal to toroidal magnetic field) predictions, etc.], comparing to the measured signals, then iterating on different ψ functions to find the solution that most closely reproduces the measured signals. The main code in the magnetic fusion community that carries out this equilibrium reconstruction is the EFIT code [5,6]. Initially at DIII-D, a single time slice per discharge would be identified, and overnight its equilibrium would be reconstructed. As computers improved, the reconstructions have been improved to be calculated both in real time for lower spatial resolution, and after the discharge for every 10–20 ms (300–600 time slices per discharge), available within minutes of the termination of the discharge given a subset of constraints (magnetic probe signals, current signals, and flux loop signals). Another set of reconstructions is calculated as soon as the magnetic pitch measurements via the Motional Stark Effect (MSE) are available, just a few minutes after the first set. The EFIT code does not explicitly provide an uncertainty on the reconstructions. But consistency from neighboring time slices provides some indication of the variability of reconstructions. There are approximately 60 million timeslices for which equilibrium reconstructions exist for the DIII-D tokamak; the outputs of the reconstructions are stored in the MDSplus storage method [2].

A recent project, EFIT-AI [7], has aimed to enhance and extend the EFIT code. In addition to modernizing the code, the project is in the process of generating a database of automated reconstructions, including storing all necessary inputs to be able to reproduce a code run or to be able to train a reduced model, such as a neural network to produce the ψ solution given a vector of inputs. The files are being stored in the hdf5 format, with a data schema given by the ITER IMAS (Integrated Modeling and Analysis Suite) data schema. This database takes up about 500 GB of space for a single year (2019) of reconstructions. In the past, DIII-D based databases have been stored at the local computing facilities of DIII-D. However, the machine learning aspect of this project requires more computing power than is available locally, and so the computing is being carried out at the NERSC HPC facility. Maintaining a copy of the data both locally and at NERSC, and keeping them in sync has various challenges, and the DVC [8] data version control software is being investigated for better control and synchronization of the database.

2.2   Event Labeling via Semi-supervised Learning

During the course of a tokamak discharge, there are several possible events that may occur. Some may correspond to pre-programmed times of changes to the actuators - where the target injected power is increased or the target shape of the plasma is changed. The plasma events of interest include the times when the plasma: transitions from a lower confinement state (L-mode) to a higher confinement state (H-mode, QH-mode, or I-mode); transitions from being a limited plasma to a diverted plasma; exhibits Edge Localized Modes (ELMs); transitions to a non-ELM state; exhibits sawteeth or other MHD modes; or abruptly ends in a disruption. A method has been devised whereby an event is labeled by hand for a small set of discharges, for a given set of measured and calculated signals, and a semi-supervised learning technique is able to apply the labeling to a broad set of discharges with high confidence. [9] While the original study only applied this to a small set of (300) discharges, simultaneous application to the entire DIII-D database would require holding all signals in memory, and then storing them together on disk for later retrieval for any retraining or validation that is carried out in the future.

2.3   Disruption Prediction via Random Forest Algorithm

One of the events that must be predicted and avoided in a tokamak is the disruption event. During a disruption, the tokamak discharge is suddenly terminated. Without the plasma, there is a leftover toroidal electric field can drive runaway electrons that are accelerated to MeV energies. These energetic electrons can impact and damage the first wall of the tokamak, if not mitigated. To predict and avoid disruptions, databases of discharges have been accumulated, and then either random forest [10] or recurrent neural networks [11] have been trained to the databases.

2.4   Validation of the TGLF Turbulence Transport Model

One of the key predictions in magnetic fusion is how the plasma transports heat out of the core, where it is heated by various actuators. The highest physics fidelity gyrokinetic turbulence models like CGYRO [12] for these processes are described in Sect. 3. The highest fidelity models are not useful for integrated modeling or control, due to their large computing resource requirements. Reduced physics fidelity models have been formulated, which calculate linearly unstable eigenmodes of the turbulence, and then the eigenmodes are used to compute approximate quasi-linear fluxes. The TGLF model [4] in particular has several quasilinear saturation rules to model the time averate turbulent fluctuation intensity. The rules have a handful of free parameters (4–9), and these have been calibrated against a smallish database ($\sim$80–300) of high fidelity CGYRO turbulence runs.

Unfortunately, the transport fluxes are not something that can be readily measured in a fusion plasma. Furthermore, the saturation rule cannot be measured. So there is not the opportunity for a direct experiment/model comparison, but there is a calculation of the power deposition in the plasma, and from that power balance calculation the fluxes can be inferred. We have assembled a database of power balance calculations (and inferred fluxes) for $\sim$2000 discharges for 9 timeslices in each discharge, for 9 radii in the plasma. The power balance fluxes have been compared to the fluxes from the TGLF reduced transport model. The comparison to the SAT1 saturation rule [13] is given in Fig. 2. An investigation into the outliers prompts a question of under which conditions the model is valid. One limitation of the turbulence model is that it does not appropriately handle macroscopic magnetic perturbations (commonly called MHD - magnetohydrodynamic - modes) in the plasma, whose signature is detected in the magnetic probes. Collecting the MHD signatures across many discharges efficiently allows us to filter out those cases with significant activity, which constituted many of the outliers from the theory experiment comparison.

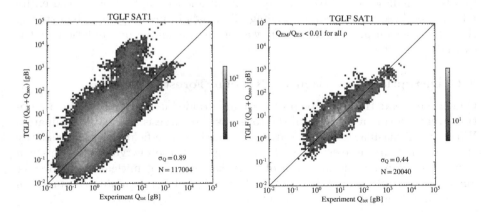

Fig. 2. 2D histograms comparing experimentally inferred fluxes to those calculated by the TGLF quasilinear turbulence code with SAT1 saturation rule for the nominal experimental parameters. (left) The unfiltered database. (right) Applying filters that exclude cases where the model is not applicable.

The comparison with the MHD mode filters (and other theory based filters) applied is shown in the right side of Fig. 2.

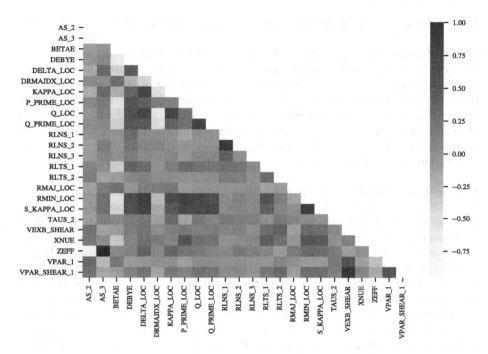

Fig. 3. Correlations between the input parameters for the database of DIII-D cases considered.

The TGLF model has 24 independent inputs for a three species plasma. A plot of the correlations between those inputs for the experimental cases reveals that there are some strong correlations and anti-correlations in the inputs, as seen in Fig. 3. This type of correlation analysis is useful for generating a database of TGLF runs from which a machine learning representation of TGLF can be devised, as it gives an indication of those parameters that need to be varied simultaneously, and not independently, which lowers the degrees of freedom that need to be scanned for the database.

2.5   Uncertainty Quantification

All of the workflows described in the previous subsections are based on evaluating the nominal experimental parameters, without any uncertainty quantification (UQ). There are three approaches to UQ that are being investigated, and have had some application to selected subsets of workflows:

- Monte Carlo
- Propagation of linear uncertainties
- Bayesian inference

Each of these has strengths and weaknesses, and implications for data storage.

Monte Carlo. For UQ via Monte Carlo, the inputs are randomly and independently changed within their uncertainties to produce an ensemble of analyses. For the equilibrium reconstruction example, there are 100's of input measurements that can be perturbed. Strict convergence studies have not been performed, but an initial assessment of an ensemble of 20 runs provides an indication of the level of uncertainties in the outputs of the reconstruction. The Monte Carlo approach is fine when all inputs are independent, but does not work well if there are correlations between the inputs.

Linear Uncertainties. There may exist correlations between the uncertainties in a code input. In fusion research this can occur as smooth curve fits are made to kinetic profiles, where the curve fit would be parameterized by multiple coefficients, and then the best fit has uncertainties in the coefficients, with correlations between the coefficient uncertainties. The ensemble of inputs for UQ in a subsequent analysis can be constructed by perturbing the inputs according to their sensitivity to the eigenvalues of the correlation matrix, with one (or two) code runs per unique eigenvalue (one-sided vs centered finite difference derivative of the result on the eigenvalue). For the power balance analysis mentioned previously, there are about 5 different profiles that are typically fit, with about 5 different parameters for each fit, resulting in the need for about 25–50 times the number of analysis runs for the nominal conditions. The linear uncertainties approach can also be applied to inputs with uncorrelated uncertainty, but with a large number of inputs, the Monte Carlo approach may be able to capture the uncertainty more efficiently than linear uncertainties.

Bayesian Inference. A more holistic approach to tokamak data analysis is to consider each raw diagnostic at the same time, including raw counts of digitizers for various spectral diagnostics or voltages and currents of magnetic pickup probes. Possible solutions to the plasma state are then constructed and synthetic diagnostic measurements are compared to the actual measurements. The current equilibrium reconstruction code - EFIT - operates in this fashion, but it is missing the kinetic data, with their associated synthetic diagnostics; as well it fails to provide uncertainties in the outputs. In the fusion community, an analysis that considers all possible data simultaneously in a Bayesian framework is referred to as Integrated Data Analysis (IDA).

There is a project underway in the ITPA (International Tokamak Physics Activity) diagnostics group to build a new IDA framework from the ground up that is ITER IMAS (Integrated Modeling and Analysis Suite) data schema compliant. It is building on the lessons learned from implementing IDA for the Asdex-Upgrade (AUG) device in Germany. One topic that came up in recent discussions on this ITPA led effort is 'What are uncertainties, and how do we store them?' In the IMAS schema, there are slots for the 'upper_error' and 'lower_error', but the uncertainties produced by IDA are not symmetric, nor Gaussian, and so these labels and locations are inadequate for capturing and storing the uncertainties. A separate approach would be to store all realizations of the solution as separate *occurences* within the IMAS storage schema, and then the uncertainty distribution could be resampled at any point in the future.

3   A Sustainable Community Fusion Simulation Database

A key scientific priority for the realization of fusion as a practical energy source is developing a *predictive transport model* suitable for burning (self-sustaining) plasma regimes. Generally speaking, a transport model computes a fast approximation to the particle and energy fluxes at a given radial location in the tokamak discharge. The accurate calculation of these fluxes is at the heart of any integrated modeling framework, and is used to optimize the reactor confinement properties. A theory-based transport model is developed with reference to high-precision, first-principles modeling of turbulence-driven transport requiring leadership-class simulations based on the so-called gyrokinetic (GK) formulation. The high-precision GK particle and energy fluxes are obtained from solution of a 5D (3D space, 2D velocity), species-dependent distribution function. From a suitable database of these expensive GK simulations, reduced transport models (semi-analytic or machine learning-based) can then be developed. These leadership-class simulations thus form the basis of the training database and enable new time-sensitive applications, such as real-time control.

In 2007, a database of over 300 nonlinear simulations [14] based on the GYRO gyrokinetic code was successfully used to calibrate the original, widely-used TGLF reduced transport model [4]. The subsequent speed and accuracy of TGLF enabled a revolution in the accuracy of modeling calculations. The original GYRO simulations incorporated only ion-scale physics, typically assumed a pure plasma (deuterium ions + electrons), and were representative of weakly-shaped core plasma parameters. Several new gyrokinetic database efforts are underway, including the US CGYRODB database at NERSC based on the CGYRO code [12], the US MGKDB [15] at NERSC based on the GENE code [16], and the European Gyro-Kinetic Database Project (GKDB) hosted at gkdb.org based on the GKW [17] and GENE [16] codes. One goal of the gyrokinetic database projects is to store not only the physics input paramaters and selected output data, but also all code-specific model and resolution parameters for reproducibility. The two US databases, CGYRODB and MGKDB, were established and are currently directly organized through projects funded by the US DOE SciDAC (Scientific Discovery through Advanced Computing) program, whose aim is to bring together physicists, computer scientists, and mathematicians to develop new computational methods for solving challenging scientific problems. These projects are AToM: Advanced Tokamak Modeling Environment (for CGYRODB) and Partnership for Multiscale Gyrokinetic (MGK) Turbulence (for MGKDB). Both CGYRODB and MGKDB are presently hosted by Community

File System (CFS) storage space at NERSC, where most of the simulations are also run with computational time in support of the associated SciDAC grants. Since the present database consists mostly of smaller-scale nonlinear simulations (e.g. ion-scale or electron-scale spatial resolution) with only highly-distilled output data, the CFS project space is presently sufficient. For example, the directory storage quota for the CGYRODB at NERSC is only 4 TB. A typical dataset for a single CGYRO ion-scale dataset is on the order of 0.1 GB.

However, for burning plasmas, these new gyrokinetic databases will need to be vastly expanded to include reactor-relevant effects that increase the computational cost as well as the data output of the first-principles simulations. This includes multi-ion physics, such as hydrogenic isotope scalings for the fuel ions, helium ash reactor byproducts, and impurity physics. For high-confinement mode (H-mode) regimes that are relevant for a reactor, the turbulence is often multiscale in nature, coupling ion scales with electron scales that are smaller by a factor of $\sqrt{m_i/m_e} \sim 60$. These simulations often require capability-class supercomputing resources, offered by programs such as the US DOE INCITE program [18], for which it may be impractical to regenerate the case from scratch to verify convergence or compute additional diagnostics. A single multi-ion, multiscale dataset from the CGYRO code is on the order of 50–100 GB in size. For example, see Fig. 4 comparing the size of a CGYRO dataset ranging from ion-scale to multiscale. Thus, a complete gyrokinetic database for fusion reactor optmization is expected to require on the order of 1 PB of data storage. Since INCITE allocations are often at specific DOE leadership computing facilities – presently Oak Ridge Leadership Computing Facility (OLCF) and Argonne Leadership Computing Facility (ALCF) – and the project storage at those facilities is limited beyond the length of these short-term projects, these large datasets need to be transferred to a different long-term storage system. Since NERSC allocations are more consistent, NERSC storage systems presently provide a more reliable host, though even this is not guaranteed.

4   Vision

The considerations of Sects. 2 and 3 lead to a vision for a US DOE-wide long-term data storage system as a science gateway for fusion experimental and HPC databases. Such a gateway may also serve the broader DOE scientific community with large projects and extreme datasets. This would presumably include existing SciDAC partnerships in climate science, fusion research, high-energy physics, nuclear physics, astrophysics, material science, and chemistry. Practical requirements for a community HPC database include:

- open access (publicly available to the scientific community)
- persistent identifier (e.g. digital object identifier)
- provenance tracking
- cross-platform accessibility across leadership-computing facilities
- longevity beyond project/allocation length
- keyword/attribute filtering

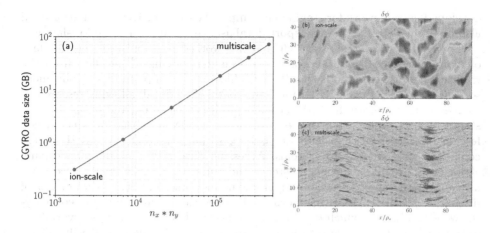

Fig. 4. (a) CGYRO dataset size, ranging from ion-scale simulations to multiscale simulations by varying the spectral spatial radial wavenumbers n_x and binormal wavenumbers n_y such that $n_x/n_y = 3$ with all other resolution parameters fixed. (b) Ion-scale and (c) multiscale electrostatic fluctuations correspondingly from CGYRO. Multiscale simulations require leadership-scale computing resources.

Open access is needed for transparency and encouraging scientific collaboration. Persistent identifiers, like DOIs, are needed for tracking datasets in models and in publications, and provenance tracking of data files within the database is needed for reproducibility and benchmarking with other codes. Data persistence and long-term availability are essential for: i) verification as new experiments and physics modules are developed, ii) recalibration of artificial intelligence and machine learning (AI/ML) and reduced analyic models, and iii) reproducibility. As many users are encouraged to contribute to the database, longevity might also include back-up protection, including version control. Finally, the ability to filter data using keywords or other attributes would facilitate access when many thousands of entries are present. These requirements are consistent with the FAIR principles of Findability, Accessibility, Interoperability, and Reuse of digital assets, and these principles will be used in the further design of these databases [19].

The ability to handle different data access patterns suggests that a combination of data support systems may be needed. For many applications, such as a fusion HPC gyrokinetic database, where data is mostly archived, the database can be supported by a low cost, high latency system like the high performance storage system (HPSS) [20]. [According to reported storage space utilization statistics provided by NERSC HPSS [21], as of May 2022, the combined usage of long-term storage for all fusion-related allocations is 1.75PB, accounting for 5.5M files, and the growth in NERSC's total storage system is approximately 1.7x per year]. However, in addition, as new machine learning-based models are developed, a framework for staging large input datasets for HPC simulations will also be needed. Unlike the transport database, this will need to be low-latency.

For DIII-D data, one approach that has worked well for accessing the data of many discharges simultaneously has been the copying of the data from the traditional storage methods to a BeeGFS filesystem and providing a convenient software stack (TOKSEARCH) for highly parallel retrieval, allowing researchers to more quickly iterate the critical data exploration, cleaning, and pre-processing stages of a project. [22] A speedup of up to 1700X has been obtained when fetching data across thousands of discharges using the TOKSEARCH system compared with traditional systems. Accessing data and analyses for so many shots easily provides excellent existence and quality assurance checks. Occasionally automated analyses encounter problems, and may not run for a number of discharges. TOKSEARCH has been used to determine which automated analyses were missing for which discharge numbers, and then the analysis workflows were relaunched for those missing discharges. In another case, a specific TOK-SEARCH analysis was able to point out that an error had crept into a traditional analysis routine for the time smoothing of some actuator inputs. While the use of TOKSEARCH continues to increase at DIII-D, future use at HPC centers to process large amounts of DIII-D data (or future ITER data) necessitates that a version of the data should be kept closer to the HPC centers. In addition, it would be useful to provide stricter versions on the data by publishing, from time to time, the whole DIII-D database – a snapshot at that point – to the previously mentioned public DOE-wide database.

In an effort to produce higher fidelity between discharge analyses, the fusion experimental community is beginning to reach out to HPC centers to be able to take advantage of their computational capabilities, which significantly exceed that available locally at the experiments. The desired timescale for turnaround of results to influence control room decisions requires a number of characteristics that are different from usual HPC practices. An initial workflow was reported in Reference [23], which outlines 7 requirements for coupling between discharge analyses to an HPC center. Based on the success of these initial pilot studies, there is a desire to routinely perform between discharge magnetic equilibrium reconstructions with higher fidelity. These reconstructions will in turn allow for further transport, stability, and actuator analysis that could influence control room decision making. Efficient interactions with data produced at an HPC center will be required; in the past the data was sent back to the experimental facility. As the amount of data increases, due to an increasing number of codes being run, there may come a time where the data is stored at the HPC center, and then efficient visualization and interaction to the HPC storage will be required.

5   Conclusion

In conclusion, the fusion community is accumulating ever more data from its experiments (both current and planned) and associated analyses, and is accumulating ever larger databases of high fidelity physics simulations that can be distilled into reduced models or even machine learning models. These faster models form the backbone of integrated modeling scenario optimization studies for reactor design and integrated real time control of those reactors as they come online. The storage of these databases can begin as high latency storage in something like HPSS, but a complementary storage in low latency form is needed for machine learning applications. Implementing a single interface to either data location type, whether that be a single dedicated facility to store these results or an API that can hide the complexity of storing different data, would provide significant improvements in accessibility and ease-of-use.

Acknowledgments. This work was supported by the U.S. Department of Energy under awards DE-FC02-04ER54698, DE-FG02-95ER54309, DE-FC02-06ER54873, and DE-SC0017992. Some material is based upon work supported by the U.S. Department of Energy, Office of Science, Office of Fusion Energy Sciences, using the DIII-D National Fusion Facility, a DOE Office of Science user facility, under Award(s) DE-FC02-04ER54698. Computing resources were also provided by the National Energy Research Scientific Computing Center, which is an Office of Science User Facility supported under Contract DE-AC02-05CH11231. An award of computer time was also provided by the INCITE program. This research used resources of the Oak Ridge Leadership Computing Facility, which is an Office of Science User Facility supported under Contract DE-AC05-00OR22725. This report was prepared as an account of work sponsored by an agency of the United States Government. Neither the United States Government nor any agency thereof, nor any of their employees, makes any warranty, express or implied, or assumes any legal liability or responsibility for the accuracy, completeness, or usefulness of any information, apparatus, product, or process disclosed, or represents that its use would not infringe privately owned rights. Reference herein to any specific commercial product, process, or service by trade name, trademark, manufacturer, or otherwise, does not necessarily constitute or imply its endorsement, recommendation, or favoring by the United States Government or any agency thereof. The views and opinions of authors expressed herein do not necessarily state or reflect those of the United States Government or any agency thereof.

References

1. McHarg, B.B.: Access to DIII-D data located in multiple files and multiple locations. In: 15th IEEE/NPSS Symposium. Fusion Engineering, vol. 1, p. 123 (1993). https://doi.org/10.1109/FUSION.1993.518297'
2. Stillerman, J.A., Fredian, T.W., Klare, K.A., Manduchi, G.: MDSplus data acquisition system. Rev. Sci. Instrum. **68**, 939 (1997). https://doi.org/10.1063/1.1147719
3. Schissel, D.P., Abla, G., Flanagan, S., Kim, L., Lee, X.: The between-pulse data analysis infrastructure at the DIII-D national fusion facility. Fusion Sci. Technol. **58**, 720 (2010). https://doi.org/10.13182/FST10-A10920
4. Staebler, G.M., Kinsey, J., Waltz, R.E.: A theory-based transport model with comprehensive physics. Phys. Plasmas **14**, 055909 (2017). https://doi.org/10.1063/1.2436852
5. Lao, L.L., St. John, H., Stambaugh, R.D., Kellman, A.G., Pfeiffer, W.: Reconstruction of current profile parameters and plasma shapes in tokamaks. Nucl. Fusion **25**, 1611 (1985). https://doi.org/10.1088/0029-5515/25/11/007

6. Lao, L.L., et al.: Equilibrium analysis of current profiles in tokamaks. Nucl. Fusion **30**, 1035 (1990). https://doi.org/10.1088/0029-5515/30/6/006
7. Lao, L.L., et al.: Application of machine learning and artificial intelligence to extend EFIT equilibrium reconstruction. Plasma Phys. Control. Fusion **64**, 074001 (2022). https://doi.org/10.1088/1361-6587/ac6fff
8. Data Version Control Software. https://dvc.org/
9. Montes, K.J., Rea, C., Tinguely, R.A., Sweeney, R., Zhu, J., Granetz, R.S.: A semi-supervised machine learning detector for physics events in tokamak discharges. Nucl. Fusion **61**, 026022 (2021). https://doi.org/10.1088/1741-4326/abcdb9
10. Rea, C., Granetz, R.S.: Fus. Sci. Tech. **74**, 89–100 (2018). https://doi.org/10.1080/15361055.2017.1407206
11. Kates-Harbeck, J., Svyatkovskiy, A., Tang, W.: Predicting disruptive instabilities in controlled fusion plasmas through deep learning. Nature **568**, 526–531 (2019). https://doi.org/10.1038/s41586-019-1116-4
12. Candy, J., Belli, E.A.: A high-accuracy Eulerian gyrokinetic solver for collisional plasmas. J. Comp. Phys. **324**, 73 (2016). https://doi.org/10.1016/j.jcp.2016.07.039
13. Staebler, G.M., Howard, N.T., Candy, J., Holland, C.: A model of the saturation of coupled electron and ion scale gyrokinetic turbulence. Nucl. Fusion **57**, 066046 (2017). https://doi.org/10.1088/1741-4326/aa6bee
14. The GYRO Nonlinear Gyrokinetic Simulation Database (J. Kinsey). http://gafusion.github.io/doc/_downloads/gyro-database.pdf
15. Hatch, D.R., et al.: Reduced models for ETG transport in the tokamak pedestal. Phys. Plasmas **29**, 062501 (2022). https://doi.org/10.1063/5.0087403
16. Jenko, F., Dorland, W., Kotschenreuther, M., Rogers, B.N.: Electron temperature gradient driven turbulence. Phys. Plasmas **7**, 1904 (2000). https://doi.org/10.1063/1.874014
17. Peeters, A.G., et al.: The nonlinear gyro-kinetic flux tube code GKW. Comput. Phys. Commun. **180**, 2650 (2009). https://doi.org/10.1016/j.cpc.2009.07.001
18. U.S. Department of Energy Innovative and Computational Impact on Theory and Experiment (INCITE) program. http://www.doeleadershipcomputing.org
19. FAIR Principles. http://www.go-fair.org/fair-principles/
20. High Performance Storage System. http://www.hpss-collaboration.org
21. National Energy Research Scientific Computing Center. http://nersc.gov/users/job-logs-statistics/storage-and-file-systems/storage-statistics
22. Sammuli, B.S., et al.: TokSearch: a search engine for fusion experimental data. Fusion Eng. Design **129**, 12–15 (2018). https://doi.org/10.1016/j.fusengdes.2018.02.003
23. Kostuk, M., Uram, T.D., Evans, T., Orlov, D.M., Papka, M.E., Schissel, D.: Automatic between-pulse analysis of DIII-D experimental data performed remotely on a supercomputer at argonne leadership computing facility. Fusion Sci. Technol. **74**, 135 (2018). https://doi.org/10.1080/15361055.2017.1390388

At-the-Edge Data Processing for Low Latency High Throughput Machine Learning Algorithms

Jack Hirschman[1,2](✉), Andrei Kamalov[2], Razib Obaid[2], Finn H. O'Shea[2], and Ryan N. Coffee[2]

[1] Stanford University, Stanford, CA 94305, USA
jhirschm@stanford.edu
[2] SLAC National Accelerator Laboratory, Menlo Park, CA 94025, USA

Abstract. High throughput and low latency data processing is essential for systems requiring live decision making, control, and machine learning-optimized data reduction. We focus on two distinct use cases for in-flight streaming data processing for a) X-ray pulse reconstruction at SLAC's LCLS-II Free-Electron Laser and b) control diagnostics at the DIII-D tokamak fusion reactor. Both cases exemplify high throughput and low latency control feedback and motivate our focus on machine learning at the edge where data processing and machine learning algorithms can be implemented in field programmable gate array based hardware immediately after the diagnostic sensors. We present our recent work on a data preprocessing chain which requires fast featurization for information encoding. We discuss several options for such algorithms with the primary focus on our discrete cosine and sine transform-based approach adapted for streaming data. These algorithms are primarily aimed at implementation in field programmable gate arrays, favoring linear algebra operations that are also aligned with the recent advances in inference accelerators for the computational edge.

Keywords: Edge · FPGA · Machine learning · Streaming · Codesign · xFEL · Fusion

1 Introduction

Data preprocessing for low-latency, high-throughput machine learning algorithms often requires efficient peak finding. There are many applications that could utilize this particular preprocessing. We focus on two such applications in this manuscript: a) analyzing electron time-of-flight spectra for X-ray pulse reconstruction at SLAC's LCLS-II X-ray Free-Electron Laser (xFEL) in a detector called the CookieBox [1] and b) analyzing Alfvén eigenmode frequency information in electron cyclotron emission (ECE) at the DIII-D tokamak fusion reactor [2]. For the xFEL case, the arriving signals are roughly 0.5 ns in width, sampled at 6 GSa/s, and arrive over the course of 500 ns. The signals within that 500 ns window are not piled up, and, in general, are sparsely distributed. The time stamps of the peaks represent arrival times of electrons at the detector and can be used to compute the electron energies. So, a precise estimate for the arrival time of the electron will directly affect the energy calculation and thus the resulting machine learning-based X-ray pulse reconstruction.

For the fusion ECE case, a time-domain signal from a multi-channel radio-frequency pickup array is first transformed into a spectrogram where well defined frequencies appear as very narrow features in the 10–200 kHz range. These sharp frequencies are sparsely distributed throughout the spectral range and so an approach identical to the one used in the Cookiebox case is used to locate–and sub-sample–these sparse features. This procedure significantly reduces the number of coefficients required to represent the spectrum. Therefore, in both use cases the problem boils down to a peak-locating algorithm that can be applied early in the signal processing pipeline, before aggregation into a multi-channel image-like representation.

There are several approaches to general peak-finding from the most basic constant fraction discrimination [3–5] to more sophisticated iterative curve fitting methods [6–8]. However, these iterative algorithms tend to require higher precision, significant run-time for convergence, and are generally less friendly for hardware targeted low-latency data processing implementations which significantly benefit from deterministic latency. Taking inspiration from the very efficient historical analog electronics like EG&G Time-to-Digital Converter (TDC) [9], we aim to use the similar approach to enhancing the resolution of peak finding for the general case, not only for the time domain signals. Since we have the freedom to use our representation mappings to move the desired signal into the known coefficients, we are also free to apply concepts like Wiener filtering [10] to these deeper representations, but doing so in the same algorithmic operation that results in the location itself. This composite algorithm transforms a relatively high-dimensional, sparse data stream into a lower-dimensional, information-rich representation for downstream inference models. Here we take the approach of using data streaming methods that leverage the capabilities of our hardware and which require a simpler peak finding method. We focus on algorithms for computing derivatives that are employed for finding zero crossings and thus the corresponding extrema in the original data.

We further show that our efficiency in information extraction also allows us to reduce the bit-depth needed to represent these coefficients. The reduced bit-depths conserve the often limited resources found in the FPGA hardware available for processing beyond this algorithm. The benefit of enforcing parsimony in the algorithm and the representation also yields very low latency when coupled with non-iterative and deterministic peak finding procedures. In this paper we compare two algorithms, a convolution method and a discrete cosine and sine transform method (DCSTM), for identifying extrema in data streaming directly from detectors. The algorithms are designed for deployment on hardware, but are first modeled here in software for development. In both cases, we identify peaks by looking for zeros in the first derivative of the signals.

2   Algorithms

This section discusses the algorithms developed for our data processing chain. We discuss two algorithms for calculating the derivative: the convolution method and the discrete cosine and sine transform method (DCSTM). Additionally, we discuss the underlying streaming discrete cosine transform method (SDCTM) used for calculating the discrete cosine transform (DCT), discrete sine transform (DST), inverse discrete cosine transform (IDCT), and inverse discrete sine transform (IDST) used within the DCSTM. Finally, we address approaches for finding peaks within the original data via zero crossings in the derivative output. The design of our algorithms are focused on implementation in hardware, such as an FPGA, so we prioritize minimizing latency and resource usage.

2.1   Convolution Method

The convolution method streams data through a stationary kernel, with a kernel choice that is dictated by the required operations. We choose a kernel that can take the derivative of our input signal. Specifically, we selected our kernel to be the derivative of a Gaussian function and arrived at this choice for two reasons. First, consider the 1-D derivative property of convolution [11,12].

$$\frac{d}{dt}(f * g) = \frac{d}{dt}(f) * g = f * \frac{d}{dt}(g) \tag{1}$$

Equation 1 shows that the convolution of the derivative of the kernel, g, and the original signal, f, is equivalent to the convolution of the derivative of f with the kernel. Then taking a Gaussian kernel, g, and convolving it with the derivative of f yields the smoothed version of the derivative of f and is known as Gaussian smoothing [13]. Therefore, we compute the derivative of this Gaussian kernel and convolve it with the original signal in order to get the smoothed version of the derivative of our signal.

For this, we start by choosing a Gaussian kernel

$$g = \frac{1}{\sqrt{2\pi}}e^{\frac{-t^2}{2\sigma^2}} \tag{2}$$

and then take the derivative to get

$$h = \frac{d}{dt}(g) = \frac{-t}{\sigma^2\sqrt{2\pi}}e^{\frac{-t^2}{2\sigma^2}}, \tag{3}$$

where σ is the kernel width, and finally convolve the kernel with the input signal.

The second benefit of this kernel shape is its ability to isolate the signal of interest in the Fourier domain. Consider multiplying the noiseless power spectrum of the data of interest and by the fourier transform of a step function, which represents a derivative [14,15]. The inverse fourier transform of the product is the analytic derivative of a Gaussian, which is exactly the kernel we chose.

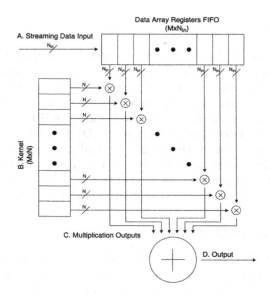

Fig. 1. Data flow for convolution method for derivative. Kernel is stored as an array with M words each of N bits. Each word gets multiplied by the corresponding word in the M word long data array registers which itself is a FIFO with the input data streaming in. Each word of this input data is N_{in} bits. These multiplications are then added together, and the result becomes one element of the derivative output. The points A, B, C, and D correspond to Table 1.

Section 3.1 discusses this second line of reasoning in the context of choosing the Gaussian derivative kernel width.

Figure 1 shows how we implement this algorithm. To perform the convolution on data streaming in, we consider the kernel to be limited in extent to a particular window size, M. Then we load our data into an array of registers equal in extent to the window size. The data is loaded in first-in first-out fashion (FIFO). Each element of the array is then multiplied by the corresponding element in the kernel and the result is summed. The summed result is then one of the output elements of the derivative. This is repeated for all the data that is streamed in, with a new element in the total convolution output available after each new piece of streaming data arrives. This convolution then takes the form of

$$y_k = \sum_{m=0}^{M} z_{k,m} * h_m \tag{4}$$

where M is the window size of the kernel, z is the array of registers piping the data in and out, and h is the stationary kernel. In this representation of convolution, for each new k, there is a new z since a new piece of data is streamed in. Therefore z has a dependence on m and k.

The final output will be valid once all of the data has been streamed through the array of registers. The exact window size and kernel width is application dependent and can be tuned ahead of time based on typical or expected feature widths. Once the kernel is chosen, it can be stored in memory as a look-up table (LUT) to be used while the algorithm is running.

2.2   Discrete Cosine and Sine Transform Method (DCSTM)

The streaming Discrete Cosine and Sine Transform Method (DCSTM) is designed to take the derivative of incoming data in a way that produces a low noise output, minimizes resource usage in the FPGA, and has high throughput and low latency. One commonly used method for calculating derivatives of functions is to use a fourier transform (FT) where one takes the FT, multiplies by a value proportional to the frequency vector, and then takes the inverse fourier transform (IFT). However, fourier transforms can both be costly in an FPGA and be an overkill in terms of what is required [16].

Here instead we use the DCT, IDCT, DST, and IDST in a way that resembles an FT [16,17]. However, for our application we cannot simply feed our data vector in. Our data is streaming in at a high rate (6 Gs/s) and may consist of over 5120 words. This could pose a problem for implementing these aforementioned transforms in an FPGA while retaining high throughput and low latency since it would require a large number of multipliers. Our algorithm instead handles incoming data in chunks which we describe as a window size. Tuning this window size is important and depends on the nature of the expected data.

Furthermore, the algorithm must be able to handle data that lands on the boundaries of windows. To handle this, we introduce a design that uses two paths for the incoming signal where each path initially applies a different filter, one path then delays its signal, both paths apply identical derivative transformations, the other path then delays its signal, and finally the two paths are recombined. Figure 2 shows the details of the algorithm.

In the block diagram on the top path, data streams in one word at a time, with each word multiplied by a particular value from a sine-squared (SIN^2) filter which was stored pre-runtime in a LUT. The period of the SIN^2 coefficient is proportional to the window size. The data splits paths again, one into a DCT block and the other to a DST block. These blocks take this streaming data and, after a window size amount of data comes in, the output is ready in parallel. Once the array of data leaves these blocks, each output word is multiplied by a value proportional to frequency. These values then go through the corresponding inverse transform blocks before being added back together. The DCT, DST, IDCT, and IDST blocks are described in Sect. 2.3.

The other data path that was not multiplied by the SIN^2 coefficients is instead multiplied by the cosine-squared (COS^2) equivalent. Then the data is delayed before going through the same series of transformations. This delay is to address capturing signal that might lie on the boundaries of the windows by providing an offset in time to move the signal away from the window size boundary in

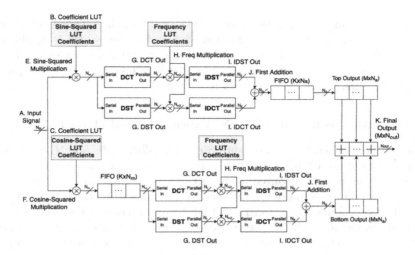

Fig. 2. Shows the data flow (left to right) for the derivative algorithm for peak identification. The original signal and a copy are multiplied by SIN^2 and COS^2 coefficients which are stored in LUTs prior to runtime. Both paths follow identical operations involving DCT and DST, multiplication proportional to frequency, and inverse DST and DCT, and finally summation. One path is delayed at the beginning of the operations and the other path is delayed following the operations in order to regain time coherence for the final, recombining addition. Points A–C and E–K correspond to Table 2 while D is in Fig. 3.

order to perform the algorithm. The data on this path then proceeds through the same series of transformations.

Finally the two paths are recombined by first delaying the original path in order to sync the two paths together, regaining temporal coherence. They are then added together and to form the final result. The multiplication by SIN^2 and COS^2 values both rolls-off the signal at the edges of the window and ensures the final recombination of the two paths leads to the proper value.

2.3   Streaming Discrete Cosine Transform Method (SDCTM)

The normalized DCT, IDCT, DST, and IDST (Eq. 5–8, respectively) are

$$y_k = 2 \sum_{n=0}^{N-1} f x_n \cos\left(\frac{\pi k(2n+1)}{2N}\right)$$

$$\text{where } f = \begin{cases} \sqrt{\frac{1}{4N}}, & \text{if } k = 0 \\ \sqrt{\frac{1}{2N}}, & \text{otherwise} \end{cases}$$

(5)

$$y_k = fx_0 + 2 \sum_{n=1}^{N-1} fx_n \cos\left(\frac{\pi n(2k+1)}{2N}\right)$$

$$\text{where } f = \begin{cases} \sqrt{\frac{1}{N}}, & \text{if } n = 0 \\ \sqrt{\frac{1}{2N}}, & \text{otherwise} \end{cases} \tag{6}$$

$$y_k = 2 \sum_{n=0}^{N-1} fx_n \sin\left(\frac{\pi(k+1)(2n+1)}{2N}\right)$$

$$\text{where } f = \begin{cases} \sqrt{\frac{1}{4N}}, & \text{if } k = 0 \\ \sqrt{\frac{1}{2N}}, & \text{otherwise} \end{cases} \tag{7}$$

$$y_k = f(-1)^k x_{N-1} + 2 \sum_{n=0}^{N-2} fx_n \sin\left(\frac{\pi(2k+1)(n+1)}{2N}\right)$$

$$\text{where } f = \sqrt{\frac{1}{2N}} \tag{8}$$

To adapt these equations for streaming data, we first realize each equation as data multiplied by coefficients that depend on the specific n and k. These coefficients then can be packaged into a matrix that is $n \times k$. By proper multiplication and addition, these functions can all be implemented.

Figure 3 shows the block diagram for these algorithms and the desired transform is selected by choice of LUT matrix for the coefficient values. We start before run-time by generating this coefficient matrix according to Eqs. 5–8 for the corresponding values of n and k. At the top of the diagram we see the data (x_{in}) streaming in one word at a time. At each clock cycle, a new word will stream in and the next column from the coefficient matrix will get loaded in parallel into the M long array of registers. So each time a piece of data comes in, that specific piece of data will get multiplied M times and accumulate in a temporary array until M pieces of data have come in and the final output vector is ready. In total, M numbers of multiplications and additions will occur at each clock cycle (this can be pipelined if needed) as well as loading the next row of the coefficient matrix. In this way, no clock cycles are wasted since M words come in and the operations are happening in sync with the data streaming in.

Of course a number of trade-offs are present in this design. For reducing resource usage, it is best to limit the size of K as this limits the number of simultaneous multiplications that need to occur (as well as additions). Additionally, constraints on the clock period can be loosened if pipelining at various stages is employed, but the ability to do this depends on latency requirements. Furthermore, we enforce symmetry and anti-symmetry in the signals streaming into the DCT and DST functions, respectively. Doing so takes advantage of the even and odd properties of these functions In software, this is accomplished by replicating data and flipping it where needed. In hardware, this is accomplished

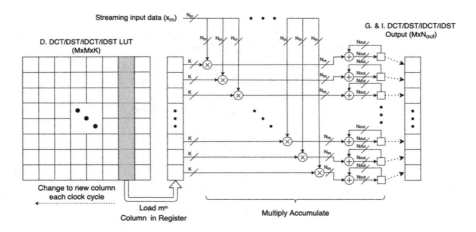

Fig. 3. This figure shows the streaming DCT, DST, IDCT, and IDST algorithms which all use this same general framework. Pre-runtime, a $M \times M$ LUT with words of K bits specific to the transform of choice is stored in memory. Each time a new piece of data streams in, a new column from the LUT is loaded into a register array. This data is simultaneously multiplied with each element in this register array. The output of this then goes into a multiply-accumulate function until M pieces of data have streamed in, at which point the process is completed. The points D, G, and I correspond to Table 2 and are used within Fig. 2.

by assigning 0 to particular computations as either the even or odd coefficient outputs will be 0 depending on if the operation is a DCT or a DST. Therefore, those computations can be ignored and will not add to the overall required number of multiplications for the DCT and DST.

2.4   Zero Crossing

The zero crossing algorithm is the final stage of finding the peaks in the data. Here we search for the x-positions–time for xFEL or frequency for ECE cases–where the derivative signals cross zero. One possible resource conserving approach to this search for streaming data is shown in Fig. 4. Given that features resemble something between a triangle and a Gaussian pulse, the derivative will also have a known shape. With this expectation, the algorithm waits for the streaming derivative input signal to pass a particular threshold, then change sign, and finally cross a second threshold. If the derivative meets these criteria, then the two positions in the data that were closest to the zero crossing are saved. In hardware, this would involve an array of predefined length for holding all of the data pairs and corresponding positions for qualifying zero crossings. A pointer in the array would then update where in the array the next data pair will be saved. In this way, if a data pair meet the first two qualifications threshold and then fail the final threshold, the saved data pair from this can be overwritten

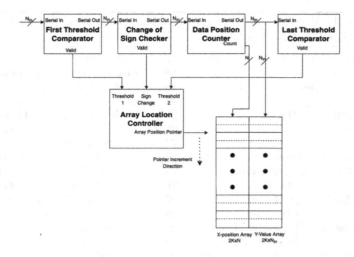

Fig. 4. Shows the process for qualifying derivative signals as a valid pulse. Three checks occur on the data. 1) threshold to see that the data goes high (low) enough; 2) checks for a change in sign from positive (negative) to negative (positive); and 3) checks that the data meets an opposite threshold that is low (high) enough. If data meets the change of sign check, the two points around this change of sign are loaded into the position and value arrays. If final disqualifies pulse, these now-invalid values will be overwritten.

by moving the pointer back. This method determines two x-axis values and two corresponding y-axis values for the points surrounding the zero crossing.

The last portion of the algorithm arrives at an estimate for the zero crossing based on these two surrounding points. In the simplest approach, the position corresponding to the value with smaller magnitude between the two can be taken as the x-axis position stamp for the zero crossing. We call this method the direct method for finding the zero crossing.

A second method uses a weighted average between the two surrounding points to elicit a better resolved x-position stamp. However, a standard weighted average is not necessarily the most conducive option for efficient implementation in an FPGA. Instead we propose a modified weighted average method. This method, shown in Algorithm 1, starts by assuming that by construction one point has negative value ($v1$) and the other has positive value ($v2$). Then it checks if either the y value of the first point (called $v1$) or the y value of the second point (called $v2$) are zero. If not, then it compares $|v1|$ and $|v2|$ in several steps. If $|v1|$ is larger than $|v2|$, then it checks how much larger. Based on how much larger, the output position (t_{out}) is assigned a corresponding proportion of $t1$ and $t2$. Specifically, we check if $|v1|$ is 2 times $|v2|$, 4 times $|v2|$, 8 times $|v2|$, or 16 times $|v2|$. This results in simple, digital operations in the FPGA design. Similarly, we do the same comparisons for the case where $v2$ is bigger than $v1$, and we handle the case where $v1$ and $v2$ are the same value by a stan-

Algorithm 1. Weighted average zero crossing calculation. $(t1,v1)$ is the first point and $(t2,v2)$ is the second point.

Require: $(v1 \leq 0 \wedge v2 \geq 0) \vee (v2 \leq 0 \wedge v1 \geq 0)$
1: **if** $|v1| == 0$ **then**
2:     $t_{out} \leftarrow t1$
3: **else if** $|v2| == 0$ **then**
4:     $t_{out} \leftarrow t2$
5: **else**
6:     **if** $|v1| \geq |v2|$ **then**
7:         **if** $|v1| \leq 2 * |v2|$ **then**
8:             $t_{out} \leftarrow (2 * t2 + t1)/3$
9:         **else if** $|v1| \leq 4 * |v2|$ **then**
10:             $t_{out} \leftarrow (4 * t2 + t1)/5$
11:         **else if** $|v1| \leq 8 * |v2|$ **then:**
12:             $t_{out} \leftarrow (8 * t2 + t1)/9$
13:         **else if** $|v1| \leq 16 * |v2|$ **then:**
14:             $t_{out} \leftarrow (16 * t2 + t1)/17$
15:         **else:**
16:             $t_{out} \leftarrow t2$
17:         **end if**
18:     **else if** $|v1| == |v2|$ **then**
19:         $t_{out} \leftarrow (t1 + t2)/2$
20:     **else**
21:         **if** $|v2| \leq 2 * |v1|$ **then**
22:             $t_{out} \leftarrow (2 * t1 + t2)/3$
23:         **else if** $|v2| \leq 4 * |v1|$ **then**
24:             $t_{out} \leftarrow (4 * t1 + t2)/5$
25:         **else if** $|v2| \leq 8 * |v1|$ **then:**
26:             $t_{out} \leftarrow (8 * t1 + t2)/9$
27:         **else if** $|v2| \leq 16 * |v1|$ **then:**
28:             $t_{out} \leftarrow (16 * t1 + t2)/17$
29:         **else:**
30:             $t_{out} \leftarrow t1$
31:         **end if**
32:     **end if**
33: **end if**

---

dard average. Additionally, the output position estimates can then be adjusted based on known adjusting constants for time-zero or other required shifts. This method leverages the ability to easily compare two values and the corresponding factors involving powers of two, which in an FPGA only requires shift-registers and comparators. The denominators for division can then be stored in reciprocal form in LUTs ahead of time for multiplication for the final output.

3   Results

In this section, we present the simulation results for the convolution method and the DCSTM for both the derivative and the final peak location estimates. We start with individual subsections on convolution and DCSTM showing how we selected algorithm specific parameters. Then we show the comparison in performance for the two algorithms on two test data use-cases– the Cookiebox time-of-flight data and the fusion ECE data. For the peak location comparisons, we use fabricated data made from Gaussian peaks placed at specific locations so that we can precisely analyze our algorithms. We compare both the direct method and the weighted average method for the final peak location estimates.

3.1   Convolution Method

The convolution method requires the kernel to be chosen ahead of run time. Specifically, the kernel length and the width need to be selected based on expected data. The kernel width, in particular, must be able to capture the width of the typical pulses. Furthermore, we want our kernel to be continuous and continuous differentiable. To find a function of this nature, we can start by considering a kernel that mimics the derivative functionality, such as a step function. Then we can inspect the noiseless power spectrum of our data. We can Wiener filter the data to get an approximation to the noiseless power spectrum and then multiply this by the Fourier transformed step function. Taking the inverse Fourier transform results in pulses that closely resemble the Wiener filtering derivative of a Gaussian pulse. We can then choose the width of the kernel, which we had originally chosen to be this derivative of the Gaussian pulse, to match the inverse of the Wiener filtered power spectrum.

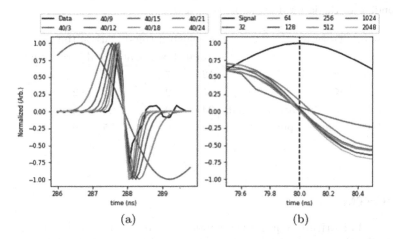

Fig. 5. Figure shows pre-runtime tuning operations for both the convolution method (a) and DCSTM (b). Specifically (a) compares the inverse transformed Wiener filtered power spectrum multiplication output (in black) and convolution kernels with window size of 40 and widths ranging from 40/3 to 40/24. (b) shows a Gaussian pulse (labeled Signal in black), a dashed line indicating the peak position of the signal, and seven versions of the derivative of the signal all using the DCSTM algorithm but with different window sizes.

Figure 5a shows derivative Gaussian kernels with a window size of 40 with Gaussian widths varying from 40/3 to 40/24. These are overlaid on the output from the inverse transformed Wiener filtered power spectrum multiplication output (labeled as Data in black). We can see that the kernel and the output overlap closely as the kernel width gets close to 40/18, and this kernel would overlap even better if the signal were truly noise free. This suggests that such a filter choice would select out the derivative of the data without emphasizing noise, and one can tune the width of the kernel to match the expected data appropriately.

For running the convolution derivative method, apart from the kernel width, the word sizes at each point in the algorithm must be chosen for the fixed point representation. Table 1 shows the selected word sizes corresponding to the different points in the convolution block diagram (see Fig. 1). The final output word size is 25 bits with 10 fractional bits for the Cookiebox data and just 25 integer bits for the fusion ECE data. The particular word sizes chosen resulted in acceptable errors for the given use-cases.

Table 1. Table shows the word sizes at each stage in the Convolution algorithm for both Cookiebox and fusion data. For each word, the total bits and the number of bits after the decimal (fractional bits) for the fixed point representation are shown. The labels for these words can be matched to the block diagram of the algorithm corresponding to the letter designator (see Fig. 1).

Label	Description	Cookiebox (bits)		Fusion (bits)	
		Total	Fractional	Total	Fractional
(A)	Input signal	12	7	13	0
(B)	Kernel	11	2	10	2
(C)	Multiplication outputs	24	10	22	0
(D)	Final output	25	10	25	0

3.2   DCSTM

The DCSTM algorithm requires the window size to be chosen ahead of run time. Additionally, the word width size–the number of bits in each word–for each stage of the algorithm must be chosen. All of these parameters can be tuned and are dependent on the expected data. The window size selection depends on the nature of the typical data, mostly the expected pulse widths. For our data we looked at how window size would affect location of the zero crossing for the derivative. Figure 5b shows how the window size can affect the derivative. This figure shows the original signal (black), a dashed black line indicating the peak location of the signal, and the derivatives calculated using DCSTM for window sizes from 32 to 2048 words for test data of similar width to our real data.

The window size needs to be larger if the pulse is wide because we must be able to capture significant portions of the pulse. We can see that for 128 and beyond, the derivative signals begin to converge. Therefore, we select 128 as the window size as we want as small of a window size as possible while still retaining accurate enough zero crossing information.

After having selected window size, bit width of the data words for each section of the algorithm were determined. We tested our selected values with test data sets from both use-cases considered in this paper.

Table 2. Table shows the word sizes at each stage in the DCSTM algorithm for both Cookiebox and fusion ECE data sets. For each word, the total bits and the number of bits after the decimal (fractional bits) for the fixed point representation are shown. The labels for these words can be matched to the block diagram of the algorithm corresponding to the letter (see Fig. 2 and 3).

Label	Description	Cookiebox (bits)		Fusion (bits)	
		Total	Fractional	Total	Fractional
(A)	Input Signal	12	7	13	0
(B)	Sine-Squared LUT	9	8	12	10
(C)	Cosine-Squared LUT	9	8	12	10
(D)	DCT/DST/IDCT/IDSCT LUT	20	18	12	8
(E)	Sine-squared Multiplication	15	10	20	5
(F)	Coine-squared Multiplication	15	10	20	5
(G)	DCT/DST Outputs	20	8	20	0
(H)	Frequency Multiplication Outputs	28	8	22	0
(I)	IDCT/IDST Outputs	25	10	23	0
(J)	First Set Additions	26	10	24	0
(K)	Final Output	27	10	25	0

Table 2 shows the chosen values for the word sizes, which correspond to the associated points in the algorithm block diagram, Fig. 2 and 3. For the Cookiebox data, the final output word is 27 bits in total with 10 fractional bits. For the fusion data, the final output word is 25 integer bits. These word sizes give errors on the derivative calculation that are acceptable for these applications.

3.3   Convolution and DCSTM Comparisons

For both algorithms, the pre-runtime parameters have to be set based on the expected characteristics of the data. First we inspect the derivative functionality of both algorithms. Figure 6a shows the convolution method derivative and DCSTM derivative applied to the Cookiebox dataset, and Fig. 6b shows the two methods applied to the fusion spectral data. Here the ground truth derivative (black) is in the center of the figures and the convolution method (red) is negatively offset while the DCSTM (blue) is positively offset for better visibility. Visually, the two algorithms align well with the ground truth derivative.

To quantify the performance of the algorithms we take the mean-squared error with the ground truth. For the Cookiebox data, the DCSTM algorithm has superior performance with an error of 1.23 while the convolution method has an error of 3.81. For the fusion data, the DCSTM also has superior performance with an error of 1.03 while the convolution method has an error of 1.26.

For further inspection, we can focus around one of the peaks in the data. Figure 6c and 6d–CookieBox and fusion ECE, respectively–show the ground truth (black) and discrete points of the convolution-based derivative (red) and DCSTM derivative (blue). In both Fig. 6c and 6d, we see that there is a slight horizontal offset of the convolution derivative output that does not show up in the DCSTM algorithm. This offset affects the points closest to the zero crossing and therefore will have an effect on the estimation methods for the peak-finding algorithms.

To better analyze how the offset and the discretization affect the zero crossing estimate, we use a generated dataset to test the peak-finding algorithms. For

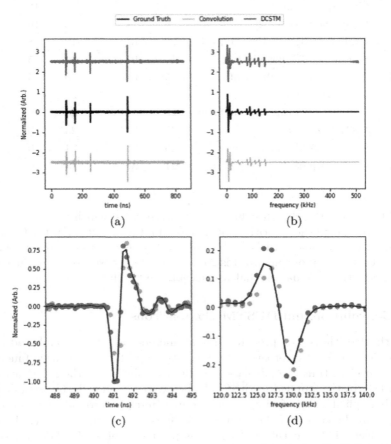

Fig. 6. Figure shows the derivative of the data collected from the Cookiebox detector – (a) and (c) – and from the fusion data – (b) and (d). The ground truth (black) is the derivative calculated using a standard software package. The remaining signals are the derivatives calculated using the DCSTM algorithm (blue) and using the convolution method (red). For visibility, (a) and (b) have the DCSTM and convolution method offset. (c) and (d) show the results zoomed on one pulse and with discrete points for the derivatives to showcase how the derivative outputs affect the zero crossing algorithms. (Color figure online)

this we use Gaussian pulses placed at specific locations. We can also get the analytic derivative of the Gaussian pulses for comparisons with the algorithms. Using both the convolution method and the DCSTM, we can test both zero crossing methods. Figure 7 shows two pulses in the dataset generated using these Gaussian pulses. Here the signal is shown in black, the analytic derivative of the Gaussian is shown as a dotted black line, the convolution method derivative is in red, the two estimates for the zero crossing–direct and weighted average–based on the convolution method are shown in red, the DCSTM derivative is in blue, and the two estimates for the zero crossing algorithm based on the DCSTM are shown in blue. The first pulse (Fig. 7a) shows an example where the peak is located off the exact time grid. The second pulse (Fig. 7b) shows an example where the peak is located on the time grid.

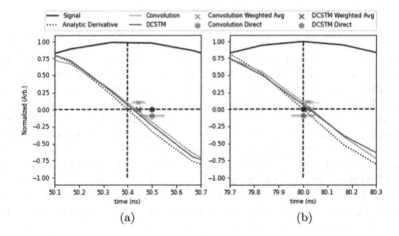

(a)   (b)

Fig. 7. Figure shows two pulses out of the total generated dataset. The signal is shown in black with a dashed line indicating the peak location. The true derivative is the analytic derivative of the Gaussian shown as a dotted black line. The convolution derivative is shown in red, and the DCSTM derivative is shown in blue. The corresponding peak estimates are shown as "x" for the weighted average and a "o" for the direct method. All of the signals have been normalized based on the maximum of the absolute value of the respective signal (across all pulses in that signal). (a) shows a pulse that does not have its center on the time grid. (b) shows a pulse that does lie perfectly on the time grid. For each zero crossing estimate, error bars based on the root mean-squared error are included. The error bars are offset from their associated points for better visibility. The RMSE for convolution weighted average is 33.8 ps, for convolution direct is 51.4 ps, for DCSTM weighted average is 24.4 ps, and for DCSTM direct is 51.4 ps. (Color figure online)

In both Fig. 7a and 7b, we see that the convolution derivative method has a larger shift from the analytic derivative. In both cases, the weighted average zero crossing has a better estimate for the zero crossing of that derivative, and this means that the peak estimate based on this method will depend how closely aligned that derivative is with the analytic derivative. For Fig. 7a where the peak is not on the time grid, the direct method zero crossing estimate is very poor, yielding a result nearly 0.1 ns wrong for both the convolution and DCSTM. However, in Fig. 7b where the peak is perfectly on the time grid, the direct method yields a very good result. This discrepancy means that the direct method is not guaranteed to deliver a valid result while the weighted average method will yield a reasonable result even for peaks that are not exactly on the grid.

To better quantify these differences, we use root mean-squared error (RMSE) for the estimated peak locations compared to their actual locations for the two versions of the peak finding for both derivative methods as given by

$$RMSE = \sqrt{\frac{1}{N} \sum_{i=0}^{N-1} (x_i - x_{\text{truth}})^2} \tag{9}$$

where N is the number of peaks identified in the data and x_{truth} is the true peak location. For this generated data, some of the peaks are located on the grid and others are not. The resulting errors are shown as error bars in Fig. 7 for the identified zero crossings. We see that the errors for the direct methods for both DCSTM and convolution methods are nearly identical and are nearly twice as large as the errors for the weighted average methods for both DCSTM and convolution. This means that even in the cases where the direct method happens to yield a closer estimate to the zero crossing because of the peak location being on a grid point, the associated error bar still gives a relatively high uncertainty. The DCSTM method using the weighted average zero crossing estimate gives the lowest RMSE of 24.4 ps for generated data in this dataset. This high resolution is in fact a factor of 2 better than that required for 0.25 eV spectral resolution with 500 eV electrons as indicated in Fig. 7 of Ref. [18].

4   Conclusions

Systems requiring live decision making, fast feedback and control, and machine learning-optimized data reduction all rely on data being fed in and pre-processed quickly and accurately. One such application is peak finding for dimensional reductive featurization of raw data. This particular application has been required in a wide range of experiments in topics spanning nuclear physics to biological applications, and the approach has involved both analog electronics with constant fraction discriminators and iterative curve fitting algorithms in software. Leveraging the computational efficiency of older approaches is seeing a resurgence given modern needs for high throughput and low latency data processing. This encourages the use of hardware-based algorithm implementations, such as on an FPGA, where highly parallel computations and real-time processing can bring the best of traditional analog approaches to more generalized digital applications in streaming data featurization. Furthermore, hardware-based approaches enable pipelined integration with detector and data acquisition systems and can be placed intimately close to the detectors and digitizers. This is the frontier of ML at-the-edge that drives in-device edge computing initiatives.

In this paper we have presented and compared two featurization algorithms designed for implementation in hardware but simulated in software. For both of these algorithms we discuss the fundamental design, the parameter selection pre-runtime, and the final results for both generated data and for real data from our use cases. We focus on two distinct use cases for in-flight streaming data processing: a) X-ray pulse reconstruction at SLAC's LCLS-II X-ray Free-Electron Laser and b) ECE as a plasma diagnostic at the DIII-D tokamak fusion reactor. The results from both show that we are able to calculate a derivative and find the zero crossings in that signal (therefore the centroids of the associated peaks) using both a convolution method and a discrete cosine and sine transform method all while keeping our bit representations quite low.

The convolution method requires, for our use cases, 40 simultaneous multiplications followed by an addition of all of those outputs. However, we are able to keep the final output size to roughly only double the initial input word size of the data. Moreover, the computations are all performed without looping or bottlenecks such that the data can continuously feed the streaming pipeline. For the DCSTM, the method requires, for our use cases, between roughly 250 and 1000 simultaneous multiplications. To keep full precision, the output bitsize, in theory, would need to be very large. Furthermore, a native version of the DCSTM that uses standard discrete sine and cosine transforms would not be able to operate on streaming data. However, our novel method of windowing the signal and using smaller discrete sine and cosine transforms to compute the total allows us to operate on streaming data while reducing the number of multipliers from roughly 5000 down to 1000 for the CookieBox data, for example. Additionally, our output word size is also roughly double the input word size even with all of these multiplications, so the hardware resources are still manageable.

The DCSTM algorithm gives a better result than the convolution method. However, the DCSTM requires significantly more resources in an FPGA. This trade-off means that applications requiring higher accuracy may choose the DCSTM but will need larger hardware to accomplish this task. We are currently working on the FPGA implementation of the DCSTM algorithm, and future work will contain a comparison, in hardware, of these two algorithms. In addition, next developments will demonstrate combinations of serial streaming and parallel burst versions of these algorithms. For example, our CookieBox data is sampled at 6 Gs/s while our FPGA clock runs slower than this sample rate. Thus, we would have access to batches of data at a given time. We are beginning to work on versions of our algorithms that will leverage this parallel data availability and vectorize some of the operations to perform streaming-vectorized operations for further reduction in latency.

Acknowledgements. This research is supported by the Department of Energy, Office of Science, Office of Basic Energy Sciences for funding the development of the CookieBox detector array itself under Grant Number FWP 100498 "Enabling long wavelength Streaking for Attosecond X-ray Science" and for funding Field Work Proposal 100643 "Actionable Information from Sensor to Data Center" for the development of the associated algorithmic methods, EdgeML computing hardware, and personnel. We also acknowledge funding for the computational method development for tokamak diagnostics by the Office of Fusion Energy Science under Field Work Proposal 100636 "Machine Learning for Real-time Fusion Plasma Behavior Prediction and Manipulation". Also, this research is funded by the Department of Defense National Defense Science and Engineering Graduate Fellowship.

References

1. Therrien, A.C., Herbst, R., Quijano, O., Gatton, A., Coffee, R.: Machine learning at the edge for ultra high rate detectors. In: IEEE Nuclear Science Symposium and Medical Imaging Conference, vol. 10, pp. 1–4 (2019)
2. Lazarus, E.A., et al.: Higher beta at higher elongation in the DIII-D tokamak. Phys. Fluids B Plasma Phys. **3**, 2220–2229 (1991)
3. Naaranoja, T.: Digital signal processing for particle detectors in front-end electronics. University of Helsinki, Master's thesis in Physics (2014)
4. Cox, S.A., Hanley, P.R.: A fast zero-crossing and constant fraction timing discriminator with emitter coupled integrated circuits. IEEE Trans. Nuclear Sci. **18**(3), 108 (1971)
5. Wall, R.W.: Simple methods for detecting zero crossing. In: IECON 2003. 29th Annual Conference of the IEEE Industrial Electronics Society, vol. 3. IEEE (2003)
6. Bevington, P.R., Robinson, K.D.: Data Reduction and Error Analysis. McGraw Hill, New York (2003)
7. Brown, A.J.: Spectral curve fitting for automatic hyperspectral data analysis. IEEE Trans. Geosci. Remote Sens. **44**(6), 1601–1608 (2006)
8. De Weijer, A.P., Lucasius, C.B., Buydens, L., Kateman, G., Heuvel, H.M., Mannee, H.: Curve fitting using natural computation. Anal. Chem. **66**(1), 23–31 (1994)
9. Maatta, K., Kostamovaara, J.: A high-precision time-to-digital converter for pulsed time-of-flight laser radar applications. IEEE Trans. Instr. Meas. **47**, 521–536 (1998)
10. Benesty, J., Chen, J., Huang, Y.A., Doclo, S.: Study of the Wiener filter for noise reduction. In: Benesty, J., Makino, S., Chen, J. (eds.) Speech Enhancement. Signals and Communication Technology, pp. 9–41. Springer, Heidelberg (2005). https://doi.org/10.1007/3-540-27489-8_2
11. Heckbert, P.S.: Filtering by repeated integration. ACM SIGGRAPH Comput. Graph. **20**(4), 315–321 (1986)
12. Simard, P., Bottou, L., Haffner, P., LeCun, Y.: Boxlets: a fast convolution algorithm for signal processing and neural networks. In: Advances in Neural Information Processing Systems, vol. 11 (1998)
13. Talbi, F., Alim, F., Seddiki, S., Mezzah, I., Hachemi, B.: Separable convolution Gaussian smoothing filters on a xilinx FPGA platform. In: Fifth International Conference on the Innovative Computing Technology, pp. 112–117 (2015)
14. Fisher, R., Perkins, S., Walker, A., Wolfart, E.: Hypermedia image processing reference, pp. 118–130. John Wiley & Sons Ltd, England (1996)
15. Gonzalez, R.C., Woods, R.E.: Digital Image Processing, 2nd edn. Publishing House of Electronics Industry, Beijing (2002)

16. Johnson, S.G., Frigo, M.: A modified split-radix FFT with fewer arithmetic operations. IEEE Trans. Signal Process. **55**(1), 111–119 (2006)
17. Lundy, T., Van Buskirk, J.: A new matrix approach to real FFTs and convolutions of length 2 k. Computing **80**, 23–45 (2007)
18. Walter, P., et al.: Multi-resolution electron spectrometer array for future free-electron laser experiments. J. Synchrotron Radiat. **28**(5), 1364–1376 (2021). https://doi.org/10.1107/S1600577521007700

Implementation of a Framework for Deploying AI Inference Engines in FPGAs

Ryan Herbst[✉], Ryan Coffee, Nathan Fronk, Kukhee Kim, Kuktae Kim,
Larry Ruckman, and J. J. Russell

SLAC National Accelerator Laboratory, Menlo Park, CA 95024, USA
rherbst@slac.stanford.edu

Abstract. The LCLS2 Free Electron Laser (FEL) will generate x-ray pulses to beamline experiments at up to 1 Mhz. These experimentals will require new ultra-high rate (UHR) detectors that can operate at rates above 100 kHz and generate data throughputs upwards of 1 TB/s, a data velocity which requires prohibitively large investments in storage infrastructure. Machine Learning has demonstrated the potential to digest large datasets to extract relevant insights, however current implementations show latencies that are too high for real-time data reduction objectives. SLAC has endeavored on the creation of a software framework which translates MLs structures for deployment on Field Programmable Gate Arrays (FPGAs) deployed at the Edge of the data chain, close to the instrumentation. This framework leverages Xilinx's HLS framework presenting an API modeled after the open source Keras interface to the TensorFlow library. This SLAC Neural Network Library (SNL) framework is designed with a streaming data approach, optimizing the data flow between layers, while minimizing the buffer data buffering requirements. The goal is to ensure the highest possible framerate while keeping the maximum latency constrained to the needs of the experiment. Our framework is designed to ensure the RTL implementation of the network layers supporting full re-deployment of weights and biases without requiring re-synthesis after training. The ability to reduce the precision of the implemented networks through quantization is necessary to optimize the use of both DSP and memory resources in the FPGA. We currently have a preliminary version of the toolset and are experimenting with both general purpose example networks and networks being designed for specific LCLS2 experiments.

Keywords: Aritifial intelligence · Machine learning · FPGA · HLS · Xilinx · Inferrence

1 Introduction

New detectors for science and other applications have exponentially increased their pixel count and their frame rate, resulting in ever larger data rates. Some

K. Doug et al. (Eds.): SMC 2022, CCIS 1690, pp. 120–134, 2022.
https://doi.org/10.1007/978-3-031-23606-8_8

of these ultra-high rate (UHR) detectors can operate at rates above 100 kHz and generate data throughputs upwards of 1 TB/s, a data velocity which requires prohibitively large investments in storage infrastructure. Machine Learning has demonstrated the potential to digest large datasets to extract relevant insights, however current implementations show latencies that are too high for real-time data reduction objectives. We intend to use machine learning inference models entirely deployed on a network of interconnected FPGAs allowing data to be pipelined for high throughput with ultra-low latency.

Edge Computing systems will receive the raw detector output and will pre-process, veto and classify the frame before sending the compressed information downstream for further analysis and/or storage. The re-programmability of FPGAs makes it possible to have a custom ML inference model for each detector and experiment. To facilitate the development and deployment of models for diverse experiments, we have created a framework (SNL) which will translate ML structures in FPGA code and deploy it to the FPGA network.

1.1   The SNL Framework

The primary goal of SNL is to produce a high-performance, low latency FPGA implementation of an AI inference engine that can accommodate reasonably sized networks and be robust enough to adapt to changes when deployed in a real-time environment. A secondary goal is to make this as easy to use as possible without sacrificing those primary goals.

C++ templates used within the Xilinx Vitis HLS development environment and modeled after the Python Keras layer procedures were chosen as the implementation method to address the performance goals and the ease of use. Dynamic loading of weights and biases was chosen to achieve robustness by avoiding re-synthesizing the network when a new set of weights and biases were needed. Once verified, deployment of a new set of weights and biases is procedurally the same as any other restart of the system.

The next two sections attempt to justify or at least explain the pluses and minuses of these decisions and how they help achieve the primary goal.

1.2   Why C++ Templates?

FPGAs work best the more that is statically known at compile/build time affording the compiler the best opportunity to optimize resources and latency/thruput. This matches well with the target SNL application, *e.g.* the topology of the inference engine is fixed, with known data sizes and loop iteration counts. Using C++ templates provides a mechanism to define this topology and, together with Xilinx HLS's palette of pragmas, allows the effective mapping of software concepts onto the FPGA resources.

The C++ templates are modeled as closely as possible in their form and function with the Python Keras layer methods. Given that a FPGA has a very different computational model from a CPU or GPU, there are necessarily differences. The design goal was not to eliminate or hide these differences, but to limit their number to what was necessary to achieve the primary goals. One of the important differences is the interface between layers is a streaming, not a memory interface. See Sect. 1.4

This approach can be contrasted with what could be called a *code that writes code* approach. The following is not meant to be promoting one over the other. As with many things, one approach's strengths are the other's weaknesses. Users should pick the approach best suited to their problem and skill set.

In general, the *code that writes code* approach is more turnkey and easier for users with minimal C++, Xilinx HLS and FPGA experience. The downside is that it is fairly rigid in its implementation and when things go wrong, even if it the user's mistake, it is often hard to track down the origin of the mistake. Even with good tools, the made-up names and layout of the generated code can become confusing and intractable.

On the flip side, while care has been taken to make SNL as easy to use as possible, it does demand more expertise on the user's part. This is a deliberate design decision. It is believed that the target application, AI at the edge, will be matched by users who have commensurate expertise in these areas. The hope is that by being just standard C++ code augmented with HLS pragmas, this gives the user greater control over the code and will allow greater performance, flexibility and the ability to track down errors when they inevitably occur. This flexibility is particularly useful when dealing with larger networks, for example allowing the user to trade performance with the finite FPGA resources.

1.3   Why Dynamic Loading of Weights and Biases?

There are two tactics one can take with the weights and biases that are calculated from the machine learning training.

– Build them into the code at synthesis time
– Load them at runtime

Building the weights and biases into the code during the synthesis allows the compiler the very real and tangible opportunity to better optimize the code. For example, weights that have little impact on the results may be pruned. It is noted that loading these at run-time eliminates this possible optimization and is at odds with the stated premium SNL places on performance. However, as in most engineering endeavors, there are trade-offs. There are two downsides to building the weights and biases into the FPGA image. Both involve operational time penalties

– The time to re-synthesize the FPGA image
– The small, but not negligible, chance that the re-synthesis will fail

An assumption is that SNL's use will be in the high stakes real-time environment of running a facility or experimental data taking, where downtime is to be minimized. Presumably a new set of weights and biases is being deployed because changing conditions demand it, *i.e* a set of new weights and biases must be deployed.

The first issue is just the reality that the time to re-synthesize networks for an FPGA can run into the multiple hours. This time is somewhat predictable and generally accepted as just the cost of using FPGAs. Said another way, it can be properly factored into the operational and scheduling,

The second entertains the possibility of the re-synthesis failing. An example of such a failure is if the previous set of weights was heavily pruned, there is no guarantee that the new set can. This could result in either FPGA resources being exhausted (admittedly less likely) or the latency drastically changing. In such a failure, the only recourse is developing a new set of viable weights and hoping they succeed. The time to do this is not predictable and certainly not welcomed if it delays operations. Using a dynamically loaded set of weights and biases will cost efficiency and the FPGA resources needed to support it may be greater but, since the FPGA image is unchanged and SNL is architected for deterministic behavior, this is a safe procedure with very predictable deployment times. It only has to be successively built once with neither the FPGA resources nor the latency changing.

When changes need to be made, many times it is in the face of multiple unrelated problems. Redeploying a new set of weights should not add to the problem list. Robustness in a real-time environment is part of good systems engineering.

1.4   Why Streaming?

A streaming interface connects the input of the current layer with the output of the previous layer. A memory interface delays the calculations of the current layer until all values of the previous layer are completed. The resulting latency accumulates though each layer using a memory interface.

In contrast, a *streaming* interface allows the current interface to start its calculations as soon as the necessary data values are available, thus decreasing the latency. In real-time applications, like triggering and feedback, latency is more valued than thru-put. The caveat is that some AI layer types are more amenable to streaming than others. For example, a Conv2D layer can, depending on options, begin when roughly the number of rows and columns equal to 1/2 kernel dimensions are available. Given most kernels are small, this delay will be small compared to the total data size. Other layers, such as the *Dense* layers, can only output their first data value when *all* the data have been processed. Thus *Dense* layers incur a heavy latency penalty. While proper coding of such layers can provide high thru-put, no coding cleverness can avoid this latency penalty. This penalty should be taken into consideration when designing a low latency network.

1.5   Overview of SNL Usage

The SNL user is presented as a collection of C++ templates that define the layer types and activators by specifying their parameters. In today's parlance, it is a header only package.

Current layers include among others, *Conv2D, MaxPooling, AveragePooling, Dense, etc.*. The template parameters follow as closely as possible, in naming, ordering and meaning, the Python Keras methods for that layer. Thus, users familiar with the Keras layer methods, should recognize their C++ template counterparts. This also has the upside that the very good documentation of the Keras layers can be referenced by the SNL user.

The user selects the layer and activator type and defines its parameters using the appropriate C++ templates. Where possible, sensible defaults are provided. These defaults are, by design, explicitly not hidden. This acts as a conspicuous prompt for the user to notice and change defaults when deemed necessary.

Finally, in strictly a mechanical step and again with the philosophy of being as transparent to the network builder as possible, the layers are gathered, in the form of a simple list, by another C++ template to form the network.

1.6   SNL Limitations, Both Correctable and Intrinsic

It is appropriate to be transparent about what SNL can and cannot do.

First SNL is not a finished product. The basic architecture is sound but missing the following (ordered from the easier to harder to address)

- Only a subset of all the Keras layers and activators are currently implemented
- Quantization of the weights and biases needs to be added
- Lack of global optimization across the network

New Layers and Activators: Adding new layers and activators is tedious, but it is a well-defined procedure. This includes a defined testing and verification method when implementing new layers. Admittedly, the somewhat obscure syntax and style of C++ templates and meta-programming is off-putting. However, this is confined to the implementer who is expected to have the necessary skills and (considering the above critique of C++ syntax) the stamina to do this. From the user's perspective, the resulting C++ templates are easy and straightforward to use. That is, the pain is confined to the few (the implementers), not the many (the users).

Quantization: The quantization of the weights and biases has been shown to greatly reduce the latency and FPGA resource usage in AI inference engine implementations. Floating point are expensive in FPGAs. Quantization replaces these with the much cheaper arbitrary precision integers and scaled integers. As an extreme case, the literature includes implementations using 1-bit integers. Adding quantization is a matter of allocating the manpower and resources..

Global Optimization: The lack of global optimization is not as easily addressed as the above two. The streaming interface defined between layers is a form of global optimization, but there are other types that, at the level SNL is implemented, fundamentally cannot be. The balancing of FPGA latencies and resources across layers is only marginally addressed by judiciously specifying pragmas that, for example, unroll loops. Consider a layer that has minimal impact on the latency, but uses a disproportionate share of FPGA resources, *e.g.* LUTs, DSPs.

A solution may be in a company Xilinx recently acquired and will soon be integrated into the HLS workflow. The product, SLX, can be described as an post-processor to the FPGA synthesis stage. Its promise is the user can specify global constraints on the resources including, not only logic resources, but also thru-put and latency. SLX will attempt to add pragmas that satisfies these constraints by considering the code in its entirety. How well this works in practice remains to be seen, but is an example of the needed solution.

2 SNL for Convolution Networks

This section is meant to give a flavor of the SNL implementation strategy using some of the layers typically found in a Convolution Network as examples. It also illustrates some of the challenges and techniques for implementing low-latency optimized code.

2.1 Data Widening

A feature common, but not exclusive to Convolution Networks, is that many times, the input is a 3D tensor. In actual usage (*i.e.* real hardware, delivering data in real-time) frequently two of these dimensions are presented serially, while the third dimension is parallelly available. An example would be an RGB image. The rows and columns are readout serially and the three colors in parallel. The pattern is a number of sensors or channels each delivering distinct serial streams in parallel. A simple scheme would be to present each value as separate data items in the input serial stream. Instead, SNL reflects the structure of the input, presenting all the channels in parallel, so instead of getting just a single data value in one FPGA clock, multiple values are fetched.

In more than one network that has been implemented, the latency is a small number of fixed cycles associated with pipeline overheads plus a larger number of cycles proportional to the input data access time. Thus the time spent accessing the input data is often a significant contribution to the total latency, so handling this efficiently is important.

The practice of widening the data path is very common in FPGA programming and fits naturally with Convolution Networks where often each channel of the initial layers is processed independently. Only latter, after the size of the data has been reduced by the initial layers, do these invoke a layer(s) that combines the channels.

Of course there are practical limits on the width. In FPGAs, a reasonable limit on the total width is 1-4K bits. Thus, inputting 3 8 bit RGB values (24 bits total) or even 64 channels of 12 bit ADCs is permissible. Given that the number of physical sensors/channels in a system is usually small, SNL currently assumes the third dimension can be always widen. Clearly there will be exceptions and one of the challenges facing SNL is how to handle this.

2.2 Controlling the Resource and Latency

The selection of which FPGA used is often determined by

- Using a familiar FPGA family
- Given the cost of a FPGA, using the smallest one capable of meeting the requirements

This translates into demanding the code squeezes as much performance using the fewest resources. High quality FPGA programming starts with selecting an algorithm and implementation that maps onto what an FPGA does well, then tuning the implementation, trying to find the sweet spot between performance and resource usage.

SNL can help in the former, selecting and carefully coding the implementation of the layers and activators to be FPGA friendly, The latter, tuning the implementation, is a challenge to do in a user blind way. In HLS, specialized pragmas[1] are the vehicle that allows the mapping of the code to hardware resources. It is through these pragmas that the performance/resource trade-off is realized. Two common pragmas determine the amount of *array partitioning* and *loop unrolling*. Both affect performance and resource usage. A future strategy will be for SNL to provide reasonable defaults, but also a user accessible method to modify these if necessary.

2.3 Scalability

The above is one of a class of scalability problems. When programming a CPU, data array sizes and loop counts can be liberally increased with the only impact being execution time. This is not true for FPGAs which have finite resources. So the challenge for SNL is how to handle cases when the finite size of an FPGA becomes a limitation. This came be summarized as

- How much can and should SNL do *under-the-hood*
- What control and how to expose that control to the user

Each path has its pitfalls.

- Can this truly be done without user input?
- Does giving the user tools to control this risk exposing details of the underlying implementation which, if the implementation needs to be modified, breaks user code?

---

[1] Pragmas are a standard C/C++ feature used to communicate information directly to the compiler.

2.4 Activators

The last step of an AI layer is the *Activator*. SNL provides class templates for the common activators such as *RELU*. From an implementation viewpoint these activators are divided into two orthogonal classes

– Natural Floating Point
– One vs two pass

Natural Floating Point: These are activators whose calculations are most naturally done in floating point and typically involve transcendentals, such as exponentials. An example would be the *Sigmoid* activator. These are computationally more expensive. Work is needed to understand their usage when doing quantized integer implementations. A look-up table would be a possible approach in this case.

One vs Two Pass: Many activators, *e.g. Relu*, can process the data in a streaming fashion. Such activators are simple functions, when handed a data value, the function immediately returns a new value. Some activators, *e.g. SoftMax*, require two passes. In the case of *SoftMax*, the sum of all the values from the first-pass is used to normalize the output.

Providing a standard interface for these is future SNL goal. The interface should allow activators to be used interchangeably. The challenge will be for SNL to avoid a *lowest common denominator* solution that unduly penalizes simple activators like *Relu* just to accommodate the more involved two-pass types.

However the reality is, independent of providing a clean interface, layers using two-pass activators are incapable of streaming. Add to this that many of two-pass activators also involve floating point operations, makes them latency-cost expensive. The take-away is, similar to certain layer types, network designers should be aware of the unavoidable cost of using such activators.

2.5 Layer Implementations: *Conv2D*

This section uses *Conv2D* as a concrete example of a typical SNL layer implementation. Two other layer types *AveragePooling* and *Dense* are used to illustrate other issues that occur.

Conv2D is an almost complete implementation of the equivalent Keras method. The following gives a flavor of the correspondence between the C++ template and Keras method. Here is the Keras method's interface:

```
keras.layers.Conv2D(filters,
                    kernel_size,
                    strides          = (1, 1),
                    padding          = 'valid',
                    data_format      = None,
                    dilation_rate    = (1, 1),
```

```
groups                      = 1,
activation                  = None,
use_bias                    = True,
kernel_initializer          = 'glorot_uniform',
bias_initializer            = 'zeros',
kernel_regularizer          = None,
bias_regularizer            = None,
activity_regularizer        = None,
kernel_constraint           = None,
bias_constraint             = None)
```

This is the corresponding C++ template with the equivalent Keras parameter specification.

```
template<typename   SRC_STREAM,         — data source

        size_t      NFILTERS,           — filters

        size_t      KERNEL_NROWS,       — kernel_size
        size_t      KERNEL_NCOLS,
        typename    KERNEL_TYPE,

        size_t      STRIDE_NROWS,       — strides
        size_t      STRIDE_NCOLS,

        Padding     PADDING,            — padding (Same or Valid)

        size_t      DILATION_NROWS,     — dilation_rate
        size_t      DILATION_NCOLS,

        size_t      GROUPS,             — groups

        typename    ACTIVATOR,          — activator
        typename    BIAS_TYPE,

        typename    DST_TYPE,
        size_t      DST_AXIS_TID   = 0,
        size_t      DST_AXIS_TDEST = 0>class Conv2D
```

The differences fall into two categories

- General differences due to differences in Python and C++ syntax
- Differences in specifying specific parameters

Parameter Defaulting: Python, with its named parameters, as opposed to C++ templates' positionally based parameters, offers much cleaner defaulting. Having said that, by design SNL avoids, though not religiously, defaulting.

Since defaults are specified in the interface, what the defaults are or even their existence is not immediately apparent when reading the code. This leaves the code vulnerable to changes in the defaults which may cause mysterious changes. SNL favors a bit more typing for the transparency it affords.

Permissible Parameter Types: Python parameters can be any legitimate Python type. C++ template parameters are limited to boolean, integer types and class types. In particular, floating point types are not permitted. To get around this, classes with purely constexpr's are used. Examples of this include the stream types (*SRC_STREAM, DST_STREAM*) and the *ACTIVATOR*[2].

Omitted Parameters: The greatest noticeable difference is the absence of the *xxx_*initializer and *xxx_*constraint parameters. These are only used for the machine learning phase, so, having no use during the inference phase, are omitted in the C++ template.

Data Types: Python deduces the data types of all the objects. For the most part this means a floating point type. With quantization and the ability to specify a wider palette of data types (half-precision, arbitrary precision integers, *etc.*), SNL must give control to the user via the *XXX_TYPE* parameters.

SRC_STREAM, DST_STREAM: This specifies the source and destination data stream as a SNL template class. It can viewed as a combination of Python's numpy shape and a HLS stream[3].

Only the source stream for the initial layer needs to be defined by the user. For subsequent layers, the source stream must be the previous layer's destination stream which can be easily referenced[4]. Furthermore, SNL can deduce the destination stream, with its stream shape being fixed by the layer type and its parameters. While the destination's stream data type can be overridden, it will default to that of the *ACTIVATOR*.

ACTIVATOR: The activator is specified as class type. SNL provides templates for the common activators such as *RELU*. See the Sect. 2.4 on activators for a more complete discussion.

2.6   Layer Implementations: *AveragePooling*

The average pooling layer is very similar to *Conv2D*. One could simply view this as a kernel with all entries equal to 1/Kernel_Size. So, *e.g.* if it were a 2 × 2 pool, then the entries would all be 1/4.

The reason this is included in the discussion is that the division by the kernel size raises two important issues

- Division in FPGAs can be expensive in resources and time
- If using integer arthimetic, the division can result in bits being lost

---

[2] Classes can be passed by reference. This technique is used to make some of the weights and biases directly available at synthesis time in the *Reservoir* layer.

[3] A HLS stream is the standard interface used to stream data between layers. It behaves like a FIFO. For technical reasons, the initial and final streams must be an AXI stream.

[4] The name of the class of the previous layer's destination stream is well-defined, for example, presuming the previous layer parameter definition is *layer2::Parameters*, then *layer2::Parameters::DstStream*.

130   R. Herbst et al.

Because this is division by a fixed value, the usual trick of multiplying by precomputed reciprocal (if floating point) or by a binary scaled factor followed by removing the scale factor with a simply shift (if integer) addresses the first issue. However, if integer arithmetic, the loss of bits still remains.

This is an issue SNL will have to be addressed when doing quantization.

2.7   Layer Implementations: *Dense*

The dense layers are an example of a layer that kills streaming. By definition, all source data values must be available before an output value can be fully computed.

The SNL implementation does calculate partial results based on the available source data. This helps increase the thru-put and at least minimize the latency, but the minimum baseline latency is set by the number of source data values. As stated previously, no amount of clever coding can be avoid this penalty. One practical consideration helps; *Dense* layers generally occur as the final layers in a network when the data sizes have been reduced. The only other option available is to avoid using layers similar to the *Dense* layers.

2.8   Adding New Layers and Activators

In implementing SNL, a standard prescription for defining new layers and activators has slowly developed. While, making no claims that it is easy, this prescription is well defined. A suite of support functions and template classes are available to assist. At the risk of becoming too meta, SNL now becomes not only a set templates to define an arbitrary network, but also a set of rules with compile-time support methods for extending the palette of layers and activators. To use an overused phrase, this make SNL more amenable to open sourcing.

Example of a Support Method: As an illustration of how similar writing a new layer is to writing a compiler, consider an implementation for a 3 × 3 2D convolution using arbitrary precision integers. This involves multiplying and adding 9 data values by 9 kernel weights, *i.e.* a common dot product. The question is: What is the data type of the dot product sum?

The compiler can easily determine the size of each multiplication. It is simply the sum of the number of bits of the two multipliers. However the data type of the sum must be wide enough to avoid overflows. In usual CPU destined code, this is solved by *overkill*; either doing things in floating point or using very wide integers. However, to minimize resource costs in an FPGA, the type and size of the data types should be kept at a minimum.

The compiler is not equipped to do this. To help, SNL uses metaprogramming features of C++ to the define a compile time method that takes the two input types and the number of summed elements and returns the appropriate data type.

    snl :: datatype :: DotType<Type0 , Type1 , Count>

For example, consider a 3×3 kernel of 8-bit signed integer weights with 12-bit unsigned data types. The minimum output data type of this convolution is a 24 bit signed integer, 20 bits from the multiple and 4 bits to cover the 9 sums. Using the above

```
// Define the dot product type
using DotProduct_t = snl::datatype::DotType(ap_uint<12>,
                                            ap_int<8>,
                                            9>;
// Do a (overly) simple implementation of a dot product
DotProduct_t sum = 0.
for (int i = 0; i < 9; i++) sum += kernel[i] * data[i];
```

3 Implementation Results: BES Network

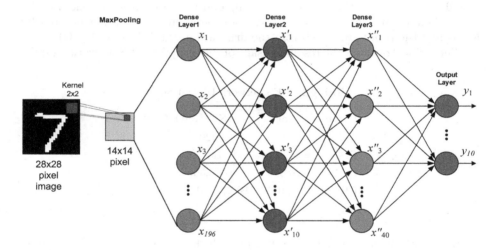

Fig. 1. BES network model

Table 1. BES network layers.

Layer(type)	Output shape	Activator
Maxpooling2D	14×14	–
Flatten	196	–
Dense	10	Leaky ReLU
Dense	40	Leaky ReLU
Dense	10	Leaky ReLU

The BES network consists of one MaxPooling2D layer and three dense layers with the Leaky-ReLU activation function. In this paper, the MNIST dataset is used to test and verify the BES network. The configuration of the network is described in Fig. 1 and Table 1. The weights and biases of each layer are calculated using the Keras and extracted for the SNL framework. The framework is verified by comparing the result of the network output with the Keras.

We were able to compile the BES network into a Xilinx KCU1500 device using the Xilinx HLS synthesis followed by a separate place and route with the HLS output included as a module in a larger VHDL based design. We used a python based software framework to load the FPGA, configure the weights and bias and to DMA image data into the FPGA in a streaming fashion. The inference results are then received via DMA using this same software.

Our python framework is able to read in the weight and bias data generated by the Keras tool directly and then formats this data to match the memory layout in the FPGA. Similarly the image data itself is read using this tool in its native format and streamed into the Xilinx FPGA. The FPGA results are stored in a custom data file and later compared to the results set generated by Keras. Our testing found perfect correlation between the results generated by Keras and the results received from the firmware in the Xilinx KCU1500.

The Table 2 outlines the resource usage of the compiled BES network module:

Table 2. BES network Ulilization.

Resource	Usage	KCU1500 Total
DSPs	298	5,520
FFs	36,901	1M
LUTs	26,016	663,360
BRAM	38 (0.7 MB)	75 Mb

In its current use the network runs at a clock rate of 250 Mhz. Based upon compilation results be believe this can be raised higher possibly to 300 Mhz or more. Further testing will allow us to determine how fast we can run this network. Given a clock rate of 250 Mhz we were able to achieve a total latency for each image frame's inference of 1.1015 uS. This is well within the target requirement for the initial application we are targeting.

The results reflect the fact that when moving an image from a dense layer to a dense layer in our current implementation does not include a pipelining stage. This saves memory in that it does not introduce additional registers at the output of each computation engine. We plan to allow a flag which will enabling the user to determine if they want to introduce pipelining at each dense layer output. The advantage of a pipeline is that it would allow a frame interval which is less than the total inference latency of the network. This will be required for larger inference networks running at higher frame rates.

4   SNL for Reservoir Networks

The Reservoir Network is included here because it uses a layer that is fairly different from other layers in the following ways

- It carries state information in the form of the previous reservoir vector
- It has two classes of weights
    - a fixed, built-in set. They are randomly initialized in the training phase, but they themselves are not trained.
    - a traditional set of weights and biases that are trained and downloaded

The other salient feature is that, because it connects all neurons, it cannot be streamed. An example network using 2 *Reservoir* layers has been implemented. A feature of these networks is the reservoir vector is large, in the 1000 s. The weight matrix connecting all the neurons of the reservoir network is thus this dimension squared. This results in a very large memory to hold it and a corresponding large number of DSPs to achieve the necessary low-latency. Such networks will need a correspondingly large FPGA. In the Xiinx series of FPGAs, choosing one with URAM is advantageous.

Again because of the large sizes involved, whereas SNL's typical target network latency is ~10 *usecs*, realistic Reservoir networks are in ~.1–10 *msecs*.

5   Conclusion

While SNL is still a work in progress, it has shown promise in implementing very low-latency networks. These latencies are very close to the best that can be expected based on the input data sizes and the unavoidable pipeline delays of the layers. The data does nicely stream through the layers.

In the future we intend to continue to add the necessary new layers and activators as stated in this document and study how their used impacts resource utilization and latency of the networks they are used in. We also plan to start implementing quantization in the models, including some novel techniques being studied by other groups such as non linear quantization. Our key concern here is to ensure we handle the overflow cases in a way which preserves the accuracy of the inference and does not introduce additional complexity in the activators.

Also now that we have a baseline framework in place we want to compare the resource usage of this framework with other frameworks that are available. Previous experience with these other frameworks indicates that they do not scale well to the network sizes we are looking at, but we intend to do direct comparisons of various size networks, starting small and scaling up to larger networks to see where the various frameworks no longer scale and how the implementation latencies compare.

References

1. Smith, T.F., Waterman, M.S.: Identification of common molecular subsequences. J. Mol. Biol. **147**, 195–197 (1981). https://doi.org/10.1016/0022-2836(81)90087-5
2. May, Patrick, Ehrlich, Hans-Christian., Steinke, Thomas: ZIB structure prediction pipeline: composing a complex biological workflow through web services. In: Nagel, Wolfgang E.., Walter, Wolfgang V.., Lehner, Wolfgang (eds.) Euro-Par 2006. LNCS, vol. 4128, pp. 1148–1158. Springer, Heidelberg (2006). https://doi.org/10.1007/11823285_121
3. Foster, I., Kesselman, C.: The Grid: Blueprint for a New Computing Infrastructure. Morgan Kaufmann, San Francisco (1999)
4. Czajkowski, K., Fitzgerald, S., Foster, I., Kesselman, C.: Grid information services for distributed resource sharing. In: 10th IEEE International Symposium on High Performance Distributed Computing, pp. 181–184. IEEE (2001). https://doi.org/10.1109/HPDC.2001.945188
5. Foster, I., Kesselman, C., Nick, J., Tuecke, S.: The physiology of the grid: an open grid services architecture for distributed systems integration. Technical report, Global Grid Forum (2002)
6. National Center for Biotechnology Information. http://www.ncbi.nlm.nih.gov

Systems and Software Advances Enabling an Integrated Science and Engineering Ecosystem

Calvera: A Platform for the Interpretation and Analysis of Neutron Scattering Data

Gregory R. Watson[✉] [ID], Gregory Cage, Jon Fortney, Garrett E. Granroth[ID],
Harry Hughes, Thomas Maier[ID], Marshall McDonnell[ID],
Anibal Ramirez-Cuesta[ID], Robert Smith, Sergey Yakubov[ID],
and Wenduo Zhou

Oak Ridge National Laboratory, Oak Ridge, TN 37380, USA
{watsongr,cagege,fortneyjm,granrothge,hugheshn,maierta,mcdonnellmt,
ramirezcueaj,smithrw,yakubovs,zhouw}@ornl.gov

Abstract. Data analysis for neutron scattering experiments is driven by the scientific needs of the instrument users and varies greatly by technique and field of study. Data from an experiment must first be "reduced" so that instrument artifacts are removed, and then scientists must choose from a wide variety of tools and applications to assemble a workflow that enables useful scientific results to be extracted. The highly manual nature of this process, combined with difficulty accessing computational resources and data when needed, puts limits on the efficiency and nature of the analysis undertaken. In addition, other activities, such as tracking data provenance to ensure the analysis is reproducible, or providing live data analysis during experiment runs, are also difficult to achieve.

Calvera is a platform that aims to solve many of the difficulties encountered by scientists as they analyze experimental neutron scattering data. In particular, the platform will provide an integration point for a range of services, such as data virtualization, remote computation, and visualization under the control of a workflow management system. In addition, the platform will handle security related issues, and maintain a history of the data sets employed during workflow execution. User's will be able to construct, manage, and share workflows via a graphical user interface, as well as script workflows via a python API. In this paper, we will describe the architecture and design of Calvera, as well as how we will address the many requirements for executing neutron science workflows in a distributed environment.

Keywords: Neutron science · Workflows · Data analysis · Ecosystem · Data management · Distributed computing · Visualization

1 Background

Oak Ridge National Laboratory (ORNL) operates two of the world's most powerful sources of neutrons for research, the High Flux Isotope Reactor (HFIR), and the Spallation Neutron Source (SNS). Neutron scattering experiments are used in

K. Doug et al. (Eds.): SMC 2022, CCIS 1690, pp. 137–154, 2022.
https://doi.org/10.1007/978-3-031-23606-8_9

a wide variety of diverse scientific disciplines in order to study the structure and properties of materials. Attached to the HFIR and SNS devices are an array of more than 30 instruments that are used for conducting different types of experiments. Scientist wishing to perform experiments using these neutron sources must plan and propose and experiment, receive an allocation and scheduling of beam time, and finally, prepare and conduct the experiment. Neutron scatting data is acquired during the course of the experiment, and transferred to a data repository where the instrument-specific data is transformed into a form that is expressed in terms of physically meaningful values, a process known as *data reduction*.

Although this reduced data is the primary artifact from neutron scattering experiments, it must undergo further processing in order to extract meaningful information that can be used for scientific discovery. This *data analysis* phase is usually carried out independently by users either during or after an experiment. Data analysis techniques vary significantly depending on the field of study, but can be broadly categorized into "structure refinement" where the structural arrangement of atoms in the material is determined and "modeling and simulation" where material characteristics are modelled and compared to actual measurements, simulated or theoretical predictions. Some analysis methods are fairly well established and have a variety of tools available, while others are highly specific to a particular area of research. However, the ability to efficiently carry out data analysis is key to scientific discovery in neutron science.

In 2019, ORNL undertook a review of data reduction, handling, and analysis at the HFIR and the SNS. This report identified a range of crosscutting needs including the integration of data management and workflows into the neutron data life cycle, the ability to undertake real-time analysis[1], visualization of large multidimensional scientific data sets, utilizing high performance computing resources, and leveraging advances in machine learning and artificial intelligence. The plan also proposed building on existing work to enable data analysis workflows[2], which has culminated in the work described here.

In this paper, we describe Calvera[3], a platform that aims to create an ecosystem of tools and applications that will solve many of the difficulties encountered by scientists as they analyze experimental neutron scattering data. The paper is structured as follows. In Sect. 2 we present an conceptual overview of the platform. In Sect. 3 we present four science use cases that have been used to drive requirements and develop workflows. In Sect. 4 we discuss the architecture and implementation of the platform. In Sects. 5 and 6, we finish with a discussion of challenges that we still need to overcome and future work.

---

[1] Real-time in this context means within the timescale of an experiment.

[2] The Integrated Computational Environment for Modeling and Analysis (ICEMAN) project that is now deployed across multiple instruments.

[3] Calvera is an X-ray source known as 1RXS J141256.0+792204 in the ROSAT All-Sky Survey Bright Source Catalog (RASS/BSC). It lies in the constellation Ursa Minor and is one of the closest neutron stars to earth. We felt the name would provide a connection between neutron science and the astronomy-themed Galaxy project.

2 A Neutrons Data Interpretation Platform

As neutron scattering experiments become increasingly sophisticated and complex, the demand for more advanced and capable data analysis methods is rising. However, it is abundantly clear that there is no single approach to analysis that can be applied to all instruments and techniques. Instead, researchers must be given the flexibility to construct analysis workflows by trying different tools, experimenting with a variety of models, utilizing different visualization techniques, or applying novel technologies such as machine learning or data analytics. Once such a data analysis workflow has been established, it, and the accompanying data, should be easily captured and be readily available for future experiments for other researchers to use. This is necessary to enable the next generation of integrated and autonomous workflows, as well as to ensure that the scientific results are both verifiable and reproducible. This process must be amenable to scientific discovery through experimentation, but also be adaptable enough to enable new approaches to be explored as they arise. Ultimately, the results of these analysis should be available to drive new experimental directions, preferably in real-, or near real-time.

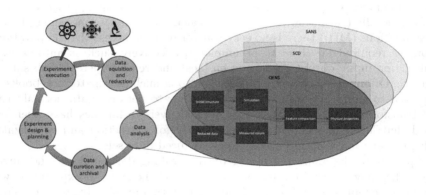

Fig. 1. Neutron scattering experiment lifecycle. Data analysis forms one part of the overall experiment lifecycle.

In the broader context, data analysis is just one part of a much larger set of activities required to undertake an experiment and deliver scientific outcomes. Others include: designing and planning the experiment; conducting the experiment; acquiring and reducing the data so that it is available for analysis; the analysis itself; and curating and archiving the results. These activities form the scientific experiment life cycle, which is sometimes referred to as a "science application". Figure 1 shows the overall neutrons experimental process and where data analysis fits into the lifecycle.

The current state of the field in data analysis for neutron scattering experiments is primarily driven by the scientific needs of the instrument users and varies greatly by technique and field of study [11]. Starting with the reduced data, scientists must rely on a variety of tools and applications that individually provide some of the capabilities they require, and hopefully, collectively all that is necessary for their analysis. Consequently, existing analysis workflows are a highly customized collection of applications, tools, and other components that are assembled into manual workflows where the user is responsible for managing data conversion and manipulation though the analysis cycle. Use of these applications must be combined with either stand-alone or integrated visualization tools (e.g. for visualizing multi-dimensional data sets, simple integration and fitting, extracting cuts and slices, etc.), and in many cases require significant expertise to correctly interpret results. Although many visualization tools are available, those used are typically also specific to the field of study or are general purpose packages that have been re-purposed for the type of visualization required. In many cases, applications are available for undertaking some analysis steps, but it may be up to the user to install these on their local resources or find pre-installed versions somewhere. These codes may be commercial, community driven, or research prototypes, each with their own unique set of issues. Some of these codes have license restrictions, may be many years old and not be well maintained, have specific operating system or other requirements, or have significant learning curves. Another problem is that even though some approaches can be useful generally (such as atomic structure calculations and/or molecular dynamics simulations (MD)) there is no easy way for users to access the computational resources required for them to be employed effectively, such as automatically transferring input/output data between local and remote systems, job submission, etc. Often interactive experimentation tools such as Jupyter notebooks are employed to gain more insight into the data or to perform data normalization and transformations. Recently, some data analysis techniques have been proposed that leverage event-based data directly for extraction and visualization tasks, rather than waiting for completely reduced data sets.

Apart from the issues pertaining to undertaking data analysis, the current approaches have other limitations. First, it is challenging to experiment with emerging technologies, such as machine learning, that are starting to be employed to undertake more sophisticated and advanced analysis. This is because users must have a deep understanding of how the technology works to integrate it into their analysis workflow. Second, manually constructed ad-hoc workflows make it very difficult to reproduce science results in a meaningful way. This is not only a problem for researchers interested in replicating published results, but also for experimental scientists wanting results that are accurate and verifiable.

Previous work we have undertaken has demonstrated that it is possible to modularize the workflow for data analysis studies for a number of neutron scattering instruments [10]. ICE-MAN provides an OClimax module to calculate the powder-averaged incoherent inelastic neutron scattering spectra (INS) of VISION and any generic direct and indirect geometry instrument from ab initio calculations, and a QClimax module that performs the general simultaneous fittings of quasi-elastic neutron scattering (QENS) data. It also showed that these components can be run effectively from docker containers orchestrated by a workflow management system that is configured and controlled via a simple user interface. Although ICE-MAN represents a step forward for neutrons data analysis, particularly for QENS, there are still a number of limitations with this approach. Demonstrating that a workflow-based modularized framework approach will be effective for creating neutron data analysis applications that will be a significant step forward in capability, however there will still be considerable work required to turn this into a generalized data analysis platform for neutron science experiments.

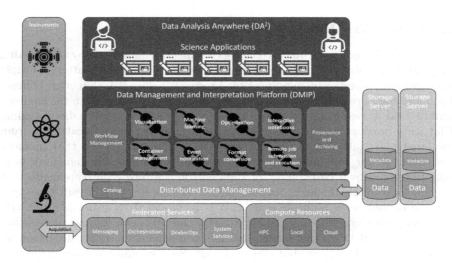

Fig. 2. Conceptual architecture for a general purpose scientific data analysis and interpretation platform. Data is acquired from instruments via a federated service using a distributed data management system (DMS). The Data Management and Interpretation Platform provides core services for managing workflows, maintaining provenance, etc. These services interact with remote computing and data resources via a virtualization layer. Users interact with web-based science applications that can be deployed using desktop or mobile devices.

We are building on this previous work to provide an extensible platform with the core functionality for creating neutron science workflows for analyzing neutron scattering data. These workflows will be deployable to researchers and users anywhere, and will provide a systemic way to employ the tools necessary to produce world class reproducible science results from reduced data. The platform is primarily responsible for integrating science workflows into a cohesive ecosystem and provides and/or exposes a number of basic services, including authentication/authorization, workflow management, provenance tracking, and distributed data management. It also utilizes a plug-in management system that will allow for the modularization of reusable components. Functionality is also provided for hosting and deploying science applications, allowing users to create and test workflows, and deploy completed workflows so they can be made available to other science users. Figure 2 shows a conceptual architecture for creating Neutron Science Applications.

3   Science Uses Cases

In this section we will present four example use cases that are being used to drive requirements and to provide initial proof-of-concept workflows for the platform.

3.1   Monte Carlo Universe (MCU)

The analysis of many neutron scattering experiments is hampered by interpreting scattering from multiple processes; especially when the neutron scatters multiple times from any number of these possible processes before it is detected. Diffraction under high pressure is an example of significant scattering from the environment around it, neutron spectroscopy measurements often require disentangling of lattice vibrations and magnetic excitations, and small angle scattering from irradiated materials is multiple scattering with different kernels that includes lead shielding, for personnel protection, around the sample. Implementation of these techniques will cover many of the neutron scattering measurements that can benefit from the inclusion of multiple scattering in the analysis. One approach to dealing with multiple scattering is to model it by using Monte Carlo Ray tracing simulations using the McStas [12] and MCViNE [8] packages to simulate the incident beam simulation and the various neutron scattering processes in the sample and its immediate environment. Such simulations have been performed [9, 13]. But the learning curve for these codes and the time of calculation has hampered broad adoption. A workflow that automates as much as possible so the user only has to concentrate on the processes in their sample and which allows compute intensive parts of the simulation to be run on large compute infrastructure, will make these tools more broadly accessible. The details of two interdependent worklflows are shown in Fig. 3.

More specifically the automated workflow shows that the Neutron Data Acquisition system is monitored for changes in incident beam condition and if a new configuration is recognized, an incident beamline simulation is launched on a gpu optimized system. The results are stored in a long-term data store that is cataloged, given a DOI and paired with the current run in the Neutron Data Catalog (OnCAT)[4]. If the incident configuration already exists, no new simulation is launched; instead only the identifier to the appropriate simulation is added to OnCAT.

For the sample simulation workflow, the user enters their sample description, an instrument name and a run number. From this information the simulation and data catalog are polled for the location of the appropriate incident beam result

---

[4] ONCAT Homepage, https://oncat.ornl.gov.

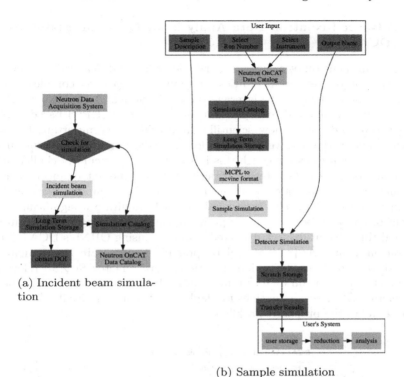

(a) Incident beam simulation

(b) Sample simulation

Fig. 3. The workflows of the overall MCU system. There are two types of workflows. The first, indicated in (a), is an automated workflow, triggered by an event on the data acquisition system, that provides a calculation for the incident beam (the neutron instrument from the source until just before the sample position) for use in the sample simulation. The second, shown in (b) is a manually launched workflow. It uses input from the users along with the output from the automated simulations to perform a sample simulation.

to load. This simulation result is then fed into the sample simulation, followed by a detector simulation for the appropriate instrument. The simulation results are in an identical format to neutron experimental data, so they will be reduced by the standard reduction software on the specified instruments [1, 4].

For understanding the instrument response for phonon and magnetic measurements usually a detailed simulation of sample shape and additional effects is not needed. In this case a resolution simulation can be helpful [7]. From a workflow perspective the resolution and the sample simulations are substantially similar, so the resolution workflow is not shown here. Nevertheless it should be noted that the codes executed in these two cases are different.

3.2   Advanced Neutron Data Analysis for Quantum Materials (DCA)

Advances in neutron scattering instrumentation and leadership computing resources promise new opportunities for solving increasingly complex scientific problems. The challenge is to leverage these advances and establish a tight link between experiments and high-performance computing (HPC) based modeling to accelerate and enable new scientific discoveries. It is important to address this challenge in the discovery process for strongly correlated quantum materials, a class of materials for which this integration is particularly challenging. In particular, for neutron scattering experiments on itinerant quantum magnets, for which we seek to understand the interaction between spin wave and continuum excitations [3]. The new capability will facilitate a significantly more efficient discovery process, where experiments are guided by theoretical input in near real time. By utilizing automated workflows using ORNL's DCA++ based neutron data analysis [2,5], it will be possible to integrate the manual steps required to predict the dynamic magnetic structure factor $S(Q,\omega)$ relevant for neutron spectroscopy on quantum materials. Machine learning will also be used to accelerate DCA++ simulations for deployment in a rapid feedback setting [6]. Figure 4 shows the proposed workflow.

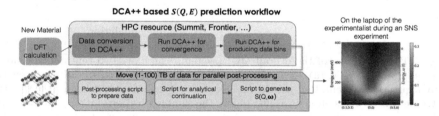

Fig. 4. Diagram of the $S(Q,\omega)$ prediction workflow. The workflow begins with a DFT calculation based on the new material of interest to build a low-energy effective model. A first DCA++ simulation is performed for convergence to self-consistency. For the problems of interest here, which require O(1000) bins of data for the four-point vertex function, a second DCA++ simulation is run to produce the binned data. The relevant observables are extracted and manipulated into a convenient form using several Python scripts. This includes the extraction of the vertex function Γ, the solution of the Bethe-Salpeter equation to generate $S(Q,\omega)$ on the imaginary frequency axis, and the analytic continuation to perform the rotation to the real frequency axis. The final product of the Python analysis is the prediction for $S(Q,\omega)$.

The ultimate goal is to allow a neutron scattering experimentalist to provide a set of very basic information, e.g., the material and the temperature for which the experiment is conducted, to launch a DCA++ simulation with automated post-processing, and receive a simulated result for $S(Q,\omega)$ that can be used for guidance on how to design the experiment and direct comparison with the experimental data. In case of discrepancies, the experimentalist will have the opportunity to revise the model by tuning basic parameters, such as the Coulomb interaction strength, to launch a new computation for improved prediction, and this process can be repeated until the model prediction matches the experiment.

3.3   Automatic Structure Refinement Platform (ASRP)

Rapidly increasing research demand for exploring material structure and its link to the performance of energy storage materials, catalysts, and functional materials, places increasing demands on neutron powder diffraction measurement and analysis. Conventional measurement-analysis workflows require humans to be heavily involved, which is error prone and quite often too time consuming to provide instantaneous feedback to the experimental loop. Automation and real-time capabilities are therefore highly desirable, in particular for the flow of data from collection to reduction, then to analysis, and finally visualization. Real-time data collection and reduction functionalities have already been developed and widely deployed on most of the diffractometers at SNS and HFIR. However, such a capability is not yet well developed to include analysis and visualization. There is an opportunity to establish an automatic measurement-reduction-analysis workflow, applying methods that include both heuristic and machine-learning methods. This will enable a live data analysis capability, and provide end-users with prompt and visible feedback. Figure 5 shows an example of this workflow.

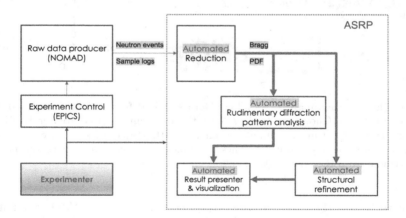

Fig. 5. Workflow diagram for automated structural refinement. Raw neutron events obtained from the NOMAD instrument are automatically reduced using live data reduction. This data is then used to perform either a diffraction pattern matching analysis or a structural refinement using Rietveld or PDF refinement using the GSAS-II and diffpy-cmi backends. Results will then be presented for interpretation and visualization.

3.4   Quasielastic Neutron Scattering (QClimax)

Quasi-elastic neutron scattering (QENS) data analysis consists of minimizing the difference between theoretical models of a QENS signal convoluted with the resolution function and the experimental spectra at each value of Q. The fitted parameters are then analyzed as a function of Q, and further fitting is required to interpret the model. The QClimax module can do global fitting procedures that minimize all data, including functional dependence of Q for some or all the parameters. The models used in the fitting of the Q dependence of the individual parameters in the global fitting of QENS data varies for samples and conditions. Hence, it is necessary to allow the users to write new functionality to customize the fitting for their own problems. The QClimax module makes it straightforward for users to add these functions if desired. Currently, QClimax is the only QENS analysis tool combining these capabilities, and it is being used to analyze BASIS data and CNCS. Figure 6 shows the workflow for QENS fitting analysis. QClimax also allows the sharing of all the information necessary to completely reproduce the calculation, making collaboration between team members more effective.

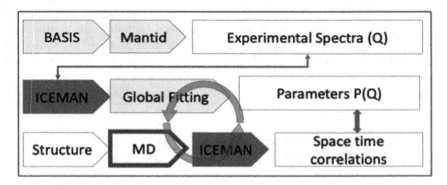

Fig. 6. QENS fitting analysis workflow. Data acquired from BASIS is reduced using Mantid. QClimax (shown as ICEMAN in the diagram) is used to iteratively perform global fitting using the input parameters. MD trajectories are used to extract parameters for localized diffusion. These parameters are compared with the parameters extracte from the QENS fittings.

There is also the need to integrate molecular dynamics (MD) simulations into QENS data analysis both for liquids and confined fluids. A workflow to use MD trajectories to extract parameters for localized diffusion in heterogeneous systems is in development. These parameters extracted from using these methods will be compared with the parameters extracted from QENS fittings. These parameters, determined from the models can be use to feedback into global fitting routines.

4 Architecture and Implementation

Although the workflows outlined in the previous section provide a good indication of the type of analysis that will be required, we are cognizant of the fact that there are over 30 different instruments, each with a very unique set of requirements for analyzing data. Many of these techniques are still being formulated, and are not currently well defined. As a result, we believed that it was important that NDIP be the core of an *ecosystem* that would enable scientists and developers to experiment with and create workflows that suited their specific requirements. This implies that NDIP must enable the development of workflows in addition to the execution of these workflows. It was also clear that many of these workflows would not be executing on a single resource, but would entail execution across a distributed range of resources, including high performance computing (HPC), virtual machines running on cloud infrastructure, and local computational resources. Using this information, we developed the architecture shown in Fig. 7.

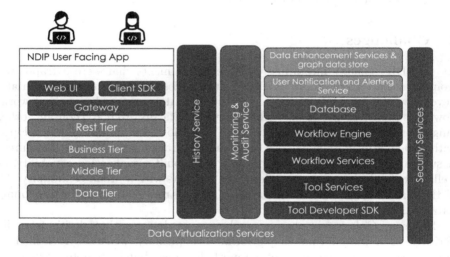

Fig. 7. Architectural design of the NDIP. On the left are the user facing components, including a web and programmatic interfaces mediated by a gateway. A tiered model is used to ensure that concerns are clearly separated. Key services depicted in the middle are the history service which is essential for provenance and reproducibility, while a monitoring and audit service ensures that users receive expedited feedback relating to the operation of the platform (via the user notification and alerting service). On the right are a range of key platform services. Security is an inherent feature of the architecture, not only for authentication, but also authorization relating to workflow execution and data access. The resource and data virtualization services mediate access to remote systems for job orchestration and data management.

Since developing an implementation of this architecture would be a massive undertaking, our approach has been to utilize existing open source technology wherever possible. No existing system will meet every requirement, however, adopting an existing platform would allow us to concentrate our development efforts on the gaps, rather than developing infrastructure that already exists in one form or another. To choose a system that most closely aligned with our needs, we developed a set of assessment criteria that could be used to evaluate existing workflow platforms in order to identify potential candidates for the NDIP. These criteria are outlined in Appendix A. Using these criteria, we assessed 34 different workflow systems, primarily derived from the WorkflowsRI community[5]. The list of workflow systems we evaluated is shown in Appendix B. Of these, we were able to immediately exclude a number that had not been updated in considerable time and were clearly inactive. We were also able to rule out a number that did not meet required criteria (e.g. no web-based GUI) Of the remaining systems, Galaxy[6] was the clear winner. However, although Galaxy met most of the assessment criteria, it still had some deficiencies, particularly in the areas of authentication/authorization and remote workflow execution. Additionally, until we had inspected the code base and understood the design principles, we still considered Galaxy to be an exploratory choice.

5 Challenges

As an NDIP, Galaxy meets many of the requirements that were extrapolated from the science use cases. In particular, it provides the ability to experimentally develop workflows while preserving a history of data manipulations and workflow executions. It also is accessible programmatically from Python and other languages, as well as Jupyter notebooks. This allows workflows to be developed within the platform, then deployed as stand-alone automated services if required. It supports a plethora of data types and has inbuilt visualization capability, as well as the ability to share workflows and datasets with a broad community. All of these features are important for creating a vibrant ecosystem for developing data analysis workflows.

However, Galaxy also has a number of weaknesses that derive from its heritage as a bio-informatics platform. The primary weakness identified in our assessment is the lack of support for distributed remote workflows, including remote job orchestration, remote data handling, and authentication/authorization issues. We will consider each of these in more detail here.

5.1 Remote Job Orchestration

Galaxy has a modular, extensible architecture that allows the addition of functions to execute jobs on remote platforms. This can be done either directly through *job runners* that connect to container orchestration services, such as

---

[5] https://workflowsri.org.
[6] https://galaxyproject.org.

kubernetes, or directly to a variety of job schedulers including PBS[7], Slurm[8], Chronos[9], or using the Distributed Resource Management Application API (DRMAA)[10]. However all these approaches require a shared filesystem between the Galaxy server and the remote computational resource. To address this limitation, a companion project, called Pulsar[11], has been developed by the Galaxy community which provides a general purpose mechanism for executing jobs on remote systems and handles transferring the input and output datasets between Galaxy and the remote resource. While this approach may be sufficient for bioinformatics applications, it suffers from scalability issues as well as performance limitations when large datasets must be transferred. Additionally, none of these approaches address the security issues related to accessing and authenticating remote resources. Rather, they rely on configuring server level access, via certificates or other techniques, which is not suitable for all environments (including ours).

5.2   Remote Data Handling

As mentioned above, Galaxy's existing remote execution mechanisms assume either a shared filesystem between the Galaxy server and the remote resource, or data is transferred to the resource prior to, and after, execution of a workflow step using Pulsar. A further complication is that in both these cases, Galaxy assumes data that is used or generated by a workflow step resides in a locally attached filesystem (which could be a shared filesystem). The platform maintains an object data store that records the location of the data along with other metadata relating to the datasets. This is a fairly significant limitation that needs to be overcome if Galaxy is going to be able to integrate with an external data management system (DMS).

5.3   Authentication/Authorization

Galaxy currently takes a fairly simplistic approach to authentication and authorization. For user management, the default is to maintain an internal database of users that is independent of any other services. It is possible to configure Galaxy to integrate with the Lightweight Directory Access Protocol (LDAP) or OpenID Connect (OIDC) so that users are authenticated using an external service. However this capability is not extended to workflow execution or data handling. This means that it is not possible for a remote resource to know the identity of the individual requesting access, nor is it possible to use this information for authorization purposes (e.g. to allow access to certain data files). Additionally, many institutions employ strong authentication practices, such as two factor authentication for accessing high profile or secure resources. Without fully integrated

---

[7] https://www.openpbs.org.

[8] https://slurm.schedmd.com.

[9] https://mesos.github.io/chronos/.

[10] https://www.drmaa.org.

[11] https://pulsar.readthedocs.io/en/latest/.

security services, it is not possible to execute autonomous workflows in this kind of environment. Again, this is a fairly significant limitation to using Galaxy in distributed computing environments that employ multiple security domains for accessing HPC resources.

6   Current and Future Work

We have developed a prototype solution to the issues outlined in the previous section. Our approach is to utilize the existing Pulsar-based remote execution approach, however we have modified Galaxy and Pulsar in a number of ways to better support distributed workflows. First, we have added support for the concept of *remote data*, which is data that is managed by an external DMS. Using Galaxy metadata, we maintain information about the dataset so that it can be manipulated (e.g. passed as an input to a tool, recorded in the history, etc.) withing the Galaxy platform as if it were local. However, accessing the data contained within the dataset triggers a call to an external DMS to fetch the contents. Additionally, Pulsar has been modified so that when it receives a remote data item, it will request the data contents via the DMS prior to invoking the tool. Once the tool has executed, any output data is handed to the DMS and only the metadata associated with the output passed back to Galaxy. To avoid a dependency on any particular DMS, we have implemented a remote data broker service that provides an abstraction layer between Galaxy, Pulsar, and the actual DMS.

In addition, we have implemented an authentication and authorization scheme that employs OIDC access tokens to provide user-level authorization for all remote operations. Once the user authenticates to Galaxy, we obtain an access token using the normal OIDC authentication flow. This access token can then be passed to the DMS or via Pulsar to the remote computational resource. Using this approach, we have implemented an OIDC Pluggable Authentication Module (PAM)[12] that enables Pulsar to execute shell commands as a specific user on a target system without requiring any special privileges or service accounts.

Figure 8 shows our current prototype implementation. We are planning to work with the Galaxy community to incorporate our solution (or an equivalent solution driven by the community) into the Galaxy code base. We are also continuing to implement demonstration workflows for the science use cases discussed previously. This will include the integration of neutrons-specific data manipulation and visualization tools (currently most data is stored in NeXus formatted HDF5 files[13]) as well as the ability to automate workflows based on certain input requirements (e.g. the acquisition of instrument data). We are also working with the neutrons community to better understand additional tools and features that would improve their ability to undertake analysis of neutron scattering data.

---

[12] https://pubs.opengroup.org/onlinepubs/8329799/toc.pdf.
[13] https://www.nexusformat.org.

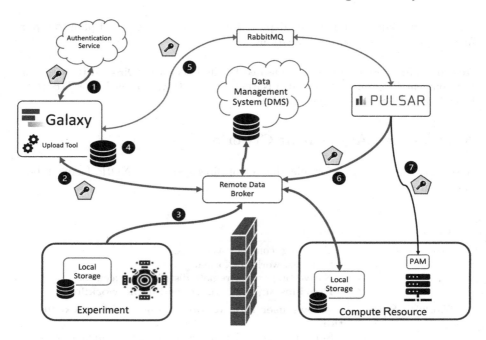

Fig. 8. The NDIP solution to remote job execution and data management using the Galaxy and Pulsar frameworks. At step 1, the user authenticates with an authentication service and obtains an access token. At step 2, the user initiates an upload using a new Galaxy upload tool and an access token is passed to the remote data broker which uploads the data to the DMS. Upon completion, at step 4, metadata about the remote data is saved in Galaxy's local storage. At step 5, the user initiates a remote workflow execution and passes the access token to Pulsar. At step 6, the access token is passed to the remote data broker along with a request to download the file to the compute resource. When this has completed, at step 7, Pulsar passes the access token to the PAM on the compute resource which executes a command using the user's credentials. On completion of the command, Pulsar request the remote data broker upload the result to the DMS and passes metadata about the output data back to Galaxy.

7   Conclusion

We have developed an architecture for a Neutrons Data Interpretation Platform that will form the central core of an ecosystem for data analysis workflows for neutrons scattering experiments. Using four science use cases to drive requirements gathering and architecture design, we chose Galaxy, an existing bio-informatics platform with a large user and developer base, as an initial candidate after an extensive analysis of existing workflow management systems. Recent work has culminated in a prototype that addresses some of the deficiencies in Galaxy and demonstrated managed workflows in a distributed remote computing and data environment that simulates the physical resources and security architecture available at ORNL. We are currently translating the science use

152   G. R. Watson et al.

cases into workflows that will be deployed using this platform and plan to report
further progress in future publications.

Acknowledgements. Research sponsored by the Laboratory Directed Research and
Development Program of Oak Ridge National Laboratory, managed by UT-Battelle,
LLC, for the U. S. Department of Energy.

A   Platform Assessment Criteria

Assessment criteria used for selecting a workflow system for NDIP. Items in bold
are required.

Category	Criteria
Workflows	– Type (e.g. control/data based) – Standard workflow format – Native support for remote distributed execution – **Provides support for reproducible workflows**
Workflow Steps	– **Allows user interaction during workflow execution** – Supports interactive and non-interactive Jupyter notebooks as workflow steps – **Workflow steps can be containerized** – Automatic dependency resolution for workflow step execution
User Interface	– Auto creation of workflow user interface – **Web-based GUI for developing and executing workflows** – **Programmatic (Python or REST) API for controlling workflow operation** – Supports different kinds of data visualization within the user interface
Architecture	– Modular architecture – Pluggable services – **Extensible components (including user interface)** – Utilizes an integrated database
Data Management	– Supports large number of built-in data types – Can add new data types – Supports remote data management (i.e. via a data management service outside the platform) – **Maintains a history of all data manipulation during workflow execution**

Category	Criteria
Reproducibility	– Maintains a history of all data manipulation during workflow execution – **Maintains a history of workflow execution** – Enforces reproducibility of workflow execution
Collaboration	– **Allows workflows to be easily shared and extended by other users** – Allows datasets to be shared
Security	– **Allows integration with external authentication services** – Enables authentication/authorization services to be used for workflow execution and data management
Community	– **Has large and active user and developer communities** – Provides comprehensive training resources – Provides documentation covering use and development

B Evaluated Workflow Systems

- AiiDA
- Apache Airflow
- ASKALON
- Cheeta
- COMPSs
- DAGman
- Dask
- Dispel4Py
- FireWorks
- Galaxy
- iDDS
- Kepler
- Makeflow
- Merlin
- Mflow
- Nextflow
- Pachyderm
- Panda
- Pegasus
- Prefect
- RADICAL
- Savanna
- SciCumulus/C2
- Snakemake
- Swift/K
- Swift/T
- Taverna
- Tigres
- Triana
- VisTrails
- WFCommons
- Workqueue
- YAWL
- YesWorkflow

References

1. Arnold, O., et al.: Mantid-Data analysis and visualization package for neutron scattering and μ SR experiments. Nucl. Instrum. Methods Phys. Res. Sect. A **764**, 156–166 (2014)
2. Balduzzi, G., et al.: Accelerating DCA++ (dynamical cluster approximation) scientific application on the summit supercomputer, pp. 433–444 (2019). https://doi.org/10.1109/PACT.2019.00041
3. Do, S.H., et al.: Damped Dirac magnon in the metallic kagome antiferromagnet FeSn (2022)
4. Heller, W.T., et al.: drtsans: the data reduction toolkit for small-angle neutron scattering at Oak Ridge National Laboratory. SoftwareX **19**, 101101 (2022)

5. Hähner, U.R., et al.: DCA++: a software framework to solve correlated electron problems with modern quantum cluster methods. Comput. Phys. Commun. **246**, 106709 (2020). https://doi.org/10.1016/j.cpc.2019.01.006

6. Li, Y., Doak, P., Balduzzi, G., Elwasif, W., D'Azevedo, E., Maier, T.: Machine-learning accelerated studies of materials with high performance and edge computing. In: Nichols, J., et al. (eds.) SMC 2021. CCIS, vol. 1512, pp. 190–205. Springer, Cham (2022). https://doi.org/10.1007/978-3-030-96498-6_11

7. Lin, J.Y.Y., Sala, G., Stone, M.B.: A super-resolution technique to analyze single-crystal inelastic neutron scattering measurements using direct-geometry chopper spectrometers. Rev. Sci. Instrum. **93**(2), 025101 (2022)

8. Lin, J.Y., et al.: MCViNE-an object oriented Monte Carlo neutron ray tracing simulation package. Nucl. Instrum. Methods Phys. Res. Sect. A **810**, 86–99 (2016)

9. Lin, J., Aczel, A.A., Abernathy, D.L., Nagler, S.E., Buyers, W., Granroth, G.E.: Using Monte Carlo ray tracing simulations to model the quantum harmonic oscillator modes observed in uranium nitride. Phys. Rev. B **89**(14), 144302 (2014)

10. Mamontov, E., Smith, R., Billings, J., Ramirez-Cuesta, A.: Simple analytical model for fitting QENS data from liquids. Phys. B **566**, 50–54 (2019). https://doi.org/10.1016/j.physb.2019.01.051

11. U.S. Department of Energy, Office of Basic Energy Sciences: Handling, and Analysis at the High Flux Isotope Reactor and the Spallation Neutron Source (2019)

12. Willendrup, P.K., Lefmann, K.: McStas (i): introduction, use, and basic principles for ray-tracing simulations. J. Neutron Res. **22**(1), 1–16 (2020)

13. Yiu, Y., et al.: Light atom quantum oscillations in UC and US. Phys. Rev. B **93**(1), 014306 (2016)

Virtual Infrastructure Twins: Software Testing Platforms for Computing-Instrument Ecosystems

Nageswara S. V. Rao[✉], Anees Al-Najjar, Helia Zandi, Ramanan Sankaran, Susan Hicks, Kevin Roccapriori, and Debangshu Mukherjee

Oak Ridge National Laboratory, Oak Ridge, TN, USA
{raons,alnajjarm,zandih,sankaranr,hicksse,roccapriorkm,
mukherjeed}@ornl.gov

Abstract. Science ecosystems are being built by federating computing systems and instruments located at geographically distributed sites over wide-area networks. These computing-instrument ecosystems are expected to support complex workflows that incorporate remote, automated AI-driven science experiments. Their realization, however, requires various designs to be explored and software components to be developed, in order to support the orchestration of distributed computations and experiments. It is often too expensive, infeasible, or disruptive for the entire ecosystem to be available during the typically long software development and testing periods. We propose a Virtual Infrastructure Twin (VIT) of the ecosystem that emulates its network and computing components, and incorporates its instrument software simulators. It provides a software environment nearly identical to the ecosystem to support early development and testing, and design space exploration. We present a brief overview of previous digital infrastructure twins that culminated in the VIT concept, including (i) the virtual science network environment for developing software-defined networking solutions, and (ii) the virtual federated science instrument environment for testing the federation software stack and remote instrument control software. We briefly describe VITs for Nion microscope steering and access to GPU systems.

1 Introduction

The next generation science workflows are expected to be supported by ecosystems of science "instruments" that range from physical systems, such as neutron and light

This research is sponsored in part by the INTERSECT Initiative as part of the Laboratory Directed Research and Development Program and in part by RAMSES project of Advanced Scientific Computing Research program, and is performed at Oak Ridge National Laboratory managed by UT-Battelle, LLC for U.S. Department of Energy under Contract No. DE-AC05-00OR22725. The United States Government retains and the publisher, by accepting the article for publication, acknowledges that the United States Government retains a nonexclusive, paid-up, irrevocable, world-wide license to publish or reproduce the published form of this manuscript, or allow others to do so, for United States Government purposes. The Department of Energy will provide public access to these results of federally sponsored research in accordance with the DOE Public Access Plan (http://energy.gov/downloads/doe-public-access-plan).

K. Doug et al. (Eds.): SMC 2022, CCIS 1690, pp. 155–172, 2022.
https://doi.org/10.1007/978-3-031-23606-8_10

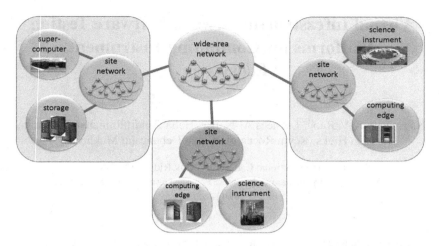

Fig. 1. Science ecosystem with computing and instrument facility sites connected over a wide-area network.

sources and microscopes, to computing platforms that execute exascale computations for the simulation and analysis of complex phenomena, as illustrated in Fig. 1. These computing-instrument ecosystems are currently under various stages of development, ranging from new designs to incremental software and hardware enhancements to current infrastructures. In these ecosystems, the computing platforms and experimental facilities are typically located at geographically distributed sites that are connected over multi-domain, wide-area networks. In several cases, these computing systems may be heterogeneous, and span the spectrum of edge, core and cloud computing platforms spread across the ecosystem. Combined with remote, automated Artificial Intelligence (AI) driven science experiments, they promise scientific discovery at unprecedented scale and scope.

Realizing the promise of these science ecosystems, however, requires overcoming multiple challenges, some of which are quite unlike in pure computing ecosystems, namely, with no physical instrument access and control. They arise from the need to explore and assess new designs, and develop and test software components to orchestrate distributed computations and physical experiments. It is often ineffective to require the access to expensive instruments, for example, neutron beam lines, for the entire software development and testing period. In particular, several science instruments, such as microscopes, are operated by single-user Windows control computers, and their dedicated use for software development potentially makes the instrument unavailable. In some cases, the ecosystems may simply be not available while new designs are being conceived and new ecosystems are being built. To address some of these challenges related to software development and testing, we propose a Virtual Infrastructure Twin (VIT) that emulates the network and computing parts of the ecosystem, and incorporates the instrument simulation software. It provides a software environment nearly identical to that of the ecosystem, which makes it suitable for software development, testing, and design space exploration. A VIT is implemented using mininet [21] to closely match the ecosystem's computing hosts and networks, and is packaged as python code or Virtual Machine (VM) to run on different computing hosts, which could be external or indigenous to the ecosystem.

The VIT concept is a refinement of the infrastructure digital twins [17] that have been used for supporting several design and development tasks of networked ecosystems. The Virtual Science Network Environment (VSNE) [24] has been developed to support the development of Software-Defined Networking (SDN) controller codes, while mitigating the potential disruptions to operational networks. Similar considerations arise in developing codes that utilize instruments, such as neutron beam line sensors, in limiting their access and exposure to early developmental codes. The Virtual Federated Science Instrument Environment (VFSIE) [16] is developed for testing the federation software stack and to provide a proof-of-principle demonstration of remote instrument control using the Experimental Physics and Industrial Control System (EPICS) [4]. A generalization of these approaches led to the VIT concept, which is described in this paper along with brief accounts of its predecessor and current implementations. We briefly describe a VIT that enabled us to develop and deploy a steering capability for Scanning Transmission Electron Microscopes (STEM) [15], and to utilize the computing platform of the ecosystem to smoothly transition the codes into operations during various development stages [31]. Due to the computational limitations of a host running the VIT, some performance measurements could be inaccurate, and we briefly describe Machine Learning (ML) methods [30] for accurate throughput profile estimation from imprecise VIT measurements of high-bandwidth data transfers.

The organization of this paper is as follows. A brief description of science workflows is provided in Sect. 2. The VIT concept is described in Sect. 3. VIT implementations and case studies are briefly summarized in Sect. 4; VSNE, VFSIE and STEM VIT are described in Sects. 4.1, 4.2 and 4.3, respectively. Extensions and limitations of VITs are described in Sect. 5.

2   Science Ecosystems

Empowered by increasingly heterogeneous and powerful computing systems at the edge, core and cloud, the science workflows are poised to become more sophisticated and solve computational problems at unprecedented scope and scale. In particular, the proliferation of AI methods enables remotely controlled and automated experiments over ecosystems of physical instruments and computing systems. Often, these resources are located at geographically dispersed sites, and need to be federated over wide-area networks to seamlessly support these workflows. The underlying tasks may involve configuring instruments, collecting and transferring measurements and analyzing them; their resultant computational results may provide parameters for the next round of remote experiments. Currently, these tasks are manually orchestrated, which may have to be repeated with different parameters for extended periods of time during the course of a complex science workflow. Such human-driven processes may limit the execution tempo of the science workflow, possibly leading to inefficient utilization of expensive resources. An automated orchestration of portions of these workflows assisted by AI methods has the potential to significantly improve the execution effectiveness of these workflows, by overcoming some of the human operator limitations.

2.1 Science Workflow Scenarios

Science workflows are composed to utilize complex computing and instrument applications in various disciplines, such as biology, astronomy, environmental science, materials science, nuclear science, and others [11]. They enable scientists to execute codes on remote systems, obtain data from instruments or databases, process the data, and run data analysis codes [28]. These workflows need to be effectively supported by the underlying ecosystems to meet the requirements typified in the following scenarios.

- *Responsive Computations*: Measurements generated by an instrument are often transported to a remote computing system for analysis to be completed within certain time period. In a cosmology scenario, the images generated by the Palomar Transient Factory (PTF) [22] survey are processed by a near-real-time computational code at a remote national laboratory to identify optical transients within minutes of images being collected. Similarly, in a material science scenario, to facilitate near-real-time analysis of organic photovoltaics (OPV) using x-ray scattering, the data generated at Lawrence Berkeley National Laboratory's (LBNL) Advanced Light Source (ALS) is moved to Oak Ridge National Laboratory (ORNL) to use its computational capability to run the analysis tool HipGISAXS [12].
- *Dynamic Monitoring and Feedback*: Data generated from a running computation or an experiment in progress at a physical instrument often needs to be dynamically monitored at the edge or streamed to remote facilities. Analyses of data sets as they are generated are critical to direct the next configuration of simulation or experiment at various facilities [11], including ALS, Spallation Neutron Source (SNS), Advanced Microscopy Laboratory (AML) at ORNL, and others.

An illustrative workflow example is the tomography based on neutron imaging, for example, using spallation neutrons and pressure diffractometer [34] at SNS, or neutron imaging facility [18] at High Flux Isotope Reactor (HFIR) at ORNL. The tomography codes use multiple images collected at these facilities for reconstruction, which requires the computational power available at remote computing resources. Since the neutron beam time to collect the images is expensive at either facility, the goal of the ecosystem is to provide access to both computing platforms and experimental facilities so that scientific team may make informed decisions for their use [25]. For example, for 3D Computed Tomography (CT) of kinetics, scans lasting under an hour have low signal-to-noise, and the reconstruction using them requires tens of scans and advanced iterative reconstruction. The scientists often pre-stage software on SNS computing systems prior to the allocated beam line time to effectively organize the workflow. The workflow involves visualization of analyses results and selection of parameters for next scans, and currently, Jupyter notebooks are used for both post-processing and visualization [19].

The ecosystems may be established in various ways to support the science workflows typified in these scenarios. For example, HFIR workflow computations specific to the instrument can be executed on a pool of computing platforms distributed across the ecosystem, some located at the edge. Operationally, these codes can be bundled into containers that can process the data streamed to hosts; for example, Jupyter notebooks may be packaged into containers and deployed on several ecosystem computing nodes [25]. Such ecosystem designs and configurations need to be developed and assessed to effectively support the workflows, and some of these tasks are accomplished using VFSIE [13] without requiring beam line allocations.

2.2 Network Capabilities

Various local, wide-area and storage networks that connect the computing and instrument systems of these ecosystems play a critical role in determining the effectiveness of workflows, which may be orchestrated manually or assisted by AI methods. They become particularly important for automated, AI-driven parts of the workflow, due to the need to sustain the tempo of automated codes. These workflows require network transfers for measurement collections, code containers migration, and control operations of instruments across the ecosystem possibly over wide-area networks. Currently, custom-designed science network connections are typically composed and configured by teams of experts. For example, Local Area network (LAN) and wide-Area Network (WAN) connections are set up by network engineers, and dedicated I/O resources and host systems are configured by systems administrators. Recent developments in SDN and related technologies [20, 23] hold an enormous promise in developing fast automatic provisioning of the underlying network paths. However, the testing of new components of workflows, such as XDD optimized for Lustre and custom Red5 streaming apps for science, requires multi-site networked infrastructure, and VSNE [24] provides an alternative development environment for significant portions of them.

The science workflows represent a different set of challenges from the data center and cloud environments where several current SDN technologies are being developed. More generally, a predominant feature of scientific ecosystems is the small number of computing and instrument systems located at known sites, which often require dedicated, precision data flows over multi-domain networks. General principles of VITs for science ecosystems and the custom implementations using mininet to emulate site hosts and networks, with additional support for instrument access and control, are described in the next two sections.

3 VIT Concept and Implementation

A VIT is a type of digital twin [32, 33] specifically designed to emulate the infrastructure of a science ecosystem to support the tasks of software development, testing, early design evaluations, and phased transitioning of solutions to deployment. Its design, implementation and packaging are guided by the following considerations.

(a) *Emulated Ecosystem:* VIT of a science ecosystem emulates its computing hosts and instruments, and also the local and wide-area networks that connect them. It provides a software environment nearly identical to the ecosystem by executing the same software as its hosts on their emulated counterparts, and utilizing the instrument simulators and system software; for example, Nion Swift STEM software [8] runs natively, EPICS areaDetector emulator [2] runs as a container, and Lustre file system run as a VM [24].

(b) *Purpose of VIT:* A VIT may be designed for specific purposes including: development of software modules; early evaluation of designs of future, current and alternative ecosystems; performance studies of software; and support for transition to deployment of software modules from early stages to final products. Its focus is primarily on the software development and functionality testing from an ecosystem perspective, which does not necessarily include aspects such as high fidelity replication of instrument physics.

(c) *VIT Functionality and Platform:* The purpose of science workflows executed on the ecosystem determines the overall functionality of its VIT, which in turn determines the software components and the platforms to support their development, testing and deployment. For example, STEM workflows require the Swift software and Pyro libraries to support the development of steering software modules [15].

(d) *Usage and Execution Mode:* A VIT may be executed on an external or indigenous host of an ecosystem, which may be running Windows, Mac or flavors of Linux OS. It may be executed as a portable VM, or natively on a selected Linux distributions such as Ubuntu. A VIT on an external host is typically used for functionality testing and early software development, and that on an ecosystem host makes it easier to transition the tested codes to the deployment; more details of these options are provided in Sect. 5.

A VIT emulates an ecosystem using virtual hosts (vhosts) that represent computing systems that execute scientific and other software, emulators and/or simulators of physical instruments, and virtual routers, switches and links for local and wide area networks. It is implemented using mininet [21] which runs as python code either natively or within a VM on a host. The vhosts inherit the user-/kernel-space computing environment of its host, which enables the software to be developed and executed on either. The network switches and routers are emulated and connected over virtual links that reflect the physical network infrastructure links. The latencies of the emulated links reflect the ecosystem connections. The instrument emulator codes can be executed on vhosts (for example, Nion Swift STEM simulator) or attached as containers, such as EPICS areaDetector software, using the containernet extension of mininet.

There is no obvious unified framework for developing various VITs. In fact, different tools, in addition to mininet, may be used for building VITs, such as containernet [27], miniNExT [6], MaxiNet [7], hypervisor-based Virtual Machines (VMs) packaged solutions, or solutions based on native Linux virtual function tools for creating processes [1], managing their namespaces and resources [5,9], and connecting them via virtual Ethernet link [10].

Some important VITs emulate the ecosystems of U.S. Department of Energy (DOE) national laboratories, and we consider three case studies involving four national laboratories in different configurations for VSNE, VFSIE and STEM VIT in the next section. Once VIT-based solutions are suitably tested, they are ready to be field-deployed and integrated into physical infrastructure, often with minimal porting requirements.

4   Implementations and Case Studies

We now consider VITs (or precursors) for specific science ecosystems that meet the requirements of software-defined networking solutions, testing of federation software

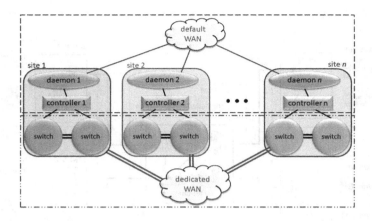

Fig. 2. VSNE framework of interconnected site daemons.

stack and remote instrument control, and steering of Nion STEM and access to GPU systems.

4.1   VSNE: Multi-VM for Software Defined Networking

The large data transfers and remote monitoring, streaming, and steering operations of science workflows require dedicated high-capacity, low-latency, and low-jitter network connections during specified periods. These connections typically span both site LAN segments and WAN connections over a dedicated high-capacity network infrastructure for data flows, as well as a persistent shared network among these sites for control traffic. These dedicated connections are typically provisioned manually by site and WAN operators, with lead times of days or longer, and the SDN technologies [20, 35] enable their automatic provisioning within seconds. The development and testing of the needed networking software and an assessment of its impacts often require installation and evaluation of untested technologies. Specifically, early developmental SDN codes can be disruptive since they can degrade the network, and in extreme cases, can flood or even crash significant portions of the network. To mitigate such effects, the VSNE emulates the host, storage, and network infrastructure of multiple sites using VMs [24]. A site is represented by a VM, wherein the hosts and LANs are emulated using Mininet, and SDN controllers and site service daemons are executed natively to support dynamic provisioning of network connections. In addition, Lustre filesystems are supported at these sites using a server VM, and the long-haul network connections are emulated using Mininet on WAN VM. Application software for tasks such as file transfer, streaming, and experiment steering, can be installed on VMs and made available to all emulated site hosts.

The SDN solution is implemented using a set of site-service daemons that provide connectivity among the sites over default IP network [24]. These daemons provide persistent connectivity among themselves and also with the local site-controllers, switches, and users, as shown in Fig. 2. A local site-service daemon receives connection requests

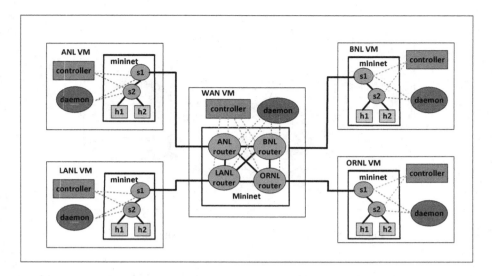

Fig. 3. VSNE of ecosystem of four sites and their LANs and WAN connections.

from its local users, automated workflow agents, or remote site-service daemons. In response, they utilize custom scripts to set up or tear down connections within the site, and generate and communicate path requests to WAN and remote site-service daemons.

A VSNE for an ecosystem that spans four DOE national laboratories, Argonne National Laboratory (ANL), Brookhaven National Laboratory (BNL), Los Alamos National Laboratory (LANL), and ORNL is shown in Fig. 3. It uses VMs, four representing the sites, ANL, BNL, LANL and ORNL, and a fifth VM emulating the dedicated ESnet [3] WAN connections among these sites. An additional VM implements the Lustre file system mounted at all four sites. Mininet [21] is used to create custom parameterized topologies on site and WAN VMs using Python code. Two vhosts $h1$ and $h2$ are connected to a virtual switch $s2$; then, another "gateway" switch $s1$ connects $s2$ to outside. Both $s1$ and $s2$ are Open vSwitches whose flows are dynamically orchestrated. Also on a site VM, a SDN controller and a site-service daemon are shown, where the latter communicates control-plane messages with other sites. Furthermore, Open vSwitches of WAN VM are used to emulate the circuits (similar to those in OSCARS [26]) among the sites, and their latency reflects the long-haul physical links. A web2py-based web service stack is integrated into the site-service daemon framework to enable the user to enter data path via client web interface.

4.2   VFSIE: VM for Federation Stack

VFSIE emulates an ecosystem of sites with computing systems and physical instruments connected over WAN, using the architecture design shown in Fig. 4. It is implemented using containernet [27] running on Ubuntu Linux. Each site consists of multiple computing resources and scientific instruments possibly located at different site facilities and connected over their individual LANs. The computing resources are emulated

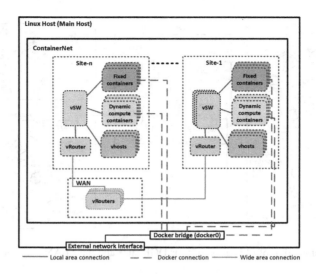

Fig. 4. VFSIE federation infrastructure design.

using vhosts that execute scientific and software stack codes, and docker containers that provide a specific service or application. The docker containers could be *fixed* to provide a service of federation stack, scientific application, or simulated instrument, which are built as part of the ecosystem. The architecture also supports *dynamic compute containers* that provide microservices the science user can execute *dynamically* without restarting VFSIE, unlike fixed containers. The dynamic compute containers are run on vhosts as needed after VFSIE is initialized. Various systems of a site facility are connected over a segmented network, which is implemented as a LAN connecting its vhosts and docker containers using virtual switches (vSW). These switches are connected to site virtual routers (vRouters), which are in turn interconnected to their peers at other sites over the emulated WAN. The routers are emulated as vhosts using *ipv4 forwarding* rules and static routing table entries that reflect WAN connectivity of the ecosystem.

A VFSIE of four DOE laboratory sites, ANL, BNL, ORNL and National Energy Research Scientific Computing Center (NERSC), which are connected over network provider ESnet, is shown in Fig. 5. This ecosystem contains multiple computing facilities, such as OLCF at ORNL and ALCF at ANL, and science target facilities, Advanced Photon Source (APS) at ANL and SNS at ORNL. These facilities are emulated using vhosts, denoted by COMP, and Docker containers, for executing the federation software stack and scientific codes as part of the science workflows. For instance, the federated facilities of APS and SNS provide access to workflow codes, including Jupyter notebooks packaged as containers, such as iMars3D [19], and to EPICS [2] control toolkit which is utilized for reconstruction measurements and for neutron/photon beamline positioning of subjects. They also provide Federation Science Analytic containers (FSA) for infrastructure performance analysis and Federation Site Repo (FdSR) as local repositories for storing local science users' codes and applications. Further details of

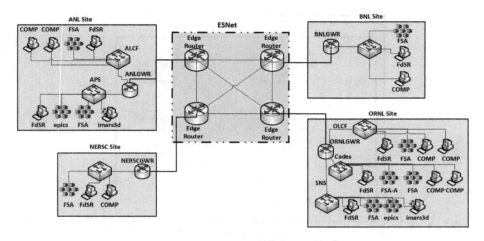

Fig. 5. VFSIE emulation of federation of four DOE sites and their LANs and the WAN connections.

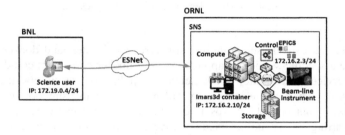

Fig. 6. A workflow demonstration using VFSIE for a science user at BNL remotely accesses beam-line instruments at SNS/ORNL.

VFSIE and a workflow demonstration of data reconstruction using measurements are provided in [14] and [13], respectively.

The VFSIE supports remote access to science instruments via EPICS and to Jupyter Notebooks running in containers at various hosts across the ecosystem. A use case scenario is demonstrated wherein a science user at BNL remotely access and controls science instruments at SNS for image reconstruction using measurements collected at neutron beam line. For this purpose, the user first remotely accesses the area detector simulator implemented and packaged as EPICS toolkit container [2] and then remotely accesses iMars3D container that includes reconstruction codes accessed via Jupyter notebook, as illustrated in Fig. 6. The BNL science user remotely accesses EPICS simulator at SNS to set the configurations, including the area detector variables, as shown in Fig. 14(c). Once the measurements are collected, the user runs the construction codes available at iMars3D container, and the remote access to that container is depicted in Fig. 14(e). Further details of this demonstration are available in [13].

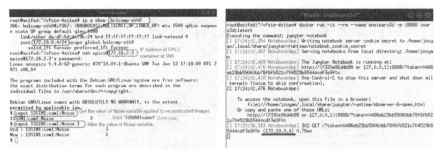

(a) Remote compute at BNL   (b) iMars3D container at SNS

Fig. 7. Illustration of instrument access and container orchestration over VFSIE.

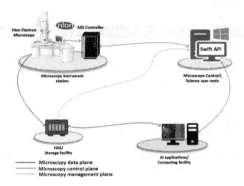

Fig. 8. Separate network channels for controlling microscope experiments using Pyro client-servers and transferring its measurements between storage system (NAS) and the computing resources; and both channels are essentials to support microscope steering and measurements collection needed for remote, automated experiments [15].

4.3   STEM VIT: VM and Native for Microscopes

A typical microscopy workflow is manually orchestrated by controlling the instrument from a co-located control computer, and collecting and transferring the measurements to computing systems located across the ecosystem. To support remote, automated execution of such workflows for STEM, an ecosystem solution is developed in [15]. An overall goal of such ecosystems is to utilize high performance computing resources combined with AI-driven methods to improve the performance of image construction and diffraction analyses codes. This solution employs separate network channels for controlling the microscope instruments and transferring measurements to computing nodes across the ecosystem, as shown in Fig. 8.

The infrastructure availability, connectivity and security challenges arise in utilizing the physical infrastructure for developing and testing the ecosystem software solutions, specifically, for microscope integration. Thus, we utilize the STEM-VIT for early development and testing of codes for remote steering of microscope over the control

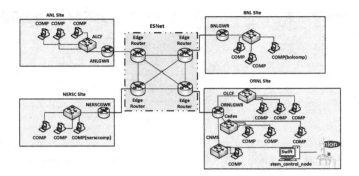

Fig. 9. STEM-VIT of four DOE lab sites connected over a wide-area network to emulate cross-facility STEM ecosystem [15].

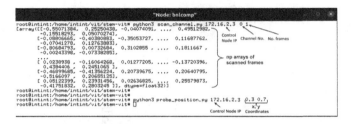

Fig. 10. Running Pyro client applications on a remote compute system at bnl (bnlcomp). The tasks illustrate scanning a microscope channel and setting a new probe position.

channel across the ecosystem. The VIT solution is successfully tested and deployed on the physical infrastructure. Its architecture is shown in Fig. 4, and unlike the somewhat more general VFSIE, its goal is specific to developing and testing microscopy ecosystem and integration solutions.

A VIT of an ecosystem spanning scientific instruments and computing systems at DOE laboratory sites, ANL, BNL, ORNL and NERSC, is shown in Fig. 9. It consists of the computing facility and CNMS microscope facility at ORNL represented by an instrument control node that supports microscope experiments. The Nion microscope is emulated using the nionswift-tool simulator [8] running on *stem_control_node* vhost, at CNMS. The tool provides Swift GUI and Python API almost identical to Swift application used for operating the physical Nion microscope. The network connectivity across the ecosystem components is emulated in a similar way to VFSIE shown in Fig. 5.

The STEM-VIT's control channel supports the remote steering of microscopy experiments by utilizing Pyro API, a Python library for distributed objects communication. It consists of two parts, Pyro server and client(s). The Pyro server runs on the control computer, and it encapsulates predefined microscopy tasks and exposes them to be accessible to Pyro client running on computing workstations across the ecosystem. Examples of microscopy tasks are *scan_channel* for scanning a microscope channel and retrieving matrices of the channel frames, and *probe_position* for changing the scanning

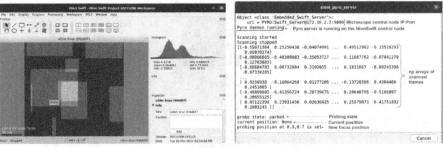

(a) Scan (HAADF) Window   (b) Script window

Fig. 11. nionswift-tool simulator runs on stem_control_node at CNMS/ORNL that provides Swift GUI and Python APIs for simulating STEM experiments. The scan (HAADF) window shows the reconstructed image while the script window shows Pyro server interaction.

focus to a specified location using geometric coordinates. These Pyro server-based tasks are called by Pyro client applications, namely *scan_channel.py* and *probe_position.py*, respectively, running on computing systems across the ecosystem. Detailed descriptions and demonstrations of STEM-VIT are provided in [15].

An example of a microscopy use case using STEM-VIT demonstrates Pyro server and client codes to scan a microscope channel, send back its frames of measurements and change the focus position of the microscope beam for the next scan. Briefly, the workflow consists of running the nionswift-tool simulator on *stem_control_node* at CNMS and initiating the Pyro server daemon for communication across the ecosystem. Then, a science user from BNL computing system accesses the nionswift simulator at CNMS for conducting the scan and retrieving the measurements, as shown in Fig. 10. After that, the user changes the scan focus to the coordinates (0.3, 0.7) for collecting the next measurements. It can be noticed that the focus position has been successfully changed to new coordinates in the Scan (HAADF) window of Swift GUI in Fig. 11(a). The detailed Pyro server interaction messages with the client applications related to the scan_channel and probe_position are shown in Fig. 11(b).

5   Extensions and Limitations

The utility of a VIT in general depends on its host's capabilities, in terms of computing power, software environment and whether it is indigenous or external, in other words, its location within or outside the ecosystem. The advantages and disadvantages of these options are summarized in Fig. 12. On an external host, the VIT is executed natively under Linux Ubuntu OS due to mininet's requirements, or inside an Ubuntu-VM under other OS, including Windows, Mac and RHEL. On an indigenous host, when VIT is executed natively, the codes developed on vhosts are readily available for direct use within the ecosystem; but when VIT is executed inside a VM, the codes need to be transferred to the host or connected via VM's interfaces. The former can be exploited to support a design-to-deployment continuum strategy [31]. When an external host is used

VIT execution

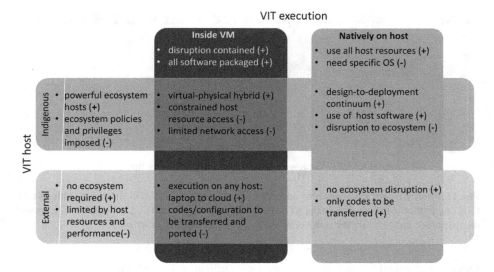

Fig. 12. VIT execution natively or inside VM on hosts indigenous and external to the ecosystem. (+) advantage, (−) disadvantage

for VIT execution, either natively or inside VM, the vhost codes need to be transferred to the ecosystem for testing and deployment. In either case, the computing power of the host together with the complexity of VIT limits the ability of its performance measurements in reflecting the ecosystem performance. In particular, the execution times of computations and throughput of network connections may significantly deviate from physical measurements when VITs emulate high performance computing and networking scenarios on workstation and laptops.

5.1 Design-to-Deployment Continuum

The development and deployment parts of VIT described in the last section are carried out on separate, disparate platforms. For example, STEM-VIT runs on VM on Windows workstation without GPUs, while its Pyro codes are deployed and tested on a powerful 80-core CPU, 2 GPU Linux ecosystem workstation. Over science ecosystems, in general, such deployments often require several critical steps including porting and refactoring code for GPUs (typically not available in VIT VMs), and this process may be repeated during the course of developing a fully operational solution. This gap may be narrowed using a design-to-deployment continuum approach, wherein codes are indigenously developed on the ecosystem and smoothly rolled into deployment.

The Continuous Design, Development, Debugging and Deployment Platform (CD4P) is proposed in [31] where in VIT runs natively on the ecosystem's own computing systems. A solution is first realized on VIT that emulates the ecosystem's hosts, networks and instruments. Codes are developed and tested using VIT's instrument simulators under the software environment identical to the ecosystem, without requiring access to physical systems. Subsequent development and testing is expanded over to

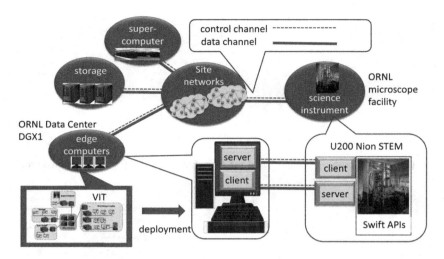

Fig. 13. ORNL Nion microscope ecosystem used for testing and deployment of VIT-developed Pyro client-server steering codes.

the ecosystem, and mature codes are deployed in-situ, as shown in Fig. 13. This platform is implemented using mininet whose vhosts inherit the host software environment so that VIT codes directly transition to the ecosystem during various cycles of development, testing and deployment.

The CD4P platform is implemented and will be demonstrated on ORNL STEM microscope ecosystem consisting of 8-GPU DGX-1 computing system and U200 Nion microscope. A workflow requiring multi-GPU codes for reconstruction using microscopy measurements is developed on DGX-1, and the same code runs on the corresponding VIT's vhost. A Jupyter notebook is developed first on VIT vhost to utilize the synthetic measurements for re-construction using DGX1 GPUs, and customize Pyro codes to collect measurements and send steering commands to Nion microscope simulator to focus on a new position. It is first developed and tested under VIT, and will be deployed on the ecosystem to control the U200 microscope by executing on DGX1 using physical IP addresses, without code refactoring and porting. We will demonstrate the potential use of this approach by utilizing multi-site VIT that emulates four national laboratory STEM ecosystem, for future use.

5.2 Throughput Profiles

VIT effectively emulates the networking functionalities as illustrated in the previous section, but Transmission Control Protocol (TCP) throughput measurements collected over its WAN connections deviate significantly from the expected, primarily because TCP dynamics are not accurately replicated in the VIT's emulation platforms, like mininet or containernet. For example, TCP throughput profile using testbed measurements, shown in Fig. 14(a), is significantly different from that based on VIT measurements shown in Fig. 14(b).

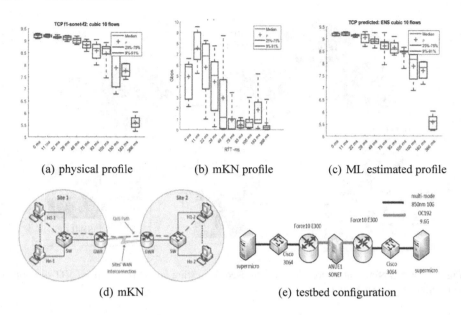

(a) physical profile   (b) mKN profile   (c) ML estimated profile

(d) mKN   (e) testbed configuration

Fig. 14. Through profiles over (a) physical (b) emulated infrastructures (c) predicted with ML model, as well as the mKN and testbed designs (d).

The *micro Kernel Network* (mKN) is proposed in [29, 30], which implements a baseline network and provides throughput measurements for a set of connections with chosen Round Trip Time (RTT) values. These measurements are used together with testbed measurements by a machine learning method to learn a map that converts the former to latter. This process is carried out in an initial step on the host by collecting mKN measurements for the range of RTTs used in VIT. Subsequently, the learned map is applied to measurements from VIT running on the same host. The ML model extrapolates mKN measurements to closely match the testbed measurements; the predicted profile in Fig. 14(c) by the ensemble of trees method is much closer to the testbed profile than that of mKN. Here, Figs. 14(d) and (e) show the mKN and the corresponding testbed, respectively. A summary and details of this method are provided in [29, 30].

6   Conclusions

To address challenges of software development, testing, and resource integration in a science computing-instrument ecosystem, we proposed a VIT that emulates its network and computing parts, and incorporates the instrument simulation software. It provides a software environment nearly identical to that of the ecosystem, which makes it suitable for software development and testing, and also for design space exploration. Earlier VITs include VSNE for developing software-defined networking solutions, and VFSIE for testing the federation software stack and remote instrument control. We described STEM-VIT that enabled the development and deployment of steering capability for a microscope ecosystem, and to utilize VIT on a computing platform of the ecosystem to smoothly transition the codes into operations. In essence, a VIT supports significant parts of software development and early analysis of ecosystem designs without needing the access to physical ecosystem.

This work constitutes only first steps towards developing virtual infrastructure twins for a variety of computing-instrument ecosystems, including automated chemistry lab with use of robots, chemical flow reactors for material design, neutron and light sources, and quantum computing and networking systems. More extensive development and testing of VITs will be of future interest including the integration of detailed physics-based digital twins. Our results also suggest several directions for future work: exploration of other network simulators and digital twin frameworks; in-situ VIT implementation on HPC systems; and ML methods for performance estimation from VIT computing and network measurements.

References

1. Clone system call. https://www.unix.com/man-page/linux/2/clone/
2. EPICS container with simulated IOCs: motor, adsim and testasynportdriver. https://hub.docker.com/r/lnlssol/epics-sim
3. ESNet: Energy sciences network. https://www.es.net/
4. Experimental physics and industrial control system. http://epics.anl.gov/
5. Linux namespaces. https://www.unix.com/man-page/linux/7/namespaces/
6. MaxiNet: A distributed network emulator. https://maxinet.github.io/
7. MiniNExT: A network emulator with process namespace isolation. https://github.com/USC-NSL/miniNExT
8. nionswift-tool. https://nionswift.readthedocs.io/en/stable/installation.html-installing-nion-swift-from-pypi-or-conda-forge
9. Unshare: Dissociating a process from the shared attributes. https://man7.org/linux/man-pages/man2/unshare.2.html
10. Veth: Virtual ethernet device. https://www.unix.com/man-page/linux/4/veth
11. Software defined networking for extreme-scale science: Data, compute, and instrument facilities. DOE ASCR Workshop, Bethesda, MD (2014)
12. ASCR network requirements review. ESNet report, Germantown, MD, 22–23 April 2015
13. Al-Najjar, A., Rao, N.S.V., Hitefield, S., Naughton, T.: Science federation emulation testbed: demonstration of VFSIE functionalities. In: Demonstrations of the 46th IEEE Conference on Local Computer Networks (LCN). IEEE (2021)
14. Al-Najjar, A., et al.: Virtual framework for development and testing of federation software stack. In: 2021 IEEE 46th Conference on Local Computer Networks (LCN), pp. 323–326. IEEE (2021)
15. Al-Najjar, A., et al.: Enabling autonomous electron microscopy for networked computation and steering. In: 18th IEEE International Conference on eScience (2022)
16. Al-Najjar, A., et al.: VFSIE-development and testing framework for federated science instruments. arXiv preprint arXiv:2101.02184 (2021)
17. Fuller, A., Fan, Z., Day, C., Barlow, C.: Digital twin: enabling technologies, challenges and open research. IEEE Access **8**, 108952–108971 (2020)
18. Neutron Imaging Facility (Imaging | CG-1D | HFIR). https://neutrons.ornl.gov/imaging
19. iMars3D: Preprocessing and reconstruction for the Neutron Imaging Beam Lines. https://github.com/ornlneutronimaging/iMars3D.git

20. Kreutz, D., Ramos, F.M.V., et al.: Software-defined networking: a comprehensive survey. Proc. IEEE **103**(1), 14–76 (2015)
21. Lantz, B., Heller, B., McKeown, N.: A network in a laptop: rapid prototyping for software-defined networks. In: Proceedings of the 9th ACM SIGCOMM Workshop on Hot Topics in Networks, p. 19 (2010)
22. Law, N.M., et al.: The Palomar transient factory: system overview, performance, and first results. Pub. Astron. Soc. Pac. **121**(886), 1395–1408 (2009)
23. Lin, Y.D., Pitt, D., Hausheer, D., Johnson, E., Lin, Y.B.: Software-defined networking: standardization for cloud computing's second wave. Computer **47**(11), 19–21 (2014)
24. Liu, Q., et al.: Virtual environment for testing software-defined networking solutions for scientific workflows. In: Proceedings of the 1st International Workshop on Autonomous Infrastructure for Science, AI-Science 2018, pp. 1–8 (2018)
25. Naughton, T., et al.: Software framework for federated science instruments. In: Nichols, J., Verastegui, B., Maccabe, A.B., Hernandez, O., Parete-Koon, S., Ahearn, T. (eds.) SMC 2020. CCIS, vol. 1315, pp. 189–203. Springer, Cham (2020). https://doi.org/10.1007/978-3-030-63393-6_13
26. On-demand Secure Circuits and Advance Reservation System. http://www.es.net/oscars
27. Peuster, M., Kampmeyer, J., et al.: ContainerNet 2.0: a rapid prototyping platform for hybrid service function chains. In: 2018 4th IEEE Conference on Network Softwarization and Workshops (NetSoft), pp. 335–337. IEEE (2018)
28. Filgueira, R., et al.: Automating environmental computing applications with scientific workflows. In: 2016 IEEE 12th International Conference one-Science (e-Science), pp. 400–406 (2016)
29. Rao, N.S.V., Al-Najjar, A., Foster, I., Kettimuthu, R., Liu, Z.: Virtual framework for science federations with instruments access and control. In: Workshop on Autonomous Discovery in Science and Engineering Report (2021)
30. Rao, N.S.V., Al-Najjar, A., Imam, N., Liu, Z., Kettimuthu, R., Foster, I.: Cross inference of throughput profiles using micro kernel network method. In: Renault, É., Boumerdassi, S., Mühlethaler, P. (eds.) MLN 2021. LNCS, vol. 13175, pp. 48–68. Springer, Cham (2022). https://doi.org/10.1007/978-3-030-98978-1_4
31. Rao, N.S.V., Al-Najjar, A., Sankaran, R.: Design-to-deployment continuum platform for computing-instrument ecosystems. In: Workshop on Modeling and Simulation of Systems and Applications (ModSim 2022) (2022, abstract)
32. Rasheed, A., San, O., Kvamsdal, T.: Digital twin: values, challenges and enablers from a modeling perspective. IEEE Access **8**, 21980–22012 (2020)
33. Schluse, M., Priggemeyer, M., Atorf, L., Rossmann, J.: Experimentable digital twins-streamlining simulation-based systems engineering for industry 4.0. IEEE Trans. Ind. Informat. **14**(4), 1722–1731 (2018)
34. Spallation Neutrons and Pressure Diffractometer (SNAP | BL-3 | SNS). https://neutrons.ornl.gov/snap
35. Xia, W., Wen, Y., et al.: A survey on software-defined networking. IEEE Commun. Surv. Tutor. **17**(1), 27–51 (2015, First Quarter)

The INTERSECT Open Federated Architecture for the Laboratory of the Future

Christian Engelmann$^{(\boxtimes)}$, Olga Kuchar, Swen Boehm, Michael J. Brim, Thomas Naughton, Suhas Somnath, Scott Atchley, Jack Lange, Ben Mintz, and Elke Arenholz

Oak Ridge National Laboratory, Oak Ridge, TN 37831, USA
engelmannc@ornl.gov

Abstract. A federated instrument-to-edge-to-center architecture is needed to autonomously collect, transfer, store, process, curate, and archive scientific data and reduce human-in-the-loop needs with (a) common interfaces to leverage community and custom software, (b) pluggability to permit adaptable solutions, reuse, and digital twins, and (c) an open standard to enable adoption by science facilities world-wide. The Selfdriven Experiments for Science/Interconnected Science Ecosystem (INTERSECT) Open Architecture enables science breakthroughs using intelligent networked systems, instruments and facilities with autonomous experiments, "self-driving" laboratories, smart manufacturing and artificial intelligence (AI) driven design, discovery and evaluation. It creates an open federated architecture for the laboratory of the future using a novel approach, consisting of (1) science use case design patterns, (2) a system of systems architecture, and (3) a microservice architecture.

Keywords: Software architecture · Federated ecosystem · Design patterns · System of systems architecture · Microservice architecture

1 Introduction

The U.S. Department of Energy (DoE)'s Artificial intelligence (AI) for Science report [41] outlines the need for intelligent systems, instruments, and facilities

Research sponsored by the Laboratory Directed Research and Development Program's INTERSECT Initiative of Oak Ridge National Laboratory. This manuscript has been authored by UT-Battelle, LLC under Contract No. DE-AC05-00OR22725 with the U.S. Department of Energy. The United States Government retains and the publisher, by accepting the article for publication, acknowledges that the United States Government retains a non-exclusive, paid-up, irrevocable, world-wide license to publish or reproduce the published form of this manuscript, or allow others to do so, for United States Government purposes. The Department of Energy will provide public access to these results of federally sponsored research in accordance with the DOE Public Access Plan (http://energy.gov/downloads/doe-public-access-plan).

K. Doug et al. (Eds.): SMC 2022, CCIS 1690, pp. 173–190, 2022.
https://doi.org/10.1007/978-3-031-23606-8_11

to enable science breakthroughs with autonomous experiments, "self-driving" laboratories, smart manufacturing, and AI-driven design, discovery and evaluation. The DoE's Computational Facilities Research Workshop report [9] identifies intelligent systems/facilities as a challenge with enabling automation and eliminating human-in-the-loop needs as a cross-cutting theme.

Autonomous experiments, "self-driving" laboratories and smart manufacturing employ machine-in-the-loop intelligence for decision-making. Human-in-the-loop needs are reduced by an autonomous online control that collects experiment data, analyzes it, and takes appropriate operational actions to steer an ongoing or plan a next experiment. It may be assisted by an AI that is trained online and/or offline with archived data and/or with synthetic data created by a digital twin. Analysis and decision making may also rely on rule-based approaches, causal or physics-based models, and advanced statistical methods. Human interaction for experiment planning, observation and steering is performed through appropriate human-machine interfaces.

A federated hardware/software architecture for connecting instruments with edge and center computing resources is needed that autonomously collects, transfers, stores, processes, curates, and archives scientific data in common formats. It must be able to communicate with scientific instruments and computing and data resources for orchestration and control across administrative domains, and with humans for critical decisions and feedback. Standardized communication and programming interfaces are needed that leverage community and custom software for scientific instruments, automation, workflows and data transfer. Pluggability is required to permit quickly adaptable and deployable solutions, reuse of partial solutions for different use cases, and the use of digital twins, such as a virtual instrument, robot or experiment. This federated architecture needs to be an open standard to enable adoption.

This paper details the Self-driven Experiments for Science/Interconnected Science Ecosystem (INTERSECT) Open Architecture, which enables science breakthroughs using intelligent networked systems, instruments and facilities. It creates an open federated instrument-to-edge-to-center architecture for the laboratory of the future using a novel approach, consisting of (1) science use case design patterns, (2) a system of systems (SoS) architecture, and (3) a microservice architecture.

2   Related Work

There are about 300 workflow solutions for instrument science and data analysis [2]. However, only very few holistic automated solutions or research and development efforts exist. None offer a federated architecture standard.

The National Energy Research Scientific Computing Center (NERSC) Superfacility framework [33] integrates instruments with computational/data facilities for automation, such as connecting the SLAC National Accelerator Laboratory's Linac Coherent Light Source via ESnet to the Cori supercomputer for photosynthesis research [43]. The RESTful Superfacility API offers access to common supercomputer functions [32]. Oak Ridge National Laboratory (ORNL) offers federated environments for connecting instruments with computational/data resources, leveraging advances in software containerization and softwarization of hardware for processing data from ORNL's Spallation Neutron Source and High Flux Isotope Reactor [1,34]. Data transfer and workflow tools developed at Argonne National Laboratory (ANL) and the University of Chicago, such as Globus Automate [17], Gladier [16] and Balsam [3], permit automated analysis of instrument data, such as by connecting ANL's Advanced Photon Source with the Theta supercomputer for real-time analysis [19]. Other solutions exist, such as the autonomous robot-controlled chemistry laboratory at the University of Liverpool [39], the FireCrest RESTful API at the Swiss National Supercomputing Centre [12], the design of experiments as a Cloud service by Kebotix [25], and robotic process automation using AI by UIPath [44].

Design patterns systematize software development using proven engineering paradigms and methodologies [6]. In object-oriented programming, design patterns provide methods for defining class interfaces, inheritance hierarchies and class relationships [15]. Pattern systems also exist for concurrent and networked object-oriented environments [40], resource management [26], and distributed systems [5]. Design patterns have been discovered in other domains, such as for natural language processing [42], user interface design [4], Web design [11], visualization [18], software security [10], high-performance computing (HPC) resilience [20,21], and data processing for automation of business processes [14].

The SoS approach designs a highly complex system by decomposing it into many smaller and easier to design systems [31,37]. The set of systems interact to provide a unique capability that none of the individual systems can accomplish on its own [22]. A SoS has five key characteristics [29]: operational independence of systems, managerial independence of systems, geographical distribution, emergent behavior, and evolutionary development. Systems are individually developed and evolved, as the architecture of a SoS is the system interfaces [30,38]. A recent example is Defense Advanced Research Projects Agency (DARPA)'s System of Systems Integration Technology and Experimentation (SoSITE) [8] System-of-systems Technology Integration Tool Chain for Heterogeneous Electronic Systems (STITCHES) [7,13]. The U.S. Department of Defense Architecture Framework (DoDAF) [46] is an overarching, comprehensive framework for the development of architectures from different viewpoints. It is used across the U.S. Department of Defense (DoD) for developing SoS architectures.

Microservice architectures emerged from service-oriented architectures, initially realized with Web services [47]. They have since become the modern approach to decompose complex software systems. For example, Netflix created an open source microservice architecture for their internal applications [35,36]. Kubernetes uses a microservice architecture for automating deployment, scaling, and management of containerized applications [28]. Cray/HPE is working on a management software solution for supercomputers using microservices [24].

3   The INTERSECT Open Architecture

The INTERSECT Open Architecture approach roughly follows the DoDAF [46] with its different architectural viewpoints, such as (i) operational scenarios, (ii) composition, interconnectivity and context, (iii) services and their capabilities, (iv) policies, standards and guidance, and (v) capability. The major difference is that the INTERSECT Open Architecture splits these views over three different parts: (1) science use case design patterns, (2) a SoS architecture, and (3) a microservice architecture.

Science use cases for autonomous experiments, "self-driving" laboratories, smart manufacturing, and AI-driven design, discovery and evaluation are described as design patterns that identify and abstract the involved components and their interactions in terms of control, work and data flow. The SoS architecture clarifies used terms, architectural elements, the interactions between them and compliance. The microservice architecture maps the patterns to the SoS architecture with loosely coupled microservices and standardized interfaces.

This approach permits separating (a) coarse-grain architectural decisions, such as what objective a particular "self-driving" laboratory has and how that objective is being achieved, from (b) mid-grain architectural decisions, such as which instruments, robots, networks and computing systems are part of this "self-driving" laboratory and how do they communicate with each other, and from (c) fine-grain architectural decisions, such as which particular experiment control, data transfer and compute microservices are being used and how. The science use case design patterns, SoS architecture and microservice architecture complement each other, just like the different viewpoints of the DoDAF. Additionally, the SoS architecture itself offers complementary viewpoints, such as user, data, operational, logical, physical and standards view.

3.1   Science Use Case Design Patterns

Machine-in-the-loop capabilities with connected scientific instruments, robot-controlled laboratories and edge or center computing and data resources that enable autonomous experiments, "self-driving" laboratories, smart manufacturing, and AI-driven design, discovery and evaluation is an inherent open or closed loop control problem. Therefore, the basic template for a science use case design pattern is defined in a loop control problem paradigm (Fig. 1). The abstract science use case design pattern consists of a behavior and a set of interfaces in the context of performing a single or a set of experiments in an open or closed loop control. Such an abstract definition creates universal patterns that describe solutions free of implementation details.

Design Pattern Format. Design patterns for science use cases are expressed in a written form and in a highly structured format, which permits quick identification of relevant patterns given a certain problem to be solved and easy comparison of patterns regarding their applicability and capabilities. The format for

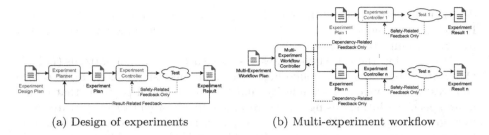

(a) Design of experiments   (b) Multi-experiment workflow

Fig. 1. Science use case anatomy as design of experiments (closed) loop control problem and as multi-experiment workflow (open) loop control problem

describing science use case design patterns consists of individual descriptions of pattern properties, including text, diagrams, and mathematical models. It can be extended over time by adding more pattern properties and their descriptions. The current science use case design pattern format is as follows:

- **Name:** A name that distinctly identifies the pattern and permits thinking about designs in an abstract manner and communicating design choices.
- **Problem:** A description of the problem, providing insight on when to apply the pattern. Multiple patterns may address the same problem differently.
- **Context:** The preconditions under which the pattern is relevant, including a description of the system before the pattern is applied.
- **Forces:** A description of the relevant forces/constraints, and how they inter- act or conflict with each other and with the intended goals and objectives.
- **Solution:** A description of the solution that defines the abstract elements that are necessary for the composition of the design solution as well as their relationships, responsibilities, and collaborations.
- **Capabilities:** The specific capabilities provided by this pattern in terms of the control problem it solves.
- **Resulting context:** A description of the post-conditions arising from the application of the pattern. There may be trade-offs between competing parameters due to the implementation of a solution using this pattern.
- **Related patterns:** The relationships between this and other patterns, which may be predecessors or successors. This pattern may complement or enhance others. There may also be dependencies between patterns.
- **Examples:** A description of one or more examples, including their properties, that illustrate the use of the pattern for solving concrete problems.
- **Known Uses:** A list of known applications of the pattern in existing systems, including any practical considerations and limitations.

Design Pattern Classification. A pattern classification helps to identify groups of patterns that address similar problems in different ways or that describe solutions at different levels of granularity or from different view points. A classification scheme codifies these relationships between patterns and enables designers to better understand individual pattern capabilities and relationships. It also helps to understand how patterns rely on each other and can be composed to form a complete solution.

At this point, there are two classes of science use case design patterns (Fig. 2): (1) strategy patterns that define high-level solutions using control architecture features at a very coarse granularity, and (2) architectural patterns that define more specific solutions using hardware and software architecture features at a finer granularity. While the architectural patterns do inherit the features of certain parent strategy patterns, they also address additional problems that are not exposed at the high abstraction level of the strategy patterns.

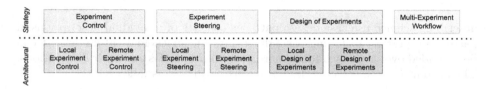

Fig. 2. Classification of the science use case design patterns

Strategy Design Patterns. The science use case strategy design patterns define high-level solutions using control architecture features at a very coarse granularity. Their descriptions are deliberately abstract to enable architects to reason about the overall organization of the used techniques and their implications on the full system design. The features of these patterns and their relationships are compared in Table 1, where Fig. 1a shows the components of the Design of Experiments pattern and Fig. 1b of the Multi-Experiment Workflow pattern. The strategy patterns solve the following problems:

- **Experiment Control:** Certain predetermined actions need to be performed while running an experiment.
- **Experiment Steering:** Certain predetermined actions need to be performed while running an experiment, depending on experiment progress.
- **Design of Experiments:** Certain predetermined actions need to be performed to run a set of similar experiments with different experiment plan parameters, depending on experiment results.
- **Multi-Experiment Workflow:** Certain predetermined actions need to be performed to run a set of experiments in serial and/or parallel.

Table 1. Features and relationships of the science use case strategy patterns

Feature	Experiment control	Experiment steering	Design of experiments	Multi-experiment workflow
# of experiments	1	1	Multiple	Multiple
Control type	Open loop	Closed loop	Closed loop	Open loop
Operation type	Automated	Autonomous	Autonomous	Automated
Extends		Experiment Control		
Uses			Experiment Control	Experiment Control
May also use or use instead			Experiment Steering	Experiment Steering, Design of Experiments

Architectural Design Patterns. The science use case architectural design patterns define more specific solutions using hardware and software architecture features at a finer granularity. They offer more detailed descriptions, conveying different design choices for implementing strategy patterns and their abstract architectural features. Architectural patterns inherit the features of their parent strategy patterns. However, they also address additional problems through specific design choices that are not exposed at the high abstraction level of the parent strategy patterns. The architectural patterns provide abstractions for different hardware and software architecture choices of implementing control and workflow, such as using experiment-local or experiment-remote computing and data resources. Figure 3 shows the Remote Design of Experiments architectural pattern as an example. Table 2 shows the science use case architectural design patterns, their relationships to the strategy design patterns and their features.

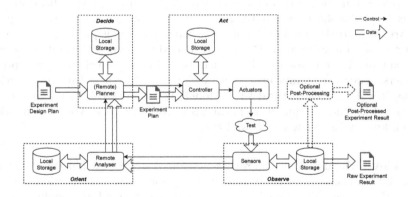

Fig. 3. Remote Design of Experiments architectural pattern

3.2 System of Systems Architecture

The SoS architecture decomposes the federated hardware/software ecosystem into smaller and less complex systems and components within these systems. It permits the development of individual systems and components with clearly defined interfaces, data formats and communication protocols. This not only separates concerns and functionality for reusability, but also promotes pluggability and extensibility with uniform protocols and system/component life cycles.

Table 2. Features and relationships of the science use case architectural patterns

Architectural pattern	Related strategy pattern	Remote components
Local Experiment Control	Experiment Control	None
Remote Experiment Control	Experiment Control	Controller
Local Experiment Steering	Experiment Steering	None
Remote Experiment Steering	Experiment Steering	Analyzer and Controller (optional)
Local Design of Experiments	Design of Experiments	None
Remote Design of Experiments	Design of Experiments	Analyzer and Planner (optional)

Instead of developing individual monolithic solutions for each science use case, the SoS architecture provides one solution that can be easily adapted to different use cases using different compositions of systems. It offers operational and managerial independence of systems and of components within systems, geographical distribution with a physically distributed and federated ecosystem, emergent behavior based on the interplay between systems and components, and evolutionary development through pluggability and extensibility.

The SoS architecture consists of various architectural views of the INTERSECT system that connects scientific instruments, robot-controlled laboratories, computational facilities, data centers, and edge computing devices to enable autonomous experiments, "self-driving" laboratories, smart manufacturing, and AI-driven design, discovery, and evaluation. The architecture specification incorporates the IEEE 42010 Standard [23], entitled "Systems and software engineering - Architecture description." It uses the concepts of multiple, concurrent views to describe a complex system. The views are used to describe the system from the viewpoint of different stakeholders, such as end-users, developers, and project managers. There are many examples of view-based architectural descriptions, such as "the 4+1 Architectural View Model" [27], the DoDAF [46], and the UK Ministry of Defence Architecture Framework (MoDAF) [45]. We use a hybrid of the well-known 4+1 view model and the DoDAF.

User View. The user view is a representation of a SoS that illustrates different human interactions with the system. It does not include interactions between systems themselves. This view highlights the human facing functionality required from the overall system. A person's view changes depending on their role, which is specific to a context. We identify the following five roles:

- **User:** This is the default role for a person interacting with a given resource in the system. Persons with this role do not own, administer, provide, or maintain the resource. Users leverage the interfaces provided by the resources in the system to compose and run scientific experiment campaigns.
- **Maintainer/Operator:** This person maintains or operates a given resource in the system. Examples include experts who configure instruments, such as a microscope, or those who maintain computational clusters.

- **Administrator:** This person performs most administrative tasks associated with a given resource, including assigning and managing maintainers/operators, granting users access to a resource, and ensuring that a resource complies with membership requirements for the system.
- **Owner:** This person is fiscally responsible for a given resource and assigns corresponding administrators.
- **Provider:** This person is a creator of software infrastructure underpinning the system or an application, such as a visualization widget or simulation module. They could alternatively be a representative of the manufacturer of resource, such as a compute cluster or an instrument.

A given person can hold multiple roles. For example, they could be the owner of a compute cluster, the administrator of three edge compute resources and a user of all other resources in the system. Roles can also be temporary and expire after a predetermined time.

The user view also provides a basic graphical representation or views of every possible interaction a person could have with the system for all relevant roles to serve as guidelines for implementors of the system. For example, the user view includes graphical representations of users logging into the system, applying for an account, viewing the catalog of resources available in the system, composing a new campaign, and monitoring or steering a running campaign. Figure 4 shows an example of graphical representations for a user configuring a dashboard for a running campaign.

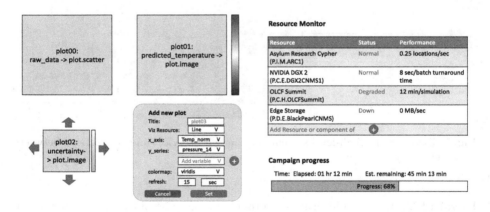

Fig. 4. Graphical representation of a user view

Logical View. The logical view addresses the logical composition and interactions between the different components in the overall system. By decomposing the overall architecture into systems, subsystems, services, capabilities and activities, it simplifies the overall design and makes it easier to architect the interactions between the different components. It contains the definition of system concepts and of system options, the system resource flow requirements, capability integration planning, system integration management, and operational planning. The logical view uses the term agent to categorize any internal or external actor that is interacting with a system or subsystem, such as humans or systems (as system agents). Additionally, it describes the resource structure of the overall system and identifies the primary systems, subsystems, performers (agents) and activities (functions), and their interactions.

Figure 5 shows an example of the system level functions and their interactions which are required for a user to configure and schedule an experiment and viewing of the experiment results after the experiment was run. Interactions are defined through interfaces, which capture the data and resource flow required to execute the different activities that comprise a capability. The data exchanged between the different system functions is captured in exchange items, which are also visible in the diagram in Fig. 5. By doing do, the logical view is tying together the data view and the operational view.

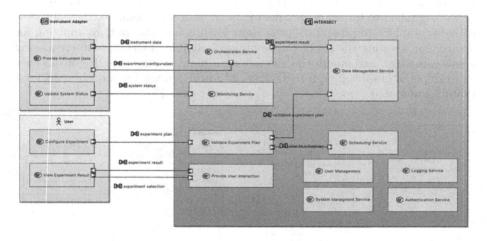

Fig. 5. Example of a high-level system diagram with services and connections between a user and an instrument

Physical View. The physical view provides a mapping of the architecture onto the physical infrastructure. This view of the environment enables system designers to determine how to decompose and place the various system components onto the resources that make up the overall system. This view provides the architecture with an understanding of the attributes of the environment, and allows the system to configure its services based on the constraints and capabilities of the underlying system components. The elements in this view consist of physical resources that provide services to the architecture as well as the network topology that connects them together. Types of physical resources include computational resources, data storage services, data sources, and network connections.

The physical view enables the enumeration of constraints placed on the overall system. These constraints can consist of capacity constraints (e.g., available storage capacity or computational elements), network constraints (e.g., available bandwidth between elements in the architecture), policy constraints (e.g., firewall rules or access control policies), and availability constraints (e.g., ability to allocate resources within necessary time frames). These constraints limit the configuration space of the architecture, and enumerate the necessary interfaces and processes required to configure the physical infrastructure to support the operations of the overall system.

Operational View. The operational view describes the tasks, activities, procedures, information exchanges/flows from the perspective of the real-world operations stakeholders, i.e., systems administrators, maintenance, facility engineers, system managers, instrument scientists. The operational view captures restrictions that may be necessary to reflect facility constraints and procedures. The intent of the view is to capture the elements needed for the operation and usage of the distributed resources in the SoS environment.

The operational view captures activities like the creation and connection of SoS services, and subsequent monitoring of services (Fig. 6), e.g., availability, health monitoring. The overall system control tree is another key component of the operational view. These control connections provide the basis for performing operations across the distributed system. The addition and removal of services within the control channel need to be clearly defined in order to maintain a coherent control network. Additionally, the registration and coordination of services must adhere to security policies. These are the types of details captured within the operational view.

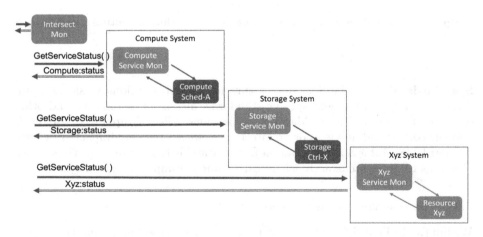

Fig. 6. Example high-level operational view diagram of service monitoring, using service adapters to connect resources to the INTERSECT environment (blue). (Color figure online)

Data View. The data view of a SoS architecture is a representation of the system from the perspective of data needs, and the data framework that needs to exist to support the INTERSECT Open Architecture. The data view is a specification for all data aspects of the system as a whole, and shall include the conceptual, logical, and physical data models. The conceptual data model provides the high-level data concepts and their relationships that are important to the SoS's operations that meet its intended purpose. Figure 7 depicts one such conceptual concept regarding building and executing a workflow in the SoS. The logical data model bridges the conceptual and physical data models and introduces the data structure for needed components. The physical data model is the actual data schema and specifications for SoS services and applications.

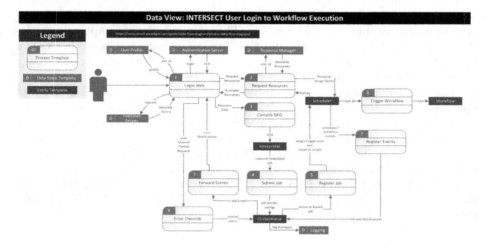

Fig. 7. Example data view of user logging in and building/executing a workflow.

Standards View. The SoS architecture incorporates various versioned standards, including instrument-specific standards, messaging standards, and other external standards. The standards view provides a list of supported standards and the corresponding views or architecture elements that are impacted by each standard (see Table 3 as an example). The standards view also provides block diagrams to illustrate exactly where each standard impacts a given system.

3.3   Microservice Architecture

Within the INTERSECT Open Architecture, the microservice architecture specification provides a catalog of infrastructure and experiment-specific microservices that may be useful within an interconnected science ecosystem (Fig. 8). All

Table 3. Example of messaging standards maintained in the standards view

Name	Version	Affected views	Affected elements
INTERSECT Core Messages	1.0	Data, Logical, Operational	Microservice Capabilities: All
Compute Allocation Capability	1.0	Data, Logical	Microservice Capabilities: Application Execution, Container Execution, Host Command Execution
Compute Queue Capability	1.0	Data, Logical	Microservice Capabilities: Compute Queue Reservation
NION Swift API	0.16.3	Logical, Operational	Systems: Electron Microscopes
Robot Operating System (ROS)	2.rolling	Logical, Operational	Systems: Additive Manufacturing

microservices are defined to facilitate composition within federated SoS architectures, where each subsystem corresponds to one or more coordinating microservices. INTERSECT infrastructure microservices represent common service functionality and capabilities, such as data management, computing, messaging, and workflow orchestration that are likely to be generally useful across many science ecosystems without the need for customization. Experiment-specific microservices, on the other hand, represent services whose implementation may require detailed application knowledge, such as experiment planning or steering services that require knowledge of experiment-specific control parameters and their associated constraints. The INTERSECT science use case design patterns help identify the relevant infrastructure and experiment-specific microservices for a given science ecosystem.

Each microservice provides a well-defined set of functions that is domain-scoped to ensure separation of concerns between differing microservices, avoid duplicate functionality, and encourage reuse. The supported functions are defined by the microservice contract, which describes the purpose for each service function and associated data (e.g., request parameters and response types). A microservice may have several different implementations, where each implementation provides the same contract but uses different underlying technologies or supports a particular deployment environment. Where multiple implementations exist, an application can choose the implementation most suitable for its environment or application needs.

Interaction Patterns. To enable federation of microservices, it is useful to understand the types of interactions a given microservice may reasonably expect from one of its clients. Figure 9 shows three common patterns that substantively cover the expected interactions: *Command*, *Request-Reply*, and *Asyn-*

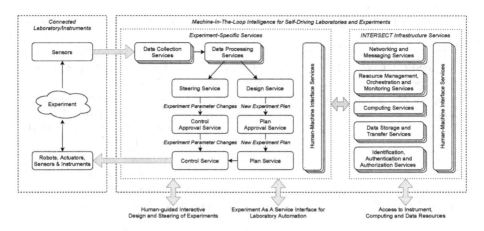

Fig. 8. Classification of INTERSECT microservices

chronous Status. The *Command Interaction Pattern* involves the client asking the microservice to do something. The microservice typically responds immediately with a simple acknowledgement that the command has been received successfully or some error status indicating why the command was not acceptable. The *Request-Reply Interaction Pattern* has the client making a request of the microservice that includes an expected reply containing pertinent information or data related to the request. Finally, the *Asynchronous Status Interaction Pattern* represents cases where the microservice generates status or event information as a result of its internal actions or state, and sends that information to one or more of its clients.

These common interaction patterns form the basis for definition of a limited set of core message types (i.e., `Command`, `CommandResponse`, `Request`, `Reply`, `Event`, and `Status`). Each message type is easily mapped to a wide variety of messaging protocols used in both RESTful client-server communication and asynchronous messaging via message brokers. The microservice architecture specifies a consistent yet flexible message structure across all message types that incorporates two sections: (1) a generic header containing information necessary for message routing and tracing, and (2) a data content section that is specific to the particular microservice function being exercised. For instance, the data contents of a `Command` or `Request` message may include function-specific parameters, while an `Event` message would include details of the associated event occurrence.

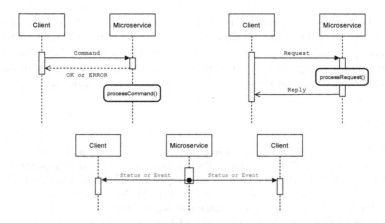

Fig. 9. Interaction patterns of INTERSECT microservices

4   Conclusion

This paper detailed the INTERSECT Open Architecture, which enables science breakthroughs using intelligent networked systems, instruments and facilities with autonomous experiments, "self-driving" laboratories, smart manufacturing and AI driven design, discovery and evaluation. The proposed open federated instrument-to-edge-to-center architecture for the laboratory of the future uses a novel approach, consisting of (1) science use case design patterns, (2) a SoS architecture, and (3) a microservice architecture.

Science use cases are described as design patterns that identify and abstract the involved components and their interactions. The SoS architecture clarifies used terms, architectural elements, the interactions between them and compliance. The microservice architecture maps the patterns to the SoS architecture with loosely coupled microservices and standardized interfaces. While there are about 300 workflow tools and only very few holistic automated scientific workflows, this is the first published work in a federated architecture standard for automated and autonomous instrument science and data analysis.

Ongoing work focuses on refining the INTERSECT Open Architecture and applying it to the following six initial science use cases at ORNL: (1) automation for grid interconnected-laboratory emulation, (2) autonomous additive manufacturing, (3) autonomous continuous flow reactor synthesis, (4) autonomous microscopy, (5) an autonomous robotic chemistry laboratory, and (6) an ion trap quantum computing resource. Detailed architecture specification documents are currently under development for the science use case design patterns, the SoS architecture, and the microservice architecture.

In the near future, we seek to publish the specification documents and reach out to research institutions world-wide for feedback, collaboration and adoption. There is also a significant amount of work needed to develop the software environment that implements this architecture, in part using existing tools, and performing the necessary research in certain critical areas, such as (1) algorithms for autonomy and AI-driven design, discovery and evaluation, (2) codesign of "self-driving" laboratories and smart manufacturing facilities, (3) data management for scientific computing and instrument science, (4) cybersecurity, and (5) distributed operating and runtime systems as enabling technology.

References

1. Al-Najjar, A., et al.: Virtual framework for development and testing of federation software stack. In: 2021 IEEE 46th Conference on Local Computer Networks (LCN), pp. 323–326 (2021). https://doi.org/10.1109/LCN52139.2021.9524993
2. Amstutz, P., Mikheev, M., Crusoe, M.R., Tijanić, N., Lampa, S., et al.: Existing workflow systems (2022). https://s.apache.org/existing-workflow-systems
3. Balsam workflows (2022). https://www.alcf.anl.gov/support-center/theta/balsam
4. Borchers, J.: A Pattern Approach to Interaction Design. Wiley, New York (2001)
5. Buschmann, F., Henney, K., Schmidt, D.C.: Pattern-Oriented Software Architecture - Volume 4: A Pattern Language for Distributed Computing. Wiley, Hoboken (2007)
6. Buschmann, F., Meunier, R., Rohnert, H., Sommerlad, P., Stal, M.: Pattern-Oriented Software Architecture - Volume 1: A System of Patterns. Wiley, Hoboken (1996)
7. Defense Advanced Research Projects Agency, U.S. Department of Defense: Creating cross-domain kill webs in real time (2022). https://www.darpa.mil/news-events/2020-09-18a
8. Defense Advanced Research Projects Agency, U.S. Department of Defense: System of systems integration technology and experimentation (SoSITE) (2022). https://www.darpa.mil/program/system-of-systems-integration-technology-and-experimentation
9. DOE national laboratories' computational facilities - Research workshop report. Technical report, ANL/MCS-TM-388, Argonne National Laboratory, Lemont, IL, USA (2020). https://publications.anl.gov/anlpubs/2020/02/158604.pdf
10. Dougherty, C., Sayre, K., Seacord, R., Svoboda, D., Togashi, K.: Secure design patterns. Technical report, CMU/SEI-2009-TR-010, Software Engineering Institute, Carnegie Mellon University, Pittsburgh, PA (2009). https://doi.org/10.1184/R1/6583640.v1
11. Duyne, D.K.V., Landay, J., Hong, J.I.: The Design of Sites: Patterns, Principles, and Processes for Crafting a Customer-Centered Web Experience. Addison-Wesley Longman Publishing Co. Inc., Boston (2002)
12. FireCrest RESTful API (2022). https://firecrest.readthedocs.io/en/latest/index.html
13. Fortunato, E.: STITCHES - SoS technology integration tool chain for heterogeneous electronic systems (2016). https://ndiastorage.blob.core.usgovcloudapi.net/ndia/2016/systems/18869_Fortunato_SoSITE_STITCHES_Overview_Long_9Sep2016_.pdf
14. Fowler, M.: Patterns of Enterprise Application Architecture. Addison-Wesley Longman Publishing Co. Inc., Boston (2002)
15. Gamma, E., Helm, R., Johnson, R., Vlissides, J.: Design Patterns: Elements of Reusable Object-Oriented Software. Addison-Wesley Professional (1994)
16. Gladier experiment steering (2022). https://labs.globus.org/projects/gladier.html

17. Globus automation services (2022). https://docs.globus.org/globus-automation-services
18. Heer, J., Agrawala, M.: Software design patterns for information visualization. IEEE Trans. Vis. Comput. Graph. **12**(5), 853–860 (2006). https://doi.org/10.1109/TVCG.2006.178
19. Heinonen, N.: Argonne researchers use Theta for real-time analysis of COVID-19 proteins (2020). https://www.alcf.anl.gov/news/argonne-researchers-use-theta-real-time-analysis-covid-19-proteins
20. Hukerikar, S., Engelmann, C.: Resilience design patterns: a structured approach to resilience at extreme scale. J. Supercomput. Front. Innov. (JSFI) **4**(3), 4–42 (2017). https://doi.org/10.14529/jsfi170301
21. Hukerikar, S., Engelmann, C.: Resilience design patterns: a structured approach to resilience at extreme scale (version 1.2). Technical report, ORNL/TM-2017/745, Oak Ridge National Laboratory, Oak Ridge, TN, USA (2017). https://doi.org/10.2172/1436045
22. ISO/IEC JTC 1/SC 7 Software and systems engineering: ISO/IEC/IEEE 21839:2019 (2019). https://www.iso.org/standard/71955.html
23. ISO/IEC/IEEE: ISO/IEC/IEEE 42010 - A Conceptual Model of Architecture Description (2019). http://www.iso-architecture.org/42010/cm/
24. Kaplan, L.: HPE cray supercomputer modernized system management and compute environment. Presentation at the 10th Accelerated Data Analytics and Computing Institute Workshop (2021)
25. Kebotix (2022). https://www.kebotix.com
26. Kircher, M., Jain, P.: Pattern-Oriented Software Architecture, Volume 3: Patterns for Resource Management. Wiley, Hoboken (2004)
27. Kruchten, P.: Architectural blueprints - the "4+1" view model of software architecture. IEEE Softw. **12**(6), 42–50 (1995). http://www.cs.ubc.ca/gregor/teaching/papers/4+1view-architecture.pdf
28. Kubernetes (2022). https://kubernetes.io
29. Maier, M.W.: Architecting principles for system-of-systems. Syst. Eng. **1**(4), 267–284 (1998)
30. Maier, M.W., Rechtin, E.: The Art of Systems Architecting (Systems Engineering). CRC Press, Boca Raton (2009)
31. Manthorpe, W.H.J., Jr.: The emerging joint system of systems: a systems engineering challenge and opportunity for APL. John Hopkins APL Tech. Digest **17**(3), 305–313 (1996)
32. National Energy Research Scientific Computing Center (NERSC): Superfacility API (2022). https://api.nersc.gov
33. National Energy Research Scientific Computing Center (NERSC): Superfacility project (2022). https://www.nersc.gov/research-and-development/superfacility
34. Naughton, T., et al.: Software framework for federated science instruments. In: Nichols, J., Verastegui, B., Maccabe, A.B., Hernandez, O., Parete-Koon, S., Ahearn, T. (eds.) SMC 2020. CCIS, vol. 1315, pp. 189–203. Springer, Cham (2020). https://doi.org/10.1007/978-3-030-63393-6_13
35. Netflix: Netflix OSS (2022). https://netflix.github.io
36. Netflix: Spring Cloud Netflix (2022). https://spring.io/projects/spring-cloud-netflix
37. Pei, R.S.: System of systems integration (SoSI) - a smart way of acquiring army C4I2WS systems. In: Proceedings of the Summer Computer Simulation Conference 2000, pp. 574–579 (2000)

38. Rechtin, E.: Systems Architecting: Creating & Building Complex Systems. Prentice Hall (1990)
39. Sanderson, K.: Automation: chemistry shoots for the moon. Nature **568**, 577–579 (2019). https://doi.org/10.1038/d41586-019-01246-y. https://www.nature.com/articles/d41586-019-01246-y
40. Schmidt, D.C., Stal, M., Rohnert, H., Buschmann, F.: Pattern-Oriented Software Architecture Volume 2: Patterns for Concurrent and Networked Objects. Wiley, Hoboken (2000)
41. Stevens, R., Taylor, V., Nichols, J., Maccabe, A.B., Yelick, K., Brown, D.: AI for science report (2020). https://www.anl.gov/ai-for-science-report
42. Talton, J., Yang, L., Kumar, R., Lim, M., Goodman, N., Měch, R.: Learning design patterns with Bayesian grammar induction. In: Proceedings of the 25th Annual ACM Symposium on User Interface Software and Technology (UIST) 2012, pp. 63–74. ACM, New York (2012). https://doi.org/10.1145/2380116.2380127
43. Troutman, K.: Superfacility framework advances photosynthesis research (2019). https://www.nersc.gov/news-publications/nersc-news/science-news/2019/superfacility-framework-advances-photosynthesis-research
44. UIPath (2022). https://www.uipath.com
45. UK Ministry of Defense: MOD architecture framework (2012). https://www.gov.uk/guidance/mod-architecture-framework
46. U.S. Department of Defense: The DoDAF architecture framework version 2.02 (2010). https://dodcio.defense.gov/Library/DoD-Architecture-Framework
47. Wolff, E.: Microservices: Flexible Software Architectures. Addison-Wesley Professional (2016)

Real-Time Edge Processing During Data Acquisition

Max Rietmann[✉], Praveen Nakshatrala, Jonathan Lefman,
and Geetika Gupta

NVIDIA Corporation, Zürich, Switzerland
mrietmann@nvidia.com
https://www.nvidia.com

Abstract. The next generation of high-intensity light sources, microscopes, and particle accelerators enable exciting new insights and discoveries. However, the data rates generated by these sophisticated instruments are exploding due to higher sensor scan rates and increased resolution. In parallel, the vision connecting experiments with real time feedback, steering, and integration demands new solutions in both hardware and software. An edge-supercomputer co-located with the sensors or instruments combined with a larger supercomputer enables real-time processing of streaming experimental data at the edge with resource intensive analysis, simulation, and reconstruction at the larger cluster.

Today, post-acquisition data processing is expensive in terms of time as well as storage, and it is scientifically costly since many opportunities are missed during data acquisition. We will describe how a small computational infrastructure can reduce the cost and latency to using the data as it is generated.

Using applications in ptychography and light sheet microscopy as examples, this paper will show how to build data streaming pipelines that form the foundation for real-time processing, visualization, feedback, and steering. We will show how a developer can write high-performance data processing pipelines using Python and C/C++ to integrate traditional processing with the latest ML and AI techniques. We highlight end-to-end performance profiling and optimization as well as the libraries and frameworks from NVIDIA to build these application-driven processing pipelines from edge to computing center.

This work pushes us towards the vision of realizing an end-to-end workflow starting with streaming directly from the instrument at the edge to the data center.

Keywords: HPC@Edge · GPU computing · Streaming processing · Visualization

1 Introduction

The next generation of high-intensity light sources and advanced microscopes will lead to exciting new scientific discoveries and insights. With enhanced resolution

K. Doug et al. (Eds.): SMC 2022, CCIS 1690, pp. 191–205, 2022.
https://doi.org/10.1007/978-3-031-23606-8_12

and increased speeds of sensor-data acquisition, these sophisticated instruments produce data at high volumes and velocities. To manage this data deluge, streaming processing pipelines are a key building block to ensuring timely results, live visualization, and feedback control. Such real-time processing of data pipelines from the edge to the computing center warrants novel software and hardware enhancements.

Often, various processing steps are involved in the analysis of data and typically, a data-processing pipeline is employed. Staging data through non-volatile I/O between these processing steps, though common, is a bottleneck to achieving real-time analysis of data at scale. To address these concerns, this paper presents a suite of solutions for developing streaming reactive pipelines, GPU-accelerated libraries for data ingestion and processing.

Despite the accelerating computational requirements, most scientists have embraced Python-based open-source frameworks because of the ease of prototyping and iterating on new implementations. Computational performance optimization is often pushed to the final stages of deployment, after a satisfactory implementation is in place. Frameworks and libraries like NumPy and PyTorch are often employed. This paper will address improving computational throughput and efficiency for real-time experiments without dramatic changes to current code bases.

This paper will cover topics including:

- Commonalities across these sensor-driven processing pipelines, particularly the transition from high-data rate processing (frame-by-frame) to high-corpus processing (collective processing and analysis of many frames).
- Example applications include x-ray ptychography and lattice light sheet microscopy; covering common workflows, data rates and processing requirements.
- Performance optimization results obtained through the adoption of GPU-accelerated frameworks like JAX and CuPy.
- Introduction of a new streaming data-processing library, NVIDIA Streaming Reactive Framework (SRF). This library enables developers to build high-performance data-pipelines containing several processing stages.
- Conclusions and discussion on what can be realized today and the future for streaming processing pipelines.

2   Common Sensor-Driven Workflows

Typical real-time sensor-driven experimental processing pipelines have common patterns. Considering scientific and manufacturing instruments, sensors generate raw data streams which are consumed and processed into downstream data components. In Fig. 1, raw data from sensors are corrected and normalized, forming sub-components of data. An example of such a process is dark current compensation for electron-counting cameras. These sub-components are further assembled into minimal data units. An example of assembling data sub-components into a minimal data unit is correcting motion from electron beam induced motion from a cryo-EM datasets [15]. Finally, minimal data units assembled or reconstructed into a complete finalized dataset. An example of creating a finalized dataset is aligning and mutually reconstructing multiple overlapping x-ray tomographic projections [5].

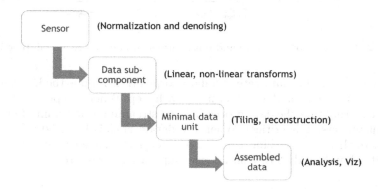

Fig. 1. Typical processing and data flows across real-time instrument processing pipelines

This generic workflow model applies to many use cases, and a critical property of these data-processing pipelines is the change of the data rate through the application and how dependencies across data units change through the pipeline.

2.1   Data Rates and Data Burden

Many applications tend to stage data through non-volatile I/O because real-time processing has not been achievable, thus data streams are stored. Using files from storage is a limitation to make real-time processing schemes; reading data from disk takes as much or more time than processing. To meet high data rates and achieve real-time data processing, it is imperative to move toward an in-memory streaming workflow. Based on our collaboration with several research groups, streaming and collective operations are a commonality among various edge processing workflows. Streaming processing relies on data with no or few dependencies and performance is typically limited by I/O throughput. Collective operations require several large blocks of data to build the final result, whether it be the final reconstructed image or 3D tomogram, for example.

These operations can be thought of as a transition from the source, raw sensor data, which typically generates data at the highest rate but with lower data amount than what goes into a minimal data unit. The transition from the data generator (sensor) to the final data product (assembled data) is visualized in Fig. 2.

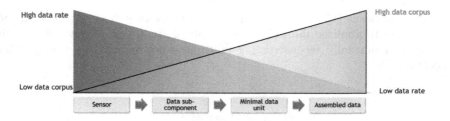

Fig. 2. Evolution of data rate and data corpus through a processing pipeline

A key factor in this data-rate and data-corpus transition is the hardware and software requirements and architecture at each step. When the peak data-rate is highest, ensuring that the data processing and streaming is not limited by I/O or inefficient processing is critical. When the data-corpus is high, I/O throughput is less critical, but processing times and potentially memory capacity become more critical and need to rely on larger computational resources.

3 Applications

With the transition from high-data rates to high-data corpus pipelines in mind, we will now introduce two application areas that fit this model, *ptychography* and *lattice light sheet microscopy*. For each of these applications, the specifics of the data flow components including data dimensions and rate for each step will show how the general concept applies and conforms to general computational workflows originating at scientific instruments.

Through representative examples from ptychography and lattice light sheet microscopy, we demonstrate the application of these technologies to enable real-time data processing and visualization at the edge.

3.1 X-Ray Ptychography

One application that we will focus on is ptychography, a growing technique using high-energy X-rays to image objects with high resolution in 2D and even 3D. The x-rays are created at a facility commonly called a "light source", which derives the x-rays from a synchrotron. The technique eschews using a lens to focus the light, and instead a sensor collects a large number of scattered images, each associated with a different scan position (due to moving either the specimen or light source), as seen in Fig. 3. This enables sharper final images as well as energy regimes where lens design and construction is very challenging or impossible. This collection of images (which visually appear only as scattered light or inference patterns) undergoes several processing steps followed by a final iterative reconstruction stage which yields an image of the scanned object [7]. Depending on the location and angle of the light source, these final scans can be associated with a particular depth, such that a collection of scans can be processed into a full 3D tomographic image allowing for non-destructive visualization of integrated circuits [8] with a resolution down to 10 nm scale [9].

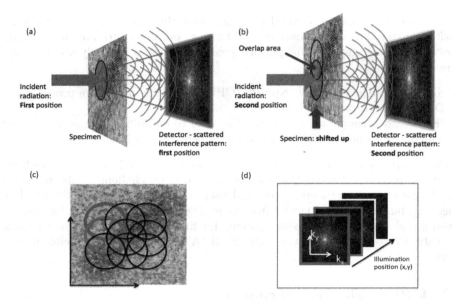

Fig. 3. Ptychography imaging overview (Image Credit: Wikipedia user 22sm22/CC BY-SA 4.0).

The data rate of ptychography is simply a product of scan rate (number of images/sec), the sensor resolution, and the image bit-depth. Current experiments produce raw data in the GB/s rate, but as sensor rates and resolutions increase, this is expected to increase to TB/s in the near term. A ptychography processing pipeline follows a common pattern:

1. Byte-level processing – arranging the raw sensor data into the image format
2. Scattered Image processing – combining multiple exposures, filtering, and image downsampling.
3. Image Reconstruction – Iteratively combine many scattered images into a single reconstructed image of the original object.

The image reconstruction is where the bulk of the algorithmic, scientific, and computational challenges are located and, accordingly, where the bulk of the development work has focused. The reconstruction algorithm itself is mostly limited by FFT throughput and performance, which is particularly well suited to GPU-accelerated FFT libraries like CUFFT. In our experience, reconstruction implementations are written using CuPy [13], PyCuda [10], and C++ with CUDA [11] and can leverage MPI to accelerate processing on multiple GPUs across many processing nodes [3,11,12]. Although most current reconstruction implementations currently require all scanned images to be present, the iterative nature of the algorithm does allow for streaming reconstruction [6], meaning that a progressive and real-time visualization of the result is possible.

Many of the codes referenced here have seen their initial processing bottleneck from step 3 to a combination of all three steps, along with any downstream processing (after step 3). This performance bottleneck is typically due to 3 factors:

1. Single-threaded Python & NumPy (CPU-only) byte and image processing.
2. Disk & File throughput limitations.
3. "Keyboard throughput" i.e., limits for users to coordinate the processing by copying files and starting scripts on a sequence of machines.

Factor 1 can be accelerated by converting the NumPy code to JAX, which we highlight in Sect. 4. Factors 2 & 3 are a more complex challenge. Files are commonly the conduit between stages, and users initiate and manage the pipeline stages by hand, transferring files from acquisition to compute nodes for preprocessing and again to multi-node systems for final analysis and reconstruction. We solve this problem in Sect. 5, using NVIDIA's SRF streaming pipeline framework.

3.2 Lattice Light Sheet Microscopy

Lightsheet microscopy is used for 3D high resolution imaging of biological samples with minimal phototoxicity and photobleaching. Images are obtained by illuminating portions of samples in the focal-plane with thin sheets of light. The fluorescence from the molecules excited within each optical section, and the field of view of the observing lens, are collected and stacked. Multiple color channels of the image correspond to different wavelengths of the light.

The data rate depends on the experiment at hand. For living and evolving biological samples, multiple image volumes are collected in short burst cycles. For dead specimens, large single volume images are acquired. Automating data acquisition will enable researchers to obtain reproducible results with minimal manual intervention, increasing experimental throughput and reliability. As a result, new techniques should be implemented to discover unique biological events. For example, cancer cells were observed splitting from 1 cell to 3 cells, instead of a canonical 1-to-2 split. This is seen in Fig. 4(a) in experimental output from the Advanced Bioimaging Center, University of California, Berkeley.

A typical data processing pipeline (Fig. 4(b)), among other processing steps, involves

1. Light sensitive camera captures a series of frames corresponding to the volume of the physical sample
2. Iterative deconvolution to filter out noise and undo the transfer function of the optical instrument
3. Deskew the 3D image volume to orient the image with respect to instrument coordinates
4. Visualizing the processed image volume in instrument coordinates

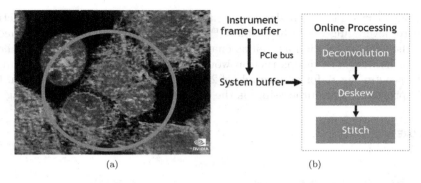

Fig. 4. (a) 3-way splitting of cancer cells (b) Typical processing steps in lightsheet microscopy

For this pipeline, visualization is desired not only as the final result, but also at several intermediate steps in the processing pipeline. A pipeline framework (see Sect. 5) can help break up the individual operations and expose the data as it moves through the pipeline to enable this visualization without a significant overhead or added implementation complexity.

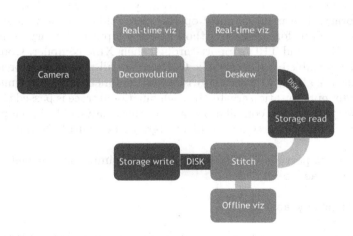

Fig. 5. SRF segment and nodes for real-time data processing. Visualization is provided for each operation of the processing pipeline.

4   High Performance GPU-Enabled Python

Working with the ptychographic imaging group at the Advanced Light Source (ALS), we were able to profile and help optimize their processing pipeline. As mentioned earlier, they put significant effort into optimizing their reconstruction software, leveraging CuPy to enable GPU-based computing, and MPI to accelerate the time-to-solution as well as enable larger working image sets. Without this acceleration, the reconstruction would be the stand-out bottleneck, but as can be seen in Fig. 6, for an example of 2500 scans of 1040×1152 resolution, the image processing (pre-processing) is the obvious next optimization goal (Fig. 5).

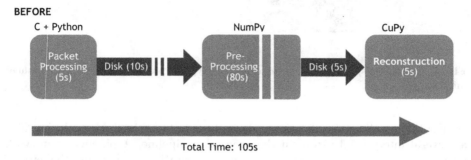

Fig. 6. Initial ptychographic processing pipeline with timing information

The pre-processing was written in NumPy with HDF5 (h5py) as the file storage library. The many NumPy operations in this processing step made it an ideal candidate for JAX, a python-based computing library from Google with CPU, GPU, and TPU support through their XLA compiler. Compared to another GPU-enabled framework like CuPy where all numerical expressions are strict, it has the ability to trace expressions at the function level at runtime. The intermediate representation created by each functional trace is passed to the XLA compiler for just-in-time compilation (jit) or other analysis like batch processing (vmap), creation of expression gradients (grad), or multi-GPU parallelization (pmap).

Superficially, porting NumPy to jax can be as simple as replacing
```
import numpy as np
```
with
```
import jax.numpy as np.
```

In practice, however, to enable all tracing features, jax enforces variable immutability. Thus any places where variables are updated using indexing, require a change in syntax from
```
imgs_out[i,:,:] = process(imgs_in[i,:,:])
```
to
```
imgs_out = imgs_out.at[i].set(process(imgs_in[i,:,:]))
```
Also any significant loops need modification to use JAX's looping mechanism so that JAX can capture the semantics of the loop without unwinding all expressions at runtime. Finally, h5py provides a convenient NumPy-like interface into the arrays stored in the HDF5 file, such that file access is on-demand and appears

to the user as simple numpy arrays. These file-access objects must be explicitly moved into JAX arrays on the GPU.

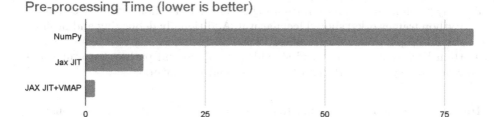

Fig. 7. Timing information for pre-processing using JAX `jit()` and `vmap()`.

Figure 7 highlights how leveraging JAX's features accelerates the preprocessing step. After applying the aforementioned changes to the processing code, including only the `jit()` operation, we already saw a 7x performance improvement from 80 s to 12 s. With some additional work to capture all processing into a single function called `def process(image)` which has only a single image as input (tensor shape = (1040, 1152)), we can leverage JAX `vmap()` operator to create a function that processes all the images (tensor shape = (2500, 1040, 1152)), which improved the runtime from 12 s to 2 s, another 6x gain for a total gain of 40x.

We additionally highlight that despite being ported to JAX, the code is still (mostly) NumPy processing code, which can be read and modified by the application scientists who first wrote and continue to maintain the code. This is a critical requirement; legibility and modifiability is critical for these smaller scale HPC applications where the user-base is small. This motivates the next section of the paper — how to chain these frequently python-based processing nodes together without losing performance (GPU data stays on the GPU) while maintaining legibility for the users.

5   Streaming Processing Pipelines

The component-wise speedups in the JAX work shown in the previous section are a critical component of the performance story of a processing pipeline, but will expose the inefficiencies in an existing file-based pipeline. Copies between CPU host memory and GPU device memory create performance bottlenecks, and using stored files as the conduit between pipeline stages only exacerbates the bottlenecks. If users manage the pipeline stages manually, often the latency they introduce will be another bottleneck, and a source of errors.

To maintain the performance gained through the use of GPU-computing we require a framework that allows us to create computational pipelines that have the following capabilities:

1. GPU-aware: Data on the GPU stays on the GPU when possible
2. Network aware: Transparent (to the user) high-performance transferring of data between physical nodes is critical because most pipelines will reach from the edge to the computing center.
3. Easy to build and maintain: Building pipelines in Python (with GPU-enabled Python frameworks) should feel natural. Additionally debugging and profiling should be possible with standard tools.
4. High Performance: Overhead should be minimal and pathways to "upgrade" pipeline stages from Python to C++ should feel natural.

Introducing SRF. Streaming Reactive Framework (SRF) is a component of NVIDIA's Morpheus (a network analysis software-development kit (SDK)) that allows users to build high-performance streaming data pipelines. It supports building complex pipelines that involve branching, joining, flow control, feedback, and back pressure. The sequence of data processing operations is captured in a computational graph. Visualized in Fig. 8, the basic building blocks of this computational graph are called nodes and segments. SRF-nodes define basic computational units, typically python functions, that perform computationally expensive operations on an input to produce an output. The connectivity of the computational graph is broken into "segments", the SRF-nodes of which are guaranteed to run on the same compute resource, meaning that node-to-node transfers remain in GPU or system memory. For segments executing on different computational resources, data transfer occurs through the network. SRF orchestrates the execution of this data pipeline by setting up an event-loop, asynchronously offloading the computation and efficiently executing the processing pipeline on the available compute-resources.

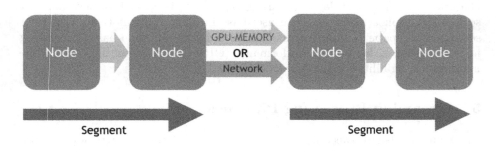

Fig. 8. SRF pipeline with several nodes connected by two segments.

SRF has a C++ runtime and the nodes typically run within a single process, and hence common debugging and profiling tooling will "just work". If several segments connect across multiple processes on different nodes, the standard tooling needs to be adapted accordingly. Nodes within SRF can be written either in Python or C++. C++ nodes are type-checked for compatibility. Python nodes simply transfer python objects from one node to the next and hence the owner-ship has to be managed by the user i.e., care must be taken to avoid modifying data downstream.

In Python, defining a segment is as simple as defining a source (see code below), processing node, and a sink (or just source & sink). In the code below, you can see an example of defining such a pipeline, where **deconvolve()** implements an image processing algorithm.

```
1    def segment_init(seg: srf.Segment):
2        source = seg.make_source("source", data_source())
3        sink = seg.make_sink("sink",
4                             sink_on_next,
5                             sink_on_error,
6                             sink_on_complete)
7
8        deconvolution_node= seg.make_node("deconvolution",
9                                          lambda x: deconvolve(x, PSF))
10       seg.make_edge(source, deconvolution_node)
11       seg.make_edge(deconvolution_node, sink)
```

A key usability feature of SRF is that nodes pass Python objects between each other, such that a deconvolution node simply wraps your existing deconvolution routine without changes, as can be seen here.

```
1    def deconvolve(img, psf, iterations=20):
2        '''
3        This function runs the Richardson-Lucy deconvolutions.
4        :img: Is the input image and it could be a numpy array or a cupy array.
5        :psf: Is the Point Spread Function and it can be a numpy array or a cupy array.
6        :iteration: Is the number of Richardson-Lucy iterations.
7        '''
8
9        # Pad PSF with zeros to match image shape
10       pad_l, pad_r = np.divmod(np.array(img.shape) - np.array(psf.shape), 2)
11       pad_r += pad_l
12       psf = np.pad(psf, tuple(zip(pad_l, pad_r)), 'constant', constant_values=0)
13
14       # Recenter PSF at the origin.
15       for i in range(psf.ndim):
16           psf = np.roll(psf, psf.shape[i] // 2, axis=i)
17
18       # Convolution requires FFT of the PSF
19       psf = np.fft.rfftn(psf)
20
21       # Perform deconvolution in-place on a copy of the image (avoids changing the original)
22       img_decon = np.copy(img)
23       for _ in range(iterations):
24           ratio = img / np.fft.irfftn(np.fft.rfftn(img_decon) * psf)
25           img_decon *= np.fft.irfftn((np.fft.rfftn(ratio).conj() * psf).conj())
26       return img_decon
```

As we saw in the JAX section, batching is a critical performance optimization in many image-processing algorithms. We can implement a batched node in a fashion similar to the code below:

```
1    def batch_pipeline(pipe_state, metadata, frame_in, frame_out):
2        ...
3        def on_next(frame):
4            i_batch = pipe_state["current_num_in_batch"]
5            pipe_state["exp_frame_batch"][i_batch, :, :] = frame_i
6            pipe_state["current_num_in_batch"] += 1
7            if pipe_state["current_num_in_batch"] == metadata["batchsize"]:
8                pipe_state["current_num_in_batch"] = 0
9                return pipe_state["exp_frame_batch"]
10
11       def on_complete():
12           if pipe_state["current_num_in_batch"] > 0:
13               batch_i = pipe_state["current_num_in_batch"]
14               return pipe_state["exp_frame_batch"][:batch_i, :, :]
15           frame_in.pipe(ops.map(on_next),
16                         ops.filter(lambda x: not isinstance(x, type(None))),
17                         ops.on_completed(on_complete)).subscribe(frame_out)
```

By maintaining a mutable state variable `pipe_state`, we gather frames into a batched image container, which is passed downstream to the next node once full (`on_next`). If the stream ends without completely filling the batch, `on_complete` sends the existing frames which ensures that we neither hang waiting for more frames nor drop frames. This enables a pipeline seen in Fig. 9. Considering the

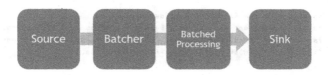

Fig. 9. Batched deconvolution pipeline

pre-processing example given in the JAX section, with this pipeline we are able to eliminate the disk stages taking the runtime from 105 s to 12 s, a speedup 9x which is highlighted in Fig. 10. By using SRF to eliminate files connecting the

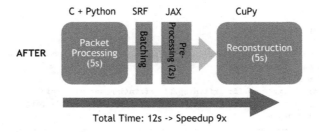

Fig. 10. Batched Ptychographic processing pipeline using JAX & SRF.

three pipeline stages we can yield a total speedup of 9x. Additionally, we can run the packet processing and image pre-processing at a node close to the sensor, and the reconstruction in a more-powerful system with pre-processed images transferred over the network.

5.1   Supercomputing as a Service (SCaaS)

With SRF, we can process and stream data from high-throughput edge hardware to larger-compute resources located at a supercomputing center to handle the high data corpus components of the processing workflow (e.g., ptychographic reconstruction) where time-to-solution and memory requirements are more demanding. With most of the processing software challenges solved, the problem becomes the ability to guarantee computing resources during data collection and stream the data from the experiment to the cluster. Recent work towards streaming Ptychography process in Switzerland at the Paul Scherrer Institute, (PSI) and the Swiss Supercomputing Center (CSCS) have managed to build streaming workflows [11] and have proven that these centers can stream results reliably and securely.

Alternatively, Globus (globus.org) is a framework and system for managing large datasets, and is a common way for scientists to transfer, manipulate, and process files across their own local systems and supercomputing resources like those found at NERSC and others. Extending Globus is *Globus Automate*, which provides the ability to write "flows" which allow the user to specify computational events triggered by files. These computational stages can be run locally or on supercomputing resources, yielding a *service* oriented structure to the computation and the center itself [4]. Assuming Ptychography or other Sensor-driven workflows are pipelined with SRF, we also require "SCaaS" to enable data to be streamed to the computing center live while avoiding expensive file-oriented designs, which limit the streaming performance to disk throughput.

The framework and the GPU optimizations highlighted in this paper have given solutions to the software architecture and performance requirements for streaming sensor processing, however we hope that supercomputing centers can use it as a benchmark for modifying and designing current and next generation systems for the expanding needs of their users.

6   Conclusion

Instruments and their research tasks have unique workflows, but have overall commonalities where best practices can be applied. Examples as diverse as particle accelerator beam lines to constantly changing novel light microscopes, we apply accelerated processing and visualization where it is most beneficial today. Each scientific domain will adopt such techniques independently.

Science and manufacturing disciplines are deploying more dynamic approaches to increase the efficiency of instrument usage: maximize data quality and minimize blind data acquisition. Developing integrated intelligent workflows as close to the sensor as possible ultimately improves data acquisition and optimizes time per experiment [14]. The demand is increasing for instruments like cryo-em, which make extensive use of automation already, but high purchase and operation costs are barriers to access [2]. National centers like NIH-funded cryo-em centers [1] are the worldwide trend. The focus is on maximizing instrument throughput and training new technologists. Globally such efforts democratize access to expensive instruments and technological best practices.

A key component to ensuring these trends continue is rapid access to data at all steps of the acquisition process. Breaking down the data acquisition process into components from raw data streams to final assembled data gives us an opportunity to apply optimal processing at each step using the right level of computational infrastructure. With access to the data, streaming visualization can be more easily implemented, giving quicker feedback for experimental adjustments and even higher-level experimental control. The GPU-accelerated Python and SRF tooling described in this paper show the advantages such workflows could provide to help the application scientists achieve the performance necessary to unlock the potential of their newest and future devices while keeping their software simple enough for them to maintain.

Acknowledgements. We thank our colleagues Jack Wells, Chris Porter, and Ryan Olson for their useful feedback. We additionally thank David Shapiro and Pablo Enfedaque at ALS for their collaboration; and Gokul Upadhyaula, Matthew Mueller, Thayer Alshaabi, and Xiongtao Ruan at the Advanced Bioimaging Center, University of California, Berkeley for their ongoing collaboration.

References

1. NIH funds three national cryo-EM service centers and training for new microscopists | National Institutes of Health (NIH). https://www.nih.gov/news-events/news-releases/nih-funds-three-national-cryo-em-service-centers-training-new-microscopists
2. The must-have multimillion-dollar microscopy machine | News | Nature Index. https://www.natureindex.com/news-blog/must-have-multimillion-dollar-microscopy-machine-cryo-em
3. Batey, D., Rau, C., Cipiccia, S.: High-speed X-ray ptychographic tomography. Sci. Rep. **12**(1), 1–6 (2022). https://doi.org/10.1038/s41598-022-11292-8
4. Blaiszik, B., Chard, K., Chard, R., Foster, I., Ward, L.: Data automation at light sources. In: AIP Conference Proceedings, vol. 2054, no. 1, p. 020003 (2019). https://doi.org/10.1063/1.5084563. https://aip.scitation.org/doi/abs/10.1063/1.5084563
5. Elbakri, I.A., Fessler, J.A.: Statistical image reconstruction for polyenergetic X-ray computed tomography. IEEE Trans. Med. Imaging **21**(2), 89–99 (2002). https://doi.org/10.1109/42.993128
6. Enders, B., et al.: Dataflow at the COSMIC beamline - stream processing and supercomputing. Microsc. Microanal. **24**(S2), 56–57 (2018). https://doi.org/10.1017/S1431927618012710. https://www.cambridge.org/core/journals/microscopy-and-microanalysis/article/dataflow-at-the-cosmic-beamline-stream-processing-and-supercomputing/2F4AD3721A36EE02C0336A8191356065

7. Guizar-Sicairos, M., et al.: High-throughput ptychography using Eiger: scanning X-ray nano-imaging of extended regions. Opt. Express **22**(12), 14859–14870 (2014). https://doi.org/10.1364/OE.22.014859

8. Holler, M., et al.: High-resolution non-destructive three-dimensional imaging of integrated circuits. Nature **543**(7645), 402–406 (2017). https://doi.org/10.1038/nature21698. https://www.nature.com/articles/nature21698

9. Holler, M., et al.: Three-dimensional imaging of integrated circuits with macro- to nanoscale zoom. Nat. Electron. **2**(10), 464–470 (2019). https://doi.org/10.1038/s41928-019-0309-z. https://www.nature.com/articles/s41928-019-0309-z

10. Klöckner, A., Pinto, N., Lee, Y., Catanzaro, B., Ivanov, P., Fasih, A.: PyCUDA and PyOpenCL: a scripting-based approach to GPU run-time code generation. Parallel Comput. **38**(3), 157–174 (2012). https://doi.org/10.1016/J.PARCO.2011.09.001

11. Leong, S.H., Stadler, H.C., Chang, M.C., Dorsch, J.P., Aliaga, T., Ashton, A.W.: SELVEDAS: a data and compute as a service workflow demonstrator targeting supercomputing ecosystems. In: Proceedings of SuperCompCloud 2020: 3rd Workshop on Interoperability of Supercomputing and Cloud Technologies, Held in conjunction with SC 2020: The International Conference for High Performance Computing, Networking, Storage and Analysis, pp. 7–13 (2020). https://doi.org/10.1109/SUPERCOMPCLOUD51944.2020.00007

12. Marchesini, S., et al.: SHARP: a distributed GPU-based ptychographic solver. J. Appl. Crystallogr. **49**(4), 1245–1252 (2016). https://doi.org/10.1107/S1600576716008074. http://scripts.iucr.org/cgi-bin/paper?jo5020. URN: ISSN 1600-5767

13. Okuta, R., Unno, Y., Nishino, D., Hido, S., Loomis, C.: CuPy: a NumPy-compatible library for NVIDIA GPU calculations. Technical report (2017). https://github.com/cupy/cupy

14. Zhang, Z., et al.: Toward fully automated UED operation using two-stage machine learning model. Sci. Rep. **12**(1), 1–12 (2022). https://doi.org/10.1038/s41598-022-08260-7. https://www.nature.com/articles/s41598-022-08260-7

15. Zheng, S.Q., Palovcak, E., Armache, J.P., Verba, K.A., Cheng, Y., Agard, D.A.: MotionCor2: anisotropic correction of beam-induced motion for improved cryo-electron microscopy. Nat. Methods **14**(4), 331–332 (2017). https://doi.org/10.1038/nmeth.4193. https://www.nature.com/articles/nmeth.4193

Towards a Software Development Framework for Interconnected Science Ecosystems

Addi Malviya Thakur[1]([✉]), Seth Hitefield[1], Marshall McDonnell[1],
Matthew Wolf[1], Richard Archibald[1], Lance Drane[1], Kevin Roccapriore[1],
Maxim Ziatdinov[1], Jesse McGaha[1], Robert Smith[1], John Hetrick[1],
Mark Abraham[1], Sergey Yakubov[1], Greg Watson[1], Ben Chance[1],
Clara Nguyen[1], Matthew Baker[2], Robert Michael[3], Elke Arenholz[4],
and Ben Mintz[1]

[1] Oak Ridge National Laboratory, Oak Ridge, TN, USA
{malviyaa,hitefieldsd,mcdonnellmt,wolfmd,archibaldrk,dranelt,
roccapriorkm,ziatdinovma,mcgahajr,smithrw,hetrickjm,abrahamme,
yakubovs,watsongr,chancebr,nguyencv,mintzbj}@ornl.gov
[2] Voltron Data, Mountain View, CA, USA
matthew@voltrondata.com
[3] Roche Sequencing Solutions, Willmington, MA, USA
[4] Pacific Northwest National Laboratory, Richland, WA, USA
elke.arenholz@pnnl.gov

Abstract. The innovative science of the future must be multi-domain and interconnected to usher in the next generation of "self-driving" laboratories enabling consequential discoveries and transformative inventions. Such a disparate and interconnected ecosystem of scientific instruments will need to evolve using a system-of-systems (SoS) approach. The key to enabling application integration with such an SoS will be the use of Software Development Kits (SDKs). Currently, SDKs facilitate scientific research breakthroughs via algorithmic automation, databases and storage, optimization and structure, pervasive environmental monitoring, among others. However, existing SDKs lack instrument-interoperability and reusability capabilities, do not effectively work in an open federated architectural environment, and are largely isolated within silos of the respective scientific disciplines. Inspired by the scalable SoS framework, this work proposes the development of INTERSECT-SDK to provide a coherent environment for multi-domain scientific applications to benefit from the open federated architecture in an interconnected ecosystem of instruments. This approach will decompose functionality into loosely coupled software services for interoperability among several solutions that do not scale beyond a single domain and/or application. Furthermore, the proposed environment will allow operational and managerial inter-dependence while providing opportunities for the researchers to reuse software components from other domains and build universal solution libraries. We demonstrate this research for microscopy use-case, where we show how INTERSECT-SDK is developing the tools necessary to enable advanced scanning methods and accelerate scientific discovery.

© The Author(s), under exclusive license to Springer Nature Switzerland AG 2022
K. Doug et al. (Eds.): SMC 2022, CCIS 1690, pp. 206–224, 2022.
https://doi.org/10.1007/978-3-031-23606-8_13

Keywords: Autonomous experiments · SDK · DevSecOps ·
Interconnected science · Edge computing · Research infrastructure ·
Scientific software · Scientific workflows · Federated instruments ·
Digital twins

1   Introduction

The future of science is a highly connected ecosystem of instruments, sensors, devices, and computing resources at the edge combined with cloud computing and centralized high-performance-computing systems that execute machine learning infused workflows to enable self-driven, automated scientific experiments. DNA sequencing is a great example of how enabling automation in a workflow has had a significant effect in science. The initial sequencing of the human genome completed in 2001 was estimated to have cost over $100M and took over 10 years. With improvements to sequencing techniques and applying automation, the cost of sequencing a whole genome is now less than $10K and takes a few days or less. The impact this has had on scientific discovery and the medical community is profound.

The potential importance of interconnected science infrastructures has caused increased interest from many areas, and systems can go by many names such as: federated systems, cognitive digital twins, or (our preferred) interconnected science ecosystems. In this push toward interconnected science systems, much of the attention is focused on the runtime and deployment aspects. However, progress must be built on transitioning from ad hoc demonstrations to a reliable, reusable, verifiable, and scientifically reproducible infrastructure that addresses the hardware, software, and wetware components.

In this paper, we will present our designs and early progress for an integrated software development kit (SDK) geared specifically for the interconnected science ecosystem. The larger initiative at Oak Ridge National Laboratory (ORNL) for interconnected ecosystems goes by the name INTERSECT, and correspondingly we call our work the INTERSECT-SDK. The development process for INTERSECT-style applications and use-cases requires many iterations between hardware, software, and human process engineering, but the core data connections and processing all live within the software space, as does this work.

Scientists are limited in many ways by the current disjointed state of experimental resources. Scientific instruments produce massive amounts of data and managing this data is not trivial. Many systems are not directly connected with each other which further complicates data movement. This results in scientists collecting data from multiple runs using pre-determined experimental conditions, and spending weeks (if not months) analyzing collected data. If those experiments do not yield desirable results, the entire process may need to be restarted causing a long time-to-result. An interconnected ecosystem will enable more efficient scientific experimentation by integrating access to computing resources, allowing resource sharing, adopting new artificial intelligence (AI) control capabilities, and improving overall system utilization. This will enable self-driven, automated experiments which can significantly reduce the overall time-to-result.

The key contributions of this paper are three-fold: (a) the design and initial implementation of a user-centric SDK for interconnected science development; (b) an evaluation of how best practices for research software engineering are adapted to such development, and; (c) a concrete demonstration of using proposed SDK in a real-world application.

In the remainder of the paper, we start by grounding the discussion using this experience with interconnecting Scanning Transmission Electron Microscopy (STEM) instruments and edge computing to enable concurrent computational analysis (Sect. 2). We then discuss our development approach (Sect. 3) and the design (Sect. 4) of our SDK. The INTERSECT-SDK design, approach, and overall infrastructure build on many examples and lessons learned from some prior work we further detail in (Sect. 5) before we conclude with our analysis in (Sect. 6).

2   Motivating Use-Case: Scanning Transmission Electron Microscope

Scanning Transmission Electron Microscopy (STEM) has long been an important technique for experimental science domains from material science to biology [26]. With the growth in computing power and data acquisition rates, microscopy has begun to study the data from Convergent Beam Electron Diffraction patterns (CBED) to greatly enhance the material properties that can be measured [25]. The combination of 2D CBED patterns, measured at the 2D spatial location of STEM produce what is known ad 4D–STEM data. The analysis of the data that comes out of the microscopes has long depended on computational analysis of the signals, but the goals for newer experimental design call for much more aggressive couplings between advanced simulation and artificial intelligence (AI) algorithms and the experimental plan. Recently, part of this team has used AI methods to develop algorithms for automatic experimental 4D–STEM acquisition [30]. A team at ORNL's Center for Nanophase Materials Sciences (CNMS), working with the larger INTERSECT community, has been working to develop a coupled platform between the microscopes and AI-guided experimental control systems to make scientific discovery faster and more repeatable.

Put simply, the goal of this project was to allow a user to put in a high-level goal for using the microscope to study a material sample, and the AI-guided process would automatically learn and guide adjustment of parameters to achieve those goals, accelerating analysis with GPU based "edge" systems. For example, a sample with a number of defects in it would be loaded in, and the experiment would be directed to find and characterize the material. The scientists would need to help define AI algorithms to identify the correct locations within a coarse-grained scan of the surface, target fine-grained examination of both 'normal' areas and the defects, and then prioritize the remaining list of potential targets against a heuristic metric of 'characterized enough'. This leverages previous work in both the electronic control of microscopes [33] and the use of AI characterization methods [30]. Incorporating this project into the interconnected

INTERSECT ecosystem and distributing various components to accelerators allows the experiment operate in real-time and introduces new opportunities and deep complexities (Fig. 1).

Beyond the science results, this 4D–STEM project also highlights some of the key difficulties in developing, sharing, and maintaining the infrastructures needed for science. As mentioned in the introduction, there are a laundry list of concerns when trying to interconnect experimental and simulation or AI components. Understanding the data flow between them so that you capture not only the correct data interface types but also the frequencies and sizes is crucial during the development process. However, this can't generally be done by taking a facility off-line for months at a time so that the hardware and software links can be co-developed. Instead, the software development program needs to progress based on 'good enough' digital twins of the instrument that can respond to controls in typical ways and time frames, and that can generate data of appropriate sizes and complexity.

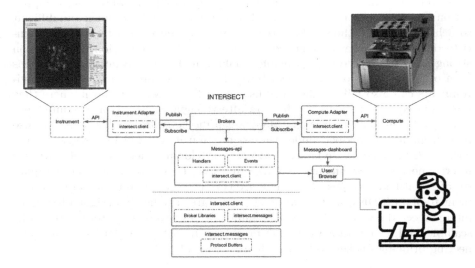

Fig. 1. SDK depiction of 4D–STEM use case in INTERSECT. The instrument control and analysis is distributed throughout the interconnected ecosystem allowing users to execute analysis remotely and take advantage of distributed accelerators.

Here, the INTERSECT 4D–STEM team helped the development process by providing expert knowledge about the Nion Swift control software and data processing pipeline for the STEM instruments [19, 24]. The synthetic data generation capabilities allow a developer to send control message to the digital twin using the exact same interfaces and response time scales as when running on a real microscope. So development can be tested, go through continuous integration, engage in test-driven development, and other similar strong research software engineering practices without the need for concurrent facility reservations. At the end of sprints, a much more limited reservation time could be utilized to assess any drift between the virtual and physical hardware behaviors.

In addition to cementing the central role of digital twins in the process of reliable development for interconnected infrastructures, the process of working on the 4D–STEM use case also highlighted the critical need for tested, stable, and reusable data management buses. It is easy enough to do a one-off demonstration, but stretching from that to a new capability is a software engineering challenge. SDK needs to be able to connect highly heterogeneous devices and needs to be able to operate seamlessly. Next we describe in detail the software engineering practices needed to make autonomous 4D-STEM experiments accessible to domain scientists.

3   Approach

As systems become more interconnected, interoperability among scientific applications and control software packages becomes increasingly complex and difficult to achieve. Because these solutions are sometimes developed by domain scientists rather than software engineers, they can lack a foundation developed on strong software engineering principles making it difficult to integrate solutions with other packages or scale them beyond a certain limit. Such software environments can also fail to efficiently use the rich hardware platform where they are deployed, and security is often an afterthought rather than a requirement during the initial development. Many scientific software applications are also monolithic and developed under the assumption it will run in a single system context. Combined, these factors can make developing scientific applications for interconnected environments a challenging task that can impact on the quality of scientific outcomes. There is a growing need for better software development toolkits (SDKs) and environments that are specifically designed to enable interconnected science ecosystems. A multi domain aware, easy-to-use, reusable, scalable, and secure framework built on strong, industry standard software engineering principles is key to fully realizing this goal.

3.1   Designing for Interconnected Science Ecosystems

Our goal is developing an SDK that seamlessly integrates instruments, computational resources, applications, tools, data, and other components into a common, connected ecosystem to simplify and accelerate scientific applications. But, we first need to have a sound understanding of example scientific use-cases and how we intend to distribute applications before we can effectively design the SDK and integrate it with those use-cases. We are using an iterative approach to design and develop the SDK which allows us to easily and quickly pivot priorities, adapt to new use-cases, develop new features, and improve existing applications.

Distributed Workflow: The STEM workflow discussed in Sect. 2 is our initial use-case that is driving the SDK design. The original workflow is a large script that includes the instrument control logic, data analysis, and the overall experiment decision logic and assumes direct access to NionSwift [34] to interface with the instrument. However, moving this fully integrated application into a distributed ecosystem where it can benefit from GPU acceleration for the AI models is a non-trivial task. The application was built assuming direct access to the control software application-programming-interface (API), so it cannot simply be moved to the edge compute system.

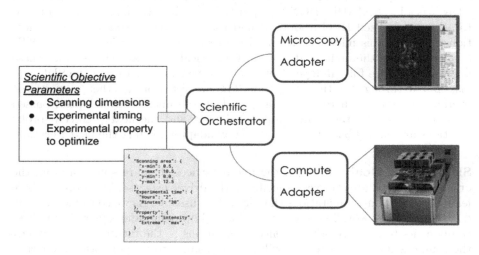

Fig. 2. Distributed version of the STEM use-case serving as the initial driver for SDK design. The original application is a single script executing in the NionSwift control application and here has been split into three main components: Microscopy adapter, compute adapter, and the scientific orchestrator.

We worked closely with the science team to understand their workflow and identified pieces that could be broken down into manageable components that could be automated and deployed. The overall approach is shown in Fig. 2 and includes three main micro-services that together comprise the workflow functionality: the Microscopy adapter, the Compute adapter, and the Scientific Orchestrator. The Microscopy adapter micro-service is responsible for handling any interaction with the instrument itself (such as moving a probe or acquiring data), the Compute adapter micro-service will analyze data using AI models, and the orchestrator will manage data movement and determine when the overall experiment is complete. All of these micro-services use a common messaging subsystem and libraries that we are developing in the SDK which is further discussed in Sect. 4.

Rather than tackling this workflow in its entirety, we are using a staged approach to develop each of the individual micro-services of the workflow. We first focused on developing the microscopy adapter and interfacing it with Nion Swift [34]. Once we identified patterns for interfacing with the microscope, these sections were moved to a separate adapter and the original code was modified to send and receive messages to a remote adapter. The next step was separating the higher-level experiment logic from the AI based analysis. The analysis service trains machine learning models and predicts the next coordinates to probe and the overall experiment orchestrator makes final decisions determining if the experiment goal was reached. Separating the higher-level logic and analysis allowed these micro-services to also be distributed at the edge. In this case, the "edge" system may not be typical of what is normally considered the edge; it is a large NVIDIA DGX-2 [13] distributed to instrument sites (compared to other centralized HPC resources) and used for accelerating the AI applications. The analysis micro-service needed to run persistently on the edge DGX accelerator, but the orchestrator could theoretically run anywhere. Once these micro-services are fully independent, they can be connected using the SDK and distributed throughout the ecosystem. The orchestrator can then manage the overall experiment where data is acquired by the microscopy adapter, passed to and analyzed by the edge compute adapter, and the next predicted probe locations are passed back to the microscopy adapter to start the next iteration.

SDK Design Goals: Initially, the micro-services that are split out from the original workflow are still very specific to the driver use-case, but stopping here leads to ad-hoc implementations that are not re-useable. As we continue to break down the STEM workflow, we are gradually improving and generalizing these components to support other science applications in the future, and we expect the components we develop now will need to change to support other scenarios. Good examples of this are the instrument adapter and the orchestrator. Our initial instrument adapter only implements the required functions to support this specific AI-infused STEM workflow, but we can continuously re-use those existing capabilities add new patterns based on other STEM workflows that use the same instruments. Similarly, the initial orchestrator is a simplified version of the original script which passes messages to the other micro-services in place of the original API calls. As we integrate other workflows, we will develop this into an intelligent orchestration engine which takes domain-specific configurations as input that include the experiment parameters such as scanning dimensions, timing, and property to optimize. This iterative approach will help us develop an SDK that enables complex systems that are easier to distribute, replicate, extend, reuse, and integrate. We can better understand what capabilities need to be fully implemented within the SDK and this allows for components to be gradually generalized and will result in re-useable and inter-operable components for future use-cases.

Our SDK will expose application programming interfaces (APIs) for services, scientific libraries, and components that can work with varied instruments across multiple sites (Fig. 4). It will support reusable, open-standards-based components to enable the interconnected science ecosystem within the Department of

Energy's (DOE) science facilities so workflows are not developed independently for each new use-case. Our standards-based, secure, and reusable framework will enable the laboratory of the future where instruments and resources are interconnected through an open, hardware/software architecture that science experiments to execute across systems and process data in a coherent fashion.

3.2 Digital Twins

Our approach includes supporting digital twin environments based on science proposals supported by the INTERSECT initiative. Digital twins are virtual environments that imitate a certain scientific instrument or setting as closely as feasible and provide the user with the same software environment as the actual system. Some of the replicated components of the twin layer's workflow will be general, while others will be instrument- and physics-specific to the selected science use-case. The digital twin environments will provide the API and SDK for users to develop scientific workflows in the virtual environments and will include the expected micro-services and access methods. Digital twins will shift how physical world experiments and processes are realized by allowing users to first develop using a virtual environment rather than the actual instrument which improves safety and repeatability and accelerates discoveries. Digital twins include: (a) Instrument models and synthetic data sources: The basis of the digital twin are models of scientific instruments from specific use-cases. These virtual instruments will model a real system and provide the same control and monitoring interface expected of a real system. (b) Computational and data resources: The digital twin systems will provide computational resources so the virtual federated environment can execute actual workflows. These can be implemented using existing virtualization capabilities such as virtual machines and containers. (c) Network resources: Networking is the last main component of the digital twin environment. This provides the simulated connectivity between disparate resources to mimic the actual environment.

3.3 DevSecOps, Process and Software Excellence

DevOps: INTERSECT-SDK seeks to shorten development cycles and enable quick response and resolution to scientific software issues, boost productivity, test new methods and algorithms, and keep domain scientists engaged by reducing complexities of development and deployment. To address these challenges, we use a full development, security, and operations (DevSecOps) environment for end-to-end testing and demonstration.

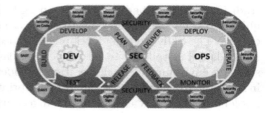

Fig. 3. DevSecsOps workflow

It supports the full OODA (Observe, Orient, Decide, Act) loop throughout development and testing [36].

As part of our DevSecOps (Fig. 3), we plan to take the following approaches: (a) Developers implement low level (unit) tests as part of the code (b) Stand up CI automation and trigger builds for every pull request to run automated low-level testing (i.e., unit tests) as well as do static code analysis to provide fast feedback for rejected changes. (c) Ensure all high-level testing (i.e., integration, system, regression, performance, etc.) is executed. (d) Implement CI practices. All developers branch from the trunk, make changes in feature branches, and submit merge requests (MRs) back to the trunk. We will use Infrastructure-as-Code (IaC) practices to capture necessary infrastructure and configuration management in version-controlled code to promote operational reproducibility and reliability.

Security: Another critical component of our SDK is the end-to-end security layer. Security in the past was isolated and added in the later stages of software development as an "after-thought" which leads to "retro-fitting" applications. Addressing vulnerabilities becomes an ad-hoc operation leading to poor accountability of critical components in production software. Thus, integrating security requirements as part of the overall workflow and system architecture is essential to build a robust foundation for the framework itself. The SDK puts security at the forefront and we are and designing end-to-end security into the core of the frameworks. This includes mechanisms such as encrypting messages for all data, application, and core services of the frameworks with end-to-end security [12]. Additionally, there needs to be a consistent method of managing authentication and user identities between multiple science domains.

Process: Developing any type of software, including scientific software, requires employing strong software engineering principles which lead to quality results. Adopting best practices helps scientific teams improve the sustainability, quality, and adaptability of their software, and ensures that the software that underpins ORNL scientific research is engineered to be reproducible and replaceable. The industry has recently shifted heavily towards using agile practices in order to rapidly develop products and meet user needs and requirements. Versus other traditional management processes, an agile approach allows software teams to quickly pivot towards new priorities as users, requirements, or available tools change. The SDK's teams development processes heavily borrow from the agile methods but is tailored to best fit our research and development and scientific software environment. Each iteration includes stages for core software engineering disciplines where teams plan for the sprint, define requirements, design tests, implement code, test and review changes, and finally release updated software. Other key features our process incorporates are user stories and issues, backlogs, and test-driven development. We also adopt other best practices into the software development life-cycle as needed.

Software Excellence: Software metrics are not like metrics in other professions in that they require context for proper interpretation. Scientific software metrics can become even more complex due to the fact the software is typically for very specific workflows which may not exist anywhere else in the world. However, both qualitative and quantitative metrics are key health indicators within the context of a project. Since our goal is enabling excellence in scientific software, we are developing a set of metrics to measure the quality and impact of the software we produce and provide a way to improve these over time. This also helps establish a road map, vision, and strategy for Scientific Software (SS) excellence across the lab by leading awareness and resources about software engineering processes and quality metrics [18].

4   INTERSECT-SDK

The INTERSECT-SDK includes several core parts, (shown in Fig. 4) including: libraries, services and APIs, digital twins, and integrated DevSecOps run-time environments and testing stacks. It is underpinned by strong software practices inspired by industry standard processes.

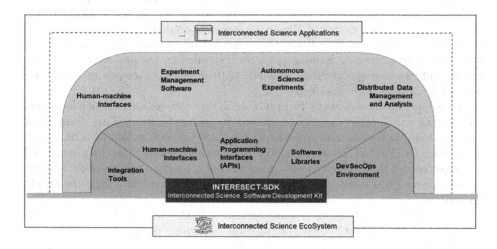

Fig. 4. INTERSECT SDK

4.1   Dev: Libraries, Services, and Adapters

Libraries: The INTERSECT-SDK provides a comprehensive set of libraries that abstract the integrated ecosystem architecture and design patterns away from the user to provide a unified method for accessing resources and instruments. They are designed to address the complexities of developing scientific applications and are cross-platform, cross-language, and reuseable to best support the unique environments that exist for different science use-cases, workflow patterns, instruments, and computing resources. The overall goal of our software stack is to be extremely flexible to easily adapt to future use-cases.

The core INTERSECT architecture is a hierarchical system-of-systems structure based on a publish-subscribe messaging architecture that allows communication between various micro-services. Two of the core libraries, *messages* and *client*, abstract the specific messaging implementations away from the user and provide the functionality to send and receive messages across the system bus. Both of these libraries implement plugins using the dependency inversion principle to be flexible and support different messaging engines and brokers. The dependency structure for the *messages* and *client* libraries is shown in Fig. 5.

The *messages* library is the message abstraction layer for all of INTERSECT and is responsible for compiling message definitions to language-specific stubs. The messages are defined by the Architectures team and can be compiled and packaged to support multiple languages and platforms. These are currently written using Google's ProtoBuf library [10] to take advantage of code generation, but this is hidden from the user and can be easily changed if needed. This library also serializes and de-serializes message objects to over the wire formats and different handlers can be used based on requirements. However, the same serialization method must be used on a single message bus in order for microservices to communicate properly. We implemented a single base message type that encapsulates all messages sent over the message bus. Several core message types exist that map to specific messaging patterns defined by the architecture. Application and use-case specific messages inherit from a core message type and are defined separately and versioned.

These specific messages can be published in separate packages which lets users only install the specific messages required for an application. This design first ensures that any service that is on a message bus can receive and understand all of the base INTERSECT messages. The application messages can be unwrapped and deserialized if the proper message version and package are installed and the messages are applicable for the current microservice; otherwise, they are simply ignored.

The *client* library handles communication with the message brokers and provides a localized view of the ecosystem from a service's perspective. It uses plugins which allows it to support several different messaging brokers based on the use-case requirements; new backends can also be easily added if needed. Messages can be transmitted using *publish* and callbacks can be set with *subscribe* for handling received messages. The *client* internally depends on the *messages* library which handles all of the message serialization and de-serialization functionality. Published messages are first passed to *messages* and serialized before sending to the broker; received messages are first passed to the de-serializer for validation before calling the application's callback handler.

Core Services: Our INTERSECT reference implementation uses component-based micro-services to support reusability and abstract functionality to reduce overhead when developing new micro-services and components and extending functionality. Our software implements some functionality of traditional workflows, but it is focused more on managing the system-of-systems environment. Being flexible in design is a high priority to our team because this is a prerequisite for wide-spread adoption; if the system design is completely inflexible and not compatible with existing workflows in any way, it would not be used.

The main two services we have implemented are the messaging broker and the discovery service. We used the RabbitMQ broker [29] as the message bus primarily because of its support for multiple protocols and since we are developing the *client* library to support different brokers. We have

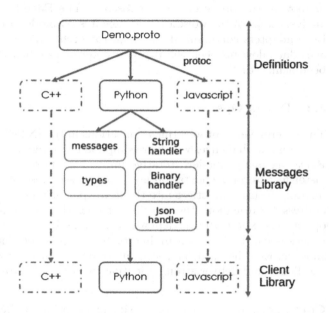

Fig. 5. INTERSECT-SDK messaging and client libraries

currently implemented both the *MQTT* and *AMQP* protocols which can be chosen based on system requirements. The *discovery* service is an important requirement for implementing a flexible messaging system. Separate INTERSECT deployments may use different messaging brokers, but the same INTERSECT-SDK software stack. The *discovery* service implements a API the client calls when first connecting to an INTERSECT deployment to determine the system messaging configuration. The client can then use this to connect to the INTERSECT messaging bus.

Adapters: Adapters within the INTERSECT context are specialized micro-services that handle interaction between the INTERSECT ecosystem and scientific systems and resources. These will implement specific capabilities that need to be exposed into INTERSECT through the *client* library and will be unique per system and/or use-case. Typically, this service will act as a bridge between a control system's API and the INTERSECT messaging bus and in some use-cases an adapter may be directly integrated into the scientific software application.

For our driver use case, we have identified two primary adapters in the workflow: the NionSwift adapter and the Edge DGX adapter. The NionSwift adapter uses a custom exposed API to communicate with the control software and exposes the higher level functions such as starting a scan, acquiring data, or moving the probe on the microscope. The Edge-DGX adapter handles the analysis steps of the workflow and executes AI models on the DGX accelerators. Both adapters communicate through the orchestrator microservice which manages data flow between the two and determines when the experiment goal has been achieved.

4.2   DevSecOps

The heterogeneity of scientific applications in the INTERESECT ecosystem provides unique challenges which are simplified by integrating DevSecOps processes. Releasing many smaller, iterative improvements over a period of time enables faster feature implementation and quicker issue resolution. Additionally, implementing security practices into the development pipeline ensures that security is addressed throughout the workflow, rather than something to be addressed by operations experts during deployment. While the initial transition to DevSecOps practices can be time-consuming for teams to adopt, these practices are extensible across other projects, streamline development, and help ensure software excellence and deliver strong scientific research software.

Containerization: The complexity of scientific applications demands consistent, segregated environments. For example, some applications (like NionSwift) require a graphical environment to successfully execute; others may demand a precise version of a plotting library due to incompatibilities with later versions or may require connections to a database or a message broker on startup. Scientific instruments also often invoke unique interactions which cannot be replicated within a generalized system; for example, a materials scientist may require working with a physical sample. To test the INTERSECT ecosystem, we require the ability to replicate a deployment of the software components of an instrument, known as a digital twin. A single scientific workflow could consist of multiple digital twins, each of which will make certain assumptions about its host system. Containerizing each application allows us to efficiently replicate its software environment without having to painstakingly recreate its environment each time we test minor modifications. As we grow the digital twin capabilities of instruments within INTERSECT, we can more easily deploy and scale an entire virtual national laboratory level deployment with container benefits. Given that we have containerized a digital twin of an electron microscope, one can envision now deploying many of these containers to resemble a microscopy User Facility. The benefits of containerization directly correlate to digital twin capabilities INTERSECT hopes to accomplish.

Infrastructure-as-Code: "Infrastructure-as-Code" (IaC) is a core DevOps practice that has emerged where teams capture system requirements for applications as code and automate creating and deploying infrastructure resources. There are many benefits of adopting IaC, including: easily reconfiguring changes across all managed infrastructure, easily scaling the managed infrastructure, and reliably deploying the infrastructure to a good, known state. Terraform[1] is used as the IaC tool to manage cloud infrastructure for hosting current INTERSECT services. IaC benefits have already affected scientific research. One such benefit is the ability to share IaC openly with other researchers to enable starting with properly configured infrastructure to run complex scientific software. An example is Google publishing open-source IaC scripts to provision infrastructure on Google Cloud Platform to run Folding@Home to support COVID-19 research.[2]

Continuous Integration: Continuous integration (CI) is accomplished by multiple levels of integrating new code changes, and ensuring high quality of software determined by the project standards. We use libraries which install pre-commit hooks on developers' local systems to enforce good practices before code can even be committed to the system. Once it is committed, it runs through additional stages of automated integration enabled by CI pipelines, which perform linting, testing, formatting, build, code coverage, etc. Using these standard software engineering practices help build reliable, high-quality scientific software.

Continuous Delivery and Continuous Deployment: Continuous delivery is a mostly automated deployment pipeline, but one that does have a manual stage for human-in-the-loop confirmation the deployment should be carried out. Continuous deployment is a fully automated deployment pipeline without any manual intervention. Continous deployment is the desired deployment approach, but sometimes the complexity necessitates using continuous delivery or even manual approaches. We deploy infrastructure to our own Kubernetes cluster in the CADES OpenStack cloud [5], to the Slate OpenShift cluster [32] inside Oak Ridge Leadership Computing Facility for HPC resources, and to ORNL's DGX Edge compute resources.

Security: For the initial implementation of authentication, tokens issued via available identity providers will be used across services. Based on existing infrastructure, authorization will first be implemented against Lightweight Directory Access Control (LDAP) and local system methods. The current web-based user interface mitigates cross-site scripting (XSS) attacks by applying a strong Content Security Policy and utilizing input-sanitizing frameworks. For ensuring security of the INTESERCT-SDK software artifacts, automated static security scanning tools, such as Bandit [28] and Harbor [11], will be set up in CI/CD for software packages and container images, respectively.

---

[1] HashiCorp's Terraform: https://www.terraform.io/.
[2] See https://github.com/GoogleCloudPlatform/terraform-folding-at-home.

4.3   Digital Twins

The last main focus of INTERSECT-SDK is developing instrument digital twins for the STEM use-case that can be deployed within our DevSecOps infrastructure. Ideally, instrument vendors would provide software, interfaces, and digital twins for their instruments, but this does not happen often. There were several major steps involved with creating and deploying the digital twin that we used for our STEM use-case.

Containerization: The NionSwift control software for the microscopes uses plugins and provides the ability to simulate STEM instruments with generated data. Our first step was integrating NionSwift and its simulator plugins into a container that could be easily deployed for testing and demonstration. NionSwift uses a graphical user interface (GUI) which introduced some initial roadblocks because containers do not typically have display servers installed. We used an existing base image that includes a X-window server which exposes a GUI over an HTTP VNC connection. This proved to be a sufficient solution for the digital twin by allowing remote access to the GUI as long as the container ports were properly mapped.

Custom Plugin: The next major hurdle is remotely accessing the digital twin from the adapter. NionSwift does have some basic APIs, but these were not adequate for handling remote control. Luckily, NionSwift is open source and the INTERSECT Integration team had developed a prototype remote API using the Pyro library (Python Remote Objects) [27] We want to reuse as much code as possible for other scenarios, so we identified generic patterns of controlling the microscope that are useful for STEM workflows. We extended the proof-of-concept server to expose new capabilities and also created a plugin that can be directly integrated into NionSwift for both the instrument and the digital twin. This simplifies the workflow even further for scientists as it is directly integrated and automatically started with NionSwift. Our NionSwift adapter connects to the API and calls the proper functions when handling INTERSECT messages.

Security: Some applications may not have INTERSECT compatible security and we must take additional steps to properly integrate them. Pyro lacks an integrated security solution, which is a major concern for the digital twin and instrument. Any user could connect to the unsecured API and run commands on the microscope without authorization. We addressed this issue by incorporating a secure socket layer to both the digital twin and the adapter to ensure only the adapter could successfully connect. This uses standard public/private certificates to validate a connecting user against a list of allowed keys. These certificates could be passed to users that need to control the microscope remotely, but ideally they should only be installed on trusted systems like the adapter.

5   Related Work

The scientific community has recently emphasized the need for intelligent systems, instruments, and facilities for enabling the science breakthroughs with autonomous experiments, self-driving laboratories, and supporting AI-driven design, discovery and evaluation [7]. Today, many scientific experiments are time and labor intensive [6]. A majority of effort is spent designing ad-hoc software stacks and data processing tools specifically for the experiments [18]. This specialization also creates interoperability challenges among scientific software tools leading to reduced automation and integration across multiple science disciplines [9]. In addition, scaling the experiments would be difficult, as the teams responsible for developing the software are domain scientists and might have inadequate experience software engineering. In brief, it would be helpful to decouple the domain science from the science of software responsible for executing the experiments. Earlier, researchers aiming to enhance interactions between traditional high performance computer resources and experimental equipment have developed a Software Framework for Federated Science Instruments [22]. The main objective of this work is the development of an interconnected SDK that would relinquish the software development by scientific domain experts, and instead benefit from a wide array of inter-connected infrastructure.

Both the System of Systems (SoS) Computing Architecture [1,9] and Artificial Intelligence brings transformative change to the scientific community and foster novel discoveries. This change largely be fueled by the scientific applications that would operate at the intersection of problem and solution space across varied domains, including materials, neutron science, systems biology, energy, and national security. While successes have been achieved by applying AI, albeit owing to its complexity and technological difficulty, AI is still limited to its domain experts and core practitioners. With the arrival of automated machine learning (AutoML) [3,8,17], there is now an unparallel opportunity to democratize the use of AI across all scientific domains and give its power in the hands of non-practitioners, too. As part of further work, we plan to extend the functionality by deploying machine learning packages and scale it through what is increasingly referred to as Machine Learning Operations (MLOps) [35] This includes model training and optimization, endpoint deployment, and endpoint monitoring for the application using ML-related functionalities.

Over the last 15 years or so, the community has recognized the key roles that Development and Operations (DevOps) play in bridging the gap between software development and deployment into production [3,17,37]. However, a skills and knowledge gap exists to realize the necessity of DevOps for scientific software development. Software for scientific experiments should require prototyping and flexibility to accommodate advances in the instrument setup and innovative, original experiments [12,20,21]. A great deal of progress has been made by trying to adopt standardized SDKs [1,8] for science. However, a feedback loop is required to rapidly adapt and modify for cutting-edge developments due to the novelty [2,23,31]. DevOps plays a crucial role in moving developers' changes from version control to a released software artifact, allowing scientists to run the latest version of the prototype. Bayser et al. [3] coined the term ResearchOps in their work where they outline the importance of a continuous cycle for research, development, and operation. This allowed for the latest prototype versions to be available in practice at the IBM Research Brazil lab (i.e., short release cycles) [3]. Our work will be the first to connect such a wide variety of devices, HPC environments, and edge federated instruments [4, 16] together under a single workflow. This brings a seamless and secure infrastructure for multi-domain science that drives the future of federated research [14, 15].

6   Conclusion

The main outcome of this work is a process toward a robust INTERSECT-SDK, a development environment for building scientific applications on an open architecture specification allowing for autonomous experiments and "self-driving" controls. The design and development of INTERSECT as a platform of transformative sciences underpins the need for a broader collaboration and coordination from computing and domain science. The proposed INTERSECT-SDK will enable the optimal use of federated architectures connecting disparate instruments and AI-driven compute for novel scientific discoveries. In addition, this will allow the research community to run multi-domain experiments virtually from distant locations, control such instruments, and process data by combining the optimal workflow. The DevSecOps capability demonstrated through this work will allow for application development and execution in an end-to-end secure environment and across different levels of access hierarchies and instruments.

Additionally, we showcased the efficacy of the proposed SDK through a case-study on Scanning Transmission Electron Microscopy. This example is an archetype of future interconnected science applications that connect experimental hardware (e.g., microscopes) and AI-guided experimental control systems to speed up and improve the repeatability of scientific discovery.

The other core outcome of this work is an articulation of the software engineering best practices for the development of scientific workflow for autonomous experiments. We propose and demonstrate early results for a complete software life-cycle framework that addresses the need to automate the development, integration and deployment of software applications in a repeatable and reproducible way. In subsequent work, we plan to complete the development of the proposed SDK with interfaces to connect with standard scientific instruments from multiple domains. In addition, we plan to develop APIs which allow for extending the SDK to new instruments. The SDK will be released as open-source, allowing the research community to benefit in their R&D work.

Acknowledgement. This manuscript has been authored by UT-Battelle, LLC under Contract No. DEAC05-00OR22725 with the U.S. Department of Energy. The United States Government retains and the publisher, by accepting the article for publication, acknowledges that the United States Government retains a nonexclusive, paid-up, irrevocable, world-wide license to publish or reproduce the published form of this manuscript, or allow others to do so, for United States Government purposes. The Department of Energy will provide public access to these results of federally sponsored research in accordance with the DOE Public Access.

References

1. Bartlett, R., Demeshko, I., Gamblin, T., et al.: xSDK foundations: toward an extreme-scale scientific software development kit. Supercomput. Front. Innov. **4**, 69–82 (2017)
2. Baxter, S.M., Day, S.W., Fetrow, J.S., Reisinger, S.J.: Scientific software development is not an oxymoron. PLOS Comput. Biol. **2**, 1–4 (2006)
3. De Bayser, M., Azevedo, L.G., Cerqueira, R.: ResearchOps: the case for DevOps in scientific applications. In: Proceedings of the 2015 IFIP/IEEE International Symposium on Integrated Network Management, IM 2015, pp. 1398–1404 (2015)
4. Brassil, J., Kopaliani, I.: Cloudjoin: experimenting at scale with hybrid cloud computing. In: 2020 IEEE 3rd 5G World Forum (5GWF), pp. 467–472 (2020)
5. CADES. CADES OpenStack cloud computing (2022)
6. Cataldo, M., Mockus, A., Roberts, J.A., Herbsleb, J.D.: Software dependencies, work dependencies, and their impact on failures. IEEE Trans. Software Eng. **35**(6), 864–878 (2009)
7. Crawford, K., Whittaker, M., Elish, M.C., Barocas, S., Plasek, A., Ferryman, K.: The AI now report. The Social and Economic Implications of Artificial Intelligence Technologies in the Near-Term (2016)
8. da Silva, R.F., Casanova, H., Chard, K., et al.: Workflows community summit: advancing the state-of-the-art of scientific workflows management systems research and development. arXiv preprint arXiv:2106.05177 (2021)
9. Eick, S.G., Graves, T.L., Karr, A.F., Mockus, A., Schuster, P.: Visualizing software changes. IEEE Trans. Software Eng. **28**, 396–412 (2002)
10. Google Developers. Protocol Buffers (2022)
11. Harbor. Harbor Website (2022)
12. Hazzan, O., Dubinsky, Y.: The agile manifesto. SpringerBriefs Comput. Sci. **9**, 9–14 (2014)
13. Hines, J.: ORNL adds powerful AI appliances to computing portfolio - oak ridge leadership computing facility, August 2019. https://www.olcf.ornl.gov/2019/02/06/ornl-adds-powerful-ai-appliances-to-computing-portfolio/. Accessed 26 June 2022
14. Li, L., Fan, Y., Tse, M., Lin, K.-Y.: A review of applications in federated learning. Comput. Ind. Eng. **149**, 106854 (2020)
15. Li, T., Sahu, A.K., Talwalkar, A., Smith, V.: Federated learning: challenges, methods, and future directions. IEEE Signal Process. Mag. **37**, 50–60 (2020)
16. Li, W., Liewig, M.: A survey of AI accelerators for edge environment. In: Rocha, Á., Adeli, H., Reis, L.P., Costanzo, S., Orovic, I., Moreira, F. (eds.) WorldCIST 2020. AISC, vol. 1160, pp. 35–44. Springer, Cham (2020). https://doi.org/10.1007/978-3-030-45691-7_4
17. Lwakatare, L.E., Kuvaja, P., Oivo, M.: Dimensions of DevOps. In: Lassenius, C., Dingsøyr, T., Paasivaara, M. (eds.) XP 2015. LNBIP, vol. 212, pp. 212–217. Springer, Cham (2015). https://doi.org/10.1007/978-3-319-18612-2_19
18. Malviya-Thakur, A., Watson, G.: Dynamics of scientific software teams. Collegeville (2021)
19. Meyer, C., Dellby, N., Hachtel, J.A., Lovejoy, T., Mittelberger, A., Krivanek, O.: Nion swift: open source image processing software for instrument control, data acquisition, organization, visualization, and analysis using python. Microsc. Microanal. **25**(S2), 122–123 (2019)

20. Mockus, A., Fielding, R.T., Herbsleb, J.D.: Two case studies of open source software development: Apache and Mozilla. ACM Trans. Softw. Eng. Methodol. **11**, 309–346 (2002)
21. Mockus, A., Weiss, D.M.: Predicting risk of software changes. Bell Labs Tech. J. **5**, 169–180 (2000)
22. Naughton, T., et al.: Software framework for federated science instruments. In: Nichols, J., Verastegui, B., Maccabe, A.B., Hernandez, O., Parete-Koon, S., Ahearn, T. (eds.) SMC 2020. CCIS, vol. 1315, pp. 189–203. Springer, Cham (2020). https://doi.org/10.1007/978-3-030-63393-6_13
23. Nguyen-Hoan, L., Flint, S., Sankaranarayana, R.: A survey of scientific software development. In: Proceedings of the 2010 ACM-IEEE International Symposium on Empirical Software Engineering and Measurement. Association for Computing Machinery (2010)
24. Nion Co., Nion Swift User's Guide (2022)
25. Ophus, C., Ercius, P., Sarahan, M., Czarnik, C., Ciston, J.: Recording and using 4D-stem datasets in materials science. Microsc. Microanal. **20**(S3), 62–63 (2014)
26. Pennycook, S.J., Nellist, P.D.: Scanning Transmission Electron Microscopy: Imaging and Analysis. Springer, New York (2011). https://doi.org/10.1007/978-1-4419-7200-2
27. Library Pyro. Github - irmen/pyro5: Pyro 5 - python remote objects for modern python versions (2022). https://github.com/irmen/Pyro5. Accessed 27 June 2022
28. Python Code Quality Authority (PyCQA). PyCQA's Bandit GitHub repository (2022)
29. RabbitMQ. RabbitMQ Website (2022)
30. Roccapriore, K.M., Dyck, O., Oxley, M.P., Ziatdinov, M., Kalinin, S.V.: Automated experiment in 4D-STEM: exploring emergent physics and structural behaviors. ACS Nano (2022)
31. Segal, J., Morris, C.: Developing scientific software. IEEE Softw. **25**, 18–20 (2008)
32. Slate. Slate: Kubernetes cluster with access to Summit (2021)
33. Somnath, S., et al.: Building an integrated ecosystem of computational and observational facilities to accelerate scientific discovery. In: Nichols, J., et al. (eds.) Smoky Mountains Computational Sciences and Engineering Conference, pp. 58–75. Springer, Cham (2021). https://doi.org/10.1007/978-3-030-96498-6_4
34. Nion Swift. Nion swift, March 2022. https://github.com/nion-software/nionswift. Accessed 26 June 2022
35. Treveil, M., et al.: Introducing MLOps. O'Reilly Media, Sebastopol (2020)
36. Zager, R., Zager, J.: Ooda loops in cyberspace: a new cyber-defense model. Small Wars J. (2017)
37. Zhao, F., Niu, X., Huang, S.L., Zhang, L.: Reproducing scientific experiment with cloud DevOps. In: 2020 IEEE World Congress on Services (SERVICES), pp. 259–264 (2020)

Deploying Advanced Technologies
for an Integrated Science
and Engineering Ecosystem

Adrastea: An Efficient FPGA Design Environment for Heterogeneous Scientific Computing and Machine Learning

Aaron R. Young[✉], Narasinga Rao Miniskar, Frank Liu, Willem Blokland, and Jeffrey S. Vetter

Oak Ridge National Laboratory, Oak Ridge, TN 37830, USA
youngar@ornl.gov

Abstract. We present Adrastea, an efficient FPGA design environment for developing scientific machine learning applications. FPGA development is challenging, from deployment, proper toolchain setup, programming methods, interfacing FPGA kernels, and more importantly, the need to explore design space choices to get the best performance and area usage from the FPGA kernel design. Adrastea provides an automated and scalable design flow to parameterize, implement, and optimize complex FPGA kernels and associated interfaces. We show how virtualization of the development environment via virtual machines is leveraged to simplify the setup of the FPGA toolchain while deploying the FPGA boards and while scaling up the automated design space exploration to leverage multiple machines concurrently. Adrastea provides an automated build and test environment of FPGA kernels. By exposing design space hyper-parameters, Adrastea can automatically search the design space in parallel to optimize the FPGA design for a given metric, usually performance or area. Adrastea simplifies the task of interfacing the FPGA kernels with a simplified interface API. To demonstrate the capabilities of Adrastea, we implement a complex random forest machine learning kernel with 10,000 input features while achieving extremely low computing latency without loss of prediction accuracy, which is required by a scientific edge application at SNS. We also demonstrate Adrastea using an FFT kernel and show that for both applications Adrastea is able to systematically and efficiently evaluate different design options, which reduced the time and effort required to develop the kernel from months of manual work to days of automatic builds.

Keywords: Design space exploration · FPGA development environment · Heterogeneous computing · Scientific computing · Machine learning

1 Introduction

Field-Programmable Gate Arrays (FPGAs) enable the development and deployment of custom hardware designs via programmable logic blocks, which can be

K. Doug et al. (Eds.): SMC 2022, CCIS 1690, pp. 227–243, 2022.
https://doi.org/10.1007/978-3-031-23606-8_14

reconfigured to perform custom functions and allow for flexible, reconfigurable computing. FPGAs excel at applications that run close to the edge (near the data collection) and for workloads that require low-latency solutions. FPGAs also excel at applications that can be expressed as data-flows between tasks and where the tasks can be implemented as a processing pipeline. Then during execution, the data flows between kernels in a stream, and the processing is done via pipelines to maximize performance.

Some examples of low-latency applications that work well on FPGAs include traditional real-time industrial control applications where fixed latencies are mandatory [4,18] and other typical low-latency FPGA applications, including financial technology [8,14,16], communication and networking [2,6,17,20], and real-time cryptosystems [9,10].

Although historically, FPGAs have been primarily used for embedded systems and custom low-level designs, FPGAs are becoming increasingly accessible as general compute accelerator cards. FPGAs are now being packaged in server-grade PCIe cards, with software support to enable quick reloading of designs and handling common tasks such as execution control and data transfer from the host to the FPGA. High-Level Synthesis (HLS) allows FPGA kernels to be written in higher-level languages like OpenCL, then compiled to the FPGA design through the HLS design flow.

Although FPGAs can now be used effectively in a shared server environment and HLS eases the complexity of FPGA kernel design, FPGA development is still challenging. Challenges with FPGA development include kernel deployment, proper toolchain setup, programming methods, interfacing with FPGA kernels, time consuming HLS compilation/synthesis time, and, more importantly, the need to explore design space choices to get the best performance and area usage from the FPGA kernel design. We present Adrastea, an efficient FPGA design environment for developing optimized kernels for high-performance applications to address these challenges. Adrastea provides an automated and scalable design flow to parameterize, implement, and optimize complex FPGA kernels and associated interfaces. In this paper, we show how virtualization of the development environment via virtual machines is leveraged to simplify the setup of the FPGA toolchain while deploying the FPGA boards and while scaling up the automated design space exploration to leverage multiple machines concurrently. Adrastea provides an automated build and test environment for FPGA kernels. By exposing design space hyperparameters, Adrastea can automatically search the design space in parallel to optimize the FPGA design for a given metric, usually performance or area. Adrastea also simplifies the task of interfacing with the FPGA kernels by providing a simplified interface API.

To demonstrate the capabilities of Adrastea, we implement a complex Random Forest machine learning kernel with 10,000 input features while achieving extremely low computing latency without loss of prediction accuracy, which is required by a scientific edge application at SNS. While developing this kernel, Adrastea was utilized to systematically and efficiently evaluate different design options, which reduced the time and effort required to develop the kernel. The

Random Forest kernel implemented with Adrastea is 5x area-efficient and can perform inference in 60 nanoseconds. We have also demonstrated the ease of using Adrastea by leveraging Adrastea to perform a design space search on a Fast Fourier Transform (FFT) kernel. We demonstrated that the Adrastea framework results in an accelerated FPGA development and optimization cycle able to perform months of effort in days. The main contribution of this paper is summarized as follows:

- We design and implement an efficient FPGA design environment Adrastea, with the capabilities of designing both the kernel implementation of FPGA and the interface, as well as the capabilities to perform FPGA optimizations;
- We demonstrate the efficiency and effectiveness of Adrastea for FPGA design on Random Forest and Fast Fourier Transform applications.

The remaining parts of this paper are organized as follows: In Sect. 2, we provide a background on FPGA design, the Xilinx Vitis Toolchain, and a brief review of related work on FPGA build frameworks. In Sect. 3, we discuss the design and use of Adrastea. In Sect. 4, we provide examples of building two applications using the Adrastea framework and discuss results from the design space explorations, followed by a conclusion and future work in Sect. 5.

2 Background

In this section, we provide more details on the principles of FPGA development and a general description of the Xilinx Toolchain.

2.1 FPGA Design

FPGAs require a different programming style from CPUs and GPUs, and code written for a CPU or GPU will likely need to be rewritten to meet the desired performance goals. When writing code for the FPGA, three paradigms are helpful to keep in mind for designing FPGA kernels [23]. These paradigms are producer-consumer, streaming data, and pipelining. Together these paradigms are a useful way to think about designing for FPGAs. Computation can be broken into tasks that operate on a data stream. These tasks then read the data from a stream, perform computation on the data, then send the output data to the next task. The tasks and communication can then be pipelined both within a task, at the instructions level, or between tasks, at the task level. The performance of the pipeline is expressed by the initiation interval (II) and the iteration latency. From this, the total latency can be computed as shown in Eq. 1.

$$\text{Total Latency} = \text{Iteration Latency} + \text{II} \cdot (\text{Number of Items} - 1) \qquad (1)$$

The total application latency is the total latency of the critical dataflow path, and the application throughput is determined by the width of the data streams and the largest II. There is a trade-off that occurs between the latency, II, area, and clock frequency of the design, and Adrastea can be used to aid in the design space search to optimize the kernel to find the best kernel design for a given application and target FPGA.

2.2 Xilinx Vitis Toolchain

The Xilinx Vitis unified software platform [11] is a comprehensive development environment to build and deploy performance-critical kernels accelerated on Xilinx platforms, including Alveo cards, cloud FPGA instances, and embedded FPGA platforms. Vitis supports FPGA accelerated application programming using C, C++, OpenCL, and RTL by providing a variety of pragmas for pipelining, dataflow, and optimizations. High-Level Synthesis (HLS) is used to convert kernels written in high-level programming languages like C, C++, and OpenCL C into RTL kernels which can then be implemented with the FPGA hardware. In addition, the Xilinx Runtime Library (XRT) provides APIs to facilitate communication between the host application and accelerators. XRT eases accelerator life cycle management and execution management. It also handles memory allocation and data communication between the host and accelerators.

2.3 Related Work

One of the recent related works is HLS4ML [5], an open-source hardware-software codesign workflow to translate machine learning kernels into hardware designs, including FPGAs. The major difference between HLS4ML and this work is the capability to explore various design choices for general FPGA designs, while HLS4ML is more focused on optimization for ML kernels.

DARClab developed an automatic synthesis option tuner dedicated to optimizing HLS synthesis options [22]. This HLS design space explorer leverages previous results to explore the HLS parameters effectively. Our work is more general on the design space knobs allowing the application developer to expose any knobs they want to explore.

Coyote is a new shell for FPGAs that aims to provide a full suite of operating system abstractions. In our work, we use the Alveo Shell from Xilinx, but Adrastea could be extended to use other FPGA tool flows and FPGA shells.

Cock et al. designed a new hybrid CPU and FPGA server system to enable hybrid systems research, and the system uses a cache-coherent socket to socket protocol to connect to the FPGA [3]. In this work, we leverage the off-the-shelf servers and a PCIe-based Alveo FPGA. Cabrera et al. explored CXL and the implications a CXL interface would have on the programming models for FPGA kernel design [1]. However, a CXL-enabled FPGA card and server are not available off the shelf at the time of writing this paper.

3 Adrastea Design Environment

In this section, we present the design of an efficient FPGA development environment, with the code name Adrastea, that we created to support the automated process of building and optimizing general FPGA hardware designs capable of deployment at the edge. Adrastea leverages and combines various related efforts from ORNL to build a powerful and efficient FPGA development environment that solves key challenges with FPGA design, including 1) setting up a scalable build environment 2) providing convenient interfaces to the FPGA kernel 3) performing design space exploration.

The FPGA build environment leverages the Vitis tool flow discussed in Subsect. 2.2 to synthesize and implement the FPGA designs. Subsection 3.1 covers the virtual machine-based deployment of the development environment, which enables sharing of computing resources, maintaining multiple versions of the toolchain, and scaling of build servers for design space experiments. Finally, CMakefiles provided by IRIS simplify the build process by generating makefiles that automate the kernel builds.

Adrastea supports easier interfacing to the FPGA kernel through the use of the IRIS runtime as specified in Subsect. 3.2. This interface allows common handling of the host communication logic and easy-to-use APIs which is common across multiple accelerator types. With this API, it is easy to have a kernel generate and run targeting multiple execution targets, including CPU, GPU, DSP, and FPGA.

By leveraging DEFFE, Adrastea can easily launch large design space search and optimization runs across multiple build servers. This capability is further discussed in Subsect. 3.3.

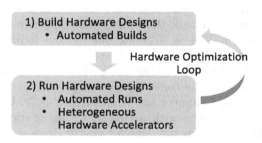

Fig. 1. Hardware optimization loop.

With all the components combined, Adrastea implements the design loop shown in Fig. 1. Step 1) leverages DEFFE to build the FPGA kernels using automated build flows. These builds can be parameterized with architecture-level parameters in addition to the synthesis and implementation flags. Different build configurations can also be run in parallel on the build servers to allow these long-running processes to execute concurrently. Once the kernel builds are finished, the designs can then move to step 2) where they are loaded and run using FPGA hardware or in emulation. As indicated by the curved arrow, the build logs and execution results collected from the FPGA implementation and can then be used to provide feedback to the automatic generation steps to improve on the resulting hardware design. This infrastructure creates a basis for performing automated hardware optimization loops and continuous integration where both building and running designs can be completely automated and scheduled.

3.1   FPGA Building Environment

There are two main challenges with this update loop: 1) the hardware builds take multiple hours to run; 2) hardware testing must be done on a system with the hardware available. Both of these issues are addressed by the toolchain infrastructure deployed on a computer cluster for experimental computing. To address the first issue, a scalable compute cluster for building is utilized to allow many hardware builds to be executed in parallel. Although there is not an easy way to accelerate a single build, multiple builds run in parallel can be used to evaluate different build configurations concurrently. To address the second issue, a system with FPGA accelerators is available for hardware execution. The Slurm job scheduler is used to allocate both build resources and FPGA hardware resources for submitted jobs. The Vitis Unified Software Development Platform is a large software installation, ~110 GB, with strict operating system requirements, and only one version of the Xilinx Runtime library (XRT) can be installed at a time. To make the setup of multiple machines and the changing of versions easier, the development platform is installed inside a Kernel-based Virtual Machine (KVM). PCIe passthrough is used to pass the hypervisor's FPGA hardware to the VM. The QCOW2 disk image format is used by the Virtual Machine (VM) so that common system files, packages, and Vitis can be installed on the backing disk image file. Then each VM instance based on that backing file uses Copy-on-Write (COW) to create overlay images that only store changes from the base image. The backing file then resides in Network File System (NFS) with the overlay images stored in a local drive of the hypervisor. This allows the unchanging, large, base files to be stored in a single shared file, with the files that change more often being stored in the faster local storage.

Slurm and GitLab-CI runners are installed in the VMs using Ansible to enable easy launching of jobs with a continuous integration (CI) pipeline or via Slurm. The FPGA is configured as a Generic Resource (GRES) in Slurm to allow Slurm to allocate the FPGA to jobs. The GitLab-CI pipelines and other automatic build launching scripts, including DEFFE, make use of Slurm to allocate build resources and coordinate the use of the FPGAs. Developers using the system also leverage Slurm to allocate resources for building and testing FPGA designs. The VMs are divided into multiple partitions in Slurm; the FPGA build partitions have nodes with the Vitis toolchain but without FPGA hardware, and the FPGA run partitions have both the toolchain and FPGA hardware. The different versions of Vitis also have their own partitions. There are two partitions, a build and a run partition, for each of the available Vitis versions. Since Ansible and VMs with overlay disk images are used, additional nodes can easily be added or removed and the Vitis version can be swapped out. Startup and teardown scripts automate the process of adding or removing new VM instances, making it trivial to change the version of Vitis that is running on the build servers. Changing the VM where the FPGA is assigned requires more steps since the process includes shutting down the VMs, changing the PCIe passthrough configuration, starting the VM with the FPGA, loading the Vitis shell which corresponds to that version, rebooting the system to load the new FPGA image, starting all the VMs on the system, loading the user shell for the FPGA, and finally using the xbutil to validate the FPGA setup.

The infrastructure enabling the design flow shown in Fig. 1 is implemented in the compute cluster as shown in Fig. 2. Figure 2 shows the same hardware optimization loop updated with the build and run nodes that are used to build the hardware in parallel and run the designs on hardware in the respective VMs as scheduled by Slurm. Since the VMs mount the same network drives and home directories, the bitfiles, runtime results, and other artifacts can easily be shared between nodes in the cluster.

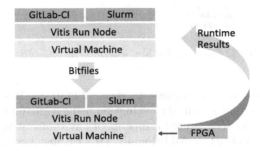

Fig. 2. Infrastructure supporting the hardware optimization loop.

3.2 IRIS

Adrastea uses the IRIS task-based programming model for interfacing with the FPGA kernels [12]. IRIS provides a unified task-based programming interface, which can be targeted for heterogeneous compute units such as multi-core CPUs, GPUs (NVidia/AMD), FPGA (Intel and Xilinx), Hexagon DSPs, etc. It also provides flexibility to the programmer to write task core kernels either using OpenMP, OpenACC, CUDA, HIP, OpenCL, etc. Memory transfers between the host and the devices are managed through IRIS's memory coherence runtime management. Through IRIS, Adrastea provides the programmer with a simplified interface which can be called using either a C++ or python application. A simple python function to call the random forest kernel to run on FPGA is shown in Fig. 3.

3.3 DEFFE

DEFFE (Data Efficient Framework for Exploration) [13] is intended for design space exploration. It is configurable with parameters (often referred to as knobs) with possible ranges of values and with cost metrics that are used for evaluation. It has the flexibility to provide a custom evaluate (Python/Bash) script to

```
import iris
def run_random_forest(args, test_data):
    features= test_data.data
    Y = test_data.target
    Y_predict = np.zeros(Y.size, dtype=np.int8)
    SIZE = Y.size
    iris.init()   # Initialize IRIS Run-time
    mem_features = iris.mem(features.nbytes)
    mem_Y_predict = iris.mem(Y_predict.nbytes)
    task = iris.task()   # Create IRIS task
    task.h2d(mem_features, 0, features.nbytes, features)
    task.kernel("rf_classifier", 1, [0], [1], [1],
        [mem_features, SIZE, mem_Y_predict], #Parameters
        [iris.iris_r, 4, iris.iris_w] )   # Parameters information
    task.d2h(mem_Y_predict, 0, Y_predict.nbytes, Y_predict)
    cu = iris.iris_cpu
    if args.cu == 'fpga':
        cu = iris.iris_fpga
    task.submit(cu)
    iris.finalize()
```

Fig. 3. Adrastea Python interface through IRIS

evaluate each set of sample parameter-value combinations. It also provides flexibility to extract the results from the evaluation using a customized extract script (Python/Bash). These scripts use arguments or environment variables to receive the parameters from DEFFE. Additionally, DEFFE has a configurable machine learning model which can be used for workload characterization. DEFFE is supported by different variants of sampling techniques such as DOEPY (Design of Experiments) [19] sampling techniques and machine learning-based sampling techniques. The configurability of DEFFE enables fast design space exploration with the parallel execution either using multi-core threading or by using a massively parallel, multiple system Slurm environment. This paper uses the build environment with Slurm as discussed in Sect. 3.1 and explores the *one-dim* sampling technique for exploring the FPGA design choices.

3.4   Experiment Setup via Git

One of the challenges with building FPGA kernels and conducting design space search experiments is tracking the history of how the experiment was performed and allowing the experiment to be easily reproducible. Source code, including source code for FPGA designs, is commonly stored in source code repositories like Git in order to track changes in the code. Git can also be used to keep track of the automatic build scripts and DEFFE experiment configurations. To ensure history tracking and reproducibility of a hardware build, we first create an experiment repository to hold the DEFFE configuration along with the scripts to automate the FPGA build. Iris and DEFFE repositories are then added as sub-modules to the repository. The generators and source code for the design can either be included in its own repository and added as a sub-module or directly included in the experiment repository. When the hardware is built, or DEFFE is run, the hash of the current commit is included in the logs of the build. That way, to reproduce the build or to rerun a DEFFE experiment, you only need to check out the same commit. The commit information is all that is needed to reproduce the experiment since the repository includes the same version of the sub-modules and all the scripts that were used for the build.

Sometimes we also want to store the history of how and when a bitfile was built. To do this we take the hash of the date, folder name, and commit id. This hash is then stored in a file that is committed to the repository and included as a read-only output in the hardware kernel. Then to reproduce the build or learn how a deployed design was built, you only need to read the hash from the kernel and search the repository for the hash. Then you know exactly the commit and, therefore, the state and folder of the repository that was used to build that hardware kernel.

The method of using Git to store the entire build process and experiment flow and keeping track of the hash with the output and result enables reproducibility and provides historical information of the artifacts.

3.5   Complete Adrastea Build Flow

By leveraging the different components that make up Adrastea, a complete FPGA design flow is built as shown in Fig. 4. As input to DEFFE, the design space knobs, cost metrics, experiment setup, and other configuration is passed to DEFFE via a config.json file. Additionally, the customized evaluate script and extract script are passed, which contain the instructions to perform the build, FPGA execution and results (cost metrics) extraction. DEFFE has more components, but the main ones used in the Adrastea build flow are shown. The design space is sampled, and the experiment folders are created. Each experiment folder contains the parameterized scripts used for the run for that set of parameters. Next, DEFFE builds the FPGA design in parallel using the build partition compute units of Slurm via the Xilinx Vitis Toolchain. The build flow used by the evaluate script for ML workloads is also shown in the figure. The ML model, along with the build knobs, is passed to an optimized ML code generator script which generates the HLS code. Then the HLS code is compiled using the Vitis and Vivado toolchains into an FPGA bitstream. After which, DEFFE uses the run partition compute units of Slurm to evaluate the FPGA kernel using the IRIS runtime. Finally, DEFFE writes the results from the design space search into a spreadsheet. This spreadsheet can then be read into a graphing program and the results from the experiment can be plotted. We use a Jupyter Notebook with Seaborn and Pandas to plot the figures shown in this paper.

4   Example Applications Leveraging Adrastea

We have evaluated the effectiveness of Adrastea for an SNS application with a Random Forest (RF) classification model deployed on Xilinx FPGAs and also deployed other state-of-the-art random forest classification models. We also used Adrastea with an FFT kernel to demonstrate how quickly and easily new applications can be built and explored using the Adrastea development environment.

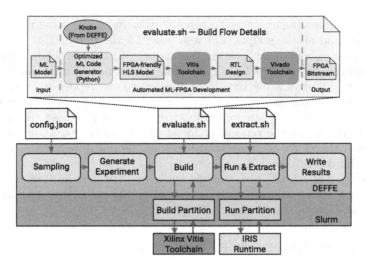

Fig. 4. Adrastea build flow

Experimental Setup. We deployed the Adrastea development environment on an experimental cluster using five servers as hypervisors. One Atipa server with dual-socket Intel Xeon Gold 6130 CPUs, 192 GiB of RAM, and a Xilinx Alveo U250 was used as the hypervisor for the *run VM*. The *run VM* was configured with 24 vCPUs, 92 GiB of RAM, and with PCIe passthrough to access the U250. Four HPE DL385 Servers with dual-socket AMD EPYC 7742 CPUs and 1 TB of RAM were used as the hypervisor for the *build VMs*. The *build VMs* are configured with 240 vCPUs and 960 GB of RAM. The Xilinx Alveo U250 board is used to evaluate the FPGA designs.

4.1 SNS and Other State-of-the-Art RF Models Design Space Exploration

The SNS facility at Oak Ridge National Laboratory (ORNL) has the world's highest pulsed power proton accelerator delivering 1.4 MW of a proton beam repeated 60 Hz onto a stainless steel vessel filled with liquid mercury to generate neutrons for material research [7]. In order to detect beam loss and abort the experiment, we designed a custom random forest implementation using Adrastea [15]. The application requires a highly complex random forest model which uses 10000 features to make a meaningful prediction and the model needs to be updated frequently. We leveraged Adrastea not only to optimize the implementation for RF models to detect the errant beam within 100ns but also for faster development, design space exploration, and deployment of the random forest model in the SNS environment FPGA hardware.

Design Parameters and Exploration. Adrastea has provided a python script to generate the Xilinx OpenCL code for the random forest model with flattened nodes while analyzing the dependency of nodes in random forest trees. It has several knobs to finetune the random forest generation and build process to explore optimal hyper parameters, such as 1) bitwise optimization flag to enable bitwise arithmetic operators instead of logical operators, 2) different type random forest tree code generation such as if-else conditional trees, flattened version of tree code generation, 3) configurable datatype of features such as floating-point (FP32), 8-bit fixed-point (FX8), and varying fixed-point bitwidth controlled by accuracy threshold percentages ranging from 10 to 100 (FT[10-100]), 4) type of fixed-point approach such as quantization or power of 2 values representation, 5) voting algorithm logic approach either with direct BRAM based array accesses, flattened approach either with or without static single assignment optimization. The design space exploration also explores the optimal frequency setting for the generated random forest kernel. The design space exploration parameters for the Adrastea-based random forest model are shown in Table 1. We have configured all these parameters in the DEFFE configuration file. DEFFE sampled the essential set of these parameter values combination and evaluated them using massively parallel Slurm jobs. Each Slurm job is configured to use eight threads, resulting in the ability to run 100 simultaneous runs across the FPGA build machines. Completed FPGA implementations were then tested serially on the run partition of Slurm where the Alveo U250 FPGA is connected. The build time of each sample evaluation is ~4 h, but the execution time on FPGA hardly takes milliseconds. Hence, it is reasonable to have multiple build systems and one FPGA run system.

Table 1. Parameters used for experiments

Parameter	Type	# of Values	Values
Frequency (MHz)	Build	5	50, 100, 200, 300*, 500
Decision tree	Generator	2	Conditional (conditional_trees), Flattened*
Bitwise optimization	Generator	2	Yes*, No (no_bitwise)
Feature datatype	Generator	12	Float (FP32), Fixed 8-bit(FX8), FT100*, FT90, FT80, FT70, FT60, FT50, FT40, FT30, FT20, FT10
Fixed point type	Generator	2	Quantization*, Power2 (no_quantization)
Voting	Generator	3	Array (array_votes), SSA*, No-SSA (no_votes_ssa)

*: Base Parameters (The best)

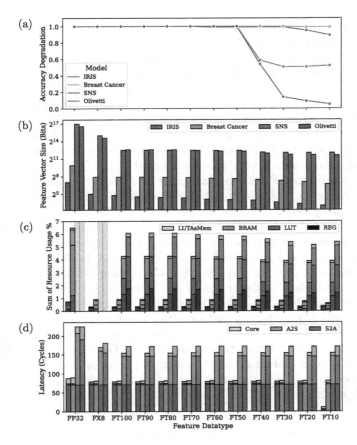

Fig. 5. Optimization metrics of interest for different input feature datatypes.

Results. We have experimented with the random forest model not only for the SNS dataset but also for other standard random forest models such as IRIS (4 features), Breast cancer (30 features), and Olivetti (4096 features) datasets which have 100 trees with maximum depth set to 20. The experiment results for varying datatype of features and its impact on the latency, resource usage, feature vector size, and prediction accuracy are shown in Fig. 5. Accuracy degradation is used instead of raw classification accuracy of the testing data since the focus is the accuracy loss from reducing the bits used to represent the input features.

It can be seen that the representation of features with FX8 will lead straight away to a 4x reduction in feature vector size when compared to 32-bit floating-point features. Further exploration of variable fixed-point datatypes with accuracy threshold will lead to higher gains. For example with 70% (FT70) threshold the multi-precision fixed-point feature vector size reduction gains are 23x for SNS, 17x for Olivetti, 4.3x for Breast Cancer, and 6.4x for IRIS, as shown in Fig. 5(b). Moreover FT70 has resulted in no accuracy degradation compared to the floating-point datatype for all benchmarks, as shown in Fig. 5(a).

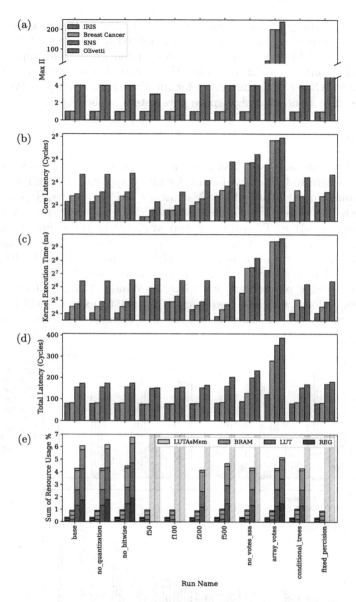

Fig. 6. Comparison with different build options.

The overall FPGA resource usage of our fixed point design of random forest models is ~2%. Figure 5(c) shows the breakdown of resource usages of registers (REG), look-up tables (LUT), block RAM (BRAM), and LUTs as memory (LUTAsMem) as a percentage of the available resources of that type.

The total latency of the models is shown in Fig. 5(d) for kernels running at 300 MHz frequency. Total latency is calculated as the sum of the latencies (cycles) for the AXI4 to stream (*A2S*) conversion for reading input features, the core functionality, which contains the random forest classifier (*Core*), and the stream to AXI4 (*S2A*) conversion for the classification output. We have also shown the effect of other design space parameters in the Fig. 6.

4.2   FFT

FFT is a data-intensive and also compute-intensive algorithm used to convert time domain data to frequency domain for many applications. FFT is an important component of an Atomic Force Microscope (AFM) and requires a very wide FFT length and size [21]. We have applied design space exploration on 1-D (single-dimensional) FFT, optimized and available in the Xilinx Vitis library. We have ported the Xilinx Vitis 1-D FFT implementation in the Adrastea environment using IRIS run-time scheduler APIs. We have applied DEFFE design space exploration on the generated FFT implementation. The FFT implementation has two design parameters, FFT length (Window) and FFT Size (number of elements), along with the frequency of kernel to explore, which will have an impact on resource utilization and runtime latency. We have measured the

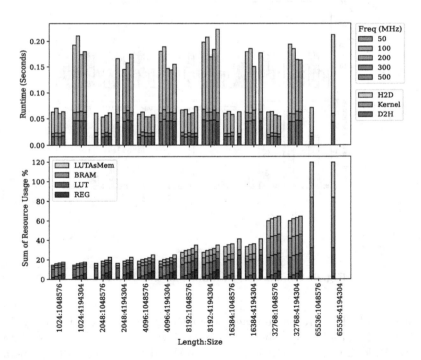

Fig. 7. FFT experiment results. Missing data points did not build successfully due to exceeded resource utilization.

latency of FFT algorithm in execution time instead of cycles as it has many iterative loops and kernel functions. The results of the design space exploration are shown in Fig. 7. FFT length is explored for the range of 1024 to very large window size of 64K (65536). The 64K FFT build was observed to be successful for 50 MHz frequency. The user can now choose the right design point for the required FFT application.

4.3 Effectiveness of Adrastea

Though there are highly efficient high-level synthesis tools for FPGA development, it is still a challenge for programmers to adapt to FPGA development. These tools simplified the FPGA core kernel programming as easy as writing C++/OpenCL code. However, it takes weeks for programmers to write interface code as they have to understand how the FPGA interface works. Using Adrastea, one can integrate their kernel in the Adrastea environment and call the kernel from the host program with a few simple function calls. This API can be called from either a C++ or a python application. Adrastea makes design space exploration as simple as providing a JSON configuration file and starting DEFFE. DEFFE then leverages Slurm to build in parallel to get the design space exploration results in a day, whereas, in the traditional FPGA design environment, manual exploration takes months to realize and perform the exploration. In summary, Adrastea enables the FPGA development from programming to deployment within a day while also conducting a design space exploration, which not only saves programmers time but also eases the FPGA development (Table 2).

Table 2. Adrastea to speedup design

	Traditional FPGA design	Adrastea based SNS random forest	Adrastea based FFT
Adrastea integration time	-	1 h (Easy setup)	1 h
Interface programming time	Weeks (Needs expertise)	1 h (Very easy similar to function call)	1 h
Build script writing	2 Days (Needs expertise)	1 h (Very easy as configuring a CMake variable)	1 h
Average build time	-	$\sim$4 h	$\sim$9 h
Number of builds	-	90	54
Design space exploration time	Months $\sim$ 13 days (SNS) $\sim$ 21 days (FFT) (Sequential build time)	$\sim$15 h	$\sim$26 h
Graphing time	6 h	3 h (Data is already tabulated)	3 h

5   Conclusion and Future Work

This paper presents Adrastea, an automated and efficient design environment to design, implement, and optimize complex FPGA kernels and their interfaces. By leveraging the power of Adrastea, we can implement and optimize complex random forest machine learning models (SNS, Olivetti, etc.,) and complex FFT kernels on a Xilinx Alveo U250 FPGA within a few days. In contrast, it would take months to design the kernel and perform the same design space exploration with a traditional FPGA design environment. This speedup is achieved from the simplified interfacing code, and parallel building of the FPGA designs in a compute cluster.

For future work, we plan to enhance Adrastea's capability further and utilize Adrastea to explore other mission-critical FPGA computing kernels. We also plan to leverage Adrastea to optimize applications that leverage multiple heterogeneous accelerator types.

Acknowledgments. This research used resources of the Experimental Computing Laboratory (ExCL) at the Oak Ridge National Laboratory, which is supported by the Office of Science of the U.S. Department of Energy under Contract No. DE-AC05-00OR22725

References

1. Cabrera, A.M., Young, A.R., Vetter, J.S.: Design and analysis of cxl performance models for tightly-coupled heterogeneous computing. In: Proceedings of the 1st International Workshop on Extreme Heterogeneity Solutions, ExHET 2022. Association for Computing Machinery, New York (2022). https://doi.org/10.1145/3529336.3530817
2. Chacko, J., Sahin, C., Nguyen, D., Pfeil, D., Kandasamy, N., Dandekar, K.: FPGA-based latency-insensitive OFDM pipeline for wireless research. In: 2014 IEEE High Performance Extreme Computing Conference (HPEC), pp. 1–6. IEEE (2014)
3. Cock, D., et al.: Enzian: an open, general, CPU/FPGA platform for systems software research. In: Proceedings of the 27th ACM International Conference on Architectural Support for Programming Languages and Operating Systems, ASPLOS 2022, pp. 434–451. Association for Computing Machinery, New York (2022). https://doi.org/10.1145/3503222.3507742
4. Dufour, C., Cense, S., Ould-Bachir, T., Grégoire, L.A., Bélanger, J.: General-purpose reconfigurable low-latency electric circuit and motor drive solver on FPGA. In: IECON 2012-38th Annual Conference on IEEE Industrial Electronics Society, pp. 3073–3081. IEEE (2012)
5. Farabet, C., Poulet, C., Han, J.Y., LeCun, Y.: CNP: an FPGA-based processor for convolutional networks. In: 2009 International Conference on Field Programmable Logic and Applications, pp. 32–37. IEEE (2009)
6. Giordano, R., Aloisio, A.: Protocol-independent, fixed-latency links with FPGA-embedded serdeses. J. Instrum. **7**(05), P05004 (2012)
7. Henderson, S., et al.: The spallation neutron source accelerator system design. Nucl. Instrum. Methods Phys. Res. Sect. A **763**, 610–673 (2014)
8. Huang, B., Huan, Y., Xu, L.D., Zheng, L., Zou, Z.: Automated trading systems statistical and machine learning methods and hardware implementation: a survey. Enterp. Inf. Syst. **13**(1), 132–144 (2019)

9. Islam, M.M., Hossain, M.S., Hasan, M.K., Shahjalal, M., Jang, Y.M.: FPGA implementation of high-speed area-efficient processor for elliptic curve point multiplication over prime field. IEEE Access **7**, 178811–178826 (2019)
10. Javeed, K., Wang, X.: Low latency flexible FPGA implementation of point multiplication on elliptic curves over GF (P). Int. J. Circuit Theory Appl. **45**(2), 214–228 (2017)
11. Kathail, V.: Xilinx vitis unified software platform. In: Proceedings of the 2020 ACM/SIGDA International Symposium on Field-Programmable Gate Arrays, FPGA 2020, pp. 173–174. Association for Computing Machinery, New York (2020). https://doi.org/10.1145/3373087.3375887
12. Kim, J., Lee, S., Johnston, B., Vetter, J.S.: IRIS: a portable runtime system exploiting multiple heterogeneous programming systems. In: Proceedings of the 25th IEEE High Performance Extreme Computing Conference, HPEC 2021, pp. 1–8 (2021). https://doi.org/10.1109/HPEC49654.2021.9622873
13. Liu, F., Miniskar, N.R., Chakraborty, D., Vetter, J.S.: Deffe: a data-efficient framework for performance characterization in domain-specific computing. In: Proceedings of the 17th ACM International Conference on Computing Frontiers, pp. 182–191 (2020)
14. Lockwood, J.W., Gupte, A., Mehta, N., Blott, M., English, T., Vissers, K.: A low-latency library in FPGA hardware for high-frequency trading (HFT). In: 2012 IEEE 20th Annual Symposium on High-Performance Interconnects, pp. 9–16. IEEE (2012)
15. Miniskar, N., Young, A., Liu, F., Blokland, W., Cabrera, A., Vetter, J.: Ultra low latency machine learning for scientific edge applications. In: Proceedings of 32nd International Conference on Field Programmable Logic and Applications (FPL 2022). IEEE (2022)
16. Morris, G.W., Thomas, D.B., Luk, W.: FPGA accelerated low-latency market data feed processing. In: 2009 17th IEEE Symposium on High Performance Interconnects, pp. 83–89. IEEE (2009)
17. Puš, V., Kekely, L., Kořenek, J.: Low-latency modular packet header parser for FPGA. In: 2012 ACM/IEEE Symposium on Architectures for Networking and Communications Systems (ANCS), pp. 77–78. IEEE (2012)
18. Rodríguez-Andina, J.J., Valdes-Pena, M.D., Moure, M.J.: Advanced features and industrial applications of FPGAs-a review. IEEE Trans. Industr. Inf. **11**(4), 853–864 (2015)
19. Sarkar, T.: DOEPY design of experiments. https://doepy.readthedocs.io/en/latest/. Accessed 30 Sept 2020
20. Sidler, D., Alonso, G., Blott, M., Karras, K., Vissers, K., Carley, R.: Scalable 10GBPS TCP/IP stack architecture for reconfigurable hardware. In: 2015 IEEE 23rd Annual International Symposium on Field-Programmable Custom Computing Machines, pp. 36–43. IEEE (2015)
21. Somnath, S., Belianinov, A., Kalinin, S.V., Jesse, S.: Rapid mapping of polarization switching through complete information acquisition. Nat. Commun. **7**(1), 1–8 (2016). https://doi.org/10.1038/ncomms13290
22. Wang, Z., Schafer, B.C.: Learning from the past: efficient high-level synthesis design space exploration for FPGAs. ACM Trans. Des. Autom. Electron. Syst. **27**(4), 1–23 (2022). https://doi.org/10.1145/3495531
23. Xilinx: Vitis high-level synthesis user guide (UG1399) (2022). https://docs.xilinx.com/r/en-US/ug1399-vitis-hls

Toward an Autonomous Workflow for Single Crystal Neutron Diffraction

Junqi Yin[1](✉), Guannan Zhang[2], Huibo Cao[3], Sajal Dash[1],
Bryan C. Chakoumakos[3], and Feiyi Wang[1]

[1] National Center for Computational Sciences, Oak Ridge National Laboratory,
Oak Ridge, TN 37831, USA
{yinj,dashs,fwang2}@ornl.gov
[2] Computational Sciences and Mathematics Division, Oak Ridge National
Laboratory, Oak Ridge, TN 37831, USA
zhangg@ornl.gov
[3] Neutron Scattering Division, Oak Ridge National Laboratory,
Oak Ridge, TN 37831, USA
{caoh,chakoumakobc}@ornl.gov

Abstract. The operation of the neutron facility relies heavily on beamline scientists. Some experiments can take one or two days with experts making decisions along the way. Leveraging the computing power of HPC platforms and AI advances in image analyses, here we demonstrate an autonomous workflow for the single-crystal neutron diffraction experiments. The workflow consists of three components: an inference service that provides real-time AI segmentation on the image stream from the experiments conducted at the neutron facility, a continuous integration service that launches distributed training jobs on Summit to update the AI model on newly collected images, and a frontend web service to display the AI tagged images to the expert. Ultimately, the feedback can be directly fed to the equipment at the edge in deciding the next-step experiment without requiring an expert in the loop. With the analyses of the requirements and benchmarks of the performance for each component, this effort serves as the first step toward an autonomous workflow for real-time experiment steering at ORNL neutron facilities.

Keywords: Autonomous workflow · Inference at the edge · Integrated ecosystem · Image segmentation

This manuscript has been co-authored by UT-Battelle, LLC, under contract DE-AC05-00OR22725 with the US Department of Energy (DOE). The US government retains and the publisher, by accepting the article for publication, acknowledges that the US government retains a nonexclusive, paid-up, irrevocable, worldwide license to publish or reproduce the published form of this manuscript, or allow others to do so, for US government purposes. DOE will provide public access to these results of federally sponsored research in accordance with the DOE Public Access Plan (http://energy.gov/downloads/doe-public-access-plan).

K. Doug et al. (Eds.): SMC 2022, CCIS 1690, pp. 244–256, 2022.
https://doi.org/10.1007/978-3-031-23606-8_15

1   Introduction

Scientific discoveries are exploratory and iterative by nature, and thus often require multi-stage decision-making along the process. Traditionally, this is achieved by involving human experts in the loop. Taking neutron scattering as an example, which is one of the most important experimental techniques to learn atomic structure and dynamics of matter, many experiments include stages of quick initial scans to identify regions of interest and long refined scans to take accurate measurements. A beamline scientist needs to review the scan images and decide the next set of experiment parameters. In some cases, the entire process can take days.

With the rise of artificial intelligence (AI), especially the breakthroughs in the field of computer vision, it now becomes a reality to have AI-enabled methods to steer the experimentation [1,2]. Thanks to the growing computing power, such AI-driven discoveries can be deployed at the edge via an autonomous workflow. In this paper, we develop an autonomous edge workflow for a neutron scattering experiment at Oak Ridge National Laboratory (ORNL).

The rest of the paper is organized as follows: in Sect. 2, we briefly review the background on the example application and related techniques. We then provide details of our deployment architectures and implementation methods in Sect. 3, and present the evaluation results in Sect. 4. We discuss the generalizability of our solution in Sect. 5, and conclude in Sect. 6.

2   Background

2.1   Bragg Peak Detection

ORNL operates two top neutron sources, the Spallation Neutron Source (SNS) and the High Flux Isotope Reactor (HIFR), that have attracted a large science user community. Here we focus on neutron diffraction data generated with the DEMAND instrument [3] at HIFR. In Fig. 1, we illustrate a typical workflow of a single crystal neutron diffraction experiment using DEMAND. The steps of current practice are,

1. Crystal screening and alignment—This is mostly performed by instrument scientists.
2. Data collection—Operate an experiment.
3. Data Reduction—Convert the collected raw data into the standard format for downstream analysis.
4. Data Analysis—Visualize and identify the Bragg peaks.
5. Repeat if Bragg peak is not clearly detected.

For most steps, knowledge about both the science domain and computer software are required, and hence a beamline scientist is often heavily involved. The outcome is that the downstream analysis takes longer time than the operation of an experiment itself, and a typical experiment needs one or two days. Furthermore,

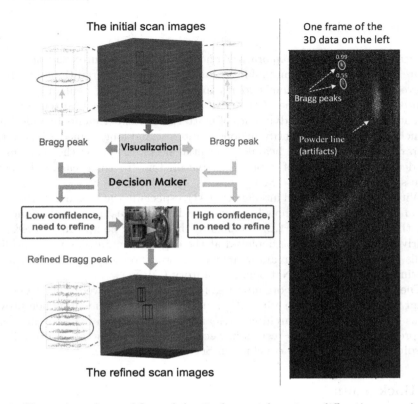

Fig. 1. Illustration of a workflow of the single crystal neutron diffraction experiment at HFIR facility of ORNL.

for current analysis software (Mantid [4]), data collection is complete, in many cases, after the experiment is finished, but the data reduction and analysis can only be performed after the experiment. This renders real-time decision-making impossible.

2.2   Image Segmentation

Image segmentation is the process of associating pixels in a image with an object type, an important task in computer vision. There are two major types of image segmentation: (1) semantic segmentation, where all objects of the same type are marked using one class label; (2) instance segmentation, where each object with the same class is marked with a separate label. With the recent breakthroughs in neural network based deep learning (DL), state-of-the-art performance [5] has been achieved with DL models on many image segmentation challenges. Typically, these DL models employ the convolution neural networks (CNN) as the backbones, given the success of CNN in extracting image features. Since the introduction of fully convolutional networks (FCN) [6] in 2014, many advance-

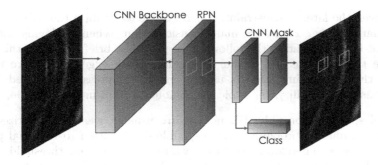

Fig. 2. Mask-RCNN architecture. It consists of a convolution neural network (CNN) backbone for feature extraction, a regional proposal network (RPN), a CNN mask head, and an object classifier.

ments have been made for both semantic segmentation (e.g., U-Net [7], FC-DenseNet [8], DeepLab [9], etc.), and instance segmentation (e.g., DeepMask [10], Mask-RCNN [11], etc.). More recently, another interesting development is to combine the semantic and instance segmentation, and the so-called panoptic segmentation [12] has obtained satisfying performance on both tasks. Considering the nature of the Bragg peak detection problem (i.e., instance segmentation) and the state of the art for instance segmentation, Mask-RCNN is employed for the task. The model architecture is illustrated in Fig. 2. Mask-RCNN is built upon the Faster RCNN (FRCNN) architecture. FRCNN predicts object class and bounding boxes in 2 stages: (1) it extracts feature maps with a CNN backbone (e.g., ResNet50) and feeds them into a region proposal network (RPN), which generates a set of regions in feature maps containing the objects. (2) a classifier predicts object class and bounding box for each proposed region. Mask-RCNN introduces an additional network branch (2 convolution layers) to predict segmentation masks on each region in a pixel-to-pixel manner. The loss of the Mask-RCNN model is then defined as,

$$\mathcal{L} = \mathcal{L}_{rpn\_class} + \mathcal{L}_{rpn\_bbox}$$
$$+ \mathcal{L}_{mrcnn\_class} + \mathcal{L}_{mrcnn\_bbox}$$
$$+ \mathcal{L}_{mrcnn\_mask}, \tag{1}$$

where $\mathcal{L}_{rpn\_class}$ and $\mathcal{L}_{mrcnn\_class}$ characterizes how well the region proposal network separates background from objects and Mask-RCNN recognizes each class of objects, respectively; $\mathcal{L}_{rpn\_bbox}$ and $\mathcal{L}_{mrcnn\_bbox}$ indicate how well RPN and Mask-RCNN localizes objects, respectively; and $\mathcal{L}_{mrcnn\_mask}$ shows how well Mask-RCNN segments objects.

2.3 Edge Inference

With a learned model for the Bragg peak detection, the ultimate goal is to obtain actionable intelligence to guide the experimentation, preferably in real time. Given the latency constraint, it is desirable to perform the inference close to the data source. There are many considerations when deploying inference models at the edge, and in the following we provide a brief review on this topic.

Since the compute and memory capacity of the edge devices are usually limited, the first optimization is usually model compression. Ordered by the level of easy applicability, the typical techniques for DL models include,

- Model sparsification. The DL models are usually over parameterized, and many parameters probably have negligible contribution to the final prediction outcome. Therefore, parameter values below certain threshold can be pruned and thus model size is reduced. Another sparsification technique is quantization, i.e. further reducing the data representation of parameters (e.g., 32 bit float to 8 bit). Both pruning and quantization are supported by DL frameworks such as TensorFlow model optimization library. Depending on applications, an order of magnitude speedup in computation and reduction in memory has been reported [13] with small accuracy loss.
- Knowledge distillation. The idea [14] is to distill the knowledge of a large model (a.k.a teacher model) to a smaller model (student model). While the training uses a teacher model to better generalize the data, the inference utilizes the student model for better computational performance. The student model learns to mimic the teacher model by optimizing a loss function with the target from teacher's output. Compared to model sparsification, knowledge distillation is more flexible and can achieve better model compression. On the other hand, it requires more tuning and exploration.
- Neural Architecture Search. This is a more general approach, and can be combined with knowledge distillation and model sparsification to pinpoint an optimal student model. Considering the trade off between the model size and computation performance, a layer-by-layer greedy search [15] can be a good starting point.

The second consideration gears towards the streaming nature of many data sources at the edge, such as image, video, and text streams. To provide real-time feedback, which requires fast and reliable message handling, a software stack that enables the data analytics on the streaming data is needed. For DL applications, this often involves input pre-processing, model inference, and output post-processing. There are several stream processing platforms, e.g., Apache Spark [16], Kafka [17], etc., and Redis [18] seems to be optimal for streaming DL inference at the edge, considering its good performance (in-memory operation) and integration with DL model serving.

Finally, the model itself sometimes needs to be updated to keep up with the change and/or drift in the distribution of data sources at the edge. This is especially the case for experimental data at scientific facilities, where characteristics (input features) of different sample materials can change dramatically. To address this problem, either a periodic re-training or some form of streaming learning [19] needs to be performed.

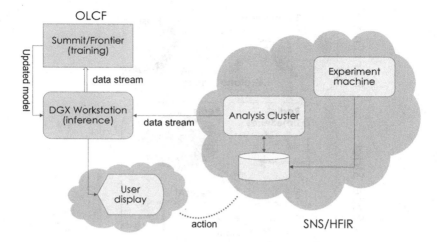

Fig. 3. Overview architecture of the workflow for Bragg peaks detection.

3   Method

3.1   Overview Architecture

In Fig. 3, we show the overview of the workflow architecture for the Bragg peak detection. The neutron experiment is performed at an instrument without direct data access. The collected data are streamed to a storage accessible by an analysis cluster. For a typical single crystal experiment, there are several thousands of images in total, and each image is of 1536×512 pixels generated every $10\,\mathrm{s}$. The image stream is then pulled by a DGX workstation, where the analyses are performed, including data processing, model inference, and time series analysis. The resulting image with predicted Bragg peak annotation, along with statistics about the peak counts and model performance, are displayed via a web portal. Periodically, the image data on the DGX workstation is pulled by an OLCF supercomputer for re-training to re-calibrate the model for different materials. We will discuss each component of the workflow in details in the following.

3.2   Transfer Learning

Image segmentation with Mask-RCNN is a supervised learning process, and it learns from the target annotated by human. In our case, specifically, it requires scanned images with marked boxes/pixels indicating region of interest by beamline experts. This is a time-consuming process and is challenging to collect large amount of data for training the model from scratch. On the other hand, considering the low-level image features (e.g., edges, blobs, etc.) are generally applicable, we use the pre-trained Mask-RCNN model on COCO dataset [20], and only finetune the model parameters of the last part of the neural network for predicting Bragg peaks. This is a common practice in DL community, and has been shown to be effective on scientific data (e.g., rock images [21]) as well.

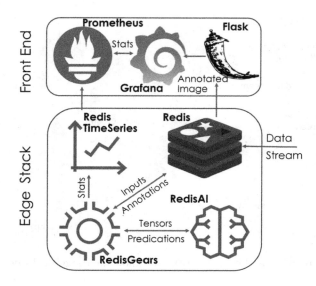

Fig. 4. Overview architecture of the workflow for the Bragg peaks detection.

3.3   Model Reduction

Table 1. The size of Mask-RCNN model with different backbones

Backbone	#Conv2D	#Parameters	Model-size
ResNet50	61	46,758,046	179 MB
ResNet101	112	65,828,510	253 MB

As discussed in Sect. 2.3, to speed up the inference at the edge, the most straightforward way is to reduce the model complexity. For Mask-RCNN model, there are many knobs related to the total number of parameters and expensive convolution operations,

- Backbone CNN. A smaller network will significantly reduce the compute operations.
- Dimensions of resized images. This effectively reduces the input data size.
- Maximum number of proposed regions and object instances.

These knobs require re-training of the model. In Table 1, the number of convolutions (Conv2D), parameters, and the model size of the Mask-RCNN models with ResNet50 and ResNet101 backbone are listed, respectively. Compared to the default ResNet101, ResNet50 backbone reduces the total number of parameters by 29%.

3.4   Solution Stack

With the optimized model in place, we employ the Redis-based software stack for model deployment at the edge, and a web application stack for analytics and interactive visualization, as shown in Fig. 4.

Edge Stack. Redis is an in-memory data structure store, and it integrates several modules to form a software stack suitable for edge applications [22]: (1) RedisAI, an inference server for executing DL models and scripts; (2) RedisGears, an engine for executing functions on Redis data flows. (3) RedisTimeSeries, a module for the time-series data structure for Redis.

The use case scenario for an input data stream is as follows,

1. Initialization of Redis server, uploading of DL models and scripts to RedisAI, loading RedisGears scripts, and creating RedisTimeSeries structures.
2. The Redis server receives the data message, and passes the input (e.g., image in bytes) to RedisGears.
3. The input is pre-processed (e.g., resizing image) and converted to tensors, and then sent to RedisAI.
4. RedisAI executes model inference and sends back the predictions.
5. The predictions are further processed, and annotations are extracted and sent to Redis server. Also, the time step statistics are sent to RedisTimeSeries.

The workflow is triggered by an input message to Redis server, and orchestrated mainly by RedisGears for all the operations on the input stream.

Front End. For the web application on the front end (see Fig. 4), we use Grafana [23] for the user interface, Prometheus [24] and Flask [25] for statistics and image stream data source, respectively. Grafana supports easily configurable dashboards and multiple data sources for visualization of analytics on a data stream. Prometheus provides functionalities to select and aggregate time-series data in real time, and has adaptor to connect with RedisTimeSeries. Flask can host annotated images streaming from the Redis server back end.

Specifically, to visualize the DL-detected Bragg peaks for an experiment at the beamline, the dashboards include not only the box annotation on the scanned image, but also the time series of current and total peak counts (within adjustable time window), and the breakdown performance of data loading, pre-processing, model inference, and post-processing. The real-time feedback enables beamline users to monitor the experiment and decide the parameters for the next scan if needed. In principle, the decision process can also be automated, should the experiment equipment be programmable.

3.5   Continuous Integration

Periodically, the Mask-RCNN model needs to be updated for new materials. To automate this re-training, a gitlab continuous integration (CI) can be created

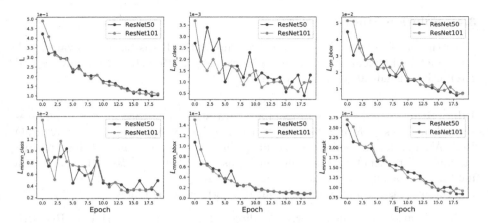

Fig. 5. The validation loss breakdown (Eq. 1) for Mask-RCNN model with ResNet50 and ResNet101 backbone, respectively.

such that both a specified schedule and/or the new dataset event will trigger a DL training job at OLCF (see Fig. 3). The gitlab runner is setup on the login node, which will pull the data from the DGX workstation and launch a job to fine tune the model on the data. The updated model is then sent back and reloaded into RedisAI.

4   Evaluation

4.1   Experiment Setup

Our edge workflow (see Fig. 3) involves an analysis cluster at the experimental facility and a DGX workstation, where we perform the evaluation. Each analysis node is equipped with an Intel Xeon Gold 6246R CPU and a Nvidia Quadro P1000 GPU with 4 GB memory. Both the CPU and GPU are shared among users. The DGX workstation is equipped with 8 V100 GPUs, and each has 16 GB memory.

The model training and inference is using TensorFlow v1.15.0. The Redis-based edge software stack is based on Redis v5.0.5 The frontend web application stack consists of Grafana v6.1.2, Premetheus v2.8.0, and Flask v2.0.3.

4.2   Results

We evaluate the computation and communication requirements for the autonomous workflow, and demonstrate the end-to-end pipeline for the application.

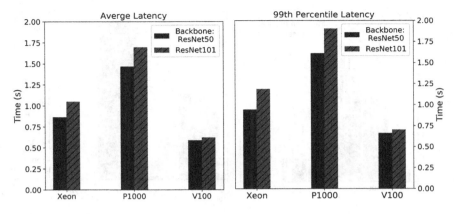

Fig. 6. The average and 99th percentile inference latency of Mask-RCNN model with ResNet50 and ResNet101 backbones on Xeon Gold 6246R CPU, Nvidia P1000, and V100 GPUs.

Computation. As discussed in Sect. 3, the default neural network backbone of Mask-RCNN model is ResNet101. Considering the trade-off between the prediction accuracy and the computational cost, we evaluate both ResNet101 and ResNet50 (see Table 1) backbones. In Fig. 5, the validation loss terms are plotted for both cases. Because of the simple features of the scanned image, the accuracy of ResNet50 backbone is on par with the more expensive ResNet101.

In Fig. 6, we compare the inference latency with ResNet50 and ResNet101 backbones on three devices: Xeon Gold 6246R CPU, Nvidia P1000, and V100 GPUs. On slower devices such as Xeon and P1000, using ResNet50 backbone can boost performance by about 20% without loss of accuracy. Overall, V100 provides the best latency, about 1.4× and 2× over Xeon and P1000, respectively. The average and 99th percentile latency behaves similarly, and the latter is about 10% larger and the impact of bigger model size seems to be bigger.

Communication. In addition to the model inference, another important factor that impacts the real-time analytics on the image stream is the communication overhead. Each image is about 3 MB and needs to be transferred from the analysis cluster at the beamline to the DGX workstation at OLCF. In Fig. 7, the histogram of the communication time of the image stream is plotted. It ranges from 300 ms to over 600 ms, with the mean value around 450 ms. In total, the end-to-end autonomous detection of Bragg peaks in a single image takes about 1.3 s.

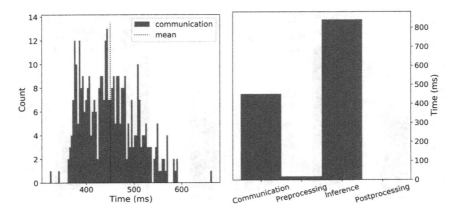

Fig. 7. The histogram of the communication overhead of the scanned image stream, and the time breakdown of the communication, pre-processing, model inference, and post-processing.

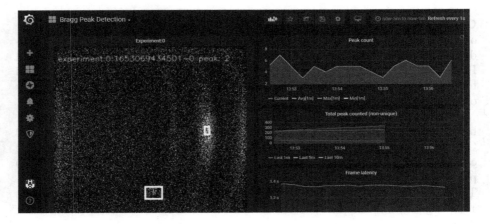

Fig. 8. Demonstration of an autonomous workflow for Bragg peak detection.

Demonstration. To put it all together, as shown in Fig. 8, we demonstrate the captured real-time analytics of a neutron scatting experiment. It includes the image display with annotation box for the predicted Bragg peaks, current and total peak counts, and performance metrics. The frame rate of this experiment (∼10 s/image) is well within the end-to-end processing capability (∼1.3 s/image), and a user can obtain real-time feedback on the experiment.

5   Discussion

The outlined solution stack is not only limited to the Bragg peak detection, but applies generally to the segmentation task of the image stream. Depending on the rate of the scanned image in an experiment, the workflow can be further optimized: (1) explore smaller model (e.g., ResNet18 backbone) and/or model sparsification to speed up the inference; (2) move the inference server closer to the beamline to reduce the overhead of data transfer; (3) obtain the data feed directly from the experiment machine to remove the intermediate I/O storage time. All of the above are worth further exploration.

6 Conclusion

We have developed an end-to-end autonomous workflow for the Bragg peak detection at the neutron facility of ORNL. We reviewed current practices for the image segmentation and edge inference, and presented an end-to-end solution from the hardware architecture to the software stack. We then evaluated the performance of each component in the workflow, and showed its capability and requirement for the real-time analytics. The output of the workflow is displayed via a frontend and ultimately can be used to steer an experiment. With improvement, the proposed autonomous workflow can be adapted generally for the online image segmentation at experimental facilities.

Acknowledgment. This manuscript has been authored by UT-Battelle, LLC under Contract No. DE-AC05-00OR22725 with the U.S. Department of Energy. This neutron data used resources at the High Flux Isotope Reactor, the DOE Office of Science User Facility operated by ORNL.

References

1. DeCost, B., Hattrick-Simpers, J., Trautt, Z., Kusne, A., Campo, E., Green, M.: Scientific AI in materials science: a path to a sustainable and scalable paradigm. Mach. Learn. Sci. Technol. **1**(3), 033001 (2020). https://doi.org/10.1088/2632-2153/ab9a20
2. Stach, E., et al.: Autonomous experimentation systems for materials development: a community perspective. Matter **4**(9), 2702–2726 (2021). https://www.osti.gov/biblio/1823639
3. Cao, H., et al.: DEMAND, a dimensional extreme magnetic neutron diffractometer at the high flux isotope reactor. Crystals **9**(1), 5 (2019). https://www.mdpi.com/2073-4352/9/1/5
4. Arnold, O., et al.: Mantid-data analysis and visualization package for neutron scattering and SR experiments. Nucl. Instrum. Methods Phys. Res. Sect. A **764**, 156–166 (2014). http://www.sciencedirect.com/science/article/pii/S0168900214008729
5. Minaee, S., Boykov, Y., Porikli, F., Plaza, A., Kehtarnavaz, N., Terzopoulos, D.: Image segmentation using deep learning: a survey. IEEE Trans. Pattern Anal. Mach. Intell. **44**(7), 3523–3542 (2022)
6. Long, J., Shelhamer, E., Darrell, T.: Fully convolutional networks for semantic segmentation. CoRR abs/1411.4038 (2014). http://arxiv.org/abs/1411.4038
7. Ronneberger, O., Fischer, P., Brox, T.: U-net: convolutional networks for biomedical image segmentation. CoRR abs/1505.04597 (2015). http://arxiv.org/abs/1505.04597

8. Jégou, S., Drozdzal, M., Vázquez, D., Romero, A., Bengio, Y.: The one hundred layers tiramisu: fully convolutional densenets for semantic segmentation. CoRR abs/1611.09326 (2016). http://arxiv.org/abs/1611.09326

9. Chen, L., Papandreou, G., Kokkinos, I., Murphy, K., Yuille, A.L.: Deeplab: semantic image segmentation with deep convolutional nets, atrous convolution, and fully connected CRFs. CoRR abs/1606.00915 (2016). http://arxiv.org/abs/1606.00915

10. Pinheiro, P.H.O., Collobert, R., Dollár, P.: Learning to segment object candidates. CoRR abs/1506.06204 (2015). http://arxiv.org/abs/1506.06204

11. He, K., Gkioxari, G., Dollár, P., Girshick, R.B.: Mask R-CNN. CoRR abs/1703.06870 (2017). http://arxiv.org/abs/1703.06870

12. Kirillov, A., He, K., Girshick, R.B., Rother, C., Dollár, P.: Panoptic segmentation. CoRR abs/1801.00868 (2018). http://arxiv.org/abs/1801.00868

13. Hoefler, T., Alistarh, D., Ben-Nun, T., Dryden, N., Peste, A.: Sparsity in deep learning: pruning and growth for efficient inference and training in neural networks. CoRR abs/2102.00554 (2021). https://arxiv.org/abs/2102.00554

14. Hinton, G., Vinyals, O., Dean, J.: Distilling the knowledge in a neural network (2015). https://arxiv.org/abs/1503.02531

15. Pasini, M.L., Yin, J., Li, Y.W., Eisenbach, M.: A greedy constructive algorithm for the optimization of neural network architectures. CoRR abs/1909.03306 (2019). http://arxiv.org/abs/1909.03306

16. Zaharia, M., et al.: Apache spark: a unified engine for big data processing. Commun. ACM **59**(11), 56–65 (2016). https://doi.org/10.1145/2934664

17. Apache kafka. https://kafka.apache.org/. Accessed 06 June 2022

18. Redis. https://redis.io/. Accessed 06 June 2022

19. Dash, S., Yin, J., Shankar, M., Wang, F., Feng, W.C.: Mitigating catastrophic forgetting in deep learning in a streaming setting using historical summary. In: 2021 7th International Workshop on Data Analysis and Reduction for Big Scientific Data (DRBSD-7), pp. 11–18 (2021)

20. Abdulla, W.: Mask R-CNN for object detection and instance segmentation on Keras and tensorflow (2017). https://github.com/matterport/Mask_RCNN

21. Mcclure, J., et al.: Toward real-time analysis of synchrotron micro-tomography data: accelerating experimental workflows with AI and HPC 1315 (2020). https://www.osti.gov/biblio/1855697

22. Redisedge. https://redis.com/redis-enterprise/more/redis-edge/. https://github.com/RedisGears/EdgeRealtimeVideoAnalytics. Accessed 06 June 2022

23. Grafana. https://grafana.com/. Accessed 06 June 2022

24. Prometheus. https://prometheus.io/. Accessed 06 June 2022

25. Flask. https://flask.palletsprojects.com. Accessed 06 June 2022

Industrial Experience Deploying Heterogeneous Platforms for Use in Multi-modal Power Systems Design Workflows

Andrew Gallo[(✉)] [iD], Ian Claydon [iD], Eric Tucker [iD], and Richard Arthur [iD]

General Electric – Global Research Center, Niskayuna, NY 12309, USA
Andrew.Gallo@GE.com

Abstract. We will present our industrial experience deploying software and heterogeneous hardware platforms to support end-to-end workflows in the power systems design engineering space. Such workflows include classical physics-based High Performance Computing (HPC) simulations, GPU-based ML training and validation, as well as pre- and post-processing on commodity CPU systems.

The software architecture is characterized by message-oriented middleware which normalizes distributed, heterogenous compute assets into a single ecosystem. Services provide enterprise authentication, data management, version tracking, digital provenance, and asynchronous event triggering, fronted by a secure API, Python SDK, and monitoring GUIs. With the tooling, various classes of workflows from simple, unitary through complex multi-modal workflows are enabled. The software development process was informed by and uses several national laboratory software packages whose impact and opportunities will also be discussed.

Utilizing this architecture, automated workflow processes focused on complex and industrially relevant applications have been developed. These leverage the asynchronous triggering and job distribution capabilities of the architecture to greatly improve design capabilities. The physics-based workflows involve simple Python-based pre-processing, proprietary Linux-based physics solvers, and multiple distinct HPC steps each of which required unique inputs and provided distinct outputs. Post-processing via proprietary Fortran and Python scripts are used to generate training data for machine learning algorithms. Physics model results were then provided to machine learning (ML) algorithms on GPU compute nodes to optimize the machine learning models based on design criteria. Finally, the ML optimized results were validated by running the identified designs through the physics-based workflow.

Keywords: Heterogeneous computing · HPC · Workflow · Metadata · Data provenance · Digital thread

1 Background

The complex design of modern systems creates challenges ranging from selecting from a myriad of trade-offs to guiding product design, manufacturability, and sustainment.

K. Doug et al. (Eds.): SMC 2022, CCIS 1690, pp. 257–273, 2022.
https://doi.org/10.1007/978-3-031-23606-8_16

Improving the performance and reliability of modern gas turbine power generation systems, for example, requires identifying actionable insights to extending asset life and operating cycles and/or improving overall aerothermal efficiency. The dimensions and applications of turbines and their components vary during the design, fulfillment, sustainment, and operational optimization phases of their product lifecycle. Design decisions must account for differences in scale, fidelity, and robustness across domains of competence, a process further confounded by the need to understand and trade-off between the multi-variate factors contributing to turbine performance. In addition to delivering the loosely-coupled and workflow-enabled functionality required to manage and resolve differences such as design contradictions, the underlying design system must enable the development and continual improvement of model-based design confidence and collaborative data-driven decision-making. The capability to capture and maintain searchable user and system-definable metadata tags, integrated with industry standard identity and access management capabilities will enable the development of digitally verifiable decision provenance [1].

We intend to demonstrate how our experience developing and deploying multiple generations of Gas Turbine products and the heterogeneous compute, modeling [2] and test platforms [3] required to design, field and sustain the same has informed the architecture, design and deployment of our next generation of digital thread capabilities [1, 4]. We show how our tooling, and that of the national labs, aligns with this model and demonstrate how our current capabilities are being used to develop, generate, orchestrate, and deliver an ensemble of design tools in service of real-world engineering design and product fulfillment challenges.

2 Advances and Outlook

We assert that four novel capabilities were required, at the advent of our work, in order advance the state of practice.

1. The ability to loosely-couple increasingly heterogenous data, tooling and compute in a modern, API-oriented manner and deliver actionable insights at all stages of the digital thread [5].
2. The ability to capture, characterize and describe data, tooling, job, and authorization information in machine-ready repositories, express their content via machine-readable metadata tags and describe their capabilities as machine-actionable verbs.
3. The interfaces and translational services required to enable the integration of machine learning capabilities into design space exploration, design space mapping, rapid candidate screening, field fault analysis, etc.
4. The establishment of sufficient modeling and simulation fidelity [6] and digital trust systems to enable human decision-makers to trust digital design systems and practices.

Having developed these capabilities, in some cases apace and in partnership with other industry, academic and government partners, we are now beginning to introduce them into practice in our next generation product design, fulfillment and sustainment practices. While the specific example articulated in this paper is partially instructive of the changes in practice underway, we believe that we are still at the very beginning of enabling the transformation in design practice first envisioned at the advent of our program.

3 Workflow Enabled Model Based Engineering

3.1 Requirements and Analysis

Identifying, characterizing, understanding, and generating actionable insights associated with the engineering design challenges noted above is best enabled through a co-design enabled approach [7] that brings together expertise in computational hardware and systems, relevant engineering domains and mathematical methods and software engineering.

Enabling the current and next generation of gas power turbines necessitates computation hardware and systems that are increasingly heterogenous. While some models benefit from access to heterogenous, hyper-converged systems, others may be better suited to loose-coupling and execution on a hyperscale cloud. At the other end of the computational spectrum, some models may run adequately on desktop-class systems, or specialized hardware embedded at or near a test stand or physical product installation. For the purposes of the example laid out in this paper, the computing environment may include a variety of architectures, including workstations and workstation-scale virtual machines, hyperscale cloud instances, and HPC servers – any of which may include accelerators such as GPUs. This provisioning of differently-abled nodes for different application purposes is typical in modern computing centers, as pioneered and advanced by the Leadership Computing Facilities at the national labs [8].

The wide array of engineering domains required to realize these actionable insights requires an equally wide array of engineering applications, each with its own performance characteristics, domain languages and interfaces. Combined with the diversity of scheduling (batch, interactive) and pre- and post-processing capabilities commonly available to engineering practitioners, further impetus is lent towards a coherent system able to provide asynchronous and loose coupling for workflows and with functionally ready integration mechanisms for interoperability and translation between domain languages and system interfaces. The loose coupling approach applies at various scales, including, as stated, between applications collaborating in an orchestrated workflow, as well as between elements of the same application, for example, in multi-physics co-simulation. In so much as a single application is not likely to elegantly encapsulate the end-to-end engineering process, it follows that figuratively "the workflow is the app." Therefore, loose coupling necessarily becomes the dominant paradigm for heterogeneous applications. Loose coupling implies contractual interfaces between collaborating components, and thus permits a wide range of implementations – in applications, in workflow constructions and executors, schedulers, and better adapting to growing diversity in the underlying hardware architectures [9]. Asynchronous loose coupling of components is often achieved with message-oriented architectures and event handlers [10].

A core tenet of co-design is pragmatism in implementation. To advance capability and performance, applications must leverage programming abstractions, composition frameworks, and numerical methods libraries which in turn conform to algorithms and data structures that efficiently exploit the state of the art in (hardware) system architecture. Advances in domain applications should proceed following technical progress in the underlying software and hardware infrastructure. The application workflow system must therefore facilitate agile adoption of improved implementations at any level of the ecosystem and communicate novel and enhanced capabilities to the users of the system.

Data produced and consumed by the workflows varies by type, size[1], and importantly by security classifications and control requirements; requirements both internal to an organization as well as established through legal and regulatory compliance. Establishing a data tenancy, or a grouping of similar authenticated users, human or otherwise, along with their access to the data required for the relevant design process/working, requires the collection, validation, storage, and processing of a complex array of metadata. A multi-tenant system must enable and allow for the establishment of logically, and sometimes physically segregated data tenancies and must contain systems and practices for storing and strictly protecting the auditable metadata required for each tenancy. In an ideal situation, every data tenancy, indeed every data element within the tenancy, is accompanied by several critical metadata elements required to enable decision provenance: *who* did or is doing *what*, *when* and *where* is it happening, and *why* [11]. Said differently, which individual or system is running each job, in what role, in each environment, and for what business purpose.

Data proliferates, and data discovery is a well-known problem [12]. To support FAIR data objectives across the heterogeneous computing ecosystem, the data tenancy metadata described previously must add descriptive metadata that includes evidence of the runtime ("the where") which produced or consumed it. When the execution is extended over a distributed multi-step workflow, it is necessary to notate the chain of jobs and their data I/O dependencies for reporting of interim results as well as end-to-end decision provenance.

Up to this point we have defined, discussed, and described solutions for use cases involving two types of workflows – one type operating intra-job (for example in-situ multi-physics workflows), and another type which chains individual jobs together into a broader workflow.[2] This second type is still intra-site, and includes the conduct of most HPC schedulers, which effectively run another job when some upstream job completes. While intra-job workflows are always executed on behalf of a single user identity, intra-site workflows may be for the same or different users within the same enterprise. An example is a GE workflow that performs physics-based computations on an HPC system and when complete triggers a second job running on dedicated GPU nodes to perform a ML training, launched under a different scheduler for the same or even a different

---

[1] Size matters – data size and locality must be addressed during workflow implementation and execution. Stated simply, the data must move to the compute, or the compute must be available where the data resides. A workflow system which provides abstractions over data location and site-specific application execution would be useful, as described in this paper, although we will not address the topic of "big data" specifically.

[2] This is like other categorizations of workflow types [13].

GE user.[3] The examples of different users being orchestrated within the same workflow include inter-departmental handoffs in an end-to-end design process.

Finally, there is an emergent third type of workflow, inter-site, in which the executing jobs span computing sites on behalf of the same user, albeit perhaps with distinct instances of their identity in each location.[4] An example of this third type is a single researcher workflow which includes jobs running sequentially on both GE nodes and under grant on national laboratory machines[5], the latter via the Superfacility API (SFAPI) [14]. A framework for rapid development of such cross-site workflows would provide encapsulated abstractions for each site's distinct authentication scheme and job running syntax, as well as translation of job status codes into some common interoperable set, and we discuss this below.

A quick scan of the online documentation for SFAPI shows RESTful endpoints in categories – "system health", "accounting information", "compute" including submit, read, and cancel job, "storage" and "utilities" providing upload and download of data, and a separate endpoint to provide the second leg of a multi-factor authentication process. Job status messages returned by these API endpoints map to those of Slurm and fall into several general categories – initializing or pending, running in some form, terminated normally or abnormally, and various informational messages [15].

DT4D or Digital Thread for Design, a system for orchestration of intra-site and inter-site workflows at GE, and discussed in more detail below, exposes its own API, with similar token validation, and endpoints which fall into several of the same general categories – run and inspect job status, transfer data.[6] Granular job profile, status and results, along with associated data tenancy metadata are captured and communicated within the system, allowing for either human or machine learning guided refactoring and optimization of the design process.

3.2 Conceptual Design of the Workflow Framework

A system for heterogeneous workflows – one for example not governed by a single scheduler or designed for single tenancy – which also meets the requirements can be conceptually thought of as having four pillars. Each pillar represents a category of

---

[3] In our compute model, as we will see below, this can be implemented as one site or two – as a single site with two distinct runtime "compute types" within it sharing the same enterprise authentication scheme, or as two distinct sites which happen to have the same authentication scheme in common.

[4] On one site the user's identity might be "sbrown", on another "Susan.Brown", etc.

[5] While the national laboratory computing facilities are valuable resources, for industrial applications their utility is practically limited to non-proprietary workloads. A further impediment to their integrated use is the necessary national laboratory security perimeter, and while the Superfacility API alleviates some of those impediments, the SFAPI is not yet deployed across all national facilities. Workflows which span sites including commercial sites like GE's have their own issues with security perimeters. As we will show later in this paper, the design of an inter-site workflow system needs to be realistic about the lack of ease of bi-directional data flow – it is not a trivial matter to open a communication channel into a corporate network, and a system which does not depend on such access likely has a higher probability of adoption.

[6] SFAPI has a richer administrative API.

contractual interfaces which must be implemented by a given collaborating computing site provider. These same pillars apply to inter-site and intra-site workflow types – a given computing site must implement these functional areas for its own purposes, and if it intends to be collaborative with inter-site workflows, it must also expose these functions.[7]

- Auth: provide for user authentication and authorization, e.g., link to a data tenancy
- Run: execute a given job or jobs in the user, workflow or otherwise determined runtime, with relevant translations across interfaces and job orchestration systems
- Repo: a means to put to and get data and its metadata from managed store(s)
- Spin: provision computing resources, e.g., in the cloud[8].

Auth takes many forms – some examples include a priori identity token dispensing to be used for just-in-time session token generation, as well as interactive logins. Run implementations are similarly diverse, but its functions fall into some general verb categories – run job, check job status, cancel job – the set of actions is notably terse. To this we add event handling for job chaining – set/unset event handler, list active handlers. Successfully implementing Repo functionality requires support for all common file system types (block, blog, object, etc.) but also necessitates interactivity with the relevant metadata. That metadata must itself be stored and made available via an enterprise metadata catalog and associated APIs. Those APIs themselves express common set of verbs: "put", "find", "get", etc. The industry has made broad advancements in Spin implementation and while the services and verbs available in these environments are broadly similar, they are often expressed within proprietary frameworks that limit portability.

The heterogeneity of computing facilities now also necessitates the Run subsystem exposing a means for declaration of the compute type on which the job needs to run. This could mean, on an HPC system for example, to target the run specifically at available GPU-accelerated nodes. In a commodity node farm, this could mean targeting at a named node type which has been pre-prepared with certain commercial engineering software.[9] Heterogeneous intra-site workflows under the same enterprise identity require a runtime model which incorporates and reconciles multiple schedulers, for example, by normalizing their job status return codes. Inter-site workflows require the same.

The concept of "job" includes not just what are traditionally thought of as tasks run by the scheduler, but also, potentially, the Repo and Spin functions as well. With event handling this permits end-to-end workflows which minimize the cost function (Fig. 1).

Upon this logical 4-part API layer, we can stack native language interfaces such as in Python, GUIs for human interaction for visibility into the running workflow and

---

[7] Intra-job i.e., in-situ workflows, do not require all these pillars – e.g., their authorization to run is validated before running, their computing pre-provisioned, etc.

[8] The GE Spin component is not yet implemented. Conceptually it utilizes existing vendor APIs such as AWS, VMWare, etc.

[9] While the use of containers is ideal for this purpose, and is implementable within DT4D, practical limitations in system security requirements, commercial software license terms, etc. necessitate the ability to sometimes understand and interface with statically configured systems and runtimes.

Fig. 1. Multi-job workflow with dynamic node provisioning

interrogation of the resulting digital thread. Under each logical section of the API, multiple implementations are possible, for example, AWS, MS Azure, and Google Cloud APIs fit under the Spin façade (Fig. 2).

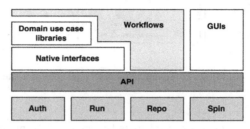

Fig. 2. DT4D API stack

3.3 Workflow Framework Implementation

The GE internal "Digital Thread for Design" (DT4D) DT4D framework has fully implemented tooling – middleware, APIs, and native interfaces – for each of the workflow types described above.

Intra-job workflows are launched on a given HPC system in a Multiple Programs, Multiple Data (MPMD) [16] modality, with our "inC2" Python / C++ library providing a simplifying messaging abstraction for extracting interim simulation results, computing derived values, using these to steer the simulation, and as desired transporting informational messages to other enterprise systems, as further described below (Fig. 3).[10]

GE enterprise intra-site multi-job workflows are enabled by the DT4D system. This system implements the key elements of the conceptual Auth, Run, and Repo subsystems.

- Auth functionality is accomplished through lightweight integration with an existing, token-based GE internal OAuth service.
- Run uses a COTS message bus to dispatch jobs to several schedulers, and job status is similarly transported on the bus. For un-clustered singleton nodes, a "Runner" agent is deployed to the node as a bus listener and assigned at runtime to a specific tenancy. All job launch information is recorded in a "Run Repo" – which tool, version, arguments, etc., as well as the full status sequence – to permit reproduction.

---

[10] An examination of prior art included ADIOS2 [17] which also provides an MPI-based transport but also implements far more functionality than our use cases demanded, and thus we erred on the side of simplicity.

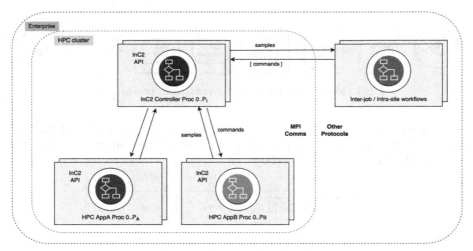

Fig. 3. In-situ intra-job workflows communicating with inter-job/intra-site enterprise workflows and interactive controllers.

- Repo implementation uses a central metadata index to front several object stores containing both data and tools which can be loaded into the job context and tracked at runtime; thus, the digital thread includes both the historical control and data flows.

The logical subsystems are exposed by a RESTful API and a native Python interface which provides the runtime harness to implement local jobs which are authenticated as first-class citizens of the ecosystems. The API is also used by a GUI which can be Web or mobile and provides a job monitoring interface,[11] system uptime information, and a metadata-driven directory tree view of data under Repo subsystem management (Fig. 4).[12]

Inter-site workflows are enabled by the "Local Workflow Manager" (lwfm) tool [18]. This thin Python façade provides native methods for the major verbs in each of the Auth, Run, and Repo subsystems. A collaborating Site implementation – be it based on the Superfacility API or GE's DT4D, or some other – is accomplished through a lightweight interface available within lwfm intended to capture 'signatures' of relevant system details. For example, the "NERSC" Site driver would translate the lwfm signatures into SFAPI calls, returning job status in lwfm canonical form. Like DT4D,

---

[11] A current side-project involves the inC2 library permitting a simulation application to transmit an informational job status message which contains a declarative GUI definition – e.g., a set of simple form control parameters. The DT4D GUI can then render this application-specific form. Use cases include interactive simulation steerage.

[12] Future work includes defining a formal interface and resolving conflicts across collaborating Auth subsystems, for example, in a situation where collaborators from multiple labs necessitates identity federation. Future run optimization can be accomplished using Run Repo and hardware profile metadata. The implementation of the Spin component is also planned.

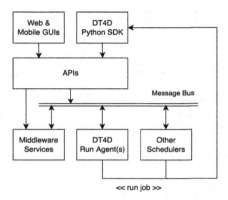

Fig. 4. DT4D high-level deployment diagram

the lwfm provides a local job status monitor service to handle workflow job chaining (Figs. 5 and 6).[13,14]

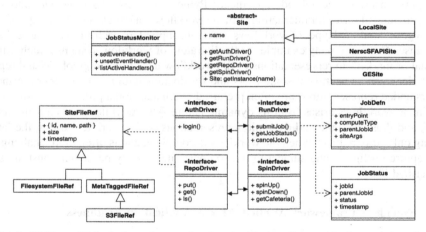

Fig. 5. UML model for lwfm software, showing the Site interface and its four sub-interfaces

In the tooling which supports each of the three types of workflows we address – intra-job ("inC2"), intra-site ("DT4D"), and inter-site ("lwfm") – we elected to represent the

---

[13] Future work includes adding a cross-site GUI which conceptually subsumes that of DT4D.

[14] Examination of prior art included ALCF Balsam [19]. We also looked at LLNL's Flux [20], and at RADICAL-Pilot [21], which seemed directed at two of the three workflow types we describe. LANL's BEE addresses reproducibility by using application containers and extending the runtime model with pre-execution CI/CD [22]. Pegasus is centered on an API for describing *a priori* DAGs. [23] Many other projects approach the workflow space from different non-comprehensive points of view, and each has its own potential strengths and weaknesses [24]. The build vs. buy decision is multi-faceted.

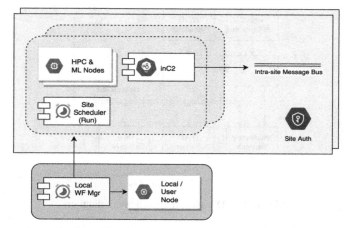

Fig. 6. lwfm orchestrating inter-site workflows, each consisting potentially of their own intra-site and intra-job workflows.

workflow in terms of actual code, specifically Python for its ease of use and wide adoption and provided libraries for interacting with the workflow constructs and APIs exposed for the type or combined types of workflows which are applied for each engineering business use case. There are many examples in the literature of workflow systems which utilize visual or marked-up representations of the workflow as a directed graph. Visual representations can be useful for some users and for documentation but for other advanced users coded representations are often preferred.[15] An additional problem in visualizing arbitrary workflows arises from its dynamic nature – the workflow can alter its future self, and thus the static and dynamic representations of the workflow differ, the latter being only fully realized when the workflow is complete, and is often more challenging to capture in-flight being subject to the compute site security perimeter constraints as described.[16]

3.4 Workflow Framework Applied: M × N Application Readiness

Complex design processes often necessitate workflows that span multiple sites and data tenancies. I.e., a researcher with access to both a company-managed supercomputer as well as one or more grant allocation on national laboratory or academic systems. When contemplating novel workloads, it would be normal to make a pre-validating run of an application on local hardware (Stage), debug it, then move the run to a larger machine for

---

[15] It's possible of course to generate a graph representation of a Python script from its abstract syntax tree – a tactic we showed to users to a somewhat unimpressive response – the raw code was the preferred medium.

[16] The visualization and navigation of dynamic and graph-oriented workflow traces, including with references to the data produced and consumed at each step, was demonstrated in the early phases of this project, but it is a subject of near-term future work to better understand how to apply such visualizations to real use cases.

the actual simulation (Production). Many applications must be recompiled,[17] and revalidated, on the target machine architecture before actual use for both basic functionality and for performance optimization. This process may need to be repeated as application code and/or underlying system operating system, kernel, library etc. changes are made. As the number of collaborating sites increases, the problem becomes burdensome. As the number of collaborating applications increases, the problem becomes intractable. Thus, assistive, and potentially democratizing tooling is required – the M application by N platform readiness problem is a use case for inter-site workflows and can be implemented with lwfm and the pertinent site drivers (Fig. 7).[18]

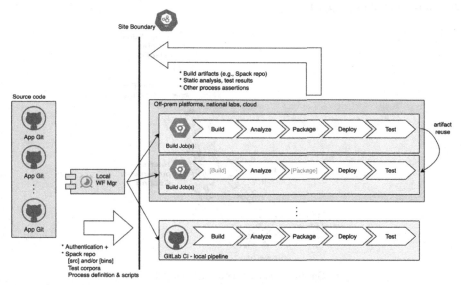

Fig. 7. MxN CI/CD – lwfm orchestrates inter-site workflows to maintain readiness of M applications on N target platforms.

4 Workflow Framework Applied: Reducing Low Cycle Fatigue

4.1 Requirements and Implementation

The flexible architecture of DT4D provides engineers the tools to orchestrate and standardize workflows, easily "get" and "put" data to storage Repos and create surrogate models of complicated components. A problem of industrial interest is that of low cycle fatigue (LCF) failure of gas turbine blades stemming from the cyclical operation of the

---

[17] The team has utilized Spack [25] and CMake in the build system. GitLab CI is used for internal CI/CD.

[18] NERSC 2021 Director Reserve Allocation, project m3952, "MxN Application Readiness", A. Gallo PI.

turbine. This weakening of the metal and continual stress-based deformation generates cracks and failures of the blade limiting the life of the blade impacting both the customer's ability to guarantee performance and the business' ability to market gas turbine products. Gas turbine airfoils, shown below, in their simplest form, can be cast metal airfoils with an array of cooling holes arranged on the surface which blanket the surface with cooling air increasing the life of the blade. The design of these airfoils is a delicate balance between two dominant factors, the LCF failure and aerothermal efficiency. These factors combine to impact business decisions ranging from duty cycle management and pricing to outage scheduling and upgrade planning. To maximize sales expediency and confidence in the ability to rapidly move from a customer's requirements to an optimized design is paramount (Fig. 8).

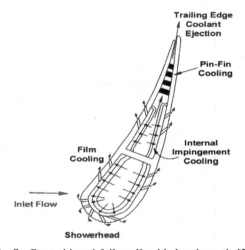

Fig. 8. Gas turbine airfoil cooling blade schematic [26]

Optimization of a blade design requires many parameters with only one discussed here; that is the cooling layout and how it impacts the delicate balance between the mechanical life of the blade and the aerothermal efficiency of the overall system. For example, an engineer could improve the longevity of the blade by overcooling the blade surface, but this additional cooling air reduces the thermodynamic performance of the engine reducing the total amount of power the engine can produce [27]. Traditionally, optimization of the arrangement of the cooling parameters has been a manual process led by domain expertise, historical design practice, and field operating knowledge generally allowing two or three designs to be analyzed prior to delivering a finalized recommendation, solution, or product to the customer. True optimization of a design requires many more iterations and must encompasses a broader variety of operating conditions and degrees of freedom than is allowed by the current state of practice. In our implementation, the DT4D system enables this by creating uniform repeatable workflows that feed into neural network (NN) training algorithms. These uniform repeatable workflows contain proprietary and commercially available analysis tools and model many different permutations of the blade and the surrounding subsystem to train a NN. These trained networks then exhaustively permutate millions of design iterations in seconds rather than the hours or days it would take to run traditional physics-based workflows. Validation of resultant optimized designs is accomplished via DT4D allowing for further development of design confidence, including through recursive iteration of workflow-enabled model training. This process can reduce design times by approximately fifty percent while providing more thoroughly optimized and validated designs.

4.2   Process Workflow Described

An optimization workflow for the gas turbine blade is comprised of three sequential steps. The first is a physics-based workflow to generate the required training data for the NN which has been previously reported in Tallman et al. [28]. The second step consists of training the NN, exhaustively exploring the designated space, and identifying the optimum results. The final step is validation of the optimum NN results which, simply put, is rerunning the physics workflow again with the design parameters identified by the NN. At their core the physics-based workflow and NN exploration algorithm are Python-based scripts that setup the requisite arguments for individual jobs including input and output lists to get from and put to the repositories along with the proper job triggering information. These workflows are designed to be repeatedly and routinely executed by a range of individual users over time.

4.3   Training Data Generation

In analyzing the gas turbine blade a physics-based workflow like that shown was utilized to improve the life of these critical gas turbine components (Fig. 9).

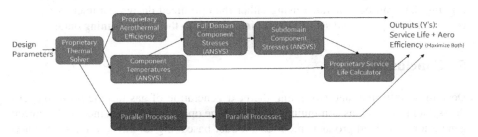

Fig. 9. Training data generation workflow

The workflow begins with the definition of the DOE design parameters which are separated into individual cases and subsequently fed into a proprietary thermal analysis tool. The outputs from this tool are then passed into three parallel processing paths including the top path which uses proprietary software to calculate the impact the design parameters have on the aerothermal efficiencies, the bottom path which simply represents any additional tools that the end user would desire to include in the design cycle, and the central path which is the focus of this discussion. All but the final element along this path involves the integration of commercial ANSYS tools into the workflow. This pathway involves calculating the component temperatures which are used to calculate full and critical sub domain component stresses. These temperatures and stresses are reunited in the final tool on this path, a proprietary service life calculator, to arrive at an array of life cycle values for the given design. The final step, alluded to in the figure, is the unification of the resulting file formats to a single format and the combination of all results into proper formats for training the NN.

4.4 Surrogate Model Creation and Execution

Leveraging open-source Python-based libraries, a NN was developed utilizing training data generated via the initial physics workflows described above. The trained NN was used to exhaustively search the area of interest for design parameters that provided optimum behavior. These design parameters were then pruned from the bulk results and formatted to be fed back through the physics workflow as a validation step utilizing the same Python code that generated the training data.

4.5 Validation and Analysis

The third workflow step is repeating the physics modeling workflow with the optimized conditions from the neural network. This necessary validation step provides multiple benefits. The first is that it identifies the true accuracy of the NN and determines the confidence in the results. If the NN is found to be accurate, it allows the engineering community to identify trends in the data that the original DOE space contains and identify trends which require expansion of the original DOE space to fully capture. Additionally, it provides training data to the NN for the next cycle of DOE points further improving accuracy of the models. If the initial NN does not possess the required accuracy, further training data can be generated using either the optimized design parameters from the NN or a newly generated set of DOE points similar to the initial training data.

5 Conclusion

Designing, fulfilling, and sustaining the next generation of gas turbine power generation systems, as well as continuing to improve the operating performance of the current generation of fielded products requires a model-based, digital thread orchestrated approach to developing product insights. The complexity of managing differences in time scale, fidelity, and robustness, combined with the desire to increase degrees of freedom and explorations of design options necessitates a design system which is capable of orchestrating workflows that span multiple heterogenous systems and data tenancies. It must also capture and communicate the metadata required to develop robust decision provenance and facilitate translation between domain languages, workflow process steps and job/solver types. Through such a system, versatile machine learning techniques can directly integrate into the design practice itself and enable continual observation and optimization of the workflows, repos and processes that underpin the design practice.

In real engineering research and development use cases, DT4D acts as a force multiplier to empower a single engineer to virtually evaluate a multitude of design permutations efficiently and effectively in a hands-off manner, while inherently more seamlessly unifying the design process workflow for collaborations among multiple engineers within a community. The system can also provide results from previously completed workflows from across the design community, potentially expediting the generation of relevant synthetic training data to create surrogate models and to validate that the models are of adequate confidence as to inform decision-making. These capabilities greatly accelerate the multidisciplinary engineering process, promote earlier discovery of design contradictions and improvements, and facilitate more agile customization of designs to meet customer specifications. The described integration of heterogenous computational platforms and software architectures provide the infrastructure for the powerful DT4D capabilities.

The Digital Thread for Design framework enables the development and continual improvement of model-based confidence and collaborative data-driven decision making and delivers significant in design-to-decision cycle time, with the opportunity to increase, by multiple orders of magnitude, the number of design alternatives considered. The framework facilitates consistency and integration of physics-based, numerical and machine learning methods for engineers to capture, execute and communicate the workflow, job, data tenancy and authentication metadata contributing to comprehensive decision provenance.

While much work remains to be done, both to augment the scope of capabilities within the framework and to expand its application within the design practice, DT4D is now in regular use providing the next generation of digital thread capabilities.

6 Areas for Further Study

There is a seemingly unending list of further areas of opportunity for focused development, study, and validation in a field of work as broad as the Model Based Engineering (MBE) of a gas turbine power generation system and the broader turbomachinery marketplace. The development, fulfillment and sustainment of the underlying workflow-enabled design framework required to sustain this MBE practice has a similarly broad and multi-variate set of opportunities. We highlight a few.

- Spin: As previously mentioned, the DT4D framework envisions and accounts for a Spin subsystem as an element of any collaborating compute site. Certainly, there is value in the ability to characterize, containerize and or configure the complete 'data+compute+job' tenancy or tenancies required for a given workflow and then to rapidly deploy that tenancy. The complexity of managing differences in functionality, interfaces, and SKUs across the proliferation of hyperscale cloud providers, the opportunity to engage across a breadth of national lab supercomputers available under grant and increasing heterogeneity of both HPC systems and computational methods on our internally developed systems all but ensure inefficiencies and lost times in design practices that rely on manual configuration and intervention.

- Multi-order modeling: While the example practice outlined in this paper incorporates iterative NN model training and design criteria refinement between a single thermal analysis tool of a given order, it is theoretically possible to orchestrate a workflow of solvers such that the level of simulation fidelity available to train the NN is varied based on the design criteria and that variability is in turn used to select the order/fidelity of the thermal analytic solver in the ensuing step. Integration of inc2 functionality for near-real time extraction of model data may further increase opportunities to reduce the cycle time to develop and validate high fidelity design recommendations. Frameworks for training and evaluating bespoke surrogate models and ensembles can further reduce development costs.
- Federated Auth for MxN: Resolving the complexity of managing person, system and data identity and the required authentication and trust systems remains an open area of research. While COTS federated authentication systems have continued to mature since the advent of our initial work on this framework, the introduction of multi-factor authentication, lack of common standards and practices associated with meeting regulatory control standards, challenges with protecting and recovering lost identities and other challenges have prevented the introduction of truly seamless, secure, and robust identity systems [29].
- Workflow Visualization, Runtime Navigation, and Democratization: The workflows described in this paper – which can dynamically at runtime set (and unset) promises for future triggered actions and spawn new jobs across a distributed computing landscape – poses significant problems relating to visualizing and debugging running workflows, and/or navigating their complete post hoc digital threads in the presence of separating enterprise security perimeters. In addition, the human experience of programming in such a heterogenous and distributed environment can be better studied, as can the potentially democratizing impact of a simplifying model of cross-site computing such as that presented in this paper.

References

1. Arthur, R.: Provenance for decision-making. In: Medium (2020). https://richardarthur.medium.com/provenance-for-decision-making-bf2c89d76ec2. Accessed 6 June 2022
2. Digital Thread for Design I GE Research. https://www.ge.com/research/technology-domains/digital-technologies/digital-thread-design. Accessed 6 June 2022
3. Feeling The Burn: Inside The Boot Camp For Elite Gas Turbines I GE News. https://www.ge.com/news/reports/feeling-the-burn-inside-the-boot-camp-for-elite-gas-turbines. Accessed 6 June 2022
4. High Performance Computing I GE Research. https://www.ge.com/research/technology-domains/digital-technologies/high-performance-computing. Accessed 6 June 2022
5. Hatakeyama, J., Farr, D., Seal, D.J.: Accelerating the MBE ecosystem through cultural transformation
6. GE Research Uses Summit Supercomputer for Groundbreaking Study on Wind Power I GE News. https://www.ge.com/news/press-releases/ge-research-uses-summit-supercomputer-groundbreaking-study-wind-power. Accessed 6 June 2022
7. Ang, J., Hoang, T., Kelly, S., et al.: Advanced simulation and computing co-design strategy (2016)

8. Compute Systems. In: Oak Ridge Leadership Computing Facility. https://www.olcf.ornl.gov/olcf-resources/compute-systems/. Accessed 6 June 2022
9. Coughlin T Compute Cambrian Explosion. In: Forbes. https://www.forbes.com/sites/tomcoughlin/2019/04/26/compute-cambrian-explosion/. Accessed 6 June 2022
10. What do you mean by "Event-Driven"? In: martinfowler.com. https://martinfowler.com/articles/201701-event-driven.html. Accessed 6 June 2022
11. Arthur, R.: Machine-augmented Mindfulness. In: Medium (2020). https://richardarthur.medium.com/machine-augmented-mindfulness-e844f9c54985. Accessed 6 Jun 2022
12. Wilkinson, M.D., et al.: The FAIR guiding principles for scientific data management and stewardship. Sci. Data **3**, 160018 (2016). https://doi.org/10.1038/sdata.2016.18
13. Deelman, E., Peterka, T., Altintas, I., et al.: The future of scientific workflows. Int. J. High Perform. Comput. Appl. **32**, 159–175 (2018)
14. NERSC SuperFacility API - Swagger UI. https://api.nersc.gov/api/v1.2/#/status/read_planned_outages_status_outages_planned__name__get. Accessed 6 June 2022
15. Slurm Workload Manager - squeue. https://slurm.schedmd.com/squeue.html. Accessed 6 June 2022
16. Multiple Program Multiple Data programming with MPI. CFD on the GO (2022)
17. Godoy, W.F., Podhorszki, N., Wang, R., et al.: ADIOS 2: the adaptable input output system. A framework for high-performance data management. SoftwareX **12**, 100561 (2020). https://doi.org/10.1016/j.softx.2020.100561
18. Gallo, A.: lwfm (2022)
19. Salim, M.A., Uram, T.D., Childers, J.T., et al.: Balsam: automated scheduling and execution of dynamic, data-intensive HPC workflows. arXiv (2019)
20. Ahn, D.H., Bass, N., Chu, A., et al.: Flux: overcoming scheduling challenges for exascale workflows, vol. 10 (2020)
21. Merzky, A., Turilli, M., Titov, M., et al.: Design and performance characterization of RADICAL-pilot on leadership-class platforms (2021)
22. Chen, J., Guan, Q., Zhang, Z., et al.: BeeFlow: a workflow management system for in situ processing across HPC and cloud systems. In: 2018 IEEE 38th International Conference on Distributed Computing Systems (ICDCS), pp 1029–1038 (2018)
23. This research used the Pegasus Workflow Management Software funded by the National Science Foundation under grant #1664162
24. Arthur R (2021) Co-Design Web. In: Medium. https://richardarthur.medium.com/co-design-web-6f37664ac1e1. Accessed 6 Jun 2022
25. Gamblin, T., LeGendre, M., Collette, M.R., et al.: The Spack package manager: bringing order to HPC software chaos. In: SC 2015: Proceedings of the International Conference for High Performance Computing, Networking, Storage and Analysis, pp. 1–12(2015)
26. Han, J.-C., Wright, L.: Enhanced internal cooling of turbine blades and vanes. In: Gas Turbine Handbook. Department of Energy - National Energy Technology Laboratory, p. 34 (2006)
27. Acharya, S., Kanani, Y.: Chapter three - advances in film cooling heat transfer. In: Sparrow, E.M., Abraham, J.P., Gorman, J.M. (eds.) Advances in Heat Transfer, pp. 91–156. Elsevier, Amsterdam (2017)
28. Tallman, J.A., Osusky, M., Magina, N., Sewall, E.: An assessment of machine learning techniques for predicting turbine airfoil component temperatures, using FEA simulations for training data. In: Volume 5A: Heat Transfer. American Society of Mechanical Engineers, Phoenix, Arizona, USA, p. V05AT20A002 (2019)
29. How Apple, Google, and Microsoft will kill passwords and phishing in one stroke | Ars Technica. https://arstechnica.com/information-technology/2022/05/how-apple-google-and-microsoft-will-kill-passwords-and-phishing-in-1-stroke/. Accessed 6 June 2022

Self-describing Digital Assets and Their Applications in an Integrated Science and Engineering Ecosystem

Dinesh Verma[1]([✉])[iD], John Overton[2], Bill Wright[3], Joshua Purcell[4],
Sathya Santhar[1], Anindita Das[1][iD], Mathews Thomas[1], and Sharath Prasad[1][iD]

[1] IBM, Armonk, NY 10504, USA
{dverma,matthom}@us.ibm.com, ssanthar@in.ibm.com,
{Anindita.Das,Sharath.Prasad}@ibm.com
[2] Kove IO Inc, Chicago, IL 60607, USA
john.overton@kove.net
[3] Red Hat, Sunnyvale, CA 94086, USA
bwright@redhat.com
[4] Red Panda, Granada Hills, CA 91344, USA
josh@redpanda.com

Abstract. An integrated science and engineering ecosystem requires the sharing of digital assets across many different participating organizations. Digital assets include data sets, AI models, system configuration, papers and technical reports etc. that are exchanged across different organizations. Due to a large diversity in the syntax and semantics of the digital assets, their use across and within organizations is fraught with difficulties. If the digital assets were self-describing, their usage and exploitation in organizations different than the ones producing them would be much simpler. However, the addition of self-description needs to be done in a light-weight and flexible manner in order to leverage the existing digital ecosystem, with the appropriate trade-off between extensibility, scalability and security. In an open-source collaborative research venture in an effort called the Enterprise NeuroSystems Group, several companies and universities are working together to create a light-weight self-description mechanism and a catalog to facilitate exchange of self-describing digital assets to support a variety of use-cases. In this paper, we describe the approach for adding self-description to existing digital assets, the architecture of this catalog, the fundamental design choices made for the approach and the architecture of the catalog, and the use-cases for collaborative science that can be enabled using such a catalog.

Keywords: Self describing digital assets · Metadata management · AI support systems

1 Introduction

Digital content is a life-blood of the modern enterprise. It has been asserted in various forums that data is the new oil [22]. During the course of the operation

K. Doug et al. (Eds.): SMC 2022, CCIS 1690, pp. 274–287, 2022.
https://doi.org/10.1007/978-3-031-23606-8_17

of any business, digital content is created, transferred, stored and analyzed. The collection and curation of data is a pre-requisite to the use of Artificial Intelligence and Machine Learning in the enterprise. As the data within the enterprise operations is processed, many types of digital assets may be created including but not limited to training data for machine learning, AI models, documents containing best practices, policies and guidelines, configuration files for system and network management, etc.

While digital content is critical to a business, a large part of the data collected within an enterprise may go unused, by some estimates close to three quarters of enterprise data falls within this category [2]. There are many reasons for the data not being used for analytics, or even existing models not being used in production. We will illustrate them when the digital asset in question is an AI model.

The development and use of AI models happens in two distinct phases. The first phase is the task of using collected data to train an AI model. This phase is resource-intensive requiring processing of a large amount of data to generate an AI model. The model may be represented in any of different formats ranging from a set of rules, decision trees, decision tables, or neural networks of different flavors. The second phase is the inference stage during which the model is used to make predictions during an operational environment.

Considering an AI model as the digital asset, it can be used only in operational/inference environments which are compatible with the training environment. The compatibility requirements could be from the environment and the type of environment used to train the model, e.g. if the AI model was trained on an environment like PyTorch [15], and the inference environment is based on TensorFlow [1], the model would typically not work. Similarly, a decision tree or even a neural network trained using scikit-learn [16] will not be compatible with inference environments based on PyTorch or TensorFlow.

While this difference in environment can be handled, there is an implicit assumption that the inference environment and training environment are the same or compatible. This implicit assumption works fine in many case, e.g. during the initial phases of a deployment, but may become a challenge over time. In many use-case scenarios, there may be a multiplicity of inference environments, and maintaining all of them in a compatible manner while upgrading the versions of different software can become a challenge.

The challenges that come with digital assets over time are well known, and documented variously as 'bit rot' [4] and manifest themselves prominently in the task of software preservation [28]. Digital assets of all types become difficult to use because their formats are no longer supported. A faster rate of rot in digital assets occurs because of many causes. These include compatibility mismatch due to version upgrades, movement of personnel leading to loss of institutional knowledge, and inadequate documentation. Digital rot leads to useful data becoming unusable over time.

These problems are well understood in the data community. Self-description of data to avoid these problems has been considered in various types of data formats and databases [11, 29]. The most common approach is to attach meta-data describing the data to make it be self-describing. However, there is a wide variety of metadata formats [19] leading to associated complexity and challenges in describing how the self-description using metadata ought to be managed.

These considerations have led to the approach for self-describing assets and the development of an utility for the same which are described in the next section.

2   Approach

While the use of a good metadata to enable self-description is understood and presented in existing works [11, 29], challenges remain in the definition of the metadata for self-description and the approach for developing this definition.

A challenge which is technical in nature is the selection of the format for the metadata which is needed to drive self-description. Formats such as XML can be viewed as approaches to enable self-describing data formats [17]. However, in any enterprise there is a significant amount of data that is not XML, and which will be too expensive to represent in XML or adorn with an XML-based description. Furthermore, there are many instances in which the nature of self-description that is needed would be very different.

As an example, when one has to describe an AI model, one would describe the environment in which it was trained if the focus is on getting it into another compatible environment. That level of self-description would be adequate for the task of model distribution. However, if the model was developed for a specific task, e.g. visual analysis of an image, and the distribution has to check that the task being done is compatible, e.g. it is not being distributed to a site involved only in the task of audio analysis, then the description of the type of task for the model will be required.

Because of the diversity of use-cases and needs within an enterprise or scientific use-case, it is very difficult to define a single common metadata format for self-description. Such a standard can become very complex and become difficult to use. On the other hand, without a set of common conventions, one cannot hope to obtain self-description capabilities in practice.

Eventually, many of these AI models will contribute data to yet another layer of AI analysis for deeper cross-correlation, and self-descriptive identification in those scenarios will become an operational requirement. We need a standard which is very light-weight, yet allows easy extension into more complex use-cases which can be customized as needed.

Assuming we could solve this technical problem and come up with such a metadata standard, another operational challenge remains. Defining such a metadata standard is not likely to be adopted if it is done by a single organization. In order to be adopted and used, this development needs to be accomplished in an open collaborative manner across many organizations.

Furthermore, just the development of an approach for self-description is inadequate. In order to be useful, the metadata standard has to come together within some common utilities and tools that make it easy to adopt the metadata specification, and promote its adoption.

As a result of these considerations, we are developing the metadata standards in an open-source collaborative consortium called the Enterprise Neurosystem Group [24]. Furthermore, as an initial utility to promote the adoption of this environment, we are developing a catalog that can be used to facilitate the distribution and exchange of self-describing assets within the same group.

In order to keep the metadata specification light, the basic standardization mechanism only asks for the specification of pointers to the digital asset and the metadata. These metadata pointer could be a remote Uniform Resource Identifier (URI) or a local description of content. An owner field identifies the organization which is defining the metadata format, which can be further defined by a subsidiary type field. The owner and the type field identify the format which the metadata is using.

In order to be useful in practice, the self-describing metadata specification needs to be coupled with an implementation of utilities that make it easy to use the metadata. At the very least, this set of utilities needs to contain a catalog which can be used to store self-describing digital assets. The catalog of self-describing assets can be used to both support new assets which include the metadata at the time of creation, or used to support legacy assets which may have a different format for metadata.

The minimal set of specification described above ensures a light-weight standard that can be customized and extended on a case by case basis. We now discuss a broad overview of a selected subset of these use-cases in the next section, focusing on how they can be enabled using the simple utility for a catalog for self-describing assets.

3 Use Cases

A catalog which contains self-describing assets can be used in many different use-cases. In this section, we look at some specific use-cases and what the metadata specification would look like for self-description in each of these use-cases. The catalog in itself can be viewed as a database of self-describing assets that is accessible via a CRUD (create, retrieve, update and delete) interface.

3.1 Use Case 1: Management of Distributed Scientific Computing Environments

Scientific computation often requires a large distributed set of resources. In some cases, these resources belong to the same organization. In other cases, different organizations come together to pool their resources. Pooling reduces the cost of any individual organization in obtaining access to a large distributed computing environment which is needed for much of scientific exploration. An example of such a collaboration is the Open Science Grid (OSG) [14]. OSG operates a pool of computing resources where many different participants provide computing resources and they can be used by the participants as the need may arise.

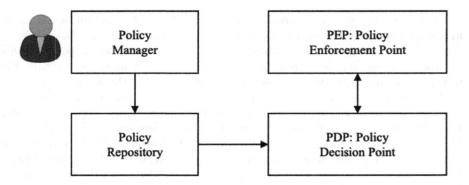

Fig. 1. The generic architecture for policy management

Whether the pool comes from a single organization or a pooled set of resources, a key requirement in these environments is that of the distribution of digital assets. One digital asset that may need to be transferred across many instances of a distributed environment is a set of configuration files or policy definitions. Architectures for using and distributing policies for Grid computing environment have been developed [23] which in turn have been inspired from policy distribution mechanisms based on network management [25]. Such distribution mechanisms typically follow an architecture shown in Fig. 1. The architecture consists of a management tool where an administrator can define policies. These policies are then stored to a policy repository. Different policy decision points take the policy definitions and use them to control the physical system through policy enforcement points. More details on the policy management architecture and its use in different scenarios can be found in the references listed earlier in this paragraph [23, 25].

Within this architecture, the task of a policy repository can be performed by the catalog of self-describing assets. The implementation of a policy repository may be done by means of a catalog of self-describing assets. The architectures used in the state of the art provide a mechanism for defining the control of policies across different architectures. The policy files that are to be distributed can considered as a single digital asset each. Although the policies can be specified in a format such as CIM-SPL [13] which is a standard specification, there are many alternative equivalent ways of specifying policies in different areas [8, 12, 21] that can be used. As a result, the distribution metadata needs to specify which language is being used, along with any identification related to the subset of policy decision points which ought to be retrieving and accessing any specific set of policy documents.

In this particular case, the physical layout of the system would be as shown in Fig. 2. When a research group obtains a set of servers from different pools of resources, e.g. from three different grid sites, it may want to provision them with appropriate policies for security, network configuration and application configuration. An instance of the catalog can be used to distribute the policies to

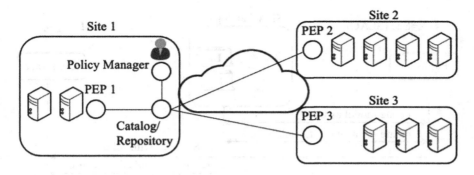

Fig. 2. Using SD-catalog for distribution of policies.

each site with the assumption of one policy decision point for each site. In the figure, the catalog is maintained at the site of the requesting party although it can belong to any other location. The metadata for each policy file would identify the type of policies it contains which can be a simple string. This setup allows each research group to manage their set of servers using policy based management techniques.

This use-case will be applicable for distribution regardless of the nature of the underlying distributed resources, such as whether the distributed infrastructure is used to manage distributed physical machines across multiple sites, virtual machines across multiple sites, Linux or Docker containers across multiple sites, and whether the resources are from a scientific grid computing environment or from a cloud computing environment.

3.2   Use Case 2: AI Model Sharing Across Two Science Organizations

A typical scientific computing environment may require the distribution of an AI model which may be trained and updated at one location, and be used across many different location. One specific use-case is sharing of these AI models across two organizations.

Let us consider a scenario where two scientists, Sue and John, one at a site like the Stanford Linear Accelerator Center (SLAC) and another one at Argonne National Laboratory (ANL) would like to collaborate on their work by sharing models. Both Sue and John have developed a significant amount of data for their research work. However, sharing of the raw data between the two researchers may not be feasible either because of the sheer volume of the data generated, or because of the sensitivity with the ownership of the research data. Sharing of the models requires the transfer of a much smaller volume of data. Furthermore, the model being shared will expose less details than that of sharing the raw data itself.

Sue and John may share many different types of digital assets as part of their collaboration, e.g. they may share some scientific papers, limited samples from

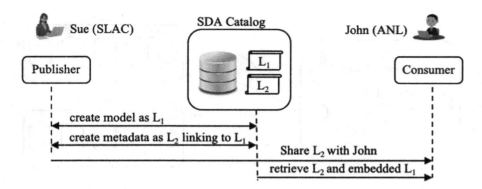

Fig. 3. Using SD-catalog for distribution of models.

data they have collected, or the models themselves. For any one of the assets, they may need to specify different types of metadata to describe the asset in a way that the receiver can use it meaningfully. The metadata description needs to be light-weight while allowing them the freedom to express a varying range of requirements.

As they are sharing the models, their work will be greatly enhanced by using self-describing digital assets stored in a catalog that they can both access. The set of exchanges that they each need to enable this exchange is shown in Fig. 3. The interacting members are Sue, John and the SD-Catalog.

1. Sue will publish the model she intends to share in the SD-catalog. The catalog will send back a link l_1 providing a reference to the model.
2. Sue will create the metadata containing the description of the model to the catalog. The metadata will include the identity of the publisher and the type description. The catalog return l_2 as the reference for the metadata.
3. Sue shares l_2 with John.
4. John uses the provided link l_2 to retrieve the metadata. The information contained there allows John to determine what type of model is being referenced, as well as the link l_1
5. John retrieves the model from link l_1

The metadata description would allow John to determine if the model is compatible with his environment. In this scenario, Sue and John can determine the type of metadata that is most appropriate to share.

3.3 Use Case 2a: AI Model Sharing Across Two Science Organizations Using an Existing Catalog

Let's looks at an extension to the above use case. Assume in this case we have a similar situation, but the model is pre-existing and stored in another catalog.

The scenario would be similar to that described earlier except that the model need not be stored, and we assume that Sue has access to a link l_1 to the model. This scenario is shown in Fig. 4 and consists of the following exchanges:

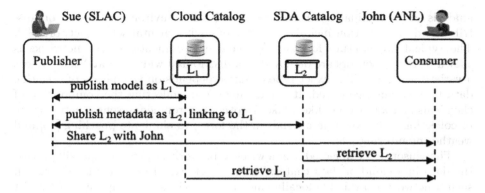

Fig. 4. Using SD-catalog for distribution of model in an existing catalog.

1. Sue will create the metadata containing the description of the model to the catalog. The metadata will include the identity of the publisher and the type description. The catalog return l_2 as the reference for the metadata.
2. Sue shares l_2 with John.
3. John uses the provided link l_2 to retrieve the metadata. The information contained there allows John to determine what type of model is being referenced, as well as the link l_1
4. John retrieves the model from link l_1.

3.4 Use Case 3: Distributed Data Collection Leveraging 5G Infrastructure

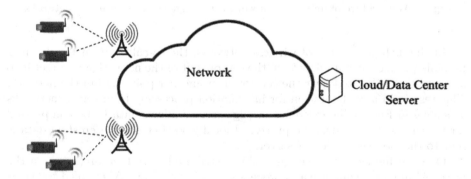

Fig. 5. Architecture of an environmental sensor network

With the advent of different types of network connected sensors and the growth of so called Internet of Things [10], data can be collected across a wide area for analysis and examination. Examples of scientific environment based on distributed data collection include a variety of environmental sensor networks [9]. The typical architecture followed by these environmental sensor networks is shown in Fig. 5. Sensors are deployed in a distributed wide area and they collect a variety of signals. The exact type of signal depends on the nature of scientific data that is being collected. It could range from collecting the composition of chemicals in a water body like a lake [7], other environmental sensor networks [9] to collection of videos from animals in the forest to eliminate poaching [10] and weather monitoring [18].

The sensors are connected over a wireless network to a server that will process the data in a cloud or data center. The network would be a cellular network if such a network is available locally since that provides the simplest logistics for data collection. If the data feeds are small, this architecture works fine. However, if the data being collected is large, e.g. images or videos, this architecture can become very expensive and bandwidth-intensive.

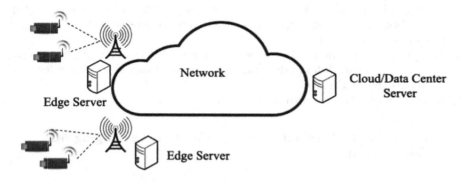

Fig. 6. Architecture of an sensor network using edge computing in 5G networks

In the fifth generation of wireless networks, the so-called 5G networks, it is possible to take the data flow from the sensors out of the network and direct it to a server that is located near the cell-tower or another point within the network. This results in a configuration for information processing from sensor networks as shown in Fig. 6. The existence of edge servers allows data to be compressed for transmission, and even be processed locally so that only *interesting* data is sent to the cloud/data center server.

One specific case for leveraging this distributed infrastructure arises in the use of AI models to analyze and process sensor information. AI enabled solutions work by processing data in two distinct stages, the first stage of using the data to train an AI model and the second stage where the trained AI model is used to make inferences on the data being received. As an example, a model to detect and classify animals may be trained from previously collected data, and then the trained model be used to do active monitoring of animals in the field. The

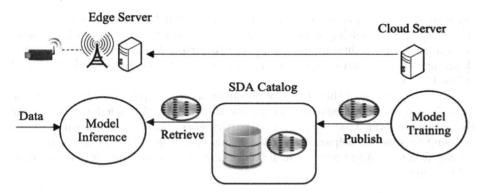

Fig. 7. AI enabled solutions in a 5G network

process works in the manner shown in Fig. 7. Models trained at a central location are moved to the edge location.

A catalog of self-describing assets can be of tremendous value in this distribution. It allows the central location to publish the models and for each edge location to retrieve the models suitable for it. Different edge servers may need different models, e.g. multiple scientific experiments, each requiring a different type of AI model, may be active at different locations. The edge servers need to get the right models, and the type of model can be specified as the metadata field associated with the model.

3.5   Use Case 4: Federated Learning

Another use-case where a catalog of self-describing assets can be used is in the enabling of federated learning. Federated learning is a technique where models are built from data present at many different sites without moving the data to a central location. It has many use-cases in enterprise [26], military [5], healthcare [27] and other contexts.

Let us consider three users, Sue from Stanford Linear Acceleration Center (SLAC), John from Argonne National Labs (ANL) and Tom from Brookhaven National Lab (BNL) who have all collected spectroscopic images from their equipment. The data at each site is too large to move across the network, but they want to train a joint AI model to classify these images using data from all the three sites. Federated Learning provides a mechanism to do that.

In federated learning, each site trains an AI model (such as a neural network) based on the data available to it. In the most commonly published algorithm in literature, training is done in multiple rounds. In each round, each site trains a model on a small set of data and exchanges that model with a fusion site. The fusion site averages the weights of the neural network, and sends them back to each site to revise and update the weights of the model for the next round of training and fusion. This process is identical to that of training a neural network at a single site, where model is trained over a small batch of data in a round, the error of the resulting model evaluated over another batch of data in the next round, and the weights updated to reduce the error. The difference in federated learning is that all sites exchange and agree upon an averaged weight at the end of each round.

In practice, one of the sites may be slower when compared to the other sites. The Fusion site would have to wait for the slowest site. When federated learning is conducted over a large number of participants, one can ignore some of the missing or slow participants. However, when only a handful of participants are engaged in federated learning, such failures can disrupt or slow down the process of training.

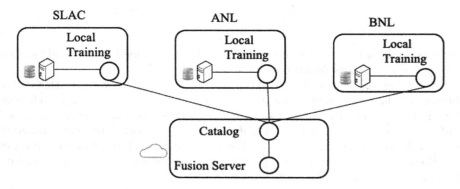

Fig. 8. Architecture of federated learning using SD-catalog to address synchronization

This synchronization can be avoided by means of an intermediary, such as the catalog of self-describing assets, as shown in Fig. 8.

Each site publishes their models in the catalog, with the round, identity of participant and version number in the metadata field to help the fusion site. The fusion site would also publish the fused model with its identity and the round in the fusion site. This allows the different sites to pick up the latest fused model, as well as enabling the fusion site to determine when to pick up the different versions from each site to include in the model fusion process. This will allow the fusion process to proceed without necessarily waiting for all the sites to synchronize. Similarly, the intermediary SD-catalog can be used as a mechanism to do an initial coordination and determine some parameters for scaling of different fields, a required pre-step for federated learning. In the diagram, the fusion server and the catalog are shown as a cloud hosted service. However, the two can be co-located at any of the three scientific sites, SLAC, ANL or BNL as well.

In summary, we see that the use of self-describing assets has several advantages. It allows for improved and efficient collaboration among several organizations. It makes it convenient for an asset to be distributed to multiple inference sites. It helps several organizations to collaborate on solving tough problems without having to share proprietary data.

4   Architecture and Implementation

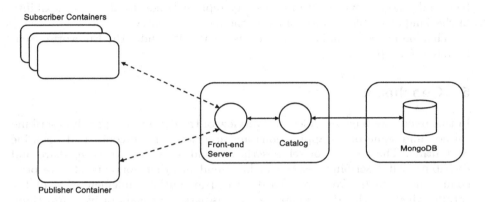

Fig. 9. System diagram.

Our proposed architecture for the catalog is outlined in Fig. 9. It consists of 3 major components: 1) Front-end Server, 2) back-end server and 3) database.

The front-end server provides an user-friendly interface for the publishers and the subscribers to access the assets stored in the catalog. It provides a form to the publisher to provide details of the assets and save the model to the database. It provides a search functionality to the user, which allows the user to search for assets provided by the catalog. It provides an interface to the user to view the details of the asset selected.

The back-end server provides access to the self-describing entries via a set of REST APIs [6]. Users are able to perform create, retrieve, update and delete (CRUD) operations using the REST APIs on the entries based on their access roles. The entries are stored as a JSON [20] object in the database.

Each self-describing entry has two components:

- **asset**: This represents an Uniform Resource Identifier (URI) for a digital asset (could be a URI for a blob in the catalog)
- **metadata**: This contains the metadata of the asset and is represented as JSON

  {``owner'': org-domain, ``type'': string, ``link'': blob}

  where **link** can have additional metadata details as desired by the publisher/context and **scope** + **type** defines the convention for the link and metadata description. For example:

```
{''owner'': slac.edu, ''type'': ''dataset'', ''link'': ''None''}
```

The back-end database stores the self-describing entries. The current implementation of the catalog consists of a MongoDB instance [3].

This three-tiered architecture allows us to scale the system as needed. The database implementation can be switched from a MongoDB instance to another type of database as needed, and additional scalability can be provided. The back-end server provides an intermediary representation to allow for flexibility in checking consistency constraints on the metadata entry.

This implementation is being done as an activity under the Enterprise Neurosystem Group [24].

5 Conclusion

In this paper, we have provided an overview of the concept of the self-describing catalog and some of its applications and use-cases in the context of scientific computing. The concept of self-description and a catalog to store, share and distribute self-describing assets can be useful in other contexts of enterprise computing as well. We have also described an initial implementation of the catalog which is being done in open-source as part of a collaborative consortium.

We are actively looking for users in different communities who will be willing to use the catalog in their use-cases and share experiences from that with the community.

References

1. Abadi, M.: TensorFlow: learning functions at scale. In: Proceedings of the 21st ACM SIGPLAN International Conference on Functional Programming, pp. 1–1 (2016)
2. Barrett, J.: Up to 73 percent of company data goes unused for analytics. Here's How to Put It to Work. Inc., Com, April 12 (2018)
3. Bradshaw, S., Brazil, E., Chodorow, K.: MongoDB: The Definitive Guide: Powerful and Scalable Data Storage. O'Reilly Media, Sebastopol (2019)
4. Cerf, V.G.: Avoiding "Bit Rot": long-term preservation of digital information [Point of View]. In: Proceedings of the IEEE, vol. 99, no. 6, pp. 915–916 (2011)
5. Cirincione, G., Verma, D.: Federated machine learning for multi-domain operations at the tactical edge. In: Artificial Intelligence and Machine Learning for Multi-Domain Operations Applications. vol. 11006, p. 1100606. International Society for Optics and Photonics (2019)
6. Doglio, F., Doglio, Corrigan: REST API Development with Node.js, vol. 331. Springer (2018)
7. Gilbert, N.: Inner Workings: smart-sensor network keeps close eye on lake ecosystem. Proc. Natl. Acad. Sci. 115(5), 828–830 (2018)
8. Han, W., Lei, C.: A survey on policy languages in network and security management. Comput. Netw. 56(1), 477–489 (2012)
9. Hart, J.K., Martinez, K.: Environmental sensor networks: a revolution in the earth system science? Earth Sci. Rev. 78(3–4), 177–191 (2006)

10. Kocakulak, M., Butun, I.: An overview of wireless sensor networks towards Internet of Things. In: 2017 IEEE 7th Annual Computing and Communication Workshop and Conference (CCWC), pp. 1–6. IEEE (2017)
11. Kuhn, M., Duwe, K.: Coupling storage systems and self-describing data formats for global metadata management. In: 2020 International Conference on Computational Science and Computational Intelligence (CSCI), pp. 1224–1230. IEEE (2020)
12. Kumaraguru, P., Cranor, L., Lobo, J., Calo, S.: A survey of privacy policy languages. In: Workshop on Usable IT Security Management (USM 07): Proceedings of the 3rd Symposium on Usable Privacy and Security. ACM (2007)
13. Lobo, J.: CIM Simplified Policy Language (CIM-SPL). Specification DSP0231 v1. 0.0 a, Distributed Management Task Force (DMTF), 10(1), 1–55 (2007)
14. OSG: The OSG Consortium. https://opensciencegrid.org/. Accessed 03 June 2022
15. Paszke, A., et al.: Pytorch: an imperative style, high-performance deep learning library. In: Advances in Neural Information Processing Systems, vol. 32 (2019)
16. Pedregosa, F., et al.: Scikit-learn: machine learning in Python. J. Mach. Learn. Res. 12, 2825–2830 (2011)
17. Ray, E.T.: Learning XML: Creating Self-describing Data. O'Reilly Media, Inc., Sebastopol (2003)
18. Singh, T., Asim, M.: Weather monitoring system using IoT. In: Singh, J., Kumar, S., Choudhury, U. (eds.) Innovations in Cyber Physical Systems. LNEE, vol. 788, pp. 247–253. Springer, Singapore (2021). https://doi.org/10.1007/978-981-16-4149-7_21
19. Smith, J.R., Schirling, P.: Metadata standards roundup. IEEE Multimedia 13(2), 84–88 (2006)
20. Sriparasa, S.S.: JavaScript and JSON essentials. Packt Publishing Ltd., Birmingham (2013)
21. Stone, G.N., Lundy, B., Xie, G.G.: Network policy languages: a survey and a new approach. IEEE Netw. 15(1), 10–21 (2001)
22. Toonders, J.: Data is the new oil of the digital economy. Wired Magazine (2016). https://www.wired.com/insights/2014/07/data-new-oil-digital-economy/
23. Verma, D., Sahu, S., Calo, S., Beigi, M., Chang, I.: A policy service for GRID computing. In: Parashar, M. (ed.) GRID 2002. LNCS, vol. 2536, pp. 243–255. Springer, Heidelberg (2002). https://doi.org/10.1007/3-540-36133-2_22
24. Verma, D., Wright, B., Overton, J., Sinha, R.: Open source collaborative AI development in the enterprise neurosystem group. In: International Conference on Empowering Smart Future through Scientific Development and Technology. MDPI (2022). https://sciforum.net/paper/view/12636
25. Verma, D.C.: Simplifying network administration using policy-based management. IEEE Netw. 16(2), 20–26 (2002)
26. Verma, D.C.: Federated AI for Real-World Business Scenarios. CRC Press, Boca Raton (2021)
27. Xu, J., Glicksberg, B.S., Su, C., Walker, P., Bian, J., Wang, F.: Federated learning for healthcare informatics. J. Healthc. Inform. Res. 5(1), 1–19 (2021). https://doi.org/10.1007/s41666-020-00082-4
28. Zaste, C.: Another bit bytes the dust: the technological and human challenges of digital preservation. Master's thesis, University of Manitoba (2016)
29. Zhang, W., Byna, S., Tang, H., Williams, B., Chen, Y.: MIQS: metadata indexing and querying service for self-describing file formats. In: Proceedings of the International Conference for High Performance Computing, Networking, Storage and Analysis, pp. 1–24 (2019)

Simulation Workflows in Minutes, at Scale for Next-Generation HPC

Allan Grosvenor$^{(\boxtimes)}$ ⓘ, Anton Zemlyansky, Dwyer Deighan, and Dustin Sysko

MSBAI, 2355 Westwood Blvd., Suite 961, Los Angeles, CA 90064, USA
`allan@msb.ai`

Abstract. As the White House pushes to decarbonize energy (https://www.atl anticcouncil.org/blogs/energysource/building-on-us-advanced-reactor-dem onstration-momentum-federal-power-purchase-agreements/), the Department of Energy (DOE)'s National Reactor Innovation Center (NRIC) has an urgent need to decrease the cost and schedule for new reactor design and construction in support of the Advanced Construction Technology (ACT) initiative. Current lead time for new reactors is 20–30 years and costs $10–$15 billion. This must be dramatically reduced to bring advanced reactors online. Digital Engineering, leveraging the best multiphysics simulation and high-performance computing (HPC), offers us a unique opportunity to lead these efforts, but a paradigm shift in engineering is mandatory: right now on the order of **only 1%** of engineers regularly use simulation as a tool in their design toolbox—meaning it is unusual for engineers to create virtual prototypes and broadly explore the available space of design options, and test and evolve them with modeling and simulation. Massive virtual prototype explorations are rarely done in new product development, because engineering modeling & simulation packages take months-to-years to learn, and setup of a new simulation can often require hours of laborious work. We must enable a new user to set up and run thousands of models quickly to evolve virtual prototypes. DOE has spent nearly $100 million (https://datainnov ation.org/2020/06/does-30-million-investment-in-supercomputing-software-will-help-maintain-u-s-top-spot/, https://insidehpc.com/2021/07/doe-funds-28m-for-scientific-supercomputing-research-projects/) in taxpayer funds, and decades of development, to advance HPC. There is massive untapped potential in the thousands of simulation packages in existence, and the commercial cloud computing that is plentiful and affordable today. Computational physics and HPC needs to be put in the hands of every engineer to begin a renaissance in construction and manufacturing. We present an autonomous system built to hyper-enable engineers, and the work we've conducted using the Summit supercomputer to pursue it.

Keywords: Digital engineering · Digital transformation · HPC · Deep learning · Reinforcement learning · Artificial intelligence

---

This research used resources of the Oak Ridge Leadership Computing Facility, which is a DOE Office of Science User Facility supported under Contract DE-AC05-00OR22725.

K. Doug et al. (Eds.): SMC 2022, CCIS 1690, pp. 288–300, 2022.
https://doi.org/10.1007/978-3-031-23606-8_18

1 Introduction

Calls to make engineering software easier to use have been made for years, and the importance of reducing simulation set up time to minutes is clear. For example:

"taking engineers 'off the line' to train them in modern modeling and simulation tools takes them away from the urgent needs of the business [and is therefore unaffordable]...many existing modeling and simulation tools ...are often too complex (Ezell and Atkinson 2016)

The White House released an Executive Order in 2021 that calls for "100% carbon pollution-free electricity on a net annual basis by 2030, including 50% 24/7 carbon pollution-free electricity". One key element to achieving 24/7 carbon pollution-free electricity is energy generated from advanced reactor projects. We expect that autonomous set up of virtual prototypes and simulation will benefit industry in general, and accelerate the pursuit of technological priorities like advanced reactors.

From the PWA web interface on the front end to MQTT orchestration on the back end, we have designed our system to maximize adoption across HPC, cloud, and mobile platforms. Our goal is to benefit the public in three tiers: 1) usability and access, 2) scalability and commercialization, 3) wider use-cases for scientific research and development. The expected outcome of this effort will be to decrease time and labor intensivity of simulation, thereby saving users money and effort, and significantly increasing the public's adoption and commercial utilization of digital engineering software packages.

2 Methodology

2.1 Designing an Autonomous System for Simulation Workflows in Minutes

GURU is a cognitive AI assistant built to be an AI layer between human and computer for engineering simulation, and has already been selected by the Air Force and Missile Defense Agency in two Phase II SBIR contracts (one focused on hypersonic CFD[1] simulation, and another focused on hypersonic threat trajectory[2] simulation). GURU is a highly modular agent-based, blackboard-driven system. At the platform level, the goal manager interprets inputs from the user ('intents' via the UI) and assembles workflows consisting of skills or capabilities trained in agents. We have chosen a common hybrid AI architecture for each agent. The hybrid of symbolic learning and geometric/machine learning enables the system to perform trusted explainable procedures while sufficiently generalizing to real-world requirements.

GURU offers the following advantages over current technology in the market:

• Enabling users to run specialized simulation software, addressing the expertise barrier to its use

---

[1] https://markets.businessinsider.com/news/stocks/evisionaries-bring-digital-engineering-revolution-1030598213.

[2] https://www.airforce-technology.com/news/usaf-selects-msbais-cognitive-ai-assistant-for-avatar-programme/.

- Addressing the time and labor intensity of using simulation, reducing the time requirements of setting up a single simulation from hours to minutes
- Our AI is not brittle – GURU leverages a hybrid AI architecture that utilizes both symbolic methods and machine learning. We have adopted a hierarchy of learning strategies to benefit from the strengths of individual methods, and cure their individual weaknesses
- GURU has an entirely new, easy-to-use user interface that runs in a browser on desktops, laptops, and mobile devices (no competitor offers this). The containerized orchestration system is based on the latest IoT technology that enables GURU to send compute-heavy jobs to any system (incl. Cloud & supercomputers) (Figs. 1 and 2).

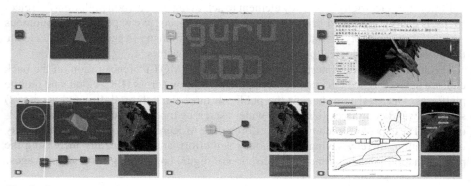

Fig. 1. Two example full workflow examples: Top—CFD application OpenFOAM, Bottom—Trajectory application SAIC (See footnote 2) **Video:** https://youtu.be/7CIQnVwiHcU

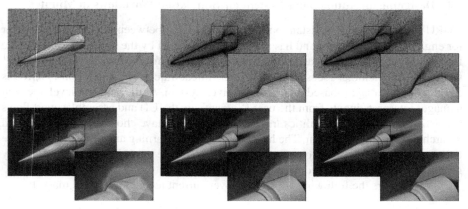

Fig. 2. Valuable application of autonomous workflow execution: Solution-adaptive mesh refinement to capture hypersonic physical phenomena (See footnote 1) (applications: Salome MESH, US3D)

GURU's interface has been designed to be highly modular, so the inputs and controls and views of models, job status, reduced data, plotting, and visualization are feasible for a broad range of applications. Both light interactive controls implemented in React, as well as full high performance Virtual Desktop Interface, rendered from the target system, are available in the modular Progressive Web App. We have a containerized orchestration system based on IoT technology, using the MQTT protocol, that enables GURU to orchestrate and deploy compute jobs to a broad range of compute systems, including commercial cloud or gov't supercomputers.

The significance of this is, anyone will be able to use simulation, data analytics, and High Performance Computing!

1. *The interface is easy to use and runs on your device in a browser*
2. *Artificial intelligence continues to learn new applications and skills*
3. *You can deploy the compute jobs where you want to*

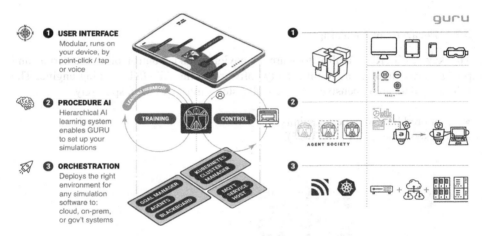

Fig. 3. Three fundamental elements to achieve simulation workflows in minutes

Three fundamental layers have been architected to fully answer the question "what would it take to enable every engineer to regularly use simulation and HPC?" (Fig. 3).

1. **Portable, modular easy-to-use interface** - The front end interface is a Progressive Web App that can be run from a browser. We have demonstrated point click, tap, and voice-driven[3] operation on multiple devices & OS
2. **End-to-end procedure learning AI** - The learning engine, Automated Reinforcement-learning-guided Tree-based hybrid-Intelligence Synthesis Trainer (ARTIST), leverages a procedure-learning AI hierarchy to enable GURU to learn complex workflows and adapt them to a new user request
3. **Multi-platform deployment** - Containerized orchestration deploys the correct software environments to a broad range of HPC systems from On-Prem, to Commercial Cloud, to Government Supercomputers (Fig. 4).

---

[3] https://youtu.be/XiFtRko0Cos.

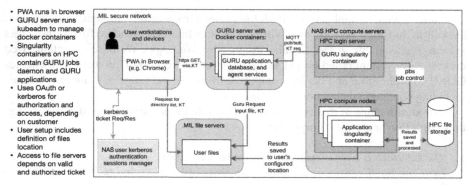

- PWA runs in browser
- GURU server runs kubeadm to manage docker containers
- Singularity containers on HPC contain GURU jobs daemon and GURU applications
- Uses OAuth or kerberos for authorization and access, depending on customer
- User setup includes definition of files location
- Access to file servers depends on valid and authorized ticket

Fig. 4. Deployment of GURU on a government system

2.2 Hierarchy of Learning

The key to GURU's ability to learn to navigate, take control of, set up, run, and post-process simulations in third-party software, is the ARTIST learning engine. The following data are expensive, so practical systems must use them sparingly:

- monitored human expert sessions
- large sets of simulations (Fig. 5).

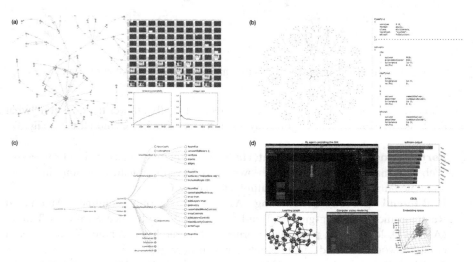

Fig. 5. Hierarchical Learning Stages—a, b) Primitives data from scanned GUIs, config files, user manuals, c) Transformers impart meaning + connections between variables & actions, d) RL completes learning of adaptable workflows. **Video:** Procedure learning hierarchy https://youtu.be/7CIQnVwiHcU?t=514, Blender geometry demonstration https://youtu.be/Ha4jG_OJ3hk

ARTIST utilizes a process that begins with collecting the cheapest 'primitives' data available to build a foundation of learned states/features/actions into sub-workflows to minimize the amount of required expensive human expert sessions to monitor or simulations to run. Key elements of this process: 'program exploration'—building state and feature graphs, training transformer-based goal estimation, and a history-aware Reinforcement Learning approach that enables the system to adapt what it has learned to fulfill new user requests (thereby, strongly distinguishing GURU from a script, macro, or Robotic Process Automation-based system).

Program Exploration

ARTIST scans every possible option in Graphical User Interfaces, and ingests corpora of configuration files, templates, and also user documentation. GUI actions (clicks, key presses, menu, and field selections) are accomplished using computer vision techniques such as Optical Character Recognition (OCR). These foundational 'primitives' are cataloged in graphs consisting of nodes and edges, which are in turn used for navigation, and the next step in training. Each node represents a program state and edges encode actions.

Embeddings

An embedding is a mapping of a discrete, categorical variable to a vector of continuous numbers, such that it can be modeled by machine learning. We map from a higher-dimensional space to a lower-dimensional space and convert the raw data available from the surrogate environment (e.g., screenshots of a GUI) using different types of embedding techniques. This unique approach possesses key advantages of representing different states (sometimes involving almost imperceptible variations) by embeddings that are very close to one another in the vector space.

Generative Pre-trained Transformers

In our applied experience, we have found it useful to run a 'predictor' step and a 'corrector' step using generative pre-trained transformers that we adapt, extend and refine for our space of applications such as GPT-Neo and GPT-J. Fine-tuning existing GPTs with primitives data described above improves the prediction of the next actions for a text-based goal, where the objective is to find optimal trajectories between different graph nodes. The program state is represented using previous actions or text from screenshots stored in the data generation process.

The combination of models already trained on massive language corpora, with additional training for specific applications offers promising advantages: 1) universal adaptability (for different languages) to predict accurate actions, 2) we can train the model on manuals and tutorials, and it provides more flexibility in transferring knowledge between different user interfaces like GUI, CLI, writing and manipulating flat files, etc.

Applied History Aware Reinforcement Learning

In Reinforcement Learning (RL), an RL agent learns from the interaction with an environment, obtaining state descriptions, S and rewards, R in order to create decisions about actions, A to perform. We previously adapted a Deep Q-learning approach to predict the next actions based on the state-action value function 'Q'-value estimation. During

training, we generated episodes using an ε-greedy policy w.r.t. the current approximation of the action-value function Q. Conventional RL algorithms tend to fail when the
state exploration space is large, and we tested adapting Distance Partial Rewards (DPR)
combined with Hindsight Experience Replay (HER) to tackle this problem, with the
following adaptation for the graph environment:

$$r(s, g) = 1 - distance(s, g)/distance(s_0, g), \qquad (1)$$

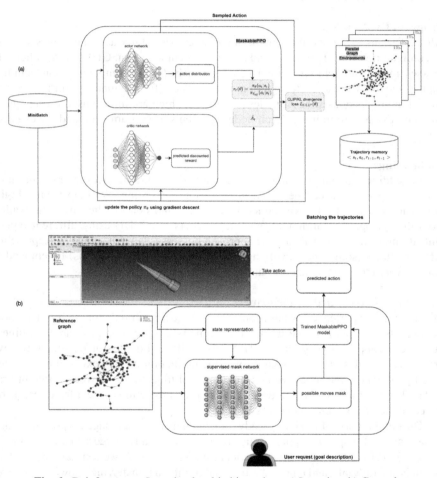

Fig. 6. Reinforcement Learning level in hierarchy—a) Learning, b) Control

Such that, s is the current state, s_0 is the initial state (before any actions) and g is
some state containing the goal. Upon encountering episodes, p1, p2, ...pT, we store
every transition pT to pT + 1 in the replay buffer, with all subsets of goals stored.

The aim of our RL system is to train an agent to navigate to desired target 'states' in
a GUI environment given an encoding/embedding (e.g., a 'picture') of the desired state.

We have also adapted these encodings to support natural language descriptions of the goals so that the system can follow verbal instructions given by the user, and to enable the system to construct language-based commands such as API calls or writing entire configuration files.

The use of graph[4]-based models of the environment built from recorded GUI navigation trajectories is an important element in training the RL system. Human expert sessions are expensive and time-consuming, so we endeavored to minimize the number required for sufficient training. We found that aiding the RL system with a supervised model, to predict which actions are currently valid, significantly improves training. Next, we combined the above approach with categorical action spaces (each category representing a different button click, for example) and Proximal Policy Optimization (PPO)—and particularly Masked-PPO[5], and this combination produced the highest performance in reaching targeted GUI states reliably.

3 Examples of Research Conducted on Summit

In real-world working environments, the human users and GURU will collaborate on design, analysis, simulation tasks, so it must be possible to resume from a variety of user interruptions (e.g., like this: https://youtu.be/E0Rc9CzVRuQ?t=46). We've found the hierarchy of methodologies described above provides GURU with an ability to recover from a broad range of interruptions, and we are working on further developing the training strategies and building more comprehensive graphs to maximize this adaptive capability.

3.1 Program exploration on Summit

The main lesson from successes achieved in recent years with AI is that it's possible to improve model performance by scaling alone [GPT3, DALLE2, GATO]. In many cases, increasing a training dataset and model size can be enough to reach state-of-the-art scores. In the case of autonomous software control, training agents require large datasets to learn how to navigate complex programs, adapt to different program states, and generalize to unseen goals. We have tested a variety of strategies, in order to compare performance and training expense by running leadership computing jobs that have utilized as much as 5-to-10% of Summit. For example, we have run massive parallel program exploration jobs.

During such exploration jobs, each resource set runs a unique session including a target program and an exploring agent. Exploring agents perform various actions reaching unseen program states. These actions and corresponding states are combined to form a large training dataset. We then build a program graph from the raw exploration data (a digital twin of a real program) that is orders of magnitude faster to navigate and drive the software application.

Examples of software we have trained GURU to drive Graphical User Interface manipulation of include ParaView, FreeCAD, Blender, and even Unreal Engine. While

---

[4] https://en.wikipedia.org/wiki/Graph_(abstract_data_type).

[5] https://arxiv.org/abs/2006.14171.

it is sometimes possible to have full source code access, and the resources necessary to prepare native ppc64le versions of application software for Summit (as we did with ParaView) there are some applications that are impractical to prepare Summit versions for. Sometimes compilation specifically for Summit is too challenging because of missing dependencies or lack of source code access. We needed a solution to continue scaling up the number of software applications we could run on Summit, and we sought options to run x86_64 emulation. A practical solution we applied successfully was hardware emulation with QEMU.

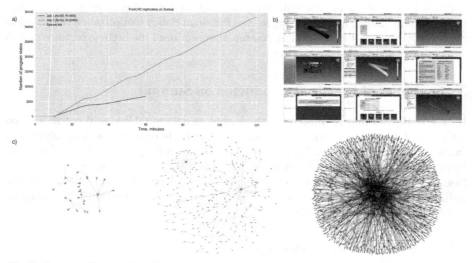

Fig. 7. Program Exploration of the FreeCAD GUI run on Summit—a) 50 compute node ensemble exploration jobs, b) sample screenshots of GUI states, c) progression of the growing program state and feature graph. **Video:** FreeCAD graph https://youtu.be/X20xXLIhaSc

When using the emulator, program exploration is performed inside a virtualized guest system that can run x86_64 binaries. This is how we ran exploration for FreeCAD, an open-source general-purpose parametric 3D computer-aided design modeler. Figure 6 presents two examples of ensemble jobs distributed over 50 compute nodes, varying the number of resource sets from 400 to 1000, varying number of CPUs per set (5 and 2), and the walltime (1 h and 2 h). Loading time of the QEMU image was a factor here, and longer queue times enabled us to complete program exploration. The tens of thousands of GUI options, including deep cascades of menus are evident in the growth progression of the graph depicted.

3.2   Leadership Computing Scale Research in Reinforcement Learning

A human can possess prior general knowledge about operating computers and navigating software interfaces, and yet they can still spend days/weeks/months learning one new software package. Not entirely dissimilarly, Reinforcement Learning agents can require tremendous amounts of data when learning to navigate and drive a new software package. Such an RL agent won't necessarily possess any prior knowledge about the world, or computers, or software in general. Performance of such agents is strongly dependent on the amount of data and training time they're given. Another important factor is their set of hyper-parameters, which define the performance of learning. We explored methods to use Summit to scale up learning, to perform massive hyperparameter searches, and to discover methods to achieve the best performance in control tasks with a particular focus on searching for most practical, data-efficient, methods.

Fundamental RL Research Motivation for Summit
Given our goal to autonomously drive third party software, a seemingly obvious strategy would be to search a GUI's program states, and use that data to build a model that can navigate a program for control purposes. However, a combinatorial explosion of the number of possible GUI program states can occur, especially considering the diverse types of files which can be loaded into a given program (e.g. number of possible text editor states is roughly: 26^n where n is the number of characters in a document). Leadership computing on a system like Summit provides a unique opportunity to achieve sufficient data from this search process, but care must be taken because there are some search processes that are intractable even for supercomputers when using brute force methods (e.g., random search). One such example would be if we searched a text editor's state space (e.g., the Infinite monkey theorem - monkeys on typewriters reproducing Shakespeare). This kind of search becomes impractical, and more intelligent approaches are obviously desirable. Fortunately, Reinforcement Learning (RL) learns to search and is therefore naturally suited to high-performance computing. In fact, the father of RL himself (Richard Sutton) declared that in RL research one of the few things that actually matters is effective leveraging of compute[6].

Evolution Strategies for Reinforcement Learning
Given this motivation we built an RL system on Summit, inspired by OpenAI's Evolution Strategies for Reinforcement Learning[7] (ES/RL), and experimented with various configurations of it applied to OpenAI's Gym (a well known RL benchmark).
    The experiments took two forms:

1. Parallel hyper-parameter (aka configuration) search - on the ES/RL algorithm itself (when applied to the Gym Benchmark)
2. Centralized parallelism - where any number of nodes can be applied to training one agent on one problem.

Both of these methods are designed to improve stability, hyper-parameter search is used because RL algorithms still need to be customized to a given set of problems. Centralized parallelism to improve stability is a powerful scaling application on supercomputer resources.

---

[6] http://www.incompleteideas.net/IncIdeas/BitterLesson.html.
[7] https://arxiv.org/abs/1703.03864.

The idea was to apply ES as-is then test if we could increase performance by also adding a few steps of PPO[8] training per generation on each worker. Interestingly, it appears that the ES was not able to reliably synergize with PPO, even though the resulting algorithm is very similar to the basic Parallelized PPO training strategy (that increased batch size via environment parallelism) which is known to work quite well (e.g. for OpenAI-five[9]). The primary difference here is that rather than increasing the batch size we add noise to the weights then apply a weighted sum.

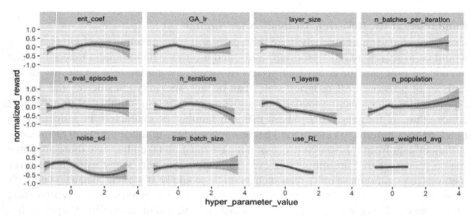

Fig. 8. Hyper-parameter influence on normalized reward

First we investigated the influence of Hyper-parameters on this system (Fig. 7), including checking whether a weighted average (e.g. such that all weights sum to 1) was better than the normalized weighted sum deployed in the default ES. We tested these settings against the gym environments: CartPole-v1, Acrobot-v1, MountainCar-v0 and Pendulum-v1. For each of the hyper-parameter experiments we normalized the total reward (aka return) across all other experiments for that environment so we could compare across them. Lastly this data was collected from a 300 compute node job run for 60 min (Fig. 10).

Observations:

- Fewer Layers appear to yield higher performance across all the environments we tested. The result wasn't necessarily expected, but other researchers have generally found a performance advantage to not going too deep with networks for RL
- Using a weighted average rather than a weighted sum actually achieved similar performance to the original OpenAI-ES algorithm
- Figure 8 demonstrates how rare it can be to arrive at high performance (e.g., the bright blue line) and that many samples are required to acquire them
- The weak scaling plot in Fig. 9 demonstrates how performance of a given run is improved by increasing the population (aka increasing parallelism)

---

[8] https://arxiv.org/abs/1707.06347.
[9] https://arxiv.org/abs/1912.06680.

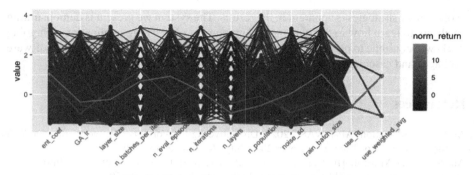

Fig. 9. Hyper-parameter vs normalized reward

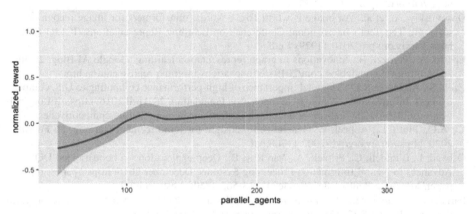

Fig. 10. Weak scaling plot: ES for RL, Ensemble Summit runs utilizing 3–400 compute nodes

- Example Demo Video: Summit ES for RL Acrobot Agent https://youtu.be/5uye_U nRmX8 – Agent on the left is random, while the agent on the right is trained using the Summit ES for RL system. The goal is to reach the robotic arm above the line as often as possible.

4   Conclusions

We presented an autonomous system that has been designed to hyper-enable engineers to build virtual prototypes and set up simulations in minutes. Details of the portable front end interface, the flexible containerized orchestration and deployment system, and the hierarchical procedure learning system were given. Applications ranging from CAD geometry generation, to trajectory and CFD simulation, and more were discussed. Research conducted using as much as 5-to-10% of the Summit supercomputer was presented. Efficient methods to explore software interfaces and populate the states and features into graph networks was presented. The challenges in applying Reinforcement Learning to this problem were presented, and fundamental research conducted on Summit and scalable strategies to maximize RL performance were tested, and the promise of evolutionary strategies is apparent in the results. The system we present is demonstrating an ability to learn how to drive an increasing number of software applications. Ongoing R&D will continue to produce improvements in performance, resulting in more software packages and associated autonomous workflows will be available to the users.

References

Air Force Association: AFA's vASC 2020: Disruptive Agility For A Disruptive World - Dr. Will Roper [Video]. YouTube, 19 October 2020. https://youtu.be/kI5_LSI04vE

Andrychowicz, M., et al.: Hindsight Experience Replay. In: 31st Conference on Neural Information Processing Systems (NIPS), 23 February 2018. https://arxiv.org/pdf/1707.01495.pdf

Chen, L., et al.: Decision transformer: reinforcement learning via sequence modeling, 2 June 2021. https://arxiv.org/pdf/2106.01345.pdf

Dosovitskiy, A., et al.: An image is worth 16x16 words: transformers for image recognition at scale. In: The Tenth International Conference on Learning Representations (ICLR) (2021). https://arxiv.org/pdf/2010.11929v2.pdf

Epasto, A., Perozzi, B.: Innovations in graph representation learning. Google AI Blog, 25 June 2019. https://ai.googleblog.com/2019/06/innovations-in-graph-representation.html

Ezell, S., Atkinson, R.D.: The vital importance of high-performance computing to U.S. competitiveness. Information Technology & Innovation Foundation, 28 April 2016. https://itif.org/pub lications/2016/04/28/vital-importance-high-performance-computing-us-competitiveness

Li, A.C., Pinto, L., Abbeel, P.: Generalized hindsight for reinforcement learning, 26 February 2020. https://arxiv.org/pdf/2002.11708.pdf

Osband, I., Blundell, C., Pritzell, A., Van Roy, B.: Deep exploration via bootstrapped DQN. In: Advances in Neural Information Processing Systems, December 2016. https://papers.nips.cc/paper/2016/hash/8d8818c8e140c64c743113f563cf750f-Abstract.html

Parisotto, E., Mohamed, A., Singh, R., Li, L., Zhou, D., Kohli, P.: Neuro-symbolic program synthesis. In: ICLR (2017). https://arxiv.org/pdf/1611.01855.pdf

Radford, A., et al.: Better language models and their implications. OpenAI, 14 February 20019. https://openai.com/blog/better-language-models/

Tirpak, J.A.: Roper reveals NGAD has flown, but doesn't share details. Air Force Magazine, 15 September 2020. https://www.airforcemag.com/roper-reveals-ngad-has-flown-but-doesnt-share-details/

The White House: FACT SHEET: The American Jobs Plan Supercharges the Future of Transportation and Manufacturing. Briefing Room, 18 May 2021. https://www.whitehouse.gov/bri efing-room/statements-releases/2021/05/18/fact-sheet-the-american-jobs-plan-supercharges-the-future-of-transportation-and-manufacturing

Scientific Data Challenges

Machine Learning Approaches to High Throughput Phenotyping

Morgan Gao[✉]

L&N STEM Academy, Knoxville, TN 37902, USA
morgangao55@gmail.com

Abstract. Image processing, extraction of appropriate data classifiers, and machine learning algorithms are key steps in plant phenotyping that connects genomics with plant ecophysiology and agronomy. Based on a dataset of labeled images from *Populus Trichocarpa* genotypes cultivated under both drought and control conditions, we are able to extract potential data classifiers such as leaf color and edge morphology, and to develop a predictive model by using PlantCV. The use of Tesseract and OpenCV has not reached the needed successes that are required for a proper workflow, such as data preparation, training the module, tuning parameters, and others. Despite many existing challenges, progresses reported here gives possible future directions can mitigate these challenges.

Keywords: Phenotyping · Image processing · Data classifier

1 Problem Description

Plant phenotyping an emerging science that links genomics with plant ecophysiology and agronomy. A grand challenge in the field of plant phenotyping is the extraction of biologically relevant features from large datasets generated by robotic, field-based instrumentation. Machine learning, as well as traditional segmentation approaches have been used for this task. Machine learning is a type of artificial intelligence (AI) that allows software applications to become more accurate at predicting outcomes without being explicitly programmed to do so. Machine learning algorithms use historical data as input to predict new output values.

In this challenge, four questions are asked to solve. Questions one is how to use optical character recognition (OCR) or machine learning techniques to "Read" the label on each tag and generate a spreadsheet contains the treatment, block, row, position, and genotype. Questions two is if machine learning can differentiate and classify different leaf morphologies among genotypes by classifying leaf shape or color characteristics. Question three is to build a predictive model using leaf morphology classifications that may indicate that a particular genotype was cultivated in a "drought" or "control" condition. Question 4 is to get GPS and other camera information from encoded in exif tags. And can this data be used to determine characteristics such as leaf size? Can other data be used to find correlations among phenotypes?

K. Doug et al. (Eds.): SMC 2022, CCIS 1690, pp. 303–316, 2022.
https://doi.org/10.1007/978-3-031-23606-8_19

The dataset consists of labeled images from *Populus Trichocarpa* genotypes culti-vated under both drought and control conditions at a common garden located in Cali-fornia. The treatment, block, row, position, and genotype are indicated on the tag. The images were collected using cell phones connected to high precision GPS instrumen-tation at a spatial resolution of 10 centimeters or better. The dataset can be accessed at: https://doi.org/10.25983/1846744, from which several representative images are presented in Fig. 1.

Fig. 1. Representative images from the provided dataset, whereas the labels contain key information on the plant. Leaf characteristics will be extracted from such images.

2 Methodology

To solve this challenge, home developed python codes using OpenCV along with "PlantCV" [1] are used. Python "pip install" is used to install OpenCV and PlantCV in conda environment. The following are the steps to install all the software packages that are used to solve this challenge.

2.1 Set Up Conda Environment

- wget https://repo.anaconda.com/archive/Anaconda3-2022.05-Linux-x86_64.sh
- ./ Anaconda3-2022.05-Linux-x86_64.sh
- conda create -n smcdc_env python=3.7
- source activate smcdc_env

2.2 Install Leptonica

- git clone https://github.com/DanBloomberg/leptonica.git
- ./autogen.sh
- /configure --prefix=$YourPath
- ./make-for-local
- ./make-for-auto
- make
- make install

2.3   Install Tesseract

- git clone https://github.com/tesseract-ocr/tesseract.git
- export PATH=$YourPath/leptonica:$PATH
- export
  PKG_CONFIG_PATH=$YourPath/leptonica/lib/pkgconfig:$PKG_CONFIG_PATH
- ./autogen.sh
- ./configure--prefix=$YourPath/tesseract
  LEPTONICA_LIBS=$YourPath/leptonica/lib
- make
- make install

2.4   Install Pytesseract, OpenCV and PlantCV

- pip install pytesseract
- pip install opencv-python
- pip install plantcv

3   Data Challenges

3.1   Question One

Is it possible to use optical character recognition (OCR) or machine learning techniques to "Read" the label on each tag and generate a spreadsheet contains the treatment, block, row, position, and genotype? Doing this would dramatically simplify data collection, as this information is usually collected manually.

Solution: Pytesseract is an OCR tool for python users to read and recognize text in images and thus has been commonly used in a variety of applications. In our home developed code (attached below Fig. 2), images were first converted to grayscale, and then the texts were extracted by: pytesseract.image_to_string(grayImage). Because all the characters in the labels are letters, numbers, comma, hyphen or underscore, function "processString ()" will match the template and remove other noisy characters.

```
import os
import cv2
import pytesseract
import numpy as np
pytesseract.tesseract_cmd = "YourPath/tesseract"
img= cv2.imread("YourPath/FC226586-D010-4E8D-A3F3-CA2EF32C1F6F.jpg")

def processString(txt):
    txt, n = re.subn('([^0-9a-zA-Z\-\,\*\_])', '', txt)
    return (txt)
def get_word(img):
    img_gray = cv2.cvtColor(img, cv2.COLOR_BGR2GRAY)
    words_in_Image = pytesseract.image_to_string(img_gray)
    return words_in_Image

print ("words_in_grayImage =", processString (get_word(img)))
```

Original Image   Gray Scale

Fig. 2. Original and processed grayscale images for text extraction.

The result from the example in Fig. 2 is

```
words_in_grayImage = eC,B1,R46,P4,BESCHOLLM
```

As one can see clearly from Fig. 2, the accuracy of the above python script is not satisfactory. In this regard, multiple remedial procedures have been tested. One option is to have these images pre-processed appropriately. Contours were first identified and a rectangular bounding box by using cv2.rectangle() to segment out the label area was then created. The outside part was cropped and only the white label area was kept, followed by using pytesseract.image_to_string() to extract the text of interest.

Fig. 3. One potential trial in order to improve the accuracy of text extraction.

However, the obtained result from Fig. 3 still has not reached the needed accuracy.

```
txt = kLMC,B1,R46,P4,BESCoMv1,r,
```

The related code is:

```
def get_contours(img):
    contours,_=cv2.findContours(process(img),cv2.RETR_TREE,
cv2.CHAIN_APPROX_NONE)
    x, y, w, h = cv2.boundingRect(max(contours, key=cv2.contourArea))
    cv2.rectangle(img, (x, y), (x + w, y + h), (255, 0, 0), 8)
    roi = img [y:y+h, x:x+w]
    return roi
```

Another trial started with an image rotation, using the following code, so that the text lines are nearly horizontal. Yet, the accuracy has not been improved either.

```
def rotate(img):
    cv2.imwrite(r'./rotate_gray.jpg',img)
    results = pytesseract.image_to_osd(r"./rotate_gray.jpg", output_type=Output.DICT)
    rotated = imutils.rotate_bound(img, angle=results["rotate"])
    cv2.imwrite(r'./rotated.jpg',rotated)
    return (rotated)
```

Further attempts have been made by using other preprocessing methods in tesseract, like thresholding, noise removal, canny edging, etc., as shown by the following code. The gain in the accuracy of textural extraction is however very minimal.

```
# noise removal
def remove_noise(image):
    return cv2.medianBlur(image,5)

#thresholding
def thresholding(image):
    return                  cv2.threshold(image,0,255,cv2.THRESH_BINARY_INV+
cv2.THRESH_OTSU)[1]

#canny edge detection
def canny(image):
    return cv2.Canny(image, 100, 200)
```

In a future research line, it is anticipated that machine learning methods can be adopted to train Tesseract on customized data. Tesseract 4.00 includes a new neural network-based recognition engine that delivers significantly higher accuracy on images. Neural networks require significantly a lot of training data and train a lot, thus leading to a slower performance than base Tesseract. Tesseract 4.00 can take a couple of weeks or more for training from scratch. While preliminary literature studies have been conducted, the team is unable to deliver sufficient training and usage of such an approach, due to limited resource and timeline at this moment for SMC conference. Further investigations are awaited in this direction (Fig. 4).

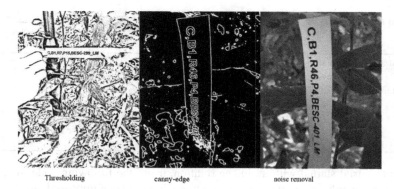

Thresholding   canny-edge   noise removal

Fig. 4. Further image processing steps that however fail to improve the text accuracy.

Fig. 5. Representative images that cannot be successfully processed from Tesseract.

Upon the above discussions on protocols and trials, the following code will generate a spreadsheet containing the text output from the given dataset.

```
wb = Workbook()
# grab the active worksheet
ws = wb.active
# Data can be assigned directly to cells
ws['A1'] = 'Treatment'
ws['B1'] = 'Block'
ws['C1'] = 'Row'
ws['D1'] = 'Position'
ws['E1'] = 'Genotype'
def write_2_excel(image)
    words_in_grayImageS = pytesseract.image_to_string(image)
    words= words_in_grayImageS.split(',')
    strVal = []
    for y in words:
        y = processString(str(y))
        strVal.append(str(y))
    if strVal != ['']:
        ws.append (strVal)
wb.save("output.xlsx")
```

Tesseract failed to extract text from a lot of images, some of which are shown in Fig. 5 and contain similar image qualities. The data set has totally 1672 images. Tesseract only able to extract 440 images and most of the readings are incorrect. Consequently, the machine learning approach discussed in the above might be a viable solution and definitely will be the next step.

3.2 Question Two

Can machine learning differentiate and classify different leaf morphologies among genotypes by classifying leaf shape or color characteristics?

Solution: The leaf edge and color information can be extracted by the following code (Fig. 6).

```
def auto_canny(image, sigma=0.33):
    # compute the median of the single channel pixel intensities
    v = np.median(image)
    # apply automatic Canny edge detection using the computed medi an
    lower = int(max(0, (1.0 - sigma) * v))
    upper = int(min(255, (1.0 + sigma) * v))
    edged = cv2.Canny(image, lower, upper)
    # return the edged image
    return edged
def detect_color(img):
    sensitivity = 20
    # Green color
    boundaries = [
        ([60 - sensitivity, 100, 100], [60 + sensitivity, 255, 255])]
    for (lower, upper) in boundaries:
        lower = np.array(lower, dtype = "uint8")
        upper = np.array(upper, dtype = "uint8")
        # find the colors within the specified boundaries and apply the mask
        mask = cv2.inRange(img, lower, upper)
        output = cv2.bitwise_and(img, img, mask = mask)
    return (output)
```

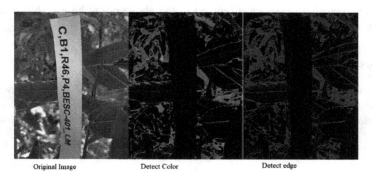

Original Image   Detect Color   Detect edge

Fig. 6. Color and edge information can be extracted from the original image.

Machine learning methods can be used to train a classifier to detect features of interest. We can capture color characteristics by RGB values of each pixel. The plantCV naive Bayes multiclass method [2] is trained using colors sparsely sampled from images. To train the classifier, we first need to build a table of red, green, and blue color values for pixels sampled evenly from each class. This data challenge has 2 classes, drought and control. For "drought" class, the white label starts with letter D. For "control" class, the label starts with letter C. To collect pixel color value, the following code is developed.

```
def get_pixel_rgb(img):
    c_f = open("pixel_value.txt", "a")
    img = Image.fromarray(img)
    R, G, B = img.convert('RGB').split()
    r = R.load()
    g = G.load()
    b = B.load()
    w, h = img.size
    for i in range(w):
        for j in range(h):
            if(r[i, j] != 0 and g[i, j] != 0 and b[i, j] != 0):
                c_f.write("%d,%d,%d\n" %(int(r[i,j]),int(g[i,j]),int(b[i,j])))
                j=j+100
        i=i+100
    c_f.close()
```

The table that was built from pixel value looks like the following. Each column in the tab-delimited table is a feature class (control class or drought class) and each cell is a comma-separated red, green, and blue triplet for a pixel. An example file is given by pixel_value.txt, as illustrated below.

Control	Drought
80,108,138	48,108,102
78,124,172	53,112,108
80,126,174	60,120,119
80,126,174	50,114,115
73,119,167	47,111,116
80,126,174	56,123,132
78,124,172	69,137,150
77,123,171	67,136,153
80,126,174	62,131,150
80,126,174	66,138,155
80,126,174	64,141,150
80,126,174	68,149,154
80,126,174	72,152,159
80,126,174	71,150,159
80,126,174	64,144,155

As stated in question one, Tesseract failed to read a lot of the labels successfully. Therefore, it remains inaccurate and not automatic in separating all the images into the above two classes. The manual intervention defies the purpose of computer automation, and consequently, there is no sufficient time for the training of the classifiers.

3.3 Question Three

Can a predictive model be built using leaf morphology classifications that may indicate that a particular genotype was cultivated in a "drought" or "control" condition?

Use plantCV the naive Bayes multiclass approach. The naive Bayes multiclass approach can be trained to classify two or more classes, defined by the user. The workflow

312   M. Gao

is described briefly here. After pixel value is saved on the above file "pixel_value.txt", the plantCV train script plantcv-train.py and input file pixel_value.txt were used to output probability density functions (PDFs) for each class. The PDF is used to specify the probability of the random variable falling within a particular range of values.

```
/bin/plantcv-train.py naive_bayes_multiclass --file pixel_value.txt --outfile naive_bayes_pdfs.txt --plots
Starting run 2022-07-05_22:43:41

Running the naive Bayes multiclass training method...
```

The output file from plantcv-train.py contains one row for each color channel for each class. The first and second column are the class and channel label, respectively. The remaining 256 columns contain the value from the PDFs for each intensity value observable in an 8-bit image (0-255).

```
naive_bayes_pdfs.txt
class   channel 0    1    2    3    4    5    6    7    8    9    10   11   12   13   14
15   16   17 18   19   20   21   22   23   24   25   26   27   28   29   30   31   32
33   34   35   36   37 38   39   40   41   42   43   44   45   46   47   48   49   50
51   52   53   54   55   56   57 58   59   60   61   62   63   64   65   66   67   68
69   70   71   72   73   74   75   76   77 78   79   80   81   82   83   84   85   86
87   88   89   90   91   92   93   94   95   96   97 98   99   100  101  102  103
104  105  106  107  108  109  110  111  112  113  114  115  116  117 118  119
120  121  122  123  124  125  126  127  128  129  130  131  132  133  134  135
136  137 138  139  140  141  142  143  144  145  146  147  148  149  150  151
152  153  154  155  156  157 158  159  160  161  162  163  164  165  166  167
168  169  170  171  172  173  174  175  176  177 178  179  180  181  182  183
184  185  186  187  188  189  190  191  192  193  194  195  196  197 198  199
200  201  202  203  204  205  206  207  208  209  210  211  212  213  214  215
216  217 218  219  220  221  222  223  224  225  226  227  228  229  230  231
232  233  234  235  236  237 238  239  240  241  242  243  244  245  246  247
248  249  250  251  252  253  254  255
   Control  hue      0.0003096585230435201       0.0003535131591506215      0.00040258268699296345
0.0004573379358379585  0.0005182719331893475  0.0005858982838145386
       0.0006607491306282733          0.0007433726751144845          0.0008343302386625414
0.0009341928505179764  0.001043537352990951  0.0011629420201091398  0.001
   292981692018223  0.0014342224340872494     0.001587215736824181       0.001752492280297207
0.001930555294729694   0.0021218735572222057  0.0023268740730754103 ....
```

Once the plantcv-train.py output file was obtained, we then proceeded with classifying pixels in a color image in PlantCV by the following code from https://plantcv.readthedocs.io/en/latest/tutorials/machine_learning_tutorial/. A test image is given in Fig. 7.

```
img = cv2.imread("./52B9FD97-534A-402F-A7DF-0038018A6CCB.jpg")
img, path, filename = pcv.readimage(filename=args.image)
mask = pcv.naive_bayes_classifier(rgb_img=img,
                  pdf_file="./img/machine_learning.txt")
control_maskpath,       control_analysis_images       =       pcv.output_mask(img=img,
mask=mask['Control'],
                              filename='control.png', mask_only=True)
drought_maskpath,       drought_analysis_images       =       pcv.output_mask(img=img,
mask=mask['Drought'],
                              filename='drought.png', mask_only=True)
classified_img = pcv.visualize.colorize_masks(masks=[mask['Control'], mask['Drought']],
                  colors=['dark green', 'green'])
control_plant = np.count_nonzero(mask['Control'])
drought_plant = np.count_nonzero(mask['Drought'])
percent_drought = drought_plant / (drought_plant + control_plant)
pcv.outputs.add_observation(sample='default', variable='percent_drought', trait='percent of
plant detected to be drought',
                  method='ratio of pixels', scale='percent', datatype=float,
                  value=percent_drought, label='percent')
pcv.outputs.save_results(filename=args.result)
```

Fig. 7. Test case for the Question Three.

Run Question_3_solution.py (box above Fig. 7), and we obtain the following output: percent of plant detected to be drought = 0.024886965781683045

```
Question_3__results.json
{"metadata": {}, "observations": {"default": {"percent_drought": {"trait": "percent of plant
detected to be drought", "method": "ratio of pixels", "scale": "
percent", "datatype": "<class 'float'>", "value": 0.024886965781683045, "label":
"percent"}}}}
```

The result for this test appears to be meaningful. As mentioned in Question Two, not sufficient data were collected, so that an accurate prediction based on a large dataset remains to be verified. Yet, the above workflow from PlantCV seems to be a proper approach to solve this challenge.

3.4 Question Four

GPS and other camera information are encoded in exif tags. Can this data be used to determine characteristics such as leaf size? Can other data, such as soil maps, weather, etc. be used to find correlations among phenotypes?

Solution: GPS and camera data can be encoded from exif tags by the following code.

```
def read_tags(img):
    tags = exifread.process_file(img)
    for key,value in tags.items():
        if 'GPS' in key:
            print(key," => ", value)
        elif 'camera' in key:
            print(key," => ", value)
        elif 'Image' in key:
            print(key," => ", value)
```

The exif data of an example image is given below:

```
Exif tag of .AE73B911-1124-42D5-A0E8-39A632ECDE98.jpg
Image ImageWidth => 3024
Image ImageLength => 4032
Image Make => Apple
Image Model => iPhone 11
Image Orientation => Horizontal (normal)
Image XResolution => 72
Image YResolution => 72
Image ResolutionUnit => Pixels/Inch
Image Software => ArcGIS QuickCapture
Image DateTime => 2021:09:03 12:47:53
Image HostComputer => iPhone 11
Image YCbCrPositioning => Centered
Image ExifOffset => 264
GPS GPSVersionID => [2, 3, 0, 0]
GPS GPSLatitudeRef => N
GPS GPSLatitude => [38, 32, 1453567/50000]
GPS GPSLongitudeRef => W
GPS GPSLongitude => [121, 47, 1950077/100000]
GPS GPSAltitudeRef => 0
GPS GPSAltitude => 8749/500
GPS GPSTimeStamp => [0, 0, 0]
GPS GPSSpeedRef => K
GPS GPSSpeed => 463/5000
GPS GPSTrackRef => T
GPS GPSTrack => 16053/100
GPS GPSImgDirectionRef => M
GPS GPSImgDirection => 405523/5000
GPS GPSMapDatum =>
GPS GPSDate => 2021-09-03
GPS Tag 0x001F => 132953/500000
Image GPSInfo => 2174
EXIF ExifImageWidth => 4032
EXIF ExifImageLength => 3024
```

Upon studies in various sources, it still appears challenging to use the above information to determine information such as the leaf size. Since the size of the white label (see various figures in this report) is already known, the nearby leaf size can be obtained by a mathematical scaling calculation. PlantCV has a workflow to analyze the shape and size of individual plants grown in a tray (https://plantcv.readthedocs.io/en/latest/tutorials/arabidopsis_multi_plant_tutorial/). But the measurement is calculated when all the objects in the image are assumed to be at the same focal distance. If the leaf is not on the same focal distance as the white label, it is hard to calculate the size. Theoretically, the camera zoom information on a pixel scale can be utilized in this regard to measure the distance of an object in photo, so that we can calculate the distance between the front and hind of the leaves. Additional troubles may arise if, for example, the leaf is not directly facing the camera, and therefore, misinterpretation and accuracy are all challenging issues.

As for the GPS information, to our knowledge, this provides the location of the camera. With the availability of other databases such as geographical information of soil, weather, etc., a connection might be made between the classifier and such additional information.

4   Summary and Future Suggestions

From the investigations for this Challenge, the team is able to extract useful information that can be potentially used for data classifier, to further connection the classifiers to genotypes and environmental conditions, and to develop a predictive model that relies on the drought and control conditions, provided that data accuracy from textural extraction and image processing is trustworthy. The use of Tesseract and OpenCV has not reached the needed successes that are required for a proper workflow, such as data preparation, training the module, tuning parameters, and others. Despite many existing challenges, working on this data challenge provides the first hands-on experience to the team on studying machine learning, its workflow and tools, as well as a practically important research topic.

References

1. https://plantcv.readthedocs.io
2. https://plantcv.readthedocs.io/en/v3.0.3/machine_learning_tutorial/#naive-bayes-multiclass

SMC 2022 Data Challenge: Summit Spelunkers Solution for Challenge 2

Thomas Fillers[1], John Maddox[1], Kevin Wang[2], Trevor Taylor[3], Reuben Budiardja[4], and Verónica G. Melesse Vergara[4(✉)]

[1] University of Tennessee, Knoxville, TN, USA
[2] University of Pennsylvania, Philadelphia, PA, USA
[3] Florida Agricultural and Mechanical University, Florida, FL, USA
[4] Oak Ridge National Laboratory, Oak Ridge, TN, USA
vergaravg@ornl.gov

Abstract. This paper investigates five separate questions regarding the usage of Summit's login nodes. We will explain the conversion of the usage logs to readable data and graphs, the comparison of usage between different timeframes like pre- and post-pandemic lockdowns or weekdays versus weekends, the comparison of usage parameters between different login nodes, the prediction of future trends of usage for Summit's login nodes, and additional patterns of interest extracted from the data.

Keywords: System utilization · Data analysis · Time series forecasting

1 Introduction

As use of high-performance computers like Summit continues to expand, there is a growing need to study and understand trends in aspects like user behavior and overall strain on Summit's resources. This will allow for future supercomputers, both new deployments and system upgrades, to be better optimized and suited for the computational needs of users, rather than being designed and built based off of data that might not accurately reflect current necessity. This has been shown most starkly with the arrival of the COVID-19 pandemic, which massively disrupted user behavior and the usage of Summit. A holistic analysis of the usage trends of Summit in multiple parameters using the usage data logs will allow for proper adjustments in the future to better prepare for events like the COVID-19 pandemic, or to adjust for inefficiencies currently shown. In this paper, we will investigate five separate questions regarding the usage of Summit's login nodes. We will explain the conversion of the usage logs to readable data and graphs, the comparison of usage between different timeframes like pre- and post-pandemic lockdowns or weekdays versus weekends, the comparison of usage parameters between different login nodes, the prediction of future trends of usage for Summit's login nodes, and additional patterns of interest extracted from the data.

K. Doug et al. (Eds.): SMC 2022, CCIS 1690, pp. 317–328, 2022.
https://doi.org/10.1007/978-3-031-23606-8_20

2 Results

2.1 Challenge Question 1: Analysis and Conversion of Data

2.1.1 Description

The first challenge question required capturing and sorting of the login node usage data. It was recommended to organize the data into an easily readable CSV file. To perform this task, code was written to sort through the data and organize it in a desired fashion.

2.1.2 Methods

The data was parsed through the usage of C++ and Java; the codes used are included in [1]. Utilizing the format of the output files to our advantage, the desired data was pulled out of the files by checking for each of the flags in the data ("w –", "endw –", "meminfo –", "endmeminfo –", etc.). These flags indicate the beginning and end of output from different commands. The flags allowed us to determine which lines were output from each command, and thus pull the necessary data from each command's output. After pulling the significant data points from each flag, those points were sorted and outputted into a formatted CSV file for easy readability and portability to applications such as Rstudio and Microsoft Excel. In RStudio, dates were converted from strings to numeric time for plotting using the `as.POSIXct()` function. Once this was done, we created separate data frames for each login node based on certain characteristics of each hour like type of day (workday, weekend, holiday), period before ORNL's COVID-19 closure and after ORNL's COVID-19 closure. Daily and Hourly averages were calculated using the `dplyr` package. Finally, utilizing Rstudio, graphs for the corresponding data sets were created.

2.1.3 Results

A	B	C	D	E	F	G	H	I	J	K	L	M	N	O	P	Q	R	S	T
	node	date	hour	users	running_p	cpu_load_	cpu_load_	cpu_load_	mem_tota	mem_avai	mem_usec	unaliased_	color_ls_ti	running_jo	total_jobs	time_to_c	disk_util	wo_ho_w	datetime
1	login1	4/1/2020	0	42	437	2.32	3.35	6.64	6.01E+08	4.96E+08	1.06E+08	0.003	0.003	57	449	23.814	12	0	4/1/2020 0:00
2	login1	4/1/2020	1	42	388	4.3	3.52	3.99	6.01E+08	4.94E+08	1.08E+08	0.003	0.003	57	460	23.817	13	0	4/1/2020 1:00
3	login1	4/1/2020	2	38	381	4.83	8.77	7.36	6.01E+08	4.87E+08	1.14E+08	0.003	0.003	58	455	24.136	15	0	4/1/2020 2:00

(a) CSV created with C++

A	B	C	D	E	F	G	H	I	J	K	L	M	N	O	P	Q	R	S	T	U	V	W
Date	Login Nod	Hour	UserCount	CPU Load	CPU Load	CPU Load	Number o	Used Mem	Running Jc	Total Job	Unaliased	Colored ls	Time to 1	rootfs Disk	Hour	User Coun	CPU Load	CPU Load	CPU Load	Number o	Used Mem	Running Jc
Apr01_202	login1	Hour 00	42 users	2.32	3.35	6.64	437 procs	1.06E+08	57 jobs	448 jobs	0m0.003s	0m0.003s	0m23.814	12%	Hour 01	42 users	4.3	3.52	3.99	388 procs	1.08E+08	57 jobs
Apr02_202	login1	Hour 00	32 users	5.12	5.2	5.29	413 procs	1.05E+08	83 jobs	420 jobs	0m0.003s	0m0.003s	0m23.559	12%	Hour 01	32 users	9.63	8.9	7.08	498 procs	1.06E+08	58 jobs
Apr03_202	login1	Hour 00	33 users	6.3	5.74	5.61	673 procs	1.1E+08	42 jobs	484 jobs	0m0.004s	0m0.003s	0m23.843	13%	Hour 01	32 users	11.82	11.52	9.52	666 procs	1.1E+08	51 jobs

(b) CSV created with Java

Fig. 1. A preview of the two CSVs that were created by this process

This process led to the creation of CSV files (Fig. 1) with columns: node, date, hour, users, running_procs, cpu_load_1_min, cpu_load_5_min, cpu_load_15_min, mem_total, mem_avail, mem_used, unaliased_ls_time, color_ls_time, running_jobs, total_jobs, time_to_create_1G, and disk_util. Additionally, one of the CSVs had a column indicating whether each hour was an hour during a weekday, weekend, or holiday.

These CSVs were used to create bar graphs and line plots. These graphs were represented in several different ways including: pre-COVID-19 and post-COVID-19 plots, weekend vs. weekday vs. holiday plots, and plots of averages for each node and the overall averages.

2.1.4   Discussion
The data and plots acquired from this challenge provided the groundwork for our analysis of login node usage on Summit. From this data we were able to compare usage during different times of the workweek, on holidays, and before and after the COVID-19. These results are expounded in later sections. One possible limitation is that pre-COVID-19 ORNL closure data is relatively small compared to the post-COVID-19 data and conclusions may be skewed by this imbalance.

2.2   Challenge Question 2: Comparison of Usage Patterns

2.2.1   Description
In this challenge question, we were tasked to find usage trends based on external events. These external events include the differences in usage on normal working days/hours compared to that of weekends and holidays. We also chose to evaluate usage differences before and after COVID-19 lockdown.

2.2.2   Methods
To perform our analysis, we started by analyzing the plots that we created previously in challenge question 1. By plotting averages over each individual node and the total averages across all nodes for weekdays, weekends, and holidays, separately, we were able to get an overview of the difference in usage during each of these time periods. After analyzing these periods, we switched to graphing the data taken before major COVID-19 lockdowns (Jan 2020–Mid March 2020) versus the data taken after. These plots allowed us to evaluate usage trends and changes before and after COVID-19.

2.2.3   Results
As expected, averages across all characteristics are generally higher during workdays rather than weekends and holidays (Fig. 2). However, not all observations were as intuitive. One such observation relates to usage during holidays compared to usage on weekends. It can be noted that most holiday averages for running jobs and CPU load are slightly higher than weekend's averages. However, when looking at the average hourly users parameter, it can be observed that the averages are still higher on weekends than holidays.

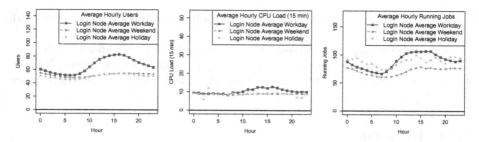

Fig. 2. Line plots comparing certain parameter averages over workdays, weekends, and holidays.

Another trend we observed and chose to investigate was usage before and after major COVID-19 lockdowns. By looking at the data before mid-March of 2020 and comparing it to the data afterwards, we were able to come up with several conclusions in regards to usage changes. It was noted that after COVID-19 more users were online later in the day, and there was a significantly higher average number of running jobs and CPU load (Fig. 3).

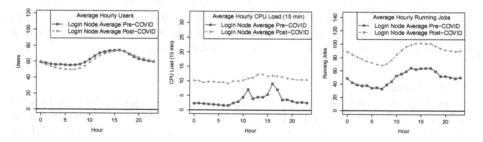

Fig. 3. Line plots comparing certain parameter averages for Pre- and Post-COVID-19 Data.

2.2.4   Discussion

Many conclusions can be drawn from the data analyzed for this section. The reasoning behind higher parameter averages on workdays rather than weekends and holidays is simply that most work will primarily be completed during working hours on workdays. However, some parameters such as running jobs and CPU load are marginally higher than those of weekends. This is likely because the holidays checked are mainly American holidays, and it is probable that users from other countries were using Summit as normal whereas weekends are universal and would be observed by all users of Summit. This would also explain why holiday trends increase and decrease more sporadically over the course of a day, as the users in other countries would be in different time zones. However, we noted that the average hourly user on holidays is still lower on holidays than weekends. At first glance this could invalidate our previous analysis of increased average usage on holidays. One explanation for this anomaly is that some Summit users login on holidays to submit jobs, then immediately log off. This would explain the higher average running jobs and CPU load even though average users is lower on holidays rather than weekends.

In the post-COVID-19 graphs, the numbers for parameters such as total users and running jobs increases from 9 to 10 AM and decreases at a slower rate all the way until midnight. Compared to the pre-COVID-19 expected increase at 8 to 9 AM and much more steep decrease from 5 to 6 PM, this pattern reflects an interesting trend for user behavior. As this pattern would reflect more usage later in the day, we believe that this could indicate users waking up later to start their work, as there is no longer the need to wake up and physically commute to work by 8 to 9 AM. Furthermore, we believe that the slow decrease until midnight is indicative of the lack of a clear separation between work life and personal life that working from home would cause. As there is no longer the need to commute back from work, and the fact that users will be in close proximity to their work laptops at most times, we believe that this pattern reflects how COVID-19 has disrupted users' clear delineation between work and personal lives, and causes users to work until much later into the night.

Likewise, we see that overall, after COVID-19 there is much higher usage of Summit resources than before COVID, as indicated in the running jobs and CPU Load graphs. We believe that this reflects the increased amount of intensive research, likely related to COVID-19 research, that took place on Summit after the lockdown. For example, in 2021 researchers used Summit to evaluate the effectiveness of 77 different drugs against COVID-19, just one example of the many experiments that likely would have used Summit to study various aspects of COVID-19 after the lockdown[1]. This would explain the increased load in most parameters of Summit after COVID-19 and provide a starting point for future address. Accounting for alternative possibilities, we collected a disproportionate amount of "post-COVID" data, from April 2020 to December 2021, compared to "pre-COVID" data, from January 2020 to March 2020. Thus, to better account for other explanations, having access to and running analysis on usage data from previous pre-COVID years would aid our analysis. Likewise, it is possible that there is simply higher usage from April to December compared to January to March, so in the future we would like to run an analysis on both time periods across two years to either eliminate or confirm the factor.

2.3   Challenge Question 3: Analysis of Inter-node Differences

2.3.1   Description

For Challenge Question 3, the task was to derive a "state" for each of Summit's five login nodes based on the different usage parameters and to compare them. The challenge recommended using multiple parameters to define the state, such as CPU usage, memory usage, and user count.

2.3.2   Methods

We chose to derive the state between the five parameters of user count, 15 min CPU load, memory used, running jobs, and running processes. We believe that these five parameters would correlate well in reflecting the usage patterns of Summit, as increases in usage for one parameter, like increased users, would tend to reflect similar increases in others because more users would lead to more processes and jobs, and therefore increased CPU load and memory usage as well.

To define three states denoted as "Intensive", "Baseline", and "Light" activity for the nodes, we chose to calculate the residuals between each hour's five selected parameters and the five average parameters of the entire data set. Summing these residuals in each hour, we calculated the "Light" state vector by creating a subset of our data with negative residual sum values and averaging each of the five parameter values. Similarly, the "Intensive" state vector was calculated by creating a complementary subset of our data with positive residual sum and averaging the five parameter values. The "Baseline" state was set to the five-parameter average vector of the entire data set. With these three state vectors, we calculated the Mahalonobis distance between each five-parameter hour vector and state vector. Hour activity was classified by using the minimum Mahalonobis distance to any of these three states.

2.3.3   Results

In Tables 1, 2, and 3, we present our results obtained after comparing the differences between each node's *state*.

Table 1. Table showing the calculated state vectors for the entire data set

State	User number	15 min CPU load	Memory used (kB)	Running jobs	Running processes
Intensive	81.02	24.64	291333900	103.761	764.318
Baseline	61.343	9.893	253065100	83.552	492.665
Light	51.868	2.794	234639000	73.821	361.866

Table 2. Table showing the tuples representing state for the baseline and the login nodes

Login node	User number	15 min CPU load	Memory used (kB)	Running jobs	Running processes
Baseline	61.343	9.893	253065079.4	83.55196	492.665
Node 1	67.339	5.988	249992476.2	83.73207	498.533
Node 2	63.637	8.624	251815472.2	83.27755	560.01
Node 3	55.145	18.422	244435642.2	83.51549	451.533
Node 4	61.479	10.477	259884698.3	83.45833	524.728
Node 5	59.436	5.662	259108407.2	83.78651	428.639

Table 3. Table showing the number of hours for each node activity classification

Login node	Light	Baseline	Intensive
Total	37043	24348	21137
Node 1	6406	4856	4608
Node 2	7214	5138	4225
Node 3	7979	5502	3299
Node 4	7711	4733	4341
Node 5	7173	4808	4535

2.3.4   Discussion

The first thing of note from this information is that all nodes have a significantly higher rate of light usage states. This makes sense when considering there is a higher number of non-working hours in a day than working hours. We found that the light, baseline, and intensive classifications for Nodes 1, 2, 4, and 5 are fairly similar to each other in scale, while the classification numbers for Node 3 are clearly discrepant from the others. Thus, the main login node of special interest is Login Node 3. The CPU Load values for Login Node 3 are disproportionately high compared to the other nodes and the baseline, while its other parameters are disproportionately lower than them instead. We believe that this could be representative of a background process running on Login Node 3 that would cause high CPU usage. Assuming that the algorithm for assigning users to login nodes is based on CPU usage levels, this would cause Login Node 3 to have less users assigned than the others, along with the highest CPU load levels. We believe that this could be responsible for the disproportionate values seen in Login Node 3.

Future research should focus on more closely analyzing the specifications of Nodes 1, 2, 4, and 5, and the more detailed and nuanced differences between them and the baseline. One way this could be achieved is by implementing a five state partitioning rather than the current three state partition. This would provide an improved distinction between nodes at the extremes of the usage spectrum and those at more moderate positions. However, it is clear that Login Node 3 is disproportionately different from the baseline in many parameters, and therefore should be specially investigated for any background processes or problems with the algorithm that would lead to this difference.

2.4   Challenge Question 4: Prediction of Future Trends

2.4.1   Description

This challenge question required us to use the provided data to come up with a mechanism that will allow us to predict future usage trends of the Summit login nodes. The challenge recommended statistical methods including correlation and regression, but also encouraged us to investigate approaches leveraging machine learning (ML)/deep learning (DL) methods.

2.4.2 Methods

Given that the provided data consists of a time series collection of usage metrics, we looked into potential machine learning (ML) frameworks that we could leverage. We decided to utilize PyTorch Forecasting [2], a relatively new ML framework specifically designed to simplify the forecasting process of time series data.

First, we used Python's Pandas package to import the CSV generated in the previous challenge questions into a dataframe. The dataset must first divided into a training and a validation dataset. Since we had two years worth of data, we selected all the data from 2020 as our training dataset. The imported validation data is stored in a dataframe that is converted to a `TimeSeriesDataSet`. This time series can be used to train the model using the PyTorch Lightning Trainer.

After the model is trained, we can evaluate it using the 2021 data as our validation dataset.

2.4.3 Results

Below we include preliminary results obtained from leveraging PyTorch Forecasting. First, we leveraged the data set to identify a suggested learning rate.

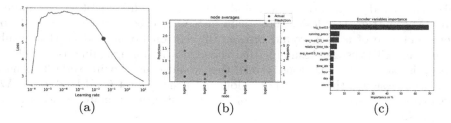

Fig. 4. PyTorch Forecasting findings: (a) identifying optimal learning rate; (b) predictions computed using the trained model; (c) identifying encoder variables of importance

2.4.4 Discussion

Accurate predictions using neural networks require large amounts of training data. In this case, we were able to use PyTorch Forecasting to identify a suggested optimal learning rate. We used that learning rate to train a model and fit it in order to predict characteristics of individual login nodes. The training was done using Google Colab and a single GPU. The training step to approximately 55 min. As shown in Fig. 4 (b), login1 and login3 result in less accurate predictions than the other three nodes. Both nodes were identified previously as outliers and these results suggest additional data may be needed to more accurately describe their behavior.

2.5   Challenge Question 5: Additional Trends and Patterns

2.5.1   Description

For Challenge Question 5, the task was to find additional trends or information in the data outside of conclusions derived from the other questions. This involved looking for significant outside events that affected the usage or regularly occurring patterns not explainable by the normal differences between working times and non-working times.

2.5.2   Methods

To approach this problem, we searched for notable outliers, sudden spikes, and sudden drops visible in the line graphs showing the averages over time and matched them to certain weeks or days. Furthermore, we looked at the timeline of major events from the beginning of 2020 to the end of 2021 to find significant events that could affect usage of Summit, such as major weather events and supercomputer announcements. After we found multiple points of interest, we would then pinpoint through the raw data the exact dates of these before running statistical analyses to create line graphs of Summit usage over those time points.

2.5.3   Results

The first major result came from looking at the different patterns of spikes and drops in the data across different parameters. We noticed that among the average daily running processes over time, the average daily memory used over time, and the average daily disk utilization over time, a matching pattern appeared in all three graphs. These three patterns are shown in Fig. 5 respectively.

We observed this matching pattern and identified out specific dates in which these sudden drops in activity occurred, finding that each drop coincided with a day where multiple hours of information were not logged, indicating a likely outage at Summit. For instance, we observed that for each drop in activity, that day would have large time periods of missing contiguous hourly data like from Hours 0 to 7, and after that from Hours 8 to 23 the activity level would be in its new, lower-level state. This pattern indicates that the average usage and activity level of each of these parameters increases steadily, peaking right before an outage. After the outage, the activity level of each feature, rather than going back to the level seen before the outage, starts at a much reduced activity level which over time increases again, repeating the cycle.

The second major result came from observing the average daily total jobs over time graph. In comparison to other parameters, which stay relatively stable close to the baseline over time, the total job amount overall increases steadily from the beginning of 2020 to the end of 2021. This pattern is shown in Fig. 6.

2.5.4   Discussion

For the first result, we believe that this pattern indicates a possible activity pattern for users of Summit. As outages to Summit are announced ahead of time, we believe that this pattern depicts users increasing their workload output

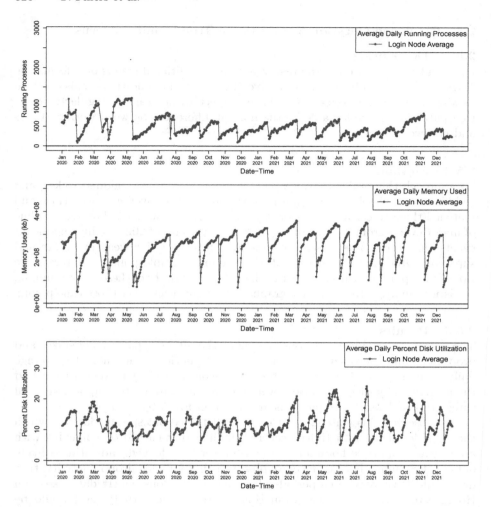

Fig. 5. Line plot showing average total jobs over time, showing an overall increase in usage.

and putting more effort towards finishing their assignments and projects before an outage. As higher levels of running processes, disk utilization, and memory used indicate an overall more intensive and higher usage of Summit as a whole, this behavior explains why the activity level of these parameters are highest right before an outage, as most users will attempt to put in the brunt of their work to finish before the outage. It would also explain the relatively low levels of usage seen after the outage, as most users would have finished their previous assignments and thus not have as many Summit-intensive processes to run. In future explorations of this data, confirming the dates of Summit outages would allow confirmation of our theory.

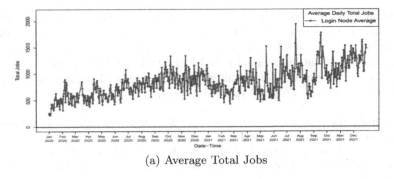

(a) Average Total Jobs

Fig. 6. Line plot showing average total jobs over time, showing an overall increase in usage.

For our second result, we believe the two-year increase in total jobs reflects the multiple closures of various supercomputers housed in the National Lab system close to the beginning of 2020. In August 2019, Oak Ridge National Laboratory shut down the prior supercomputer, Titan, and in January 2020, Argonne National Laboratory decommissioned the Mira supercomputer [3,4]. Furthermore, on January 31st, 2020, Lawrence Livermore National Laboratory also decommissioned their supercomputer, Sequoia [5]. We speculate that the decommissioning of these supercomputers, especially Titan, would have driven an influx of users who were previously accustomed to using these supercomputers to using Summit instead. At that point, Oak Ridge National Laboratory supercomputer users would mostly likely transition to using Summit, their closest alternative, and Argonne National Laboratory had not yet released Polaris for public use [6]. The other parameters of Summit staying at a relatively stable usage would reflect this as well, as Summit would still only be able to handle a certain amount of running jobs and processes, but the total job count increasing would reflect this growth in reliance on Summit. Furthermore, it is unlikely that this increase shown only in total jobs would be a reflection of increased usage after the COVID-19 pandemic, as then the increase would be similar in other parameters as well, which is not seen. An expanded timeline of Summit user data from before 2020 showing the total number of jobs would help to supplement this theory. There are other possible explanations for this trend, such as increase in worker productivity or something yet unexplored, which would be a good focus on future research.

3   Conclusions

The Summit login node data has provided useful insight into the changes and trends of Summit usage in the past two years. During our analysis, we evaluated differences between usage on weekends and holidays compared to normal workdays. While some of these observations were to be expected, others provided unique insight into how people work during otherwise non-working hours.

Additionally we observed the increases in usage after other significant external events such as the rise of COVID-19 and the decommissioning of supercomputers. Furthermore, we used forecasting software methods to predict future usage trends. This data can be invaluable in its ability to provide expectations for the Summit supercomputer's future usage and the usage of future supercomputer such as the upcoming Frontier supercomputer.

Acknowledgements. Major thanks to Oak Ridge National Laboratory for providing the Summit login data and general support for this paper.

This research used resources of the Oak Ridge Leadership Computing Facility, which is a DOE Office of Science User Facility supported under Contract DE-AC05-00OR22725.

References

1. "Summit Spelunkers." https://github.com/HomeworkThomas/SummitSpelunkerS MDC22
2. "PyTorch Forecasting." https://pytorch-forecasting.readthedocs.io/en/stable/
3. "Farewell to Titan." https://www.olcf.ornl.gov/2019/06/28/farewell-titan/
4. "Decommissioning Mira." https://www.alcf.anl.gov/support-center/miracetusves ta/decommissioning-mira
5. "Sequoia Decommissioned Making Room for El Capitan." https://www.hpcwire. com/2020/02/27/sequoia-decommissioned-making-room-for-el-capitan/
6. "Polaris Supercomputer Announced." https://www.datacenterdynamics.com/en/ news/hpe-to-build-argonne-national-labs-44-petaflops-polaris-supercomputer/

Usage Pattern Analysis for the Summit Login Nodes

Brett Eiffert[✉] and Chen Zhang

Computer Science and Mathematics Division,
Oak Ridge National Laboratory, Oak Ridge, USA
`eiffertbc@ornl.gov`

Abstract. High performance computing (HPC) users interact with Summit through dedicated gateways, also known as login nodes. The performance and stability of these login nodes can have a significant impact on the user experience. In this study, the performance and stability of Summit's five login nodes are evaluated by analyzing the log data from 2020 and 2021. The analysis focuses on the computing capability (CPU average load, users and tasks) and the storage performance, along with the associated job scheduler activity. The outcome of this study can serve as the foundation of a predictive modeling framework that enables the system admin of an HPC system to preemptively deploy countermeasures before the onset of a system failure.

Keywords: Summit · HPC · Performance analysis

1 Introduction

Summit, the world's fourth fastest[1] high performance computing system (HPC), is the result of the Collaboration of Oak Ridge, Argonne and Livermore (CORAL) project [1] aimed to bring near-exascale systems to researchers in the fields of natural science, energy, environment, and national security. Located at Oak Ridge National Laboratory, Summit can provide an average performance of 122.3 petaflops and a peak performance of near 200 petaflops, thanks to its modern hybrid computing architecture. Since its first commission in 2018, Summit

---

6th Annual Smoky Mountains Computational Sciences Data Challenge (SMCDC22)
This manuscript has been authored by UT-Battelle, LLC, under contract DE-AC05-00OR22725 with the US Department of Energy (DOE). The US government retains and the publisher, by accepting the article for publication, acknowledges that the US government retains a nonexclusive, paid-up, irrevocable, worldwide license to publish or reproduce the published form of this manuscript, or allow others to do so, for US government purposes. DOE will provide public access to these results of federally sponsored research in accordance with the DOE Public Access Plan (http://energy.gov/downloads/doe-public-access-plan).

[1] At the time of writing, the world's fastest HPC system is Frontier, the successor of Summit.

K. Doug et al. (Eds.): SMC 2022, CCIS 1690, pp. 329–344, 2022.
https://doi.org/10.1007/978-3-031-23606-8_21

has been a powerhouse that helps advance scientific discoveries in astrophysics [2], materials science [3], medical research [4], and biology [5,6].

As a centralized computing system where the computing jobs are scheduled and distributed to worker nodes via a scheduler, Summit's users generally need to interact with Summit's mainframe through a gateway, also known as login nodes. There are currently five login nodes to facilitate the interaction between the users and Summit's mainframe, and the performance and stability of these login nodes can impact the user experience as well as job scheduling. In order to improve the performance and stability of Summit, a usage pattern analysis, similar to the one performed on its predecessor Titan [7], is carried out in this study.

In this manuscript, Sect. 2 describes the steps to pre-process the raw log entries into more efficient DataFrames, followed by detailed analysis with respect to computing, storage and job scheduling in Sect. 3. The findings are summarized in Sect. 4, along with suggestions on modeling these usage patterns to assist the system admin such that preemptive measures can be taken before the onset of a system failure.

2   Data Processing and Feature Extraction

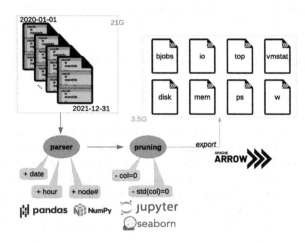

Fig. 1. The raw data is parsed and pruned into eight individual DataFrames, which are saved to disk using the Apache Arrow toolbox.

The log data [8] is an hourly snapshot from various system monitoring processes concatenated into a single plain text file for each login node per day for the duration of 2020 and 2021. As the unstructured format of these log entries cannot be directly parsed by standard data processing libraries, a customized parser[2] is created to convert these log entries into pandas.DataFrame [9] objects

---

[2] https://github.com/brettceiffert/summit-data-challenge.

for the subsequent data analysis. More specifically, the customized parser goes through all 3522 raw data files[3] to extract the log information into eight individual DataFrames, including **w**, **meminfo**, **vmstat**, **ps**, **bjobs**, **io**, **disk**, and **top** (Fig. 1). During parsing, dates and hours are added based on the filename and the embedded timestamp, along with the corresponding login node number. Additional feature pruning is also performed for all eight DataFrames so as to remove features with zero values or near-zero variance. The resulting DataFrames are compressed and saved to binary archives using the Apache Arrow toolbox.

3 Usage Pattern Analysis

3.1 Computing Pattern

The general usage pattern of the Summit login nodes, as shown in Fig. 2, exhibits a multi-level oscillating pattern, the periodicity of which varies with respect to the feature of interest as well as the corresponding observation scope. For instance, when analyzed from the scope of 24 h, the number of users logged in gradually increases after midnight, peaking at around 16:00 in the afternoon, then decreasing again until midnight (Fig. 3). A similar pattern can also be observed when viewed from the scope of a week (Fig. 4), where the number of users for all five login nodes starts relatively low on Mondays, jumping to a relatively high number for the middle of the week (Tuesday, Wednesday and Thursday), dipping back slightly on Fridays, followed by a sharp decline on the weekends. When viewed from the scope of both years, the number of users stays relatively stable for the first three quarters of each year, followed by a slight decline in the last one, which corresponds to the holiday season in the North American region. Using the common work schedule in the US as a frame of reference, the pattern above indicates that Summit's users prefer to use the system during the working hours on weekdays, and the login nodes are generally less occupied during the holiday season, which matches the results shown in Fig. 5. This distinctive collective usage pattern from all Summit users indicates that the majority of Summit users are most likely from US or non-US institutions that follows a similar work schedule to the US. Additionally, login node one and two tend to have more users than login node four and five, while login node three seems to be operating under a different set of rules, resulting in its smaller but more stable user numbers. Interestingly, the beginning of the COVID-19 pandemic in March 2020 that forced a nation-wide lockdown did not have any visible impact on the usage patterns, except for a small window around the announcement of lockdown where all five nodes seem to be offline as indicated by the lack of log data. However, there is a small and gradual decline in the total number of logged-in users after the end of the federal mask mandate[4],

---

[3] Although the theoretical number of data files should be $2 \times 365 \times 5 = 3650$, there are 128 records missing due to maintenance or other issues that led to unscheduled down time.

[4] On 2021-03-08, the CDC announced that fully vaccinated people can resume indoor working without a mask.

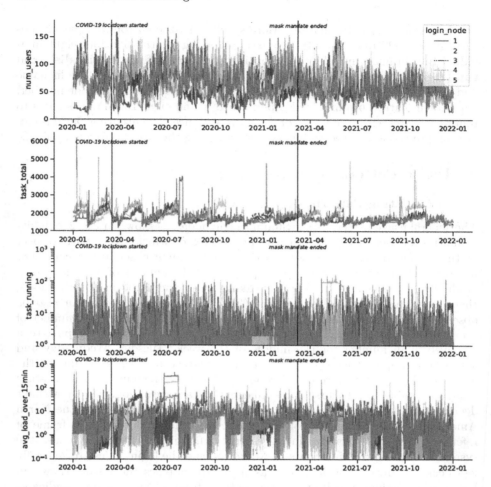

Fig. 2. The number of users (first row), total number of tasks (second row), active number of tasks (third row), and the load average from the last 15 min (bottom row, in unit of percentage) for all five login nodes fluctuated periodically in the short range, but overall exhibited a stable pattern for the duration of the COVID-19 pandemic with occasional exceptions.

which could be the result of some Summit users shifting their focus from running computations on Summit remotely to accommodating the transition to an on-site working schedule.

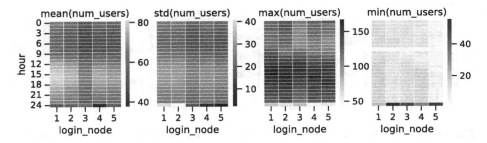

Fig. 3. The heat map of number of users for each login node with respect to hour of the day.

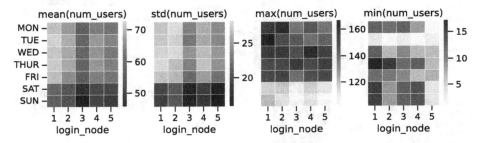

Fig. 4. The heat map of number of users with respect to day of the week and login node shows that there are more users during the weekdays.

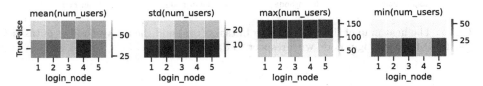

Fig. 5. The heatmap of the number of users for each login node with respect to whether the given date is a US federal holiday (24 holidays).

The usage patterns of tasks and average load share some similarities with the pattern of logged-in user numbers, but they also have their own distinctive features.

The total number of tasks follows a similar 24-h pattern (Fig. 6) and the weekday pattern (top row in Fig. 7). When viewed from the scope of two years (second row in Fig. 2), the total number of tasks does not seem to have a strong pattern that correlates with the holiday season, which is consistent with the results shown in Fig. 8. However, it does follow a distinct pattern where the total number of tasks accumulates gradually for some time, followed by a sharp decline, then the cycle begins anew. Since all five login nodes seem to experience the sharp drop around the same time, it is possible that these sharp drops are the results of the system auto purging stagnated processes to improve system

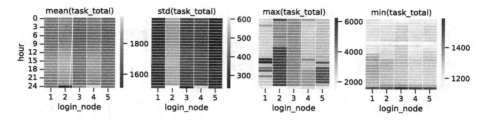

Fig. 6. The heat map of the total number of tasks for each login node with respect to hour of the day.

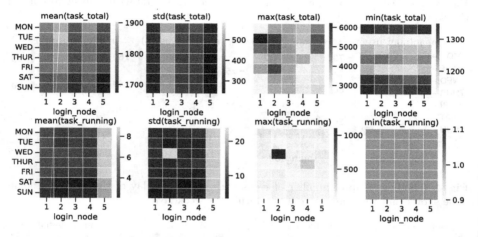

Fig. 7. The heat map of the total number of tasks (top) and the active number of tasks (bottom) for each login node with respect to day of the week.

performance. Despite the volatility of the total number of tasks with respect to time, the number of active tasks is much smaller and more stable (third row in Fig. 2) while exhibiting a slight decrease during the holidays (bottom row in Fig. 8). In addition, all five nodes seem to have very similar active running tasks patterns (bottom row in Fig. 7), except for login node five which has a persistent high number of active tasks. The relatively high number of active tasks in login node five could be the result of some persistent services that are unique to login node five.

The average load over 15 min (Fig. 9), a representation of the CPU load state, exhibits a much weaker pattern in the 24 h scope. A similar conclusion can also be drawn in the scope of week where the average load is relatively stable, with some slight increases in the middle of the week (Fig. 10). However, the average load pattern does show a strong correlation with US federal holidays as shown in Fig. 11 where all five login nodes are significantly less busy during the holidays. During the analysis of the dynamic range of the CPU load during 2020 and 2021, it is observed that the average CPU load for all five nodes are kept below

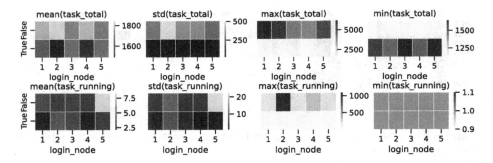

Fig. 8. The heat map of the number of all tasks (top) and the active tasks (bottom) for each login node with respect to whether given date is a US federal holiday.

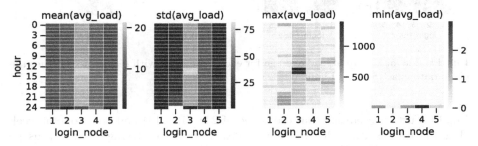

Fig. 9. The heat map of load average for each login node with respect to hour of the day.

1000 %, about one third of the total computing capability of each node.[5] This phenomenon could be a direct result of the Summit login node policy where long or heavy computational jobs are prohibited and subject to termination without notice. Interestingly, login node three has the highest average CPU load while having fewer tasks and users, which further indicates that login node three is operating under a different set of rules, or possibly reserved for projects with priorities.

Theoretically, the information about system memory state can be extracted from both **top** and **meminfo**. However, the data from 2020 and early 2021 in **top** is truncated due to using 1 kB as the smallest unit, which renders them unsuitable for system memory analysis. Therefore, the following memory usage analysis is based on the information extracted from **meminfo**.

The active memory (top row in Fig. 12) and free memory (second row in Fig. 12) exhibit complimentary patterns, sharing almost identical periodicity for the duration of 2020 and 2021. However, this periodicity varies slightly from one cycle to another, and it does not seem to be affected by the holiday season as well as the COVID-19 pandemic, which can be confirmed by the statistics shown in

---

[5] Each login node has 32 processors, therefore 3200 % is the theoretic full load for each node.

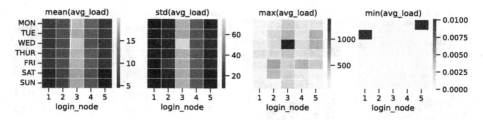

Fig. 10. The heat map of load average over 15 min for each login node with respect to the day of the week.

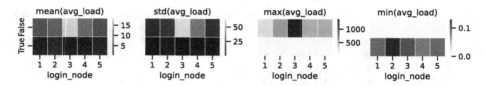

Fig. 11. The heat map of load average for each login node with respect to whether the given date is a US federal holiday.

Fig. 13. Further analysis from the scope of 24 h (Fig. 14) and the scope of week (Fig. 15) reveals that all five login nodes have stable average memory usage patterns regardless of the hour or the day. However, the peak memory usage occurs more around midnight as well as in the middle of the week, contradicting the general patterns observed from number of users and average CPU load. Given the observations above, it is important to consider the system memory as an independent factor when designing the load balancer and potential predictive modeling.

Besides the general memory usage trend, there are some other interesting observations from **meminfo**'s data as well. For example, the kernel estimated memory[6] (third row in Fig. 12) shows that all five login nodes stay in a relatively safe region where the kernel estimate memory is well below the total amount of physical memory, with a few exceptions where the peak estimate shoots over the total physical memory available. Most of the time, these rare peaks are quickly corrected as indicated by the following sharp decline. However, there are two exceptions where login node three and login node five have projected memory usage slightly above the physical memory for a noticeable amount of time, which also matches the pattern of active running tasks shown in Fig. 2. Another interesting case related to the hardware performance of the memory is observed - login node one has a persistent, large (about 130 kB) corrupted page whereas login nodes two to five have none. This indicates that a small portion of the memory in login node one has a constant memory error, triggering Error Correcting Code (ECC) to mark the corresponding page as "corrupted".

---

[6] A projected memory load from kernel to avoid an out of memory issue for the entire system. Most modern kernels tend to overestimate to provide a larger safe margin.

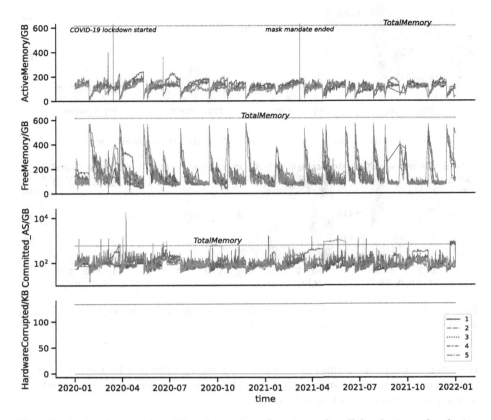

Fig. 12. Active (top row) and free (second row) memory for all five login nodes during 2020 and 2021. The kernel estimate memory is shown in the third row, and the detected hardware memory corruption is shown at the bottom. The total memory on each node drops slightly from 615.61 GB at the beginning of 2020 to 615.56 GB at the beginning of the fourth quarter of 2021.

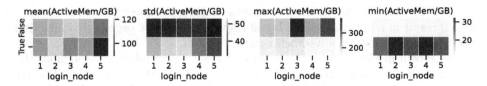

Fig. 13. All five login nodes have similar average active memory. However, the peak active memory only occurs during non-holiday time.

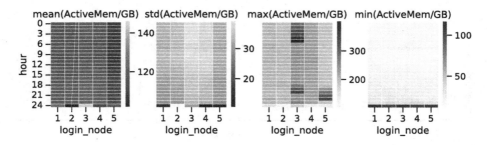

Fig. 14. Active memory stays relatively stable throughout the day.

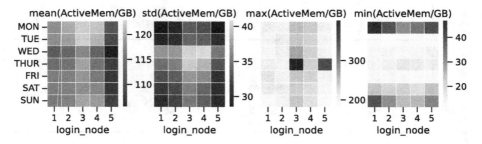

Fig. 15. The average active memory is relatively stable across the week, but the peak usage occurs during the middle of the week.

However, such phenomenon is missing from login node two to five, indicating either their memory is more reliable or the accompanied ECC is turned off, leaving the memory error undetected.

3.2 Storage Utilization and Responsiveness

Input and output (I/O) response time is a good indicator of disk drive health, making it an important factor to consider when evaluating the overall performance of Summit's login nodes. In this study, the overall health of the storage system is evaluated by analyzing the read and write response times of each login node. Only around one percent of all real system response times across all five login nodes were below the ≈ 0.0167 s threshold,[7] indicating the storage system remained stable for the majority of 2020 and 2021. A slower frame refresh rate would result in a human seeing a lag in response, therefore negatively impacting the user experience when interacting with Summit.

As shown in Fig. 16, the slow response cases occur randomly throughout the day, and slightly more in 2021. For instance, login node one has significantly slower response times around July and August 2021, which was followed by it going offline, indicated by the lack of log data. This correlation suggests that

---

[7] This threshold is chosen based on the common refresh rate, 60 FPS of most modern televisions and monitors.

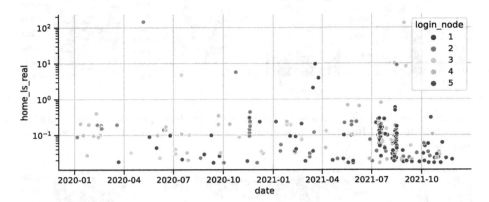

Fig. 16. A scatter plot of the home_ls_real response times (in seconds) slower than 0.0167 s (60 FPS) from running an "ls" command on each login node.

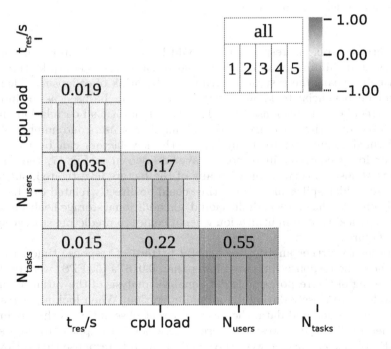

Fig. 17. Correlation analysis of system response time (home_ls_real, t_{res}/S) with respect to CPU load, number of users (N_{users}) and number of tasks (N_{tasks}). The horizontal bar in each glyph represents the correlation calculated using aggregated data from all login nodes whereas the vertical bars below it represent the corresponding correlation value calculated using data from a specific node.

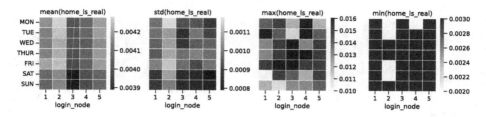

Fig. 18. A heat map of the number of seconds it takes to respond to an "ls" command for each login node. Response times greater than 0.0167 s (60 FPS) are excluded from analysis.

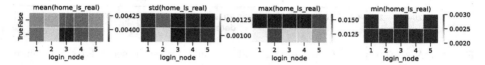

Fig. 19. A heat map of the number of seconds it takes to respond to an "ls" command for each login node on a federal holiday or not. Response times greater than 0.0167 s (60FPS) are excluded from analysis.

a concentrated spike in response time could be a good indicator of a potential storage system failure for a given node. However, a concentrated spike in response time usually means the system is already on the brink of collapsing. Therefore, it would be beneficial to know if certain factors can be used as an indicator for the irregularity in response time. To this end, additional correlation analysis between response time, average CPU load, number of users and number of tasks is performed to investigate if any one of the key factors can be used as an indicator for irregularity in response time. As shown in Fig. 17, the response time has almost no correlation with any of the factors investigated, suggesting that these sudden spikes in response time could be directly related to a hardware issue. Therefore, the system admin should add additional storage health monitors instead of tracking system utilization when it comes to predicting storage system related failures.

In order to further analyze the general pattern of response times, irregular cases where the response time was slower than 0.0167 s (60 FPS) were excluded. This filtering of the response time data enables analysis of the variance for each login node more closely during its normal operation. When looking at response times by login node and data, the most apparent observation is that login node two generally has the slowest response. There does not appear to be a strong correlation between specific week days and login node response times. However, the disk response does generally improve during the weekend as shown in Fig. 18.

When analyzing the response time data along the holiday season axis, it is clear that the disk responses are slightly faster during the holiday season (Fig. 19), which is expected since the total number of users are lower during this period.

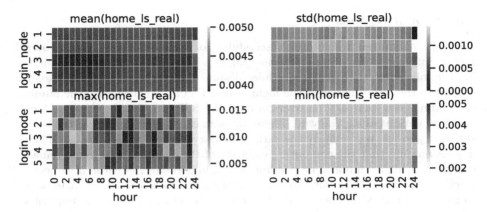

Fig. 20. A heat map of the number of seconds it takes to respond to an "ls" command for each login node with respect to hour of the day. Response times greater than 0.0167 s seconds (60 FPS) are removed.

Similarly, the analysis in the scope of 24 h (Fig. 20) reveals that the disk response time is slower starting from the late morning and continuing into the late afternoon, which corresponds to the day shift schedule commonly found in the North American region.

Interestingly, the average disk response times for all five login nodes in 2020 are slightly better than those in 2021 (Fig. 21), which could be an indicator of the associated physical storage device degradation during the continuous service.

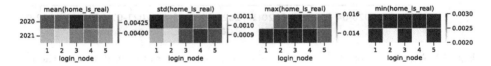

Fig. 21. The heat map of the number of seconds it takes to respond to an "ls" command for each login node with respect to year. Response times greater than 0.0167 s (60 FPS) are excluded from analysis.

Another interesting finding when performing the storage usage analysis is that fewer and fewer disk drive rebuilds happen as time goes by, indicating that the overall storage system is becoming more stable over the two years. More specifically, there are some large, temporary snapshot drives that appear in the storage utilization log for a specific period of time, which could be the result of the storage system trying to recover from its hourly backup due to some run-time failure. This phenomenon occurs less frequent in 2021 than 2020, suggesting that 2021s storage system is more stable and requires less frequent recovery from backups.

3.3 Submitted Jobs

The jobs submitted to Summit's scheduler for execution can provide useful insight into the overall Summit usage pattern. This section focuses on analyzing the jobs submitted to the scheduler despite that their status is not directly related to the performance of the login nodes. Figure 22 shows that the number of pending jobs increases on average over the full two years with some localized fluctuations along the way. There are noticeable declines during the major vacation periods, particularly the early calendar year and the beginning of summer. Assuming that the computing capacity of the Summit mainframe remains constant, a higher number of pending jobs could be an indicator of a heavier workload, which could indirectly lead to an increased workload for login nodes as users might need to check and update their submitted jobs more frequently.

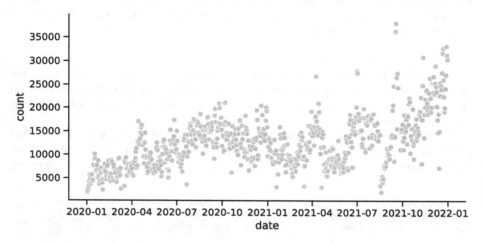

Fig. 22. A scatter plot of the total number of jobs pending at each date over the two year period.

Another interesting finding from the analysis of submitted jobs is shown in Fig. 23, which demonstrates the distribution of submitted job size (SLOTS) for the two-year period. More specifically, the majority of the submitted jobs are "small" jobs using about 40 SLOTS, which is within the vicinity of a single node's computing capacity. Jobs with more than 1×10^3 SLOTS make up about one tenth of the total jobs submitted and the largest jobs (greater than 1×10^5 SLOTS) account for only about 1 %. In other words, finding an efficient way to schedule the "small" and "middle" size jobs are critical in improving Summit's utilization.

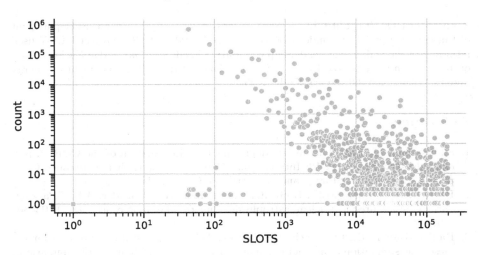

Fig. 23. A scatter plot showing the number of slots (CPUs) used by all jobs run on Summit over the two year period.

4 Summary and Future Work

This study presents a usage pattern analysis of Summit's five login nodes using log data collected from 2020 and 2021. The analysis reveals that the number of logged in users and total number of tasks generally follows a multi-level oscillation pattern where the corresponding periodicity correlates with the general work schedule in the North American region. Although both average CPU load and memory usage show similar oscillation patterns, they are not correlated with working hours or the holiday schedule. This is most likely due to the automated and manual measures taken to balance the CPU and memory usage during production, the details of which are not available to the authors at the time of writing. The irregular spikes in system response time could be a good indicator of a potential system failure. However, system response time is not directly correlated with the number of users and CPU load, therefore a continuous monitoring of the storage system health provides a more useful insight when it comes to forecasting storage related system failures. Although not directly related to the login node performance, the distributions related to the submitted jobs can be used to improve the performance of the scheduler by prioritizing "small" and "medium" sized jobs. Overall, the findings from this study indicate that the usage patterns of Summit's login nodes are not completely chaotic, and it is possible to model these patterns such that the system admin can use them to predict potential system failures and deploy corresponding countermeasures preemptively.

Acknowledgements. This research used resources of the Oak Ridge Leadership Computing Facility at the Oak Ridge National Laboratory, which is supported by the Office of Science of the U.S. Department of Energy under Contract No. DE-AC05-00OR22725.

Support for DOI 10.13139/OLCF/1866372 dataset is provided by the U.S. Department of Energy, project DLSW under Contract DE-AC05-00OR22725. Project DLSW used resources of the Oak Ridge Leadership Computing Facility at Oak Ridge National Laboratory, which is supported by the Office of Science of the U.S. Department of Energy under Contract No. DE-AC05-00OR22725.

References

1. Sudharshan, S. et al.: The design, deployment, and evaluation of the CORAL pre-exascale systems. In: SC18: International Conference for High Performance Computing, Networking, Storage and Analysis, pp. 661–672. IEEE (2018)
2. Berry, D.K., Caplan, M.E., Horowitz, C.J., Huber, G., Schneider, A.S.: "Parking-garage" structures in nuclear astrophysics and cellular biophysics. **94**(5), 055801 (2016)
3. Radhakrishnan, B., Eisenbach, M., Burress, T.A.: A new scaling approach for the mesoscale simulation of magnetic domain structures using Monte Carlo simulations. **432**, 42–48 (2017)
4. Tourassi, G., Yoon, H.-J., Songhua, X.: A novel web informatics approach for automated surveillance of cancer mortality trends. **61**, 110–118 (2016)
5. Nakano, C.M., Byun, H.S., Ma, H., Wei, T., El-Naggar, M.Y.: A framework for stochastic simulations and visualization of biological electron-transfer dynamics. **193**, 1–9 (2015)
6. Agarwal, P.K.: A biophysical perspective on enzyme catalysis. **58**(6), 438–449 (2019)
7. Iserte, S.: An study on the resource utilization and user behavior on titan supercomputer. In: Nichols, F., et al. (eds.) Driving Scientific and Engineering Discoveries Through the Integration of Experiment, Big Data, and Modeling and Simulation. Communications in Computer and Information Science, vol. 1512, pp. 398–410. Springer International Publishing, Cham (2022). https://doi.org/10.1007/978-3-030-96498-6_23
8. Maheshwari, K., Wilkinson, S., Ferreira da Silva, R.: Pseudonymized user-perspective summit login node data for 2020 and 2021 (2022)
9. Reback, J., et al.: pandas-dev/pandas: Pandas 1.4.3 (2022)

Finding Hidden Patterns in High Resolution Wind Flow Model Simulations

Tianle Wang[1]($\boxtimes$), Bigeng Wang[2]($\boxtimes$), Elisha Siddiqui Matekole[1], and Mohammad Atif[1]

[1] Computational Science Initiative, Brookhaven National Laboratory,
Upton, NY, USA
[2] Department of Physics and Astronomy, University of Kentucky,
Lexington, KY, USA
bwa271@g.uky.edu

Abstract. Wind flow data is critical in terms of investment decisions and policy making. High resolution data from wind flow model simulations serve as a supplement to the limited resource of original wind flow data collection. Given the large size of data, finding hidden patterns in wind flow model simulations are critical for reducing the dimensionality of the analysis. In this work, we first perform dimension reduction with two autoencoder models: the CNN-based autoencoder (CNN-AE) [1], and hierarchical autoencoder (HIER-AE) [2], and compare their performance with the Principal Component Analysis (PCA). We then investigate the super-resolution of the wind flow data. By training a Generative Adversarial Network (GAN) with 300 epochs, we obtained a trained model with 2× resolution enhancement. We compare the results of GAN with Convolutional Neural Network (CNN), and GAN results show finer structure as expected in the data field images. Also, the kinetic energy spectra comparisons show that GAN outperforms CNN in terms of reproducing the physical properties for high wavenumbers and is critical for analysis where high-wavenumber kinetics play an important role.

Keywords: Data exploration · Machine learning · Autoencoder · Super-resolution · Generative Adversarial Network

1 Background and Related Work

In recent years, machine learning based models for several fluid flow applications have shown many promising results. Supervised learning based models for super-resolution reconstruction of turbulent flows are difficult to implement as they require huge amounts of trained data sets. However, unsupervised learning based methods have shown much promise. For example, autoencoder based methods for low dimensional mapping for microscale windflow dynamics proposed in [2,3] has demonstrated superior performances. In particular, it was shown in [2] that hierarchical autoencoder (HIER-AE) utilizing Convolutional Neural Network (CNN) has a strong potential as the nonlinear low-dimensional

K. Doug et al. (Eds.): SMC 2022, CCIS 1690, pp. 345–365, 2022.
https://doi.org/10.1007/978-3-031-23606-8_22

mapping function. However, since the training method used by them is probabilistic, the mapping of the turbulent flow field in the latent space is not unique. Cycle-consistent generative adversarial network (GAN) has been used to reconstruct high-resolution (HR) flow field when the low-resolution (LR) and HR field data are unpaired [4].

Recent approach to generate HR climate data is deep learning based super-resolution (SR). Single-image SR takes LR image and produces an approx HR version of it. Deep CNN with adversarial training has been developed for SR image processing [5]. The authors showed that SRGAN with deep residual network (ResNet) was able to preserve the small-scale structures of the image, and enhance the coarse climate data [6]. The ResNet is used to solve the problem of vanishing gradients in the training. It includes skip-connections which connect activation of a layer to further layers by skipping some layers in between. In general, the layer that reduces the performance is skipped using regularization. The reconstructions obtained from SRGAN method were found to be more *photo-realistic* than SRCNN methods.

In this paper we first look at the statistics of the data, and then implement two types of autoencoder: CNN-AE and HIER-AE, to perform dimension reduction and capture important features of the LES simulation data of wind velocity field, and compare them with PCA. We then apply SRCNN as well as SRGAN for up-scaling the low-resolution LES simulation data. Autoencoder have been shown to be powerful in some 2D and 3D problems [2,3]. In this work, we compare the performance of AE with the classical PCA method used in dimension reduction problems. From a qualitative comparison of the linearity of PCA and non-linearity of the AE, we conclude that AE does not always work better than PCA and one needs to evaluate the cost and benefit of AE while applying dimension reduction for a specific problem. We propose to consider the correlation between the hyperparameter n_γ, the latent vector size, and the number of dominating modes encoded in the physics of the problem.

As for the super-resolution problem, we compare the results of GAN with the results of CNN, and GAN results show finer structure as expected. In addition, while we find the loss of GAN generator is larger than that of the CNN given the same data sets, the kinetic energy spectra comparison show that GAN outperforms CNN in terms of reproducing the physical properties for high wavenumbers and is critical for analysis where high wavenumber kinetics play an important role. We also conclude that the kinetic energy spectrum is a better metric compared to MSE and should be used to evaluate the results for super-resolution problems when fine structures also play an important role.

2   Exploratory Data Analysis and Visualization

In this section we begin by introducing the data followed by a discussion on data analysis and visualization. We use the ERA5 data obtained from [7] which contains timeseries of x and y components of velocity and temperature at a singular point. In addition to the ERA5 data, we have the timeseries of LES simulation

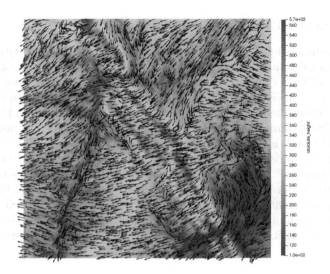

Fig. 1. Visualization of the high resolution LES data over the domain: the background color represents the surface height and the arrows indicate the direction of the wind. (Color figure online)

at two grid resolutions. The LES data are timeseries of fields of velocities and temperature in a domain divided into 96×96 and 192×192 for low (LES96) and high (LES192) resolution grids respectively. Figure 1 visualizes the high resolution LES data at the initial time-step over the domain. Here, the background color represents the height and the arrows indicate the direction of the wind.

Table 1. Averages of the ERA5 and LES data. The average horizontal and vertical components of the wind speed are given by u and v respectively in m/s.

Data	u (m/s)	v (m/s)
ERA5	0.905466	-1.0331627
LES96	0.71078604	-1.0271654
LES192	0.6988208	-1.0105036

We first compare the temporal average of the ERA5 data with the spatiotemporal average of the two LES data as shown in Table 1. We observe that while the average of v obtained from the LES data is close to the ERA5 data, the average of u from the LES data shows approximately 22% deviation. Here, u is the average U component of the wind speed along the x-axis, and v is the average V component of the wind speed along the y-axis. The units of the wind speed are m/s.

348   T. Wang et al.

2.1   Systematic Bias in the Data

Next, we compare the timeseries of spatially averaged LES data with the ERA5 timeseries to gain an understanding of the bias. To this end, we first calculate the average of LES data over x and y coordinates which is a timeseries of the same length as the ERA5 data, and then compute the difference between the two for u, v. Figure 2a and Fig. 2b depict this difference along with the difference between LES192 and LES96 data for u and v respectively. It shows that the bias of LES192 and ERA5 is substantial whereas the bias of LES192 and LES96 is negligible. To understand the spatial dependence of the bias we evaluate the time average of the LES96 and LES192 data. We then subtract the time average of ERA5 data from each grid point of the time-averaged LES data. Figures 3 and 4 show the aforementioned difference and one can observe a spatial dependence of time-averaged u and v fields. Thus the bias is found to depend on the spatial location as well as it shows fluctuations in time for spatially averaged velocity fields.

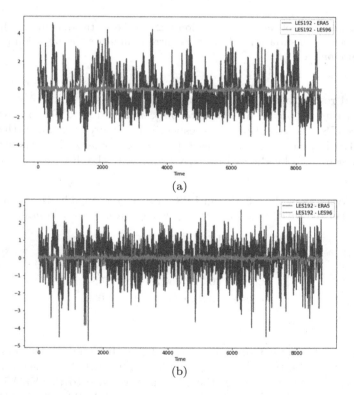

(a)

(b)

Fig. 2. (a) Bias of spatially averaged u – the x component of velocity. In case of LES192 and LES96 the bias is negligible. However, for LES192 and ERA5 the bias is quite pronounced. (b) Bias of spatially averaged v – the y component of velocity. In case of LES192 and LES96 the bias is negligible. However, for LES192 and ERA5 the bias is quite pronounced.

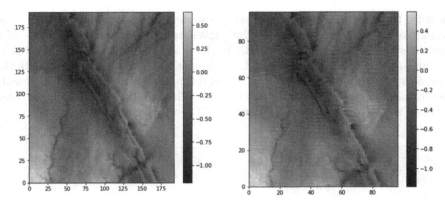

Fig. 3. Bias of time-averaged u from LES and ERA5 − LES192 (left) and LES96 (right).

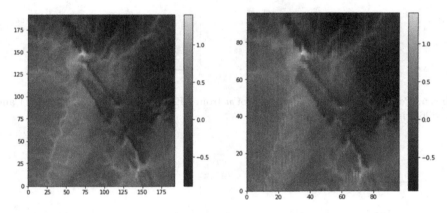

Fig. 4. Bias of time-averaged v from LES and ERA5 − LES192 (left) and LES96 (right).

2.2 Data Correlation

The ERA5 data is singular in space. Hence, its spatial standard deviation is zero, thus the spatial correlation will be ill-defined. However, we can compute the spread of temporal Pearson correlation coefficient of the LES data with the ERA5 data. The Pearson correlation coefficient is a widely employed metric to measure the relation between two variables. Here, we first evaluate the spatial average of the LES velocity fields which gives us a time stream. We then calculate the standard deviation of the ERA5 data, and the covariance of the ERA5 stream and the spatially averaged LES streams and use them to calculate the coefficient. It can be seen from Figs. 5 and 6 that in the majority of the domain the correlation coefficient is larger than 0.9. This signifies a strong correlation between the ERA5 and the LES data.

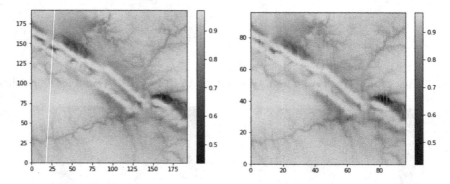

Fig. 5. Pearson correlation coefficient of u from LES and ERA5 – LES192 (left) and LES96 (right).

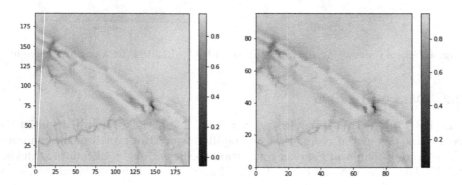

Fig. 6. Pearson correlation coefficient of v from LES and ERA5 – LES192 (left) and LES96 (right).

It can thus be concluded from the analysis that a strong correlation exists between the LES simulations and the ERA5 data despite the spatio-temporal average of u showing a significant deviation. This deviation could be attributed to the lack of information on the location of the point of ERA5 data sampling.

3   Dimension Reduction

Table 2. The architecture of Encoder and Decoder used in this work. The latent_dim represents the dimension of the latent space.

Encoder		Decoder	
Layer	Data shape	Layer	Data shape
Input	(192, 192, 2)	Dense (576)	(576)
Conv2D (3, 3, 16)	(192, 192, 16)	Reshape	(3, 3, 64)
BatchNormalization	(192, 192, 16)	Conv2D-T (3, 3, 64, s = 2)	(6, 6, 64)
LeakyReLU	(192, 192, 16)	BatchNormalization	(6, 6, 64)
MaxPooling2D	(96, 96, 16)	LeakyReLU	(6, 6, 64)
Conv2D (3, 3, 16)	(96, 96, 16)	Conv2D-T (3, 3, 64, s = 2)	(12, 12, 64)
BatchNormalization	(96, 96, 16)	BatchNormalization	(12, 12, 64)
LeakyReLU	(96, 96, 16)	LeakyReLU	(12, 12, 64)
MaxPooling2D	(48, 48, 16)	Conv2D-T (3, 3, 32, s = 2)	(24, 24, 32)
Conv2D (3, 3, 32)	(48, 48, 32)	BatchNormalization	(24, 24, 32)
BatchNormalization	(48, 48, 32)	LeakyReLU	(24, 24, 32)
LeakyReLU	(48, 48, 32)	Conv2D-T (3, 3, 32, s = 2)	(48, 48, 32)
MaxPooling2D	(24, 24, 32)	BatchNormalization	(48, 48, 32)
Conv2D (3, 3, 32)	(24, 24, 32)	LeakyReLU	(48, 48, 32)
BatchNormalization	(24, 24, 32)	Conv2D-T (3, 3, 16, s = 2)	(96, 96, 16)
LeakyReLU	(24, 24, 32)	LeakyReLU	(96, 96, 16)
MaxPooling2D	(12, 12, 32)	Conv2D-T (3, 3, 16, s = 2)	(192, 192, 16)
Conv2D (3, 3, 64)	(12, 12, 64)	LeakyReLU	(192, 192, 16)
LeakyReLU	(12, 12, 64)	Conv2D (3, 3, 2)	(192, 192, 2)
MaxPooling2D	(6, 6, 64)	-	-
Conv2D (3, 3, 64)	(6, 6, 64)	-	-
LeakyReLU	(6, 6, 64)	-	-
MaxPooling2D	(3, 3, 64)	-	-
Flatten	(576)	-	-
Dense (latent_dim)	(latent_dim)	-	-

There are various dimension reduction techniques. Principal Component Analysis (PCA) is a widely used linear, non-trainable dimension reduction method. However, its linear nature makes it difficult to capture non-linear features in the data. With the development of machine learning, several unsupervised learning methods which capture non-linearity in the data have been well developed. In this work, we are most interested in the technique called autoencoder (AE). An AE usually includes two main components: an encoder network

Table 3. Hyper parameters used in this work.

Parameter	Value	Parameter	Value
Number of epochs	7000	Number of training data	5112
Number of validation data	1704	Number of testing data	1704
Batch size	128	Optimizer	Adam
Learning rate	0.001	Pooling size	(2,2)
α in LeakyReLU	0.2	-	-

Table 4. Performance of PCA, CNN-AE and HIER-AE with various dimension of latent space (n_γ). Here the performance metric is chosen to be pixel average of mean square error (MSE). As we increase n_γ, the error becomes smaller. The CNN-AE works best when n_γ is small (4, 9, 18 and 36), while PCA works better when n_γ is large (72 and 144). The HIER-AE almost always performs worse than CNN-AE.

Architecture	MSE	Architecture	MSE
PCA ($n_\gamma = 4$)	0.648	AE ($n_\gamma = 4$)	**0.366**
PCA ($n_\gamma = 9$)	0.432	AE ($n_\gamma = 9$)	**0.269**
PCA ($n_\gamma = 18$)	0.293	AE ($n_\gamma = 18$)	**0.215**
-	-	HIER-AE ($n_{sub} = 2, n_\gamma = 18$)	0.232
PCA ($n_\gamma = 36$)	0.196	AE ($n_\gamma = 36$)	**0.169**
-	-	HIER-AE ($n_{sub} = 2, n_\gamma = 36$)	0.183
PCA ($n_\gamma = 72$)	**0.126**	AE ($n_\gamma = 72$)	0.145
-	-	HIER-AE ($n_{sub} = 2, n_\gamma = 72$)	0.145
-	-	HIER-AE ($n_{sub} = 4, n_\gamma = 72$)	0.157
PCA ($n_\gamma = 144$)	**0.080**	AE ($n_\gamma = 144$)	0.114

and a decoder network. The encoder maps the high dimensional input into a low dimensional representation (latent vector) in the latent space of dimension n_γ, and the decoder maps the latent vector back to the original high dimensional space in order to reconstruct the input. Researches have shown that by using a deep neural network with non-linear activation function as both encoder and decoder, AE is capable of capturing non-linear features of the input data.

3.1 Methods

We first look at a conventional CNN-based AE (CNN-AE). The structure of CNN-AE is shown in Table 2. We introduce 6 convolutional layers in the encoder, with a small kernel size of 3 × 3. Different from Ref. [1] where the number of kernels decrease as we go deeper in the network, here the number of channels is larger in deeper layers. This is designed to compensate for the information loss due to the max pooling layer. Meanwhile, as we go deeper, the receptive field gets larger so that the model can learn more complex features, and it is

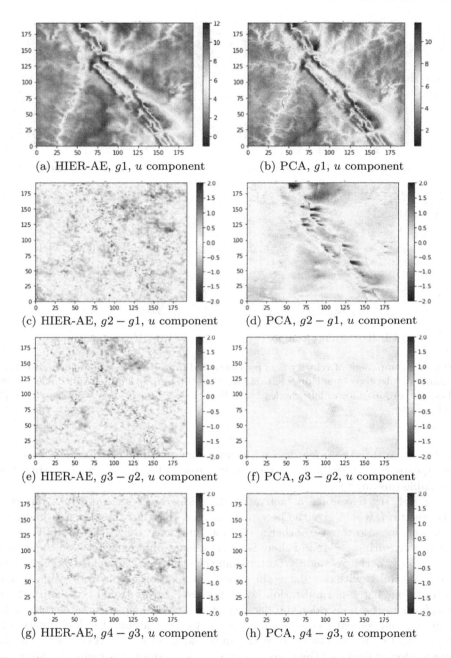

Fig. 7. First column (top to bottom): u component of velocity field reconstructed from HIER-AE with first, second, third, and fourth group of components of latent vectors. Each group has 18 components of latent vector. Second column (top to bottom): u component of velocity field reconstructed from PCA with modes 1–18, modes 19–36, modes 37–54 and modes 55–72.

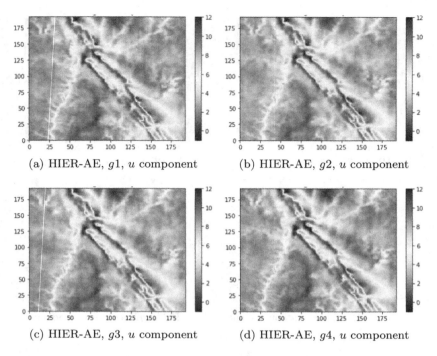

(a) HIER-AE, $g1$, u component   (b) HIER-AE, $g2$, u component

(c) HIER-AE, $g3$, u component   (d) HIER-AE, $g4$, u component

Fig. 8. u component of velocity field reconstructed from HIER-AE model with different number of latent vectors. Upper left: modes 1–18 (first group); upper right: modes 1–36 (first two groups); lower left: modes 1–54 (first three groups); lower right: modes 1–72 (all groups).

easier to capture those features with more channels. For the decoder, we use a *transposed* convolutional layer instead of upsampling layer, which enables the learnable upsampling.

In Ref. [1], five different activation functions are tested and it is reported that the *tanh* would give the best performance, as it has the best non-linearity. However, we also test two other activation functions: ReLU, LeakyReLU along with *tanh*, with $n_\gamma = 4$, and there is no significant difference between them, and LeakyReLU performs slightly better than the other two. Therefore, we choose to use LeakyReLU with $\alpha = 0.2$ as the activation function in this work. We also add in total four batch normalization layers between convolutional layer and activation layer for both encoder and decoder, which could help with accelerating the training, and reducing generalization error. In the training, the loss function is chosen to be the grid-average of the mean squared error (MSE) between the input velocity field and the decoder outputs. To perform the training, the training input data is prepared based on LES data [8] with two channels, u and v, which represent the wind speed along the x-axis and the y-axis, respectively. We then preprocess the data to remove those time frames which have "nan" in velocity field. After that we split the data into train/validation/test set with a ratio of 60%/20%/20%. Other important hyper parameters can be found in Table 3. In the training, we also introduce learning rate decay where the learning rate decays by a factor of two after 3500 epochs. This reduces the possibility that the model converges to a local minimum, while it keeps the training at a steady pace.

However, in contrast to PCA, where the order of eigenvalue represents the importance of each component of the latent vector, one disadvantage of this CNN-AE is the lack of *interpretability* of each component of the latent vector. Because of that we then look at a natural extension of AE called hierarchical autoencoder (HIER-AE) [2]. The HIER-AE can be defined recursively: It is composed of n sub networks. The first sub-network is the same as CNN-AE, and we first train that network the same way we train a CNN-AE. After the training of the first sub-network is finished, its encoder E_1 will capture the most important information of the original velocity field and transform that into the low dimensional representation γ_1. We then build the second network, where most of the architecture is identical to the first sub-network, with the exception that we will first concatenate γ_1 from the first sub-network with the low dimensional representation γ_2 generated from this second sub-network, and feed that into the decoder of the second sub-network. We then train the second sub-network while fixing the first sub-network. After the training of the second sub-network is finished, γ_2 should represent those most important features in the original velocity field that the first sub-network failed to capture. We then build the third sub-network, concatenate γ_1 and γ_2 from the first two sub-networks with γ_3 generated from the encoder of the third sub-network, and feed into the decoder of the third network. We then train the third sub-network while fixing the first two sub-networks. We continue this process until we go through all sub-networks, and $\gamma_1, \gamma_2, ..., \gamma_n$ are the low dimensional representation of the input velocity field, where initial γ should capture more important features.

In this work, we choose the number of sub-networks to be two/four, and instead of trying to interpret each component of the latent vector, we interpret each group of components of the latent vector (there are in total two/four groups). We need to mention that while in theory, the HIER-AE is capable of interpreting each individual component of the latent vector, it requires training a HIER-AE with n_γ sub-networks. This could take a substantial amount of computational time in this problem, as n_γ could be really huge ($O(100)$) if we want to reconstruct the velocity field with high quality.

3.2   Results

In this work we use PCA as a baseline of the performance. We compare PCA with CNN-AE and HIER-AE for several different values of n_γ and two values of number of sub-networks (two and four). The results are summarized in Table 4. As we can see, the performance of PCA is much worse than CNN-AE and HIER-AE when n_γ is small, but as we increase n_γ, the PCA becomes better. One possible reason is that the structure of CNN-AE and HIER-AE are fixed as we vary n_γ. However, as n_γ increases, the encoder network needs to extract more information from the data, which suggests that we need a larger network. However, when we try to increase the size of the channels of convolutional layers in the network, the performance on the training data decreases, while the performance on the validation data does not decrease, which suggests that we overfit the model. We propose to consider the correlation between the hyperparameter n_γ, which is the latent vector size, and $n_{\gamma,\text{phys}}$, which is the number of dominating modes encoded in the physics of the problem. On the one hand, when the actual n_γ used is less than $n_{\gamma,\text{phys}}$, AE may be better because of the non-linear properties. On the other hand, if the n_γ used is larger than $n_{\gamma,\text{phys}}$, the linear operations of the PCA may also yield good enough results by capturing the main features while the AE network may have overfitting problem. Therefore by evaluating the PCA and AE results, we can estimate the number of dominating modes and use it to guide our choice of either AE or PCA for dimension reductions. To further alleviate the effects of overfitting, we tried various regularization methods including adding L1/L2 regularization and adding dropout layers, but both make the performance even worse.

Another interesting observation is that despite HIER-AE gives us more interpretability, its performance is almost always worse than CNN-AE. One possible reason could be overfitting, as we find the training loss is always at least 16% lower than the validation loss which alludes to overfitting. This can be understood if we look at the parameters: With $n_\gamma = 72$, in CNN-AE, the number of trainable parameters is 264906, while in HIER-AE with four sub-networks, that number becomes 872784, about 3.3 times larger than the former one.

Another thing we can look at is the interpretability of the latent vector in HIER-AE. In Fig. 7 we plot the reconstruction results of the u-component of the velocity field from each group of components of latent vector, generated from HIER-AE with $n_\gamma = 72$ (that means each group includes 18 components of latent vector). The way we generate the ith plot is to reconstruct the velocity field with first $(i-1)$ group and first i group, and then compute their difference. We compare that with PCA reconstruction results, where we set $n_\gamma = 18, 36, 54$ and 72. The results show that 1). The first group encodes the most important features of velocity field, while the other three groups encode less important features. This shows the hierarchical nature of the model; 2). For latent vector in group 2–4, HIER-AE encodes more local features than PCA. The decoded latent vectors from HIER-AE and reconstructed modes from PCA are plotted in Fig. 7. By comparing these outputs from each group in pairs in Fig. 7, we find that both HIER-AE (left column) and PCA (right column) results have similar patterns which indicate consistent modes extracted in the process. Compared to PCA, HIER-AE results have more finer structure.

We now answer the questions proposed in the data challenge.

Comparison Between Standard Dimension Reduction Approach and Autoencoders: 1). PCA is a linear technique, while other deep learning techniques (for example, CNN-AE and HIER-AE) can be implemented using non-linear activation functions to capture non-linear features in the input data. 2). PCA does not involve any learning, while other deep learning models are *learnable*, which means the model parameters are learned from the input data.

Latent Space Interpretability: The latent space should encode the modes (important features) of the input data. For CNN-AE, we can not interpret each component of the latent vector separately, as they are trained at the same time. For HIER-AE, the group trained from earlier sub-network should encode more important modes (features) of the input data.

Regeneration of Full Grid: The second half of AE is the decoder. It serves the purpose of regenerating the full grid from the latent vector, which is the small, low-dimensional representation of the input data. It means that given a time series of latent vector obtained from the encoder network, we can regenerate a time series of the full grid. However, we need to remind the reader that in general, we can not regenerate a full grid that is identical to the initial input grid. This can be understood in terms of information loss: As long as the dimension of the latent vector is smaller than the dimension of input data, by encoding the input we lose some information, and that information can not be retrieved when we decode the latent vector.

Visual Insights from Latent Space: The decoded latent vectors are visualized in Fig. 7 and 8. From these two figures, we can see that 1). The first 18 modes can describe the most important features in the input data. 2). The next 54 modes obtained from HIER-AE encode more fine structures of the input data than those in PCA.

4   Up-Scaling from a Low-Resolution (LR) to High-Resolution (HR) Grid

We view the problem of up-scaling from a LR to HR grid as a single-image super-resolution(SR) problem [9]. Data from a specific time slice from Wind Flow Model Simulations, i.e. Large Eddy Simulation (LES) has the same structure as data describing images:

- pixels ↔ grid points
- RGB values to specify color ↔ horizontal components of the wind flow

In addition to a simple SR problem, we expect the HR grid obtained, reflects physical fine-scale details in order to provide physical insights. Therefore, we tackle the wind flow up-scaling problem using state-of-art single-image SR algorithm: generative adversarial networks (GAN). The application of GAN to the SR problem of the wind flow problem has been explored in [5]. In this work, we implemented and evaluated two models using CNN and GAN respectively. We would like also to explore and improve the model by examining and tuning the parameters.

4.1   Data and Methodology

In order to use the data for neural network training, we process the original wind flow data (ERA5) and Large Eddy Simulation (LES) data in the following way:

- Remove not-a-number (NAN) data in the data sets: there are NAN-data in the data sets. We first scan through the data set and identify the pattern where NAN data appears. Except for the data set "absolute height" which is irrelevant in our model, we find that the NAN pattern is consistent for all data in the same time slices. However, time slices with NAN for LR and HR data sets are different. Therefore, we remove the time slices with NAN (whether LR or HR data sets) for both LR and HR data sets to reserve the one-to-one mapping between the LR and HR data for all time slices without NAN values.
- Standardize the data sets for training: for input $\mathbf{x}$:

$$\mathbf{x}_{\text{std}} = \frac{\mathbf{x} - \langle \mathbf{x} \rangle}{\text{std.dev.}(\mathbf{x})}, \tag{1}$$

where $\langle ... \rangle$ and "std.dev." denotes the mean and standard deviation over the data sets.

GAN. A GAN usually consists of two components: In addition to a CNN generator G, a discriminator neural network D is introduced to enhance the performance of the generator to produce more physical data. The discriminator is trained to distinguish whether the HR grid obtained is real (physical) or not. The generator and discriminator are trained against each other, and the generator loss function is given in Eq. 2,

$$\mathcal{L}_G(\mathbf{x}, \mathbf{y}) = \mathcal{L}_{\text{content}}(\mathbf{x}, \mathbf{y}) + \alpha \mathcal{L}_{\text{adversarial}}(\mathbf{x}, \mathbf{y}), \tag{2}$$

where $\mathcal{L}_{\text{content}}(\mathbf{x}, \mathbf{y})$ is the content loss function defined as the pixel average of square difference between the HR image (y) and SR image (G(x)) generated from the corresponding LR image, as shown in Eq. 4

$$\mathcal{L}_{\text{content}}(\mathbf{x}, \mathbf{y}) = ||\mathbf{y} - G(\mathbf{x})||^2, \tag{3}$$

and $\mathcal{L}_{\text{adversarial}}$ is the adversarial loss introduced by the discriminator as shown in Eq. 4

$$\mathcal{L}_{\text{adversarial}}(\mathbf{x}, \mathbf{y}) = -\log(D(G(\mathbf{x}))), \tag{4}$$

and α is a tunable weighting factor. For simplicity, we use the mean-squared error (MSE) over all grids.

Generator Network. The Generator network includes two rounds of training. The first round is when the network is *pretrained*. The pretraining does not include the discriminator in order to give the generator a head-start. The aim of pretraining the generator is to teach the generator how to map from low-resolution (coarse data) to high-resolution output. The deep-CNN training is equivalent to our "pretraining" stage in GAN. Next we describe our deep *Generator* network architecture that we use for pretraining. We take inspiration from the work presented in [6].

We implement a deep CNN network with 16 residual blocks and "skip connections". The convolutional *kernels* are of size 3 with a *stride* of 1 and 64 *feature maps*. We use "ReLU" as the activation function in our model. The super-resolution is applied by including two CNN at the output of the residual blocks [10]. We use a resolution ratio of 2 between the output and input such that the super-resolved image has dimensions $2W \times 2H \times C$. Unlike the architecture presented in [6], we do not include batch normalization in the generator pretraining. We train the generator using *Adam* as the optimizer with learning rate = 1e−4, $\beta_1 = 0.9$, and $\beta_2 = 0.999$ and use only content loss as the loss function for 1000 epochs.

In our results shown in Table 6, we observe that the validation loss is higher than the training loss, hence there is over-fitting in our model. This can be fixed by tuning the hyperparameters of our model. For example, we can include kernel regularization (L2) with some learning rate, as well as include dropout regularization to our CNN layers. Another way to deal with this issue is to scale the dimensions of the image, which will increase the resolution and do the training on this scaled data set.

Discriminator Network. For the discriminator, we implement a deep CNN network with 8 residual blocks with discriminator loss function defined in Eq. 5,

$$\mathcal{L}_D(\mathbf{x}, \mathbf{y}) = -\langle [\log(D(\mathbf{y})) + \log(1 - D(G(\mathbf{x})))] \rangle, \tag{5}$$

where $\langle ... \rangle$ denotes the mean over samples. As shown in Table 5, while we also train the discriminator network using Adam as the optimizer function, the loss function converges faster than that of the generator network. We did some tuning over the learning rate and finally decide to use 4×10^{-5} as the learning rate for the discriminator. As we calculated the loss function, we also obtained the ratios of: true positive, true negative, false positive, and false negative. These values are evaluated along with the loss function in our analysis of the discriminator performance.

As mentioned in Ref. [5] that the GANs training procedure works best when the discriminator loss remains around 0.5, we also noticed that when the discriminator loss gets significantly lower than 0.5, the discriminator works so effectively that it becomes much harder for the generator to improve, and GANs training procedure yields no improvement compared to a single CNN generator.

GAN Training Steps. To make the GANs training procedure work efficiently by maintaining the balance between the generator and discriminator, in each GAN training step, we use an adaptive training scheme similar to the one used in [5] with some improvements:

- Firstly, we evaluate the generator network. If the discriminator loss is lower than 0.5, we need to enhance the generator because the generator works poorly in producing a physical grid. For such case, within the maximum generator training steps: 40, unless the discriminator loss gets larger than 0.5, we will continue training the generator while keeping the discriminator unchanged.
- Secondly, we evaluate the discriminator network. If the discriminator loss is larger than 0.65, we need to enhance the discriminator because the discriminator works poorly in distinguishing a real grid data and a generated data. For such case, within the maximum discriminator training steps: 40, unless the discriminator loss gets smaller than 0.65, we will continue training the discriminator while keeping the generator unchanged.

Table 5. Optimizer and learning rates used in our pretraining and GAN training procedure.

Neural network	Optimizer	Learning rate
Generator (CNN/GAN)	Adam	10^{-4}
Discriminator (GAN)	Adam	4×10^{-5}

The networks are trained using GPU-accelerated nodes with NVIDIA A100 Tensor Core GPUs based on the NVIDIA Ampere GPU architecture on Perlmutter cluster at National Energy Research Scientific Computing Center (NERSC). We pretrained the generator network for 1000 epochs through the 8520 training examples and saved the pretraining weights. At the beginning of the GAN, we loaded the pretraining weights and performed 300 epochs of GANs training.

For each epoch, we obtain outputs including generator loss, discriminator loss, generator training counts and discriminator training counts and using validation data sets to evaluate and monitor the performance of the current model. As shown in Table 6, the values of loss functions obtained from the validation data are very close to the training data which implies that there is no obvious overfitting problem in our training procedures.

Comparison Between GAN and CNN. First we compare the values of the full-generator loss function of GAN and the generator loss function of CNN using the test data set. As shown in Table 7, the value of CNN $\mathcal{L}_{G}$ (the content loss) is smaller than the generator content loss of GAN. This is within our expectation that the introduction of the discriminator will constrain the generator and a generator trained to yield physical grids may have higher content loss value than a simple CNN generator.

The ratios as benchmarks of the GAN model performance are evaluated using validation data set at several epoch and listed in Table 8. We find that the performance becomes stable after 230 epochs and the TP and TN rate stay

Table 6. The model evaluation outputs from epochs in the GANs training procedure, with training data and validation data.

Epoch index	Model evaluation outputs				
1	Training	$\mathcal{L}_G$	$\mathcal{L}_D$	n_g	n_d
		0.014066	0.633818	40	50
	Validation	$\mathcal{L}_G$	$\mathcal{L}_D$	$\mathcal{L}_{content}$	$\mathcal{L}_{adversarial}$
		0.013259	0.643441	0.012493	0.765912
151	Training	$\mathcal{L}_G$	$\mathcal{L}_D$	n_g	n_d
		0.012632	0.462197	65	40
	Validation	$\mathcal{L}_G$	$\mathcal{L}_D$	$\mathcal{L}_{content}$	$\mathcal{L}_{adversarial}$
		0.014685	0.483555	0.013467	1.218270
300	Training	$\mathcal{L}_G$	$\mathcal{L}_D$	n_g	n_d
		0.013175	0.466602	62	40
	Validation	$\mathcal{L}_G$	$\mathcal{L}_D$	$\mathcal{L}_{content}$	$\mathcal{L}_{adversarial}$
		0.015172	0.477748	0.013973	1.198851

Table 7. The loss function values from GAN and CNN. The CNN loss function value is obtained from the "pretrain" stage of GAN in the absence of a discriminator.

Loss function	GAN	CNN
$\mathcal{L}_{content}$	$\sim$0.014	$\sim$0.012

Table 8. The GAN model performance evaluated using validation data set.

Epoch index	True Positive	True Negative	False Positive	False Negative
1	0.63850	0.73357	0.26643	0.36150
151	0.73298	0.89554	0.10446	0.26702
300	0.79930	0.83392	0.16608	0.20070

reasonable, which indicates our training is successful. To further examine the difference between the CNN and GAN, on the one hand, we compare the super-resolution (SR) images generated by CNN and GAN with the original HR image. As shown in Fig. 9, for both u and v components, the GAN SR data yields more fine-scale details than the CNN SR data and the fine-scale details are consistent with the ground truth HR data.

On the other hand, we examine the kinetic energy spectra of images of LR, HR, and SR (both CNN and GAN) data fields as shown in Fig. 10. We use the HR data field as a reference for physical behavior. We find in Fig. 10 that for the low wavenumber k values, the LR kinetic energy spectrum is quite consistent with the HR spectrum while for wavenumber larger than $\sim$120, the LR spectrum deviates from the HR spectrum and has an obvious cutoff at wavenumber $\sim$150. From the

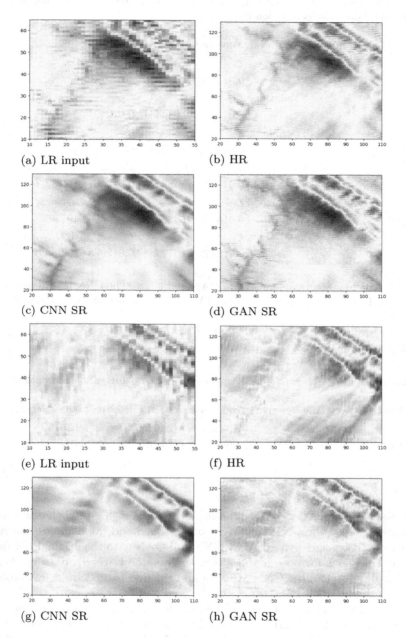

Fig. 9. (a–d) The u-component of the LES data and SR data generated by CNN and GAN. (e–h) The v-component of the LES data and SR data generated by CNN and GAN

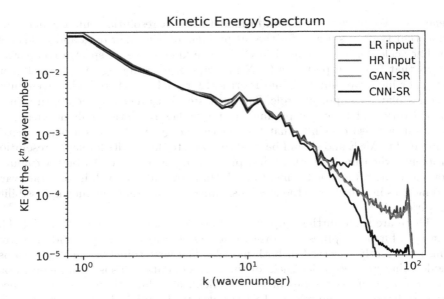

Fig. 10. The kinetic energy (KE) spectra for low-resolution, high-resolution data fields and super-resolution data fields obtained using CNN and GAN.

LR input, the CNN SR produce a smooth behavior similar to the HR spectrum in this window of wavenumber $\sim[120, 150]$ with a large discrepancy. In contrast, the GAN SR reproduce the HR spectrum behavior all through this wavenumber window with a very high precision. In the earlier paragraphs, we mention that the value of CNN $\mathcal{L}_\mathrm{G}$ (the content loss) is smaller than the generator content loss of GAN because the discriminator will constrain the generator and a generator trained to yield physical grids may have higher content loss value. Therefore, when comparing CNN and GAN SR in our case, in addition to the generator loss based on MSE, the kinetic energy is an ideal metric to check quantitatively the physical quality of the SR data fields. Here our data shows that the GAN SR reproduces HR physical features as expected.

5   Conclusion and Outlook

In this work, we first perform dimension reduction with two autoencoder models: The CNN-AE, and HIER-AE, and compare their performance with PCA. We find that the autoencoder models perform better when n_γ is small, and become worse than PCA when n_γ gets larger. We also look at the interpretability of the latent vector obtained from HIER-AE, and find that unlike CNN-AE, the HIER-AE is capable of interpreting the latent vector by introducing some hierarchy when generating different components of the latent vector.

We then perform single-image super-resolution using SRCNN and SRGAN. The SRCNN trains a deep CNN model, which is later fine tuned in GAN as the generator. We obtained a generator model with 2× resolution enhancement, and show that GAN is suitable for the SR problem of wind flow data and yields better fine-scale details compared to CNN. The kinetic energy spectra comparison shows that GAN outperforms CNN in terms of reproducing the physical properties for high wavenumbers and is critical for analysis where high wavenumber kinetics play an important role. The next step is to increase the depth of neural network and tune the parameters for higher resolution enhancements. In addition, we also conclude that the kinetic energy spectrum is a better metric compared to MSE and should be used to evaluate the results for super-resolution problems when fine structures also play an important role. To better evaluate how close the SR grid is to the physical wind flow data, we will incorporate various metrics in addition to the MSE loss function, including the incompressibility conditions.

There are some further improvements that we can make on our model: The first is to further suppress the overfitting. As described in Sect. 3 and 4, overfitting is currently observed in both models. The next thing we can try is to use models that are better designed for timeseries of data. This is because our input data are actually timeseries of velocity field, and data at different time slices are correlated. For example, an LSTM-autoencoder might be a better model for dimension reduction, and we can use some ideas from video super resolution to perform SR for velocity field.

Acknowledgements. This work was supported by Brookhaven National Laboratory, which is operated and managed for the U.S. Department of Energy Office of Science by Brookhaven Science Associates under contract No. DE-SC0012704. This research used resources of the National Energy Research Scientific Computing Center (NERSC), a U.S. Department of Energy Office of Science User Facility located at Lawrence Berkeley National Laboratory, operated under Contract No. DE-AC02-05CH11231.

A   Appendix

Open-source code and visualizations can be accessed via the Github page: https://github.com/GKNB/data-challenge-2022.

References

1. Murata, T., Fukami, K., Fukagata, K.: Nonlinear mode decomposition with convolutional neural networks for fluid dynamics. J. Fluid Mech. **882**, A13 (2020)
2. Fukami, K., Nakamura, T., Fukagata, K.: Convolutional neural network based hierarchical autoencoder for nonlinear mode decomposition of fluid field data. Phys. Fluids **32**(9), 095110 (2020)
3. Milano, M., Koumoutsakos, P.: Neural network modeling for near wall turbulent flow. J. Comput. Phys. **182**(1), 1–26 (2002)
4. Kim, H., Kim, J., Won, S., Lee, C.: Unsupervised deep learning for super-resolution reconstruction of turbulence. J. Fluid Mech. **910**, A29 (2021)

5. Stengel, K., Glaws, A., Hettinger, D., King, R.N.: Adversarial super-resolution of climatological wind and solar data. Proc. Natl. Acad. Sci. **117**(29), 16805–16815 (2020)

6. Ledig, C.: Photo-realistic single image super-resolution using a generative adversarial network (2016)

7. Hersbach, H.: ERA5 hourly data on single levels from 1979 to present. Copernicus climate change service (C3S) climate data store (CDS). https://doi.ccs.ornl.gov/ui/doi/385. Accessed 05 Apr 2022

8. Data source. https://doi.ccs.ornl.gov/ui/doi/385

9. Yang, C.-Y., Ma, C., Yang, M.-H.: Single-image super-resolution: a benchmark. In: Fleet, D., Pajdla, T., Schiele, B., Tuytelaars, T. (eds.) ECCV 2014. LNCS, vol. 8692, pp. 372–386. Springer, Cham (2014). https://doi.org/10.1007/978-3-319-10593-2_25

10. Shi, W., et al.: Real-time single image and video super-resolution using an efficient sub-pixel convolutional neural network. In: 2016 IEEE Conference on Computer Vision and Pattern Recognition (CVPR), pp. 1874–1883 (2016)

Investigating Relationships in Environmental and Community Health: Correlations of Environment, Urban Morphology, and Socio-economic Factors in the Los Angeles Metropolitan Statistical Area

Eyrin Kim[✉]

Farragut High School, Farragut, TN 37934, USA
S931665@student.knoxschoools.org

Abstract. Environmental characteristics, urban morphologies, and socio-economic factors co-evolve as urban areas grow. Investigating the interactions between these components is important as they directly impact community health and city sustainability. This research examines correlations among building density, temperature distribution, and socio-economic composition within an urban setting. The research is conducted as a case study of the Los Angeles Metropolitan Statistical Area (LAMSA). The results demonstrate that varying degrees of correlations exist among the LAMSA's built urban environment, natural environment, and demographic composition. Further, the incorporation of community health data underscores marginalized groups that may potentially experience disproportionate effects of evolving climactic events. Finally, as the general framework of analysis can be applied to other cities, this research provides a set of steps in understanding the connections among these domains to shift towards more sustainable urban futures.

Keywords: Community health, · Urban morphology, · Socio-economic factors

1 Introduction

In urbanized areas, built environment factors, natural environment factors, socio-economic variables, and infrastructural systems interact with one another to lay the foundational network of a region. These interactions are critical in determining the resilience and overall health of a community [16]. However, variances among environmental, socio-economic, and infrastructural compositions create nuanced differences in the strengths (and by extension, vulnerability) of regions [17]. Hence, the purpose of this research is to investigate the relationships between key factors- such as the density of buildings, heat distributions, and regional demographics- and examine their impact on the sustainability of a city, especially as interactions among these facets are still being understood [22]. To support the analyses, various geo-processes were performed using commercial GIS software.

K. Doug et al. (Eds.): SMC 2022, CCIS 1690, pp. 366–383, 2022.
https://doi.org/10.1007/978-3-031-23606-8_23

1.1 Case Study Area

The case study area for this research is defined as the Los Angeles Metropolitan Statistical Area (LAMSA). This region, consisting of Los Angeles, Long Beach, Anaheim, and the California Metropolitan Area, is particularly vulnerable to extreme heat and droughts. The Los Angeles area is expected to have 37 extreme heat days annually; in addition, the presence of an urban heat island has resulted in an up-to nineteen degrees Fahrenheit temperature difference between urban and non-urban areas [15]. The LAMSA is also one of the largest metropolitan regions in the United States, with a population of over 13 million residents that are 70.8% either Hispanic and/or of color [1]. As a result, the LAMSA was a suitable region to investigate in terms of correlations between morphological characteristics, demographic distributions, and environmental patterns. In consideration of the scale of the LAMSA and the consistency of the datasets, point-based data (building information, temperatures) and image data (land cover types) were adjusted to a tract level.

1.2 Data Sources

The data used in this study falls into three categories: built environment (morphological characteristics of buildings), natural environment (annual daytime/nighttime temperatures, land use), and socio-economic (demographics). An additional variable, the uninsured population of Los Angeles County, was investigated to answer an extended challenge question. Figure 1 displays the datasets of (1) U.S. Census tracts, (2) buildings, (3) temperatures, and (4) land cover uses in a portion of downtown Los Angeles.

Data regarding socio-economic factors was obtained from the 2020 U.S. Census [2] and given in tract units ($n = 2,971$). The U.S. Census Bureau also provided state-based Metropolitan and Micropolitan Statistical area maps, which were used to inspect variables visually [3]. In addition, Oak Ridge National Laboratory, the Department of Energy (DOE), and other partners made available building data of Los Angeles and its surrounding areas [4]. Building archetypes were primarily used to classify building use type while Los Angeles Urban Parameters were utilized to derive building dimensions (building areas, heights, and densities by tract). With respect to the environmental aspect of this research, temperature data for the year of 2020 was provided by the Moderate Resolution Imaging Spectroradiometer (MODIS) Land Surface Temperature dataset [5]. Information regarding classification by land use was derived from the National Land Cover Database (NLCD) [6, 7]. Finally, to analyze community health, uninsured population data was obtained from a public Los Angeles data portal [8].

2 Methodology

The data sources used in this study were aggregated on a tract level and created as a set of GIS files via the *spatial join* process. This aggregation facilitated the integration of key socio-economic information available on the tract scale into the research [2]. Most variables were also logarithmically transformed during pre-analysis to correct skewness [9]. To drive statistically significant impressions, correlation analysis, multivariate

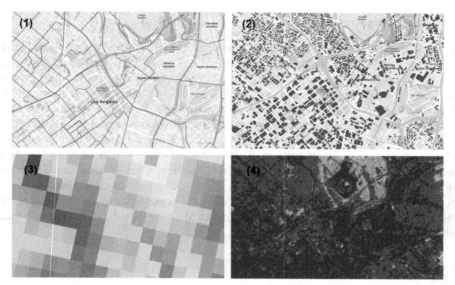

Fig. 1. Data used for analysis: (1) Tract data from the U.S. Census, (2) Building data from ORNL and DOE, (3) Annual temperature data from MODIS LST datasets, (4) Land cover usage data from NLCD.

regression, and clustering methods were conducted using *Excel Data Analysis tools* and *ArcGIS Pro* online.

As a note for clarity regarding the analysis, this study investigates four selected challenge questions from the 2022 SMC Data Challenge and integrates an extended question that derives public health implications with the provided datasets (Fig. 2).

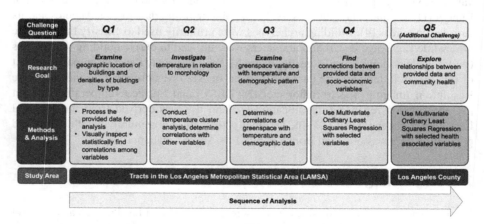

Fig. 2. Sequence of analysis: data challenge questions 1–5.

Q1. What is the distribution of commercial, industrial, and residential buildings within each geographic location? Do these distributions correlate with density of building size & volume by tract in LAMSA?

This challenge question centered around the distribution of commercial, industrial, and residential buildings and their correlation with building factors. The first step in addressing this question was to aggregate individual building data to match Census tract levels. To achieve this, the area of each building was multiplied by its height, determining building volume. Then, the resulting values were summed by tract and divided by the area of the tract to calculate building density.

Similarly, NLCD data was aggregated after converting the image data into a point layer using the *raster to point* tool in ArcGIS. This data was initially categorized into 17 land use type classes [6, 7]. However, for a more effective analysis, these classes were regrouped into six major categories that appropriately suited the composition of the LAMSA: water-dominated area, developed open space, developed area with low to intermediate density, developed area with high density, forest greenspace, and general greenspace (Table 1). Analyses were conducted to determine the correlation r between the building density per tract (by are), building density per tract (by volume), density of residential area per tract, and density of commercial/industrial area per tract. Building density values were evaluated from both an area perspective and a volume (area $\times$ height) perspective as it was predicted that the quantity of multi-story buildings in a metropolitan region like Los Angeles could cause significant differences between the two parameters.

Table 1. Summary of the classifications of land cover uses and their prevalence.

Class	Description	# of cells (%)
Water	Areas of open water	27,010 (0.54%)
Developed, open space	Some constructed materials but mostly vegetation Detached housing units, golf courses, parks	362,249 (7.17%)
Developed, low to intermediate intensity	Constructed materials and vegetation, single family housing units	3,132,449 (62.02%)
Developed, high intensity	Highly developed areas, commercial/residential buildings, apartment complexes	999,724 (19.79%)
Forest Greenspace	Deciduous, Evergreen, or mixed forest	28,375 (0.56%)
General Greenspace	Shrubs, grasslands, cultivated lands, wetlands	500,900 (9.92%)

Q2. *Using temperature data from a source of the participant's choosing, are there locations within the city that tend to be warmer than others? How does this relate to building density and building type?*

First, two temperature datasets (2020 annual daytime and nighttime median temperature data) were procured from the Moderate Resolution Imaging Spectroradiometer Land Surface Temperature (MODIS LST) database [5]. The MODIS LST data used in this study were collected four times a day at spatial resolutions of 1 km, then composited over an eight-day period to reduce internal noise [18–20]. The datasets were also converted to discrete observations via geoprocessing. Lastly, LST temperature values were converted to Fahrenheit using the Python command below (the conversion formula was derived from the LP DAAC2Disk guideline) [10].

$$Fahrenheit\ conversion\ from\ LST\ =\ \{LST*0.02-273.15\}*9/5+32. \quad (1)$$

The *Optimized Hot Spot Analysis* tool was then used to investigate statistically significant clusters of warmer areas in the LAMSA. This tool categorizes data (in this case, tracts) into three groups (hotspot/coldspot/insignificant) using *Getis-Ord Gi** statistics. Given a set distance band, the *Getis-Ord Gi** function minimizes variance within a particular group while maximizing variances between groups (please refer to references [11] and [21] for detailed equations and information about the *Getis-Ord Gi** tool in GIS) [11, 21]. Therefore, the tool isolates clusters if there are prominent changes in variable values within a defined region. Additionally, descriptive statistical values (max, min, average, and difference) of daytime and nighttime temperatures were determined, as seen in Table A-3. Given these characteristics, hotspots- areas of significantly high temperature- and coldspots- areas of significantly low temperature- at 95% or 99% of significance levels were delineated.

Finally, correlations among pairs of variables were calculated to investigate any potentially pronounced relationships. These variables were: average daytime temperature (*daytemp*), average nighttime temperature (*nighttemp*), the density by building area (*DensityA*, given in square kilometers) and building volume (*DensityV*), the density of residential area per tract (*DenResi*), and the density of commercial/industrial area per tract (*DenComin*).

Q3. *Using the included land use data, how does greenspace vary with urban temperature and demographic distribution?*

Greenspace data was categorized into two types: general greenspace and forest greenspace (see Table 1). This was because the broader groups within the Anderson Classification System distinguishes forest land cover from rangeland and wetland [7]. Even with these distinctions, however, an overarching 'general greenspace' variable (all greenspace values combined) was tested for correlation as well. To remove extreme skewness of variables for analysis, tracts from the datasets with zero greenspace and their corresponding temperature values were not considered. Finally, three demographic variables were used to investigate covariation with greenspace: population (*Pop*), the number of households (*Household*), and median household income (*HH_Median*).

***Q4.** Using demographic data from a source of the participant's choosing, how does the built environment and the local scale experience of heat co-vary with socio-economic and demographic characteristics of residents?*

To determine if the local scale heat distribution and built environment correlated with the socio-economic attributes of LAMSA residents, demographic variables taken from the 2020 U.S. Census [2] were juxtaposed against average temperatures (*Avgtemp*) and density by building area (*DensityA*).

Multivariate OLS regression was conducted for two sets of models relevant to the challenge question using the Exploratory Regression tool (see Table 2). This tool identifies the model that best explains a specified dependent variable. A key consideration in building the best fit model is avoiding multicollinearity between the explanatory variables; hence, many iterations of model are constructed until the best set of explanatory variables have been selected [9].

Table 2. Summary of variables chosen for the multivariate regression models.

Dependent variables	Socio-economic factors (8)*
Model 1: *Avgtemp* Model 2: *DensityA*	Socio-economic: Median Household Income (*HH_Median*), the number of Households (*Household*), Population (*Pop*), Median Age (*MedAge*) Race: Hispanic, White, Black, Asian**

* Log-transformed variables for socio-economic factors were also tested. ** See Fig. A-1 in the Appendix for a display of the pattern of race variables and the correlation coefficients of each model.

***Q5.** The health of a community is closely linked to the built environment of a region. One variable that is strongly representative of the health of the community is health insurance. In terms of community health disparities, what socio-economic, morphological, or land use related factors correlate with the uninsured population of LA County?*

According to the 2020 U.S. Census, 7.3% of Californian residents lack health insurance [12]. This statistic doubles in Los Angeles County (where nearly 15% of residents are currently uninsured), highlighting a potential healthcare disparity. Further, residents lacking health insurance are particularly vulnerable to health conditions impacted by the built environment, socio-economic factors, and land use as they are significantly less likely to receive essential medical treatments and checkups [13]. Addressing these barriers is key to expanding healthcare access [14]; thus, it is important to investigate if there exist certain critical factors that help predict the uninsured population of an area. Multivariate OLS regression was conducted for the rate of uninsured population by tract (*Uninsured*) [8] 16 selected socio-economic variables were prepared for the study area of County of Los Angeles (See Table A-1 in the Appendix to see a complete list of variables).

3   Results and Impressions

For the purposes of this analysis, a correlation coefficient of $r \approx 0.6$ or greater was considered noteworthy as it is usually an acceptable indicator of a strong relationship when socio-economic variables are involved in calculations [9]. However, it is worth noting that only a few correlation coefficients were very high. For multivariate Ordinary Least Squares (OLS) regression models, only the best fit models from the model specifications were reported.

Analysis of Q1. What is the distribution of commercial, industrial, and residential buildings within each geographic location? Do these distributions correlate with density of building size & volume by tract in LAMSA?

As illustrated in Fig. 3-(1), the density of buildings is concentrated in the center of the LAMSA. This trend was demonstrated less clearly in Fig. 3-(2). Both the density of residential areas (*DenResi*, Fig. 3-(3)) and commercial/industrial areas (*DenComin*, Fig. 3-(4)) appear to have a similar pattern; however, nuanced differences exist within the two distributions. The distribution of building densities (*DensityA* and *DensityV*) and *DenResi* also seemed to have a relationship, albeit not as pronounced. Finally, the density by building volume per tract (*DensityV*) did not noticeably correlate with land use data.

To examine these relationships statistically, correlations were calculated across *DensityA*, *DensityV*, log transformed *DenResi* (*LgDenResi*), and log transformed *DenComin* (*LgDenComin*) [The latter two variables were logarithmically transformed to correct for skewness of the dataset]. The most notable correlation was found in the relationship between density by building area and density of commercial/industrial areas ($r = 0.592$) (see Table A-2). This suggests that regions with a prominent quantity of commercial/industrial buildings likely also have a greater area of buildings per land area. Note that the correlation between density of commercial areas and density by building area is low ($r = 0.148$), confirming that their distributions differ significantly. This may not have been apparent upon visual inspection of Fig. 3.

Analysis of Q2. Using temperature data from a source of the participant's choosing, are there locations within the city that tend to be warmer than others? How does this relate to building density and building type?

Figure 4 displays the distribution of annual temperatures in the LAMSA (including log transformed data to account for skewness in the original dataset). Initial visual analysis suggested that there was little difference in the pattern between original temperature values and log-transformed temperature values. However, it is clearly shown that there are significant spatial differences in daytime and nighttime hotspot temperatures (see Fig. 5-(1) and (3)). For example, while daytime temperatures are hottest in the center of the region, nighttime temperatures are hottest in the outskirts.

Figure 4-(1), the daytime temperature map identified major hotspots of intense heat areas in the northwestern, northeastern, and central regions of the LAMSA. These hotspots correlate to (a) the central city, Los Angeles, (b) densely populated residential

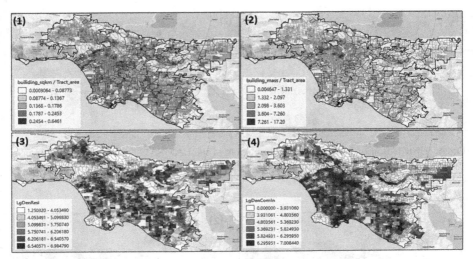

Fig. 3. Distribution of (1) Density by building area per tract (*DensityA*), (2) Density by building volume per tract (*DensityV*), (3) Density of residential area per tract (Log transformed; *LgDenResi*), (4) Density of commercial/industrial area per tract (Log transformed; *LgDenComin*).

tracts in the northwest, and (c) large industrial tracts in northeast. As a result, it can be concluded that significantly dense areas (residual, downtown, and industrial/commercial) experience greater daytime heat than the remainder of the LAMSA.

In Fig. 4-(2), the nighttime map displays major clusters of high nighttime temperature regions in the northwestern, northeastern, and southeastern corners of the LAMSA. There is also a small cluster on a coastal pocket, which geographically approximates to the city of Long Beach (d). However, despite its urbanity, the city of Los Angeles was outlined as a 'coldspot' during the night.

Other factors that may have influenced temperature distribution include nearness to the ocean and population activity. For instance, Fig. 4-(1) displays that coastal areas are likely to be coldspots during the day, and while the presence of coldspots spreads inwards during the night, areas with high human activity (Region D) and industrial areas (Region C) retain heat. Hence, more population-active areas may experience less temperature variability.

As presented in Fig. 3 and 5, initial visual analysis suggested that there may be notable correlations between *DensityComin* and annual daytime temperatures (*Avgtemp*). However, when calculated, all correlations between temperature and building density/area classification were insignificant (see Table A-4). Thus, it can be concluded that there exists no particular relationship between the temperature of a tract and its urban composition in context of the data used in this particular analysis.

Analysis of Q3. *Using the included land use data, how does greenspace vary with urban temperature and demographic distribution?*

General greenspace and forest greenspace areas are found in the outskirts of the LAMSA as mapped in Fig. 6-(1) and 6-(2), respectively. Two demographic variables,

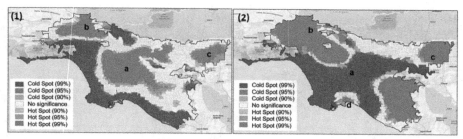

Fig. 4. Distribution of hot/cold temperature spots in the LAMSA: (1) Annual daytime temperature, (2) Annual nighttime temperature (Red: Hot temperature cluster, Blue: Cold temperature cluster).

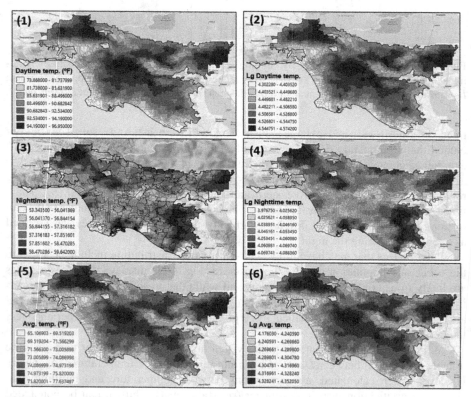

Fig. 5. Spatial distribution of annually averaged daytime/nighttime temperatures: (1) Daytime, (2) Log-transformed Daytime, (3) Nighttime, (4) Log-transformed Nighttime, (5) Average temperature, (6) Log-transformed Average temperature.

population by tract (*LgPop*) [Fig. 6-(3)] and household median income (*HH_Median*) [Fig. 6-(4)], were selected for analysis with greenspace. [Note: Median household data was not log transformed as it displayed little to no skewness]. Maps from Fig. 6 indicate that most of the greenspace in the LAMSA lays near the edges of the region while maps from Fig. 3 indicate that density by building area is highest in the center of the region. These variables possessed a statistically significant correlation ($r = 0.659$), as seen in Table 3. A modestly strong correlation was present for density by building area and household median income ($r = 0.519$). In addition, the density by building area and general greenspace presented a significant negative correlation ($r = 0.659$). Intuitively, this follows reason as less buildings would likely be found in a region with more greenspace. However, the density of forest greenspace (*FGreens*) and other variables had no notable correlations, implying that forest coverage is a less relevant aspect of greenspace in the LAMSA. Finally, average temperature values presented a slight negative relationship with median household income values ($r = 0.510$) and weak but potentially inverse correlation with greenspace area ($r = 0.327$).

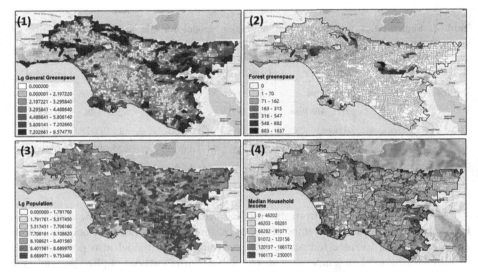

Fig. 6. Distribution of (1) Log-transformed general greenspace, (2) Forest greenspace, (3) Log-transformed Population, and (4) Median Household Income.

Analysis to Q4. Using demographic data from a source of the participant's choosing, how does the built environment and the local scale experience of heat co-vary with socio-economic and demographic characteristics of residents?

Multivariate OLS regression was performed for a total of nine variables to explain *Avgtemp* (Model 1) and *DensityA* (Model 2). The best fitting model is formulated below, and all coefficients of the variables were tested based on t-statistics at $p < 0.05$. The best-fit Model 1 consists of four variables: median household income, number of households, Hispanic population, and Asian population. As summarized in Table 4, the multiple correlation r for this was 0.633. However, the *Adjusted* r^2 was 0.401 (model F-test significance $p < 0.0001$), indicating that covariation with temperature may not be as strong as the r value suggests.

Table 3. Correlations among selected variables to investigate $Q3$.

Variables	Avgtemp	LgGreens	DensityA	LgPop	HH_Median	FGreens
Avgtemp	1.000					
LgGreens	**–0.327**	1.000				
DensityA	0.112	**–0.659**	1.000			
LgPop	0.073	0.0162	0.041	1.000		
HH_Median	**–0.510**	**0.519**	–0.358	–0.068	1.000	
FGreens	–0.254	–0.042	–0.336	–0.150	0.007	1.000

Note: Variables that were not logarithmically transformed were kept in their original formats as they had more significant r values than their log-transformed counterparts

Table 4. Summary of the multivariate regression model for the Model 1: Correlation of demographics with annual average temperature.

Results	Variables	Coefficients	Std. Error	t- Stat	p-value
Multiple $r = 0.633$ Adjusted $r^2 = 0.401$	Intercept	75.47	0.115	654.8361	0.000
	HH_Median	–0.000018	0.000	–20.2338	0.000
	Asian	0.0004	0.000	11.20478	0.000
	Hispanic	0.0005	0.000	22.9094	0.000
	Household	–0.0009	0.000	–16.2547	0.000

An important takeaway from this model is that the median household income is inversely related to average temperature, indicating that more affluent neighborhoods experience lower average temperatures. Interestingly, this model also possesses two racial factors to explain temperature distributions (initial analysis implied that only the Hispanic population had significant ties to other variables). Thus, it is possible that these two races are commonly patterned in less favorable health environments with high heat exposure. This is important as LAMSA uniquely hosts high Hispanic and Asian populations (50% and 16%, respectively [2]).

For Model 2 (dependent variable: *DensityA*), Table 5 shows that the best model consists of the same variables in the Model 1. The multiple r is decent; however, the *Adjusted r^2* is only 0.164, implying that building morphology in the LAMSA is not keenly reflected by socio-economic variables. The impression concurred with the results in the answers of $Q1$ and $Q3$.

Analysis to Q5. The health of a community is closely linked to the built environment of a region. One variable that is strongly representative of the health of the community is health insurance. In terms of community health disparities, what socio-economic,

Table 5. Summary of the multivariate regression model for the Model 2: Correlation of demographics with building density.

Results	Variables	Coefficients	Std. Error	t- Stat	p-value
Multiple r = 0.405	*Intercept*	0.178562	0.0033	54.3353	0.0000
Adjusted r² = 0.164	*HH_Median*	−0.000001	0.0000	−22.4993	0.0000
	Asian	−0.000005	0.0000	−4.8846	0.0000
	Hispanic	−0.000005	0.0000	−7.6105	0.0000
	Household	0.000017	0.0000	10.6623	0.0000

morphological, or land use related factors correlate with the uninsured population of LA County?

Exploratory analysis began by examining correlations among variables listed in Table A-5. [As uninsured population data was limited to the LA county borders, the original variables used in this study were focused to match this area. Thus, conclusions for this challenge question may differ from those in previous questions]. The variables median household income, daytime temperature, Hispanic population, and log-transformed residential area were selected as the best fit model (Table 6). The model produced both a significant multiple r (0.711) and significant *Adjusted r²* (0.504). The model also has a minute significant F-value ($p < 0.0001$), attesting to its validity.

Table 6. Summary of the multivariate regression model for the uninsured population.

Results	Variables	Coefficients	Std. Error	t- Stat	p-value
Multiple	*Intercept*	0.01379	0.02348	0.587	0.5571
r = 0.711	*HH_Median*	0.00000	0.00000	−11.675	0.0000
Adjusted r² = 0.504	*Daytemp*	0.00110	0.00025	4.342	0.0000
	Hispanic	0.00001	0.00000	18.627	0.0000
	Log Residential	−0.00697	0.00041	−17.020	0.0000

In detail, Fig. 7 confirms how the patterns between the uninsured population of a tract and each explanatory variable chosen in the Model 2 covary. The more a tract reflects the upper right corner color of the map legend, the more highly positively correlated the two variables are within the tract. The Hispanic population distribution has a positive relationship with uninsured population distribution, signifying that areas with a greater uninsured population (e.g., the center and north of LA county) are likely to also have larger Hispanic concentrations.

Daytime temperature was also positively patterned with the uninsured population. Though the results do not provide a direct interpretation, previous results demonstrate that locations with high urban temperatures and high Hispanic populations are positively

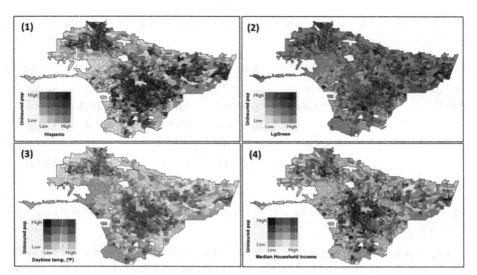

Fig. 7. Multivariate correlations of variables to uninsured population: (1) Hispanic (+), (2) Log Residential Area (–), (3) Daytime temperature (+), and (4) Median Household Income (–).

correlated. Thus, a further investigation of the correlations between temperature hotspots and ethnic clusters should be conducted to investigate the issue of equitable community health in the LA county.

4   Conclusions and Future Research

The answers to the five selected challenge questions provide important information regarding the relationships between built environment, temperature patterns, and socio-economic characteristics. No extremely prominent statistical relationships were determined between variables in the LAMSA, but the modest correlations that were found suggest that there may be a model that better explains the connections between the three domains. Nevertheless, this research is meaningful as it takes exploratory steps in further understanding the complex interactions among these facets. For instance, this analysis demonstrates that the LAMSA is clearly clustered regarding temperature, but variations in clustering between daytime and nighttime values indicate that deviations of correlations may exist across variables. Further, results reflect that the distribution of commercial/industrial buildings has a modest correlation with overall density by building area, hinting towards the potential existence of a relationship between land use type and building density. Finally, this study attempts to identify explanatory variables for the regional uninsured population as a representation of community health. Multiple regression models enable the conclusion that urban temperatures may be affected by racial distribution and median household income. In terms of policy applications, this finding could recommend that key socio-economic variables be considered more heavily when developing legislation that addresses barriers to healthcare access as prescribed in the analysis.

Future research should consider incorporating a wider range of variables into this case study or changing the scope of the analysis. For instance, commercial building data and industrial building data could be distinguished for comparison on a microscale. The framework of analysis in this research could be replicated to analyze other cities as well; in fact, this research is limited in that the geographic extent of the analysis depends on the margins of the tested region. Interestingly, when correlation analysis was conducted between building area density and the density of commercial/industrial areas, the r value of LA County was slightly greater than that of the LAMSA ($r = 0.591$ and $r = 0.617$, respectively). In addition, as implied in Table A-6, the range of temperatures varied depending on the extent of study areas (note that the temperature range of the LA county is slightly greater than the LAMSA), which may alter modeling processes. Since these discrepancies imply that even small alterations in geographic boundaries during analyses could invalidate results, it will be important to explore locational differences in the future as well. Finally, this research reflects a specific time frame. However, results indicate that extended research is necessary as the impact of variables can gradually manifest and alter (Table A-7).

Appendix

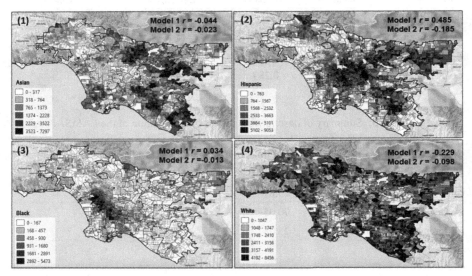

Fig. A-1. Distribution by race (1) Asian, (2) Hispanic, (3) Black, (4) White; The coefficients r to the dependent variable of Model 1 and 2 is presented in each Figure.

Table A-1. Summary of variables for multivariate OLS regression model ($n = 2,315$ tracts).

Model	Socio-economic (5)*	Built environment (7)*	Environment* (2)
Rate of Uninsured population *(Uninsured)***	Median Income Hispanic White Black Asian	Density of buildings (Area) Density of buildings (Volume) Water area Residential area Commercial/Industrial area Greenspace (General) Greenspace (Forest)	*Daytemp* *Nighttemp*

Note: *All variables were tested in their log-transformed or original variable formats. The listed variables above were determined to be the most effective set of independent variables.
** To fix the skewness of original variable (uninsured population by tract), the variable is calculated as rate to generate a more reliable statistical result.

Table A-2. Correlation matrix among four variables.

Variables	*DensityA*	*DensityV*	*LgDenResi*	*LgDenComin*
DensityA	1			
DensityV	0.557	1		
LgDenResi	0.170	− 0.224	1	
LgDenComin	0.592	0.289	0.148	1

Table A-3. Summary of descriptive statistics of temperature of the LAMSA.

Statistics	Daytime temp.	Nighttime temp.
max	96.95	59.64
min	73.87	53.34
average	90.65	57.39
Difference (max-min)	23.08	6.30

Table A-4. Complete correlation matrix for Q2.

	Daytime	Nighttime	Avgtemp	LgDaytemp	LgNightemp	LgAvgtemp	DensityA	DensityV	LgDenResi	LgDenComin
Daytime	1.000									
Nighttime	0.216	1.000								
Avgtemp	0.983	0.390	1.000							
LgDaytemp	0.999	0.219	0.983	1.000						
LgNightemp	0.217	1.000	0.391	0.220	1.000					
LgAvgtemp	0.983	0.389	1.000	0.984	0.389	1.000				
DensityA	0.108	0.067	0.115	0.108	0.068	0.114	1.000			
DensityV	−0.077	0.190	−0.037	−0.076	0.188	−0.038	0.558	1.000		
LgDenResi	0.268	−0.036	0.246	0.267	−0.034	0.247	0.180	−0.21	1.000	
LgDenComin	0.186	0.098	0.193	0.184	0.099	0.193	0.569	0.284	0.166	1.000

Table A-5. Complete correlation matrix for extended Q5.

	daytime	nighttime_	DensityA	DensityV	LgDenComin	LgDenResi	LgNightemp	LgDaytemp
daytime	1.0000							
nighttime	0.2260	1.0000						
DensityA	0.0964	0.1075	1.0000					
DensityV	−0.1007	0.2519	0.5497	1.0000				
LgDenComin	0.2189	0.1133	0.6175	0.2807	1.0000			
LgDenResi	0.2897	−0.0976	0.1294	−0.2450	0.1519	1.0000		
LgNightemp	0.2272	0.9999	0.1083	0.2501	0.1143	−0.095	1.0000	
LgDaytemp	0.9995	0.2302	0.0967	−0.0987	0.2179	0.2895	0.2314	1.0000

Table A-6. Summary of descriptive statistics of temperatures of the LA County.

Statistics	Daytime temp	Nighttime temp
Max	97.04	59.60
Mean	90.82	57.34
Min	73.90	53.32
Range (Max-Min)	24.94	6.28

Table A-7. Summary of descriptive statistics of temperatures of coldspot and hotspot clusters by daytime and nighttime.

Statistics	Daytime			Nighttime		
	Coldspot Cluster (C)	Hotspot Cluster (D)	Range (D-C)	Coldspot Cluster (E)	Hotspot Cluster (F)	Range (F-E)
Max (A)	90.38	96.95	6.57	58.43	59.64	1.21
Mean	85.10	93.72	8.62	56.83	57.98	1.15
Min (B)	73.87	89.09	15.22	53.34	55.72	2.38
Range (A-B)	16.51	7.86	-	5.09	3.92	

References

1. DATAUSA. Profile of Los Angeles, Long Beach and Anaheim. https://datausa.io/profile/geo/los-angeles-long-beach-anaheim-ca. Accessed 23 May 2022
2. U.S. Census Bureau. U.S Tract 2020 data (2020). https://www.census.gov/geographies/mapping-files.html. Accessed 15 June 2022
3. U.S. Census Bureau. U.S. Census Metropolitan Statistical Area map. 2020 State-based Metropolitan and Micropolitan Statistical Areas Maps (2020). https://www.census.gov/geographies/reference-maps/2020/demo/state-maps.html. Accessed 18 June 2022
4. New, J., Bass, B., Adams, M., Berres, A., Luo., X.: Los Angeles County Archetypes in Weather Research and Forecasting (WRF) Region from ORNL's AutoBEM (2021). https://doi.org/10.5281/zenodo.4726136
5. Hengl, T., Parente, L.: MODIS LST monthly daytime and nighttime low (0.05), median (0.50) and high (0.95) temperatures for year 2020 at 1-km (v1.1) (2021). https://doi.org/10.5281/zenodo.4527052
6. Multi-Resolution Land Characteristics (MRLC) Consortium. The National Land Cover Database (NLCD) (2019). https://www.mrlc.gov/. Accessed 24 May 2022
7. Multi-Resolution Land Characteristics (MRLC) Consortium. National Land Cover Database (NLCD) Class Legend and Description (2022). https://www.mrlc.gov/data/legends/national-land-cover-database-class-legend-and-description. Accessed 24 May 2022
8. County of Los Angeles Enterprise GIS Data Gallery. https://egis-lacounty.hub.arcgis.com/. Accessed 23 June 2022
9. McClave, J., Benson, G., Sincich, T.: Statistics for Business and Economics, 13th edn. Pearson, New York (2017)
10. USGS. LP DAAC2Disk Download Manager (HTTP/FTP Download Tool) User Guide (2014). https://lpdaac.usgs.gov/tools/daac2diskscripts/#documentation. Accessed 18 June 2022
11. Getis, A., Ord, J.K.: The analysis of spatial association by use of distance statistics. Geogr. Anal. **24**(3), 189–206 (1992)
12. Statista. Health insurance status distribution of the total population of California in 2020 (2022). https://www.statista.com/statistics/238714/health-insurance-status-of-the-total-population-of-california/
13. Office of Disease Prevention and Health Promotion (ODPHP). Access to Health Care (2020). https://www.healthypeople.gov/2020/topics-objectives/topic/social-determinants-health/interventions-resources/access-to-health#11
14. U.S. Environmental Protection Agency (EPA). Heat Island Impacts (2022). https://www.epa.gov/heatislands/heat-island-impacts. Accessed 23 June 2022

15. Southern California Association of Governments (SCAG) (2020). Extreme Heat & Public Health Report, https://scag.ca.gov/sites/main/files/file-attachments/extremeheatpublichealthr eportfinal_09302020.pdf?1634674354

16. Cardona, O.D., et al.: Determinants of risk: exposure and vulnerability. In: Managing the Risks of Extreme Events and Disasters to Advance Climate Change Adaptation. Field, C.B., et al., (eds.) A Special Report of Working Groups I and II of the Intergovernmental Panel on Climate Change (IPCC). Cambridge University Press, Cambridge, UK, and New York, NY, USA, pp. 65–108 (2012)

17. Gencer, E., et al.: Disasters and risk in cities. In: Rosenzweig, C., Solecki, W., Romero-Lankao, P., Mehrotra, S., Dhakal, S., Ali Ibrahim, S. (eds.) Climate Change and Cities: Second Assessment Report of the Urban Climate Change Research Network, pp. 61–98. Cambridge University Press, New York (2018)

18. Wan, Z.: Collection-6 MODIS land surface temperature products users' guide. ICESS, University of California, Santa Barbara (2007). https://icess.eri.ucsb.edu/modis/LstUsrGuide/usr guide_8dtil.html#alg

19. Hu, L., Brunsell, N.A., Monaghan, A.J., Barlage, M., Wilhelmi, O.V.: How can we use MODIS land surface temperature to validate long-term urban model simulations? J. Geophys. Res.: Atmos. **119**(6), 3185–3201 (2014). https://doi.org/10.1002/2013jd021101

20. Jonsson, P., Eklundh, L.: TIMESAT-a program for analyzing time-series of satellite sensor data. Comput. Geosci. **30**, 833–845 (2004)

21. "Hot Spot Analysis (Getis-Ord Gi*) (Spatial Statistics)." Hot Spot Analysis (Getis-Ord Gi*) (Spatial Statistics)-ArcGIS Pro, https://pro.arcgis.com/en/pro-app/latest/tool-reference/ spatial-statistics/hot-spot-analysis.htm

22. Singh, R., Dumas, M.A.: Esxploring the spatial relationship between demographic indicators and the built environment of a city. In: Driving Scientific and Engineering Discoveries Through the Integration of Experiment, Big Data, and Modeling and Simulation, vol 1512. Springer, Cham (2022) https://doi.org/10.1007/978-3-030-96498-6_27

Patterns and Predictions: Generative Adversarial Networks for Neighborhood Generation

Abigail R. Wheelis[1]([✉]), Levi T. Sweet-Breu[2], and Melissa R. Allen-Dumas[2]

[1] Centre College, Danville, KY, USA
`abby.wheelis@centre.edu`
[2] Oak Ridge National Lab, Oak Ridge, TN, USA
{`sweetlt,allenmr`}`@ornl.gov`

Abstract. Urban climate patterns affect the quality of life of growing urban populations. Studying microclimate patterns, particularly relating to heat, is key to protecting urban residents. The morphology of urban neighborhoods affects local weather patterns, and the development of new neighborhoods could potentially affect future weather. Given the complexity of these relationships, machine learning is a perfect candidate for analyzing the data. This study leverages an adversarial network, containing two competing models, to predict future neighborhood possibilities given the land cover in the area. The model has been trained on data from Los Angeles, California, with the images divided into residential, commercial, and mixed neighborhoods. These divisions allow for patterns and predictions to be analyzed on a neighborhood-specific level, addressing the effects of building distribution on localized weather patterns. Once these predictions have been made, they can be fed into existing models and the impact on climate can be examined.

Keywords: Urban morphology · Generative adversarial networks · Machine learning

1 Introduction

Planning the development of a new neighborhood requires the careful consideration of dozens of factors because urban areas are complex and ever-changing. The study of urban structures and the patterns and processes that connect them

This manuscript has been authored by UT-Battelle LLC under contract DE-AC05-00OR22725 with the US Department of Energy (DOE). The US government retains and the publisher, by accepting the article for publication, acknowledges that the US government retains a nonexclusive, paid-up, irrevocable worldwide license to publish or reproduce the published form of this manuscript, or allow others to do so, for US government purposes. DOE will provide public access to these results of federally sponsored research in accordance with the DOE Public Access Plan (http://energy.gov/downloads/doe-public-access-plan).

K. Doug et al. (Eds.): SMC 2022, CCIS 1690, pp. 384–397, 2022.
https://doi.org/10.1007/978-3-031-23606-8_24

is called urban morphology [10]. These patterns can be referred to as urban tissues: an organic whole seen through different levels of resolution [10]. Urban tissues comprise features such as buildings, roads, and green spaces. The tissues vary from city to city, but also vary within a city. For example, an area containing new apartment buildings will have distinct characteristics from an area with older industrial plants. Planning or creating urban neighborhoods is complex and time consuming because urban tissues, and the factors that influence them, are so intricate. However, data-driven artificial intelligence and machine learning techniques mimic brain function and have the ability to build and strengthen connections upon receiving input and feedback. These techniques provide new avenues for insight and prediction as more data about urban tissues and the way they interact with the natural world becomes available.

2   Challenge Question and Proposed Solution

Challenge question two seeks connections between building classifications and other building characteristics. By connecting building classifications, such as residential or commercial, to other characteristics of an area, it is possible to determine how resources are used to fit different needs. This study connects current land cover classifications to the buildings present in each area. It also generates potential building geometries for an area based on the current land cover. To accomplish this task, a generative adversarial network (GAN) is trained on pairs of land cover and building footprint images. The GAN learns to generate new neighborhoods based on land cover characteristics alone. By dividing the training pairs into three neighborhood types (residential, commercial, and mixed) current morphological patterns are revealed and future possibilities for new developments can be tested. Training the GAN on different neighborhood types provides insight into challenge question number two, examining the impact of building types on climate factors. This study has not addressed all challenge questions, but rather takes a deep dive into a technique that could be a powerful tool in predicting the future of urban neighborhoods and microclimates. These predictions allow for the development of more sustainable cities.

3   Background

A survey of GAN publications found that their application is rapidly increasing across disciplines and noted common applications in medicine, three-dimensional image generation, and object detection [1]. One particular study written by Stanislava Fedorova successfully leveraged GANs to generate small segments of urban tissue based on the learned characteristics of a specific city [4]. Other relevant work includes the creation of fake satellite images depicting cities, accomplished by spoofing satellite images with models trained on specific areas [12]. These studies support the idea that a GAN is a good candidate for working with image data and is particularly suited for the complexity of an urban environment.

As Fedorova points out, urban design is a good candidate for machine learning techniques because of the many interconnected parameters and the long-lasting effects of urban developments [4]. The use of machine learning in this application is groundbreaking because previous work in the generation of urban tissues relied on the explicit definition of parameters. In order to facilitate the recognition and generation of urban tissues that matched different cities, Fedorova trained one model for each city. Through training on tailored image pairs, the GANs learned to infill city blocks consistent with characteristics of the surrounding areas. The approach was proven effective across diverse urban tissues in both qualitative and quantitative terms. Qualitatively, the results were validated by classifying the generated images according to city using a convolutional neural network. Quantitatively, the outputs were proven realistic by comparing aggregate statistics about the generated images to the same statistics for the cities themselves.

Fedorova constructed the models for each city using an image translation GAN put forward by Isola et al. [7]. The image-to-image GAN builds on a conditional adversarial network, with the input image serving as the condition. This architecture is one of several variations that have been proposed since Goodfellow first published on generative adversarial networks. At its core, a GAN is composed of a generator and a discriminator that are set against each other in a minimax two-player game [6]. In this game, the generator seeks to create convincing fake images while the discriminator seeks to accurately classify an image as either real or fake. Theoretically, the model will eventually be so well trained and the fake images so realistic that the discriminator must guess with 50/50 odds. In a traditional GAN, the generator receives a random vector as input. In the image-to-image GAN, an image is provided as input [7]. The generator then creates an output image and the discriminator discerns whether the provided pair of images are real or fake. In the previous study, Fedorova trained models on pairs of diagrammatic representations of city zones. The input images contained a small blank section and the target images contained the same section filled with existing buildings [4]. Therefore, the models sought to fill in the blank spaces in a way that convincingly fit with the surroundings and represented the city of interest.

4   Approach

The use of a GAN to generate parts of the urban tissue is not unique. Both Fedorova's study [4] and a study by Xu and Zhao [12] used GAN models to create images representing built up areas. Fedorova trained a GAN to infill city blocks with a conditional GAN, and the other study created fake satellite images of settlements using a standard GAN. However, we seek to extend previous applications by training models using more abstracted images. Whereas Fedorova trained on pairs that only differed in a small segment, training in this study was conducted on image pairs in different color schemes with different meanings. Following the procedure outlined by Fedorova [4], this study uses a conditional adversarial network for image-to-image translation [7] to propose buildings given a swatch of land cover data. In this way, the input images represent land cover and the target images represent buildings. In addition, the categorization of training data into neighborhood types allows the model to learn the characteristics of how land is used for different purposes. As a result, predictions for specific types of new neighborhoods given intended land cover can be made using an image-to-image GAN approach.

4.1 Data Preparation

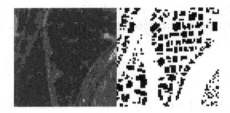

Fig. 1. Example pair of land cover and building images

Fedorova trained five models on image data from five different cities and proved the GAN could accurately learn and recreate the urban tissues of different cities [4]. In a similar manner, this study trained three models with image data from Los Angeles, California specified to residential, commercial, and mixed neighborhoods. A neighborhood is defined by a square tile measuring 1.92 km by 1.92 km for this application. By using land cover and building data, the relationship between the two is examined, and neighborhood types are divided to provide different contexts for those relationships. Land cover data used for this project is from the National Land Cover Database (NLCD) [3], which classifies 30-meter resolution patches of land according to their cover. The cover classifications include woodland types (greens), scrublands (tan), and different densities of developed land (reds). With developed land in particular, darker shades of red represent more dense urban areas, but the data does not include individual buildings. To create the building imagery, the building polygons (obtained from Model America [9]) were rasterized, aggregated to a 30-meter resolution to match the NLCD data, and given height as the raster value. This raster value means that the darker the grayscale in a certain area, the taller the building in that location. After rasterization, the datasets were split into square neighborhood tiles. A simple Python script was needed to ensure the naming conventions from the two data sets matched and that the tiles were properly paired. A sample pair is shown in Fig. 1, with land cover on the left and building representations on the right. From the building data, the tiles were divided into neighborhood types based on building volume.

4.2   Model Architecture

Following the structure put forth by Isola et al., the GAN constructed for this study consists of a generator with skips (Unet) and a PatchGAN discriminator [7]. The Unet structure allows for low-level features such as roads and waterways to flow through the generator from layer i to layer $n - i$, where n is the number of layers. These skips speed up the encoding and decoding processes in the generator by limiting the bottle-necking that takes place at the central layer. The PatchGAN structure discriminates the generated image on a patch basis, meaning feedback is provided for sections of the generated image, not just the image as a whole. This discriminator is run convolutionally across the image to provide output. The model was created using PyTorch, a machine learning library for Python. PyTorch is user-friendly, includes the capability to train on GPUs, and is extensively documented. Code for this implementation has been based, in part, on [11].

4.3   Optimization

Both the generator and the discriminator use an Adam optimizer initialized with a learning rate of 0.0002 and betas of 0.5 and 0.999. These parameters and techniques follow what was implemented in the Fedorova study regarding the generation of urban tissues [4]. Both the generator and the discriminator utilize a binary cross-entropy loss function, which is a common loss function used in binary classification models [5]. While the model is generating images, these images can be classified as either real or not real. The generator has an additional loss component of lasso regression, designed to prevent over-fitting in the deep-learning model [8].

4.4   Model Training

With the architecture of the image-to-image translation network, the models were trained using mini-batch stochastic descent [7]. For each iteration of training, the discriminator was tested on a batch of real image pairs. Next, fake images were generated by the generator net. Then the discriminator was tested on the fakes and updated based on the error from the real and fake images. Finally, the discriminator was tested on the fake images again and the error was used to improve the generator. This framework was used because it continually updates both the generator and the discriminator such that one does not outperform the other. Figure 2 illustrates the GAN and the ways the generator, discriminator, and loss, or error, interact.

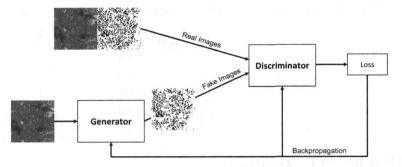

Fig. 2. Overview of GAN architecture, including inputs to generator: land cover, and discriminator: land cover paired with generated or real buildings, alongside backpropagation of error during training.

4.5 Evaluation

The best manner to evaluate the output from a GAN is one of the most pressing questions in the rapidly developing field of machine learning. A general consensus is that "visual examination of samples by humans is one of the common and most intuitive ways to evaluate GANs" [2]. This study relies on visual examination alongside the loss calculated during the training process to perform a preliminary evaluation of the generated images. Further evaluation of quality was conducted using metrics discussed in Sect. 5. Evaluation found these techniques to be effective, so no significant alterations have been made to model architecture or parameters from what was used in [4] as proposed by [7].

Fig. 3. Overall workflow proposed by this study

Once quality building representations have been obtained, their effect on local weather patterns can be analyzed using existing numerical weather modeling tools. The workflow in Fig. 3 demonstrates the overall process of this approach. As described, data is prepared and the GAN models are trained for different neighborhood types. Then, projected land cover can be provided to the generator as input. Finally, existing frameworks can break down the impacts of the predicted buildings.

Table 1. Improvement in PSNR and SSIM over prolonged training.

NumEpochs	PSNR(db)	SSIM
1	1.27	0.009
50	16.7	0.468
250	22.9	0.946
500	25.0	0.980

5 Results and Discussion

In the early phases of model development, it was necessary to determine a sufficient training duration. Training for too few epochs yielded patchy outputs that were not sufficiently similar to the targeted building images. As the models continue to train, one of the characteristics learned is the black and white pixelated appearance of more convincing outputs. An example of this well-trained output is shown in Fig. 4, produced after training for 500 epochs. The training process provides feedback that rewards the grayscale pixels. Further training produces more realistic outputs that are closer fits to the ground truth images. The similarity between generated and ground truth images can be calculated with a variety of metrics. Two metrics for image quality, peak signal to noise ratio (PSNR) and structural similarity index measure (SSIM) have been calculated for outputs from the GAN over different points in training. It is clear from the increase in both measures, as seen in Table 1 that prolonged training yields sufficiently convincing results.

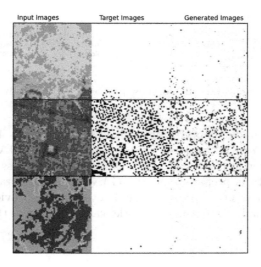

Fig. 4. Produced from 500 epochs of training on residential LA tile pairs with a batch size of 32. SSIM after training of approximately 0.965.

Once an adequate training period was determined, all three models trained for 500 epochs with a batch size of 32, which yielded varying total numbers of iterations. A selection of outputs was then captured from the validation stage of training on the final iteration of each model. Figures 4 through 6 display a grid of outputs from each model. Each row represents the land cover, actual, and generated buildings for a different neighborhood. Variation in size between the data sets of each neighborhood type created a variation in total training iterations. A uniform batch size and number of epochs was prioritized so each model had equal opportunity to train on each training image. In machine learning, there are many parameters that can be tuned in order to facilitate better training. To achieve these results, a batch size, number of epochs, and number of GPUs across which training was chosen and kept constant to maintain uniformity. Further experimentation in this line of study could include studying the impact of adjusting other hyperparameters.

Figure 4 shows results from the residential model. The characteristics of the outputs correspond to the patterns learned by the model. One such pattern is the correspondence of lower-density urban land cover to smaller and more spread-out buildings. In residential areas, these buildings might be houses. Many residential areas are tightly packed, as shown in the central row. However, the buildings in the dense areas are still relatively small. Other residential neighborhoods are slightly less populated. The buildings are small and there is significant space between the individual buildings as well as between the groups of buildings.

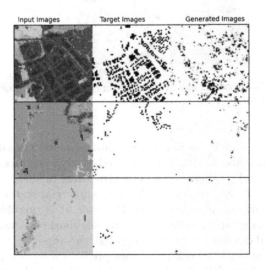

Fig. 5. Produced from 500 epochs of training on commercial LA tile pairs with a batch size of 32. SSIM after training of approximately 0.959.

On the other hand, commercial buildings tend to be much larger and sometimes closer together, as shown in Fig. 5. The larger buildings are clear in the top row. As in residential areas, the commercial buildings are clustered together, interrupted by divisions like roads or undeveloped land. The selection of outputs presented in the figure contains several areas with very few buildings. These tiles, such as those in the bottom row, are classified according to the buildings they contain, even if there are very few buildings. In the future, these undeveloped areas might become more dense urban areas. Investigation of results obtained through providing forecast land cover as input could be of interest in further studies.

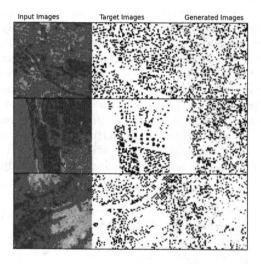

Fig. 6. Produced from 500 epochs of training on mixed LA tile pairs with a batch size of 32. SSIM after training of approximately 0.970.

The selection of mixed tiles in Fig. 6 contain characteristics of both residential and commercial neighborhoods. There is a relatively even mix of larger, densely packed buildings and smaller, spread-out structures in these areas. The central row is an example of such variety. Unlike the commercial and residential samples, these areas are fairly evenly developed. However, it is possible that the use of the land could change and projecting future neighborhoods would be beneficial.

Once predicted developments are generated, the impact of those buildings can be studied with existing numerical weather prediction models and climate modeling frameworks. A modeling system called Neighborhood Adaptive Tissues for Urban Resilience Futures (NATURF) will generate data on 132 different urban parameters. These parameters can then be input into the Weather Research and Forecasting model (WRF). The workflow utilizing NATURF and WRF has the power to evaluate the impact of the buildings generated by the GAN on microclimate factors. Outputs from the GAN have been successfully tuned to represent realistic building placements through many iterations of training. Therefore, the design and functionality of the GAN developed in this study are useful in the development of future cities where environmental, geographical, and infrastructural impacts are given balanced priority.

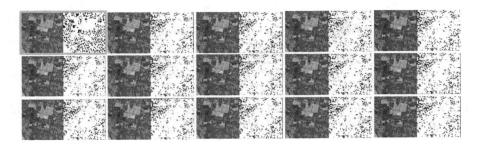

Fig. 7. Output over the same residential tile in 14 distinct iterations of training. Land cover inputs (colored) are shown to the left of their corresponding building outputs (grayscale). Box highlights the ground truth pairing.

The goal of examining the outputs is to select future neighborhood plans which best meet the needs of stakeholders. Choosing between neighborhoods requires multiple options, which drove the examination of multiple outputs from the GAN model over the same input. Early captures of outputs were taken over the same input image on the same model iteration. However, this showed no variation between the group of generated images due to the lack of random noise input. Many GANs utilize random noise as a primary or supplemental input into the generator, but this model does not include any because the authors who developed the image-to-image GAN found the model ignored any random input [7].

In order to capture more variation, the output was gathered every ten iterations for the last 150 iterations out of 6,000. Such results for a single residential tile in Los Angeles, California are displayed in Fig. 7. Upon first glance, there is little difference between the outputs captured on different iterations. Upon zooming into select pockets, there are some differences. While small on the scale of 1.92 km squared, these differences in building size and density are significant on the scale of actual development - typically occurring just a few blocks at a time. This study has succeeded in proving the concept of neighborhood generation compatible with analysis and comparison in the existing climate modeling frameworks.

During training, the loss calculated for the generator and discriminator is captured and displayed in the format of a line graph. These graphs are an indicator of how well the models are performing. Figures 8 through 10 contain the loss graphs for the GANs trained on commercial, residential, and mixed tiles during training. Each of the graphs shows significant rates of loss in the first 200–500 iterations, representing the initial failure of the generator to produce

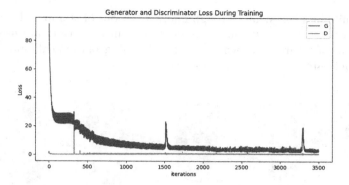

Fig. 8. Generator and discriminator Loss over 500 epochs of training with residential neighborhood input tiles using a batch size of 32.

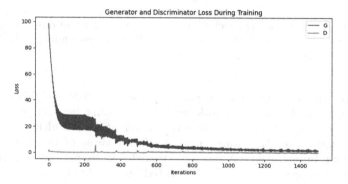

Fig. 9. Generator and discriminator Loss over 500 epochs of training with commercial neighborhood input tiles using a batch size of 32.

convincing outputs. The number of iterations required to reach convincing output varies between neighborhood type, which reflects the difference in number of training images available for that neighborhood type. As training progresses, the loss decreases and remains low, with the exception of occasional spikes in generator loss. It is difficult to know what causes these spikes, though they indicate the continued change and learning process of the model.

In initial testing, the GAN was trained on a personal computer. The runtime to train for just 2 epochs on the full set of Los Angeles, California tiles was approximately 40 min. When the model was trained for two epochs on the computing resource, it only took 32 s. Training the model on two GPUs through the computing resource sped up the process by approximately 70 times. This increase in speed reflects the power of advanced computing resources in the sphere of machine learning. Access to computing resources and libraries to optimize code to run on those resources, such as PyTorch, allow for machine learning algorithms to train to a point of usefulness in a very short period of time. Mak-

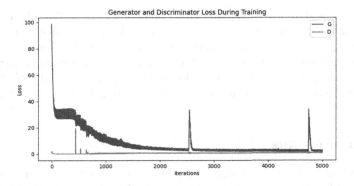

Fig. 10. Generator and discriminator Loss over 500 epochs of training with mixed neighborhood input tiles using a batch size of 32.

ing machine learning more accessible has the power to impact many of the most pressing issues in the scientific world, such as climate change.

6   Conclusions

This study has succeeded in obtaining compelling preliminary results through careful selection of an image-to-image GAN and clever testing to create different outputs. The models' architecture facilitated the learning of correlation patterns between land cover and existing buildings. The separation of data into residential, commercial, and mixed neighborhoods allowed the three separate models to specialize in the generation of each type of urban tissue. Outputs obtained from each model clearly show the differing developments within urban areas of Los Angeles, California. Therefore, the approach effectively explores the patterns within the city and makes predictions based on those patterns. Prolonged training has yielded outputs that are closely styled to the ground truth images and therefore are compatible with analysis and comparison in the existing climate modeling frameworks (NATURF and WRF). The capture of outputs corresponding to the same land cover from different iterations of a model has proven the generation of options for future neighborhoods with this method plausible. Therefore, this study has succeeded in leveraging the power of deep learning through GANs to detect patterns and predict future neighborhoods based on land cover classifications.

While the study was successful, there are several factors that should be considered in the extension of this work. Further experimentation with hyperparameters and training duration may be necessary to create optimal outputs. An adaptive learning rate was cited by Fedorova as leading to better results [4], but that optimization was not included in this study's code. It is possible that an adaptive learning rate, training for a longer time, or locating the cause of the spikes could improve performance or eliminate the spikes in loss observed during training. The rapid recovery from these spikes as well as the overall performance of the model are promising signs of the increased understanding of urban morphology that could come of this work. A critical next step of this work is testing outputs from the GAN with weather modeling frameworks, as proposed, to create an effective workflow and analyze the utility of the process in making predictions about neighborhoods and their interactions with weather and climate.

7   Contributions

Abigail Wheelis tuned the design, conducted the experiment, and analyzed the results. Levi Sweet-Breu produced the data used in this research, processing the land cover and building raster as described in the data preparation subsection. Melissa Allen-Dumas contributed to the development of the original concept and to the scientific analysis design. All contributed to writing and editing the manuscript.

Acknowledgements. This work was supported in part by the U.S. Department of Energy, Office of Science, Office of Workforce Development for Teachers and Scientists (WDTS) under the Science Undergraduate Laboratory Internship program.

This research used resources of the Compute and Data Environment for Science (CADES) at the Oak Ridge National Laboratory, which is supported by the Office of Science of the U.S. Department of Energy under Contract No. DE-AC05-00OR22725.

Support for DOI 10.13139/ORNLNCCS/1774134 dataset is provided by the U.S. Department of Energy, project Automatic Building Energy Modeling (AutoBEM) under Contract DE-AC05-00OR22725. Project Automatic Building Energy Modeling (AutoBEM) used resources of the Oak Ridge Leadership Computing Facility at Oak Ridge National Laboratory, which is supported by the Office of Science of the U.S. Department of Energy under Contract No. DE-AC05-00OR22725

This study was completed under the sponsorship of the DOE Office of Science as a part of the research in Multi-Sector Dynamics within the Earth and Environmental System Modeling Program as part of the Integrated Multiscale Multisector Modeling (IM3) Scientific Focus Area led by Pacific Northwest National Laboratory.

References

1. Aggarwal, A., Mittal, M., Battineni, G.: Generative adversarial network: an overview of theory and applications. Int. J. Inf. Manag. Data Insights **1**(1), 100004 (2021)
2. Borji, A.: Pros and cons of GAN evaluation measures. Comput. Vis. Image Underst. **179**, 41–65 (2019)
3. Dewitz, J.: National land cover database (NLCD) 2019 products. Data release (ver. 2.0, June 2021), U.S. Geological Survey (2021). https://doi.org/10.5066/P9KZCM54
4. Fedorova, S.: GANs for urban design. CoRR, abs/2105.01727 (2021)
5. Godoy, D.: Understanding binary cross-entropy/log loss: a visual explanation (2018). https://towardsdatascience.com/understanding-binary-cross-entropy-log-loss-a-visual-explanation-a3ac6025181a

6. Goodfellow, I.J., et al.: Generative adversarial networks (2014)
7. Isola, P., Zhu, J.-Y., Zhou, T., Efros, A.A.: Image-to-image translation with conditional adversarial networks. In: Proceedings of the IEEE Conference on Computer Vision and Pattern Recognition, pp. 1125–1134 (2017)
8. Karim, R.: Intuitions on L1 and L2 regularisation: explaining how L1 and L2 work using gradient descent (2018). https://towardsdatascience.com/intuitions-on-l1-and-l2-regularisation-235f2db4c261
9. New, J., Adams, M., Berres, A., Bass, B., Clinton, N.: Model America-data and models of every us building. Technical report, Oak Ridge National Lab. (ORNL), Oak Ridge, TN (United States) (2021). https://doi.org/10.13139/ORNLNCCS/1774134
10. Oliveira, V.: Urban Morphology: An Introduction to the Study of the Physical form of Cities. Springer, Cham (2016). https://doi.org/10.1007/978-3-319-32083-0
11. Sharma, A.: Pix2Pix: image-to-image translation in pytorch & tensorflow, October 2021. https://learnopencv.com/paired-image-to-image-translation-pix2pix/
12. Xu, C., Zhao, B.: Satellite image spoofing: creating remote sensing dataset with generative adversarial networks (short paper). In: Winter, S., Griffin, A., Sester, M. (eds.) 10th International Conference on Geographic Information Science (GIScience 2018). Leibniz International Proceedings in Informatics (LIPIcs), vol. 114, pp. 67:1–67:6, Dagstuhl, Germany. Schloss Dagstuhl-Leibniz-Zentrum fuer Informatik (2018)

Author Index